TYPE & TYPOGRAPHY

Type &

Typography

*Highlights from Matrix, the review
for printers and bibliophiles*

MARK BATTY PUBLISHER · LLC

West New York, New Jersey

2003

The articles in this book are collected from the first 20 years of the annual publication
Matrix: a Review for Printers and Bibliophiles

The Introduction for this edition © 2003 John D. Berry
'The Genesis of *Matrix*' © John Randle

Matrix 1981 - 2003 © The Whittington Press
Lower Marston Farm, Risbury, Herefordshire, U.K.

Special thanks to Adobe Systems for assistance with type for this book.
Special thanks to Tim Johnson, Special Collections & Rare Books Department; and Chuck Thomas, Digital Collections Unit, who with Erin Bender, Ahn Na Brodie, and Phil Dudas supplied digital materials used in the design of the book. The Whittington Press archives are housed at the Elmer Anderson Library at the University of Minnesota Libraries, Minneapolis, MN.

Library of Congress Cataloging-In-Publication Data:

Type & typography: highlights from Matrix, the review for printers and bibliophiles.
p. cm.
Includes bibliographical references and index.
ISBN 0-9715687-6-6 (alk. paper) – ISBN 0-9724240-8-3 (special ed. : alk. paper)
1. Type and type-founding History. 2. Type designers – History. 3. Printing – History.
I. Title: Type and typography. II. Matrix.
Z250.A2T95 2003
686.2'21 – dc21
2003004228

Printed and bound in the United Kingdom.

First Edition
10 9 8 7 6 5 4 3 2 1

This edition © 2003
Mark Batty Publisher, LLC
Tower West Suite 2H
6050 Boulevard East
West New York, NJ 07093 USA

www.MarkBattyPublisher.com

ISBN: 0-9715687-6-6 Hard Cover
ISBN: 0-9724240-8-3 Special Edition

Table of Contents

Type & Typography: A Matrix Anthology

Contents

Type & Typography: A Matrix Anthology

Contents

Shakespeare Head Brewhouse Kelmscott Spiral   Hogarth Cranach Aylesford *Scotch Roman*   Doves
Golden Cockerel *Plantin* I. M. Imprimit Bird & Bull   Gregynog *Caslon* Corvinus Heyeck   *Walbaum*
Franciscan Hague and Gill St Mary's Nonesuch   Curwen Warren Plough   Imprenta Glorias Ashendene   St Dominic's
Primrose Hill Hammer Creek Taller Martin Pescador   Weather Bird *Matrix* 20   Tallone Sylvan Reagh   Vale   Ritchie Stourton Castle
Plum Tree *Garamond* Darantiere *Van Dijck*   Florin   Nag's Head   &   *Centaur* Canopy   *Blado*   Old School *Gill Sans*
Paulinus *Lutetia* Editions de Minuit Three Candles   &   *Perpetua* *Bell*   Bella Fortuni   Draeger   Stanbrook Abbey Pear Tree
Hand & Eye Compulsive Hermetic Bieler Rampant Lions   Rocket Fleece   Red Hen   St Albert's   *Janet* Plain Wrapper Wayzgoose
Imprimerie Nationale Bodger *Bodoni* Circle Tiessen *Modern no. 20* Cadenza   Tragara   *Times* *Baskerville*   Kelly-Winterton *Mediaeval*
Folio Fleuron Allen Incline Teriade Ganymed Stigbergets Goncharova Bowne   Windover   Golgonooza   Wulling *Regulus* Old Stile Arion
Hammer *Fournier* Boar's Head Allix Beaumont Cherub Bremer Cuckoo Hill   Five Seasons   Cummington   Perdix Perpetua Yellow Barn
Kat Ran Libanus Cresset *Ehrhardt* Cuala Dun Emer Eragny Essex House   *Goudy Modern*   Merrymount   Strawberry *Bembo* St Martin's Tern
Red Ozier   Old Bourne *Holywell* Nine Elms Horton Tank   Midnight Paper   *Union Pearl*   Moreland Moschatel Burning Book
Arrighi   Kis   Lubbock Willow Waugh Tuscany Alley   Schmied *Bifur*   Celtic Cross   Hayloft p's & q's Dropmore Redlake
Sceptre   Malaprop   Primavera Hermit Oxbow Hedgehog   Mountain House   Cloanthus   Lion & Unicorn *Emerson* Gogmagog
Swan   *Poliphilus*   Goudy Jericho San Serriffe *Romulus*   *Sheldon* Thistle   *Fell*   Dale Guild   Spoon Print Rosbif Trajanus *Trafton*
Delos   Froshaug Flying Sugar Enschede Elzevir Eggebricht   Kynoch Monotype   C.U.P.   September   Pentagram Keepsake Enitharmon
O U P   *Friar* Alembic Talbot Hampden *Kayo* Janus   Epinal *Haarlemmer*   Parrot   Perishable   *Elizabeth* Fanfare Gehenna Samson
Cochin   Officina Bodoni *Village* John Roberts   *Dartmouth* Petropolis   Acorn   Pennyroyal   Workshop   Barbarian *Robin*
Fulcrum   *Casey/Bulmer* Daedalus   D'Ambrosio Riverside Insel   Vine   Black Sparrow   Gruffyground
Latin *Bixler*   Plantin Shenval *Hammer* Trianon   Stellar *Montallegro*   & Tabard

Matrix 20: a review for printers & bibliophiles

Introduction

BY JOHN D. BERRY

In the world of printing and book publishing, type and typography play a very large role. The private press movement began with the creation of new typefaces, based in older traditions, as a reaction against the famously spindly, anemic text types and the extravagantly ornamented display types of the Victorian era. William Morris commissioned his Golden Type; other printer/publishers made theirs. One of the very first of the periodicals aimed at improving printing, *The Imprint* (published in the early teens), gave its name to the typeface it introduced – which was meant to show that a machine-made type, designed and manufactured for the Monotype rather than for setting by hand, could be used to make fine books. The ongoing program of typeface development at Monotype, best known in the 1920s and 1930s when it was headed up by Stanley Morison, involved both the creation of new designs and the revival of old ones from the best periods out of more than 400 years of printing. The other type manufacturers, both of foundry type for hand-setting and of the matrices that produced metal type from typesetting machines, had their own programs – some visionary, some just following fashion – of type revival and typeface development.

Although we are in the midst of another period of ferment and transition in printing and design (one that may well be in need of its own typographic revival), the craft that was perfected in the first half of the 20th century is still being practiced today, and the lessons learned then are useful ones to look at in a later, digital era.

The pleasures of a well-made book are many. The most commercial of books can be a pleasure to handle and read; conversely the most rarified of special editions can be badly made. But a well-made book, whether it's humble or grand, is first and foremost a pleasure to *read*. The volumes of *Matrix* certainly fill the bill. In a simple, usually consistent format of plain Caslon type on a comfortably proportioned page, they are printed on excellent paper and skillfully bound, with specially printed samples and examples occasionally tipped in. Each volume is a book that you can comfortably hold in your hand or on your lap or desk and read, page after page. Although the heft and texture of the original letterpress volumes cannot be reproduced in a book typeset digitally and printed on an off-set press, this anthology serves as a medium for conveying some of the words and images that first appeared in the issues of *Matrix*.

The essays in this book come from two decades of *Matrix*, but they stretch back much farther in their reach; they conduct a dialog with printers, typographers, and type designers of the past as well as the present.

And the authors certainly don't all agree with each other.

The field of typography has seen some strong-willed people during the 20th century. The writers of the first few essays in this book concentrate on several of the personalities of the type world whose ideas and influence are important today.

Perhaps most influential of all, especially in British book publishing, was Stanley Morison, who managed to be typographic advisor simultaneously to both the Monotype Corporation, makers of the most extensively used typesetting equipment in the UK and much of the world, and Cambridge University Press, where the typefaces he developed at Monotype were often put to their first use. From the 1920s on, he gave book designers some of their most useful tools, in the form of Monotype's text faces, and he supported and encouraged their use with extensive writing on the history and practice of type and printing.

Morison was hardly alone in his influence, however. His fellow Englishman Eric Gill, the sculptor/letterer known for his high principles and his eccentric practice, set his stamp on the visual world in the years between the wars. In France, Maximilien Vox not only tirelessly promoted imaginative printing and showed repeatedly how it should be done, he also created one of the most extensive systems ever devised for classifying the unruly families of typefaces, and he organized an annual encounter of type professionals that is still going, decades after his death. Victor Hammer, the German punchcutter who immigrated to the United States, bringing the uncial style of type with him, was a quieter personality; his influence, too, is quiet but persistent. The upright, austere Dutch type designer Jan van Krimpen found it hard to bend to the winds of machine composition, and in an essay reprinted here he was outspoken in his opposition to adapting and reviving the past in a compromised form.

Other writers here deal with the effects of the typographic revival of the 1920s and '30s, which dramatically raised the quality of printed matter of all kinds, especially books. The heart of this renaissance was in Britain, although of course it had many divergent streams and sometimes clashing proponents. As Sebastian Carter says, in 'Type for Books, and Books for Type': 'What characterised the period between the Wars was the uniquely seductive alliance of new typesetting technology with the craft skills of traditional letterpress.' The necessity of change became an opportunity for revival.

Besides the tools for typesetting books, some of the essays printed here deal with the design of the books themselves: from the revolutionary experimentation of El Lissitzky in the newly created Soviet Union to the skilled and nuanced book jackets being produced in Germany today by the consummate calligrapher and type designer Hermann Zapf. The awkward art of turning poetry into printed books appears in these pages, as does an examination of how French typesetters in the 1920s produced galleys from the challenging English prose of James Joyce.

Individual typefaces figure prominently in these essays, and twice an account of their historical roots is followed by a presentation of their revival and adaptation to digital form. (What would Jan van Krimpen have made of this? It's tempting to imagine a dialog between Van Krimpen and, say, Justin Howes, who digitized the typefaces of William Caslon directly from printed specimens, avoiding as much as possible any smoothing or cleaning up of the original imperfections.) Besides the familiar Caslon types and Eric Gill's much-admired Golden Cockerel, these pages feature many of the popular book faces used in the last century, and a variety of little-known or unusual types. Paul Luna writes about two Bible types developed for Oxford University Press – the tiny typefaces that make portable Bibles possible. J. F. Coakley describes the creation of Robert Proctor's Greek types, also for Oxford, for setting the classics, and Fiona Ross and Graham Shaw describe Bengali and Modi types designed in the 19th century for some of the many languages of India. Modern Irish type, although it is in the Latin alphabet, has a tradition that recalls the look of medieval handwriting, and must somehow preserve that tradition and be usable in the present-day world; Dermot McGuinne describes an attempt in the 1930s to achieve this difficult feat. Beyond alphabets entirely, several writers deal with the craft of setting music and mathematics in metal type.

Still farther afield, and yet right next to us at every moment, lie the non-typographic elements of typesetting: the decorative elements, from centuries-old printers' flowers to modern designs for creating complex rules and borders. The tradition of large, decorated initial letters receives consideration here, as both anonymous 17th-century copper engravings and the 20th-century wood engravings of Eric Gill.

Finally, the actual techniques of the craft of punchcutting, and even creating the punchcutting tools themselves, are preserved in practical form, along with meditations on the reasons for continuing this practice in a digital age.

Context matters. It's important to remember what type *was* when the fine printing movement started. Type was a physical object, something you could hold in your hand; it was used to impress the ink onto (and sometimes slightly into) the paper, which was then almost invariably bound in sewn signatures. None of the limitations of these statements is true today. Type is generally a bit of digital information, and if it's still printed on paper the printing is done on an offset press (which quite literally makes no 'impression' on the paper, but only an image) or on a laser printer (the source of enormous amounts of ephemeral printing, but also a means of reaching an audience quickly and easily). Sometimes, these days, the type appears in its final form as an electronic display on some kind of screen, not on paper at all. Most printed books are perfect-bound (the edges glued directly to the spine); even where a book is bound in signatures, they are generally glued rather than sewn, and the result is a volume that does not lie flat when it's open.

Matrix is the latest in a long series of publications devoted to fine printing and the well-made book. *Matrix* started at a time when this tradition was fading in practice, or at least when letterpress printing was becoming obsolete for anything but specialist uses. All around the world – especially the English-speaking world – there are small workshops of individuals laboring slowly and carefully to produce a usually small edition of a book intended for an appreciative audience of bibliophiles. Sometimes these books are aimed largely at collectors, and the content is almost beside the point. But other printers are passionately engaged in disseminating good literature to the world, not in a mass way but in a very personal, direct way. Nobody does it as a way to get rich, although there is enough support to make a living at it; most do it because they want to have an effect. And they do it because the work itself is satisfying: it's literally hands-on work, without the intermediary of a huge printing industry, and this kind of printing lends itself to contemplation rather than to rush and hurry. It is a craft, and one that's still inherently useful, even if it's not in the commercial mainstream anymore.

Fine printers are the ones who maintain the traditions of letterpress printing and still practice this craft today. Through their practice, as well as through their words in publications like *Matrix*, they preserve the continuity of skills and knowledge. There is a wealth of knowledge in these pages.

Matrix affords its writers an opportunity to extend their minds, to record their traditions, and to write calmly and intelligently, without hype, for their colleagues and peers, and for interested others. The circulation of *Matrix* is fairly small, and as time goes on the earlier issues become unavailable except to collectors. Yet the material deserves to be made available again and again, to new readers and old. The purpose of this anthology is to extend the circle of those 'interested others.'

Ultimately, type and printing and the publishing of books are all about the transmission of culture. By publishing *Matrix*, John Randle participates in this ongoing conversation, and he makes it possible for us to join in.

1. The type used for the poster showing Whittington Press's complete range of founder's Caslon type. The text is a letter written by Eric Gill in 1917 extolling the virtues of Caslon type (photo: Ski Harrison).

The Genesis of *Matrix*

BY JOHN RANDLE

There was never much doubt about the typeface that was to be used in *Matrix*. When I first entered the school press as a boy of fourteen, the first things that hit me were, apart from the intoxicating smells of printing ink, paraffin and damped hand-made paper, the sight of three massive Albion presses and behind them the racks of Caslon type in sizes from 10- to 72-point.

Caslon entered the psyche subtly and insidiously, to such effect that other faces began to seem nothing more than unnecessary distortions of William Caslon's creation.

The Marlborough College Press had been started some twenty years before I joined its number by a master named Edward Walters, a fine wood-engraver and printer whose work was described and illustrated in *Matrix* 1 and 2. He had learned to print with Hilary Pepler (whose work was described in *Matrix* 3 and 13) at the St Dominic's Press in 1927. Pepler's enthusiasm for Caslon was shared if not encouraged by his partner at the Guild of St Dominic, Eric Gill. Thus it was passed on to Edward Walters and thence to the Marlborough College Press where I encountered it thirty years later. *Matrix* 2 contains our tribute to Gill and Caslon in the form of a broadsheet set in 12- to 72-point Caslon, using the text of a letter written by Gill in 1917 that extolls the virtues of Caslon type.

If intuition led to the choice of a typeface for *Matrix*, then osmosis dictated its use. Towards the end of the seventies it seemed that foundries such as Mould-type, Riscatype and Western Typesetting who supplied private presses (and others) with founts of Monotype may not be around for ever. At about the same time the economics of desktop publishing finally rang the death knoll for Mono-type, and an avalanche of casters, keyboards, diecases and all the other mass of paraphernalia that accompanied this extraordinary invention began to become available. It was all there for the taking, and we rushed about to secure the most interesting ranges of diecases, most notably from Western Printing Services in Bristol and from Riscatype in Wales.

As noted in *Matrix* 4, whereas Monotype sold some 40,000 diecases of 10-point Times, sales of more exotic faces in the larger sizes struggled to reach

2. Oxford University Press's seventeenth-century Fell type is stored at Whittington in these large Barge cases and then transferred to standard cases for hand-setting. The drawers under the Fell cases contain the large collection of wood-engravings at the Whittington Press.

double figures, and it was these that we were in a hurry to procure, and were largely successful in doing so: for example 16-point Garamond and 14-point Centaur. Later on, in 1986, the contents of Oxford University Press's Monotype collection found their way to Whittington, leaving us with one of the largest collections of Monotype faces assembled under one roof. The OUP collection included such rarities as Bruce Rogers' Bible Centaur, adapted for the Press in 1929.

In 1980, however, I had bought at an auction in Gloucester a keyboard, caster, and diecases for 10- and 12-point Caslon, and just as importantly found at the same sale George Wiggall, a retired and highly skilled Monotype operator about whom I wrote in *Matrix 7*. The idea of *Matrix* came about at around the same time. We had a reasonable amount of 26-em furniture and leads, and so the first issue was put together, largely from items that were too short or specialised to make into a separate book, but which nevertheless needed to be published, and the idea evolved to put them together and publish them under the masthead of *Matrix*. The choice of title was encouraged by the chance to begin it with the Caslon swash *M*, a character for which I had always had a particular liking.

The first few galleys were proofed and it was soon apparent that the 26-em measure was really too short for the 7½-inch page width, which was in turn dictated by the maximum sheet size of our Wharfedale SW2 cylinder press (which was used to print the first four issues of *Matrix,* after which the much faster Heidelberg SBB was bought to cope with the larger extent and longer run). To overcome the narrow text measure the running heads and page numbers were put in the outer margins, which seemed to solve the problem, and so evolved the basic typographic layout of *Matrix* for the first twenty-two issues.

This simple layout has provided a structure upon which we can hang the plethora of tip-ins, fold-outs, sew-ins and other sometimes three-dimensional objects that have found their way between the covers of *Matrix.* The structure provides the solid building blocks that can be added to in an apparently endless variety.

Other faces creep in on a fairly regular basis, usually because they have some bearing on the article in hand, or sometimes just to add typographic variety, and then sometimes printed on a different stock. In the early days they were often used out of simple exuberance or because they had just been acquired. This is especially true of the front covers. Up till about *Matrix* 17 the front covers described the contents of the issue. For example, *1* was set in Caslon, *2* in Gill, *3* in Cochin, *4* in 16-point Centaur, *5* in Walbaum, *6* in Bulmer, *7* in 14-point Centaur, *8* in Lutetia, *9* in Goudy Modern, and so on. Often the appearance of a face can date its arrival at Whittington, particularly with the more exotic founts.

The order forms vary considerably in style and are one of the few occasions when the Press uses typographic ornament, often mirrored from its use elsewhere in the same issue. The order forms are the last part of the job, a relaxation from the concentration that each issue of *Matrix* demands.

Within each issue, we only deviate from Caslon for a reason. A change of typeface can however strike a new note occasionally and lend variety to the issue. For example, Garamond was used in *6* to go with Miriam Macgregor's wood-engravings, as her favourite face; Cochin lent a French flavour to articles on *Les Images d'Epinal* (*13*), a poem by Cocteau (*14*), and illustrations by Matisse (*16*). Walbaum accompanied engravings by John Craig in *1* and *7* (his favourite face), and was used for Hellmuth Weissenborn's obituary in *2* (the German connection).

Similarly, Gill has been used for the Russian constructivists (*17*), Centaur with italic handwriting (*14*), Goudy Modern to go with engravings of iron hand-presses (*12*), Romulus and Haarlemmer for an essay by Van Krimpen (*11*), and Bembo for Guido Morris (*18*) and Vivian Ridler (*19*), their favourite face, and Fournier to strike a literary note for T. S. Eliot (*21*).

An important facility for a letterpress journal is the ability to print type as an illustration from the metal. Clearly there is no better way of showing off a face than to print it by the process for which it was designed. So long as a type is .918 in. high, it can be printed in the same forme or even line as our 12-point Caslon, regardless of its age, provenance, or type size.

Thus we have printed an extraordinarily delicate Syriac in *10*; Proctor's Greek in *13*; Dard Hunter's magnificent but dreadfully cast fount in *19*; numerous Egyptian heiroglyphics in *10* (including a transliteration of '*Matrix 10*' for the half-title), and *21*; and the sorts cast for James Mosley when he was a student in *21*. In *17* we set a facsimile page from *Lady Willoughby's Diary* of 1844, preceded by the facing page set as a facsimile in Justin Howes' digitised 18-point Caslon and printed by litho. It is hard to tell one from the other typographically.

But whatever the typeface, they all come from the same stable. Whether they be modern, sans, old face or transitional, one attribute they will all share is perfection in spacing. Set, alignment and letterspacing on the Monotype are immutable, handed down to us by God and Stanley Morison. Even on our elderly machines, with technology over a century old, the new technology has a job to keep up with us typographically. This is the reason we have stuck with Monotype, and until someone comes up with something better, we shall continue to do so.

3. The keybars that control the operation of the Monotype keyboard are housed in these wooden boxes, with the name of the fount written on each box

TYPE & TYPOGRAPHY

Matrix 4

Matrix 5

Matrix 6

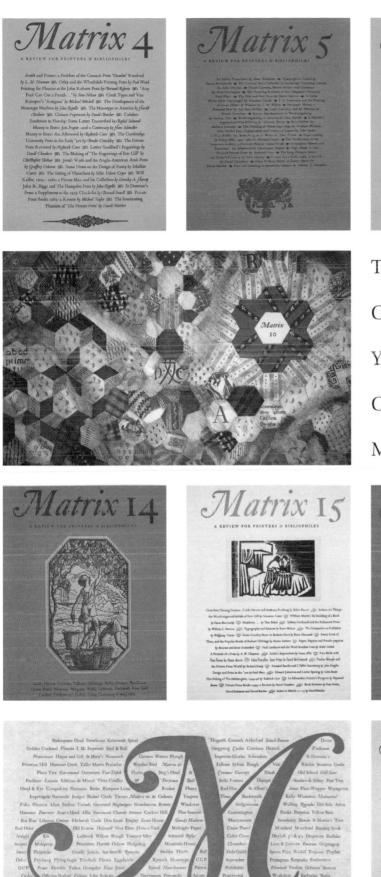

TWENTY-

ONE

YEARS

OF

MATRIX

Matrix 14

Matrix 15

Matrix 16

Matrix 21

* A *

abcde

BCDEF

fghijklmn

GHIJKLM

opqrstuvxyz

NOPQRST

nmlkjihgf

VWXY

edcba

* Z *

Stanley Morison's Times New Roman typeface, the digitized version from Monotype

Logic, Lucidity, and Mr Morison[1]

BY BROOKE CRUTCHLEY

As a towering figure in the 'typographic ferment' of the 1920s and 1930s, Stanley Morison was more responsible than anyone else for the revival of both type design and typography in the first half of the 20th century. Brooke Crutchley's essay in Matrix 5 (1985) shows how the traditionalist Morison was a major force in favor of functionality and simplicity in printed work.

When it comes to judging any piece of industrial design, there are two questions to ask. First: 'Does it work?' Second: 'Does it look good?' (There are, of course, other questions, e.g. about durability and ease of maintenance, but these are not relevant to the present study.) The assessment of looks must be subjective; what pleases one pair of eyes, or one generation, will not necessarily please another. But whether a thing works or not is a practical issue. Does a kettle pour? Does a car go?

With printing the question 'Does it work?' is somewhat complex, as there is an intellectual dimension, of a kind not to be found in any other artifact, at any rate to the same extent. It is not enough that the eye can take in the words, can pass from one line to the next without losing its way, is not distracted by eccentric letter-forms or by uneven inking or by rivers running down the text. These things have their importance but they are incidental. What matters to the reader of a book or the peruser of a notice is the message – the meaning of what has been set down. Does this come through clearly, so that there is no waste of time or danger of misunderstanding? Only then can that piece of printing be said to work.

To Stanley Morison this was the vital issue. In that seminal essay of his, *First Principles of Typography*, published in 1930, he could surprise, even shock, professed connoisseurs of fine printing by a statement that has become famous. 'Typography,' he declared, 'is the efficient means to an essentially utilitarian and only accidentally aesthetic end.' And elsewhere he asserted: 'The primary claim of printing is not to be an art, but to be the most responsible of our social, industrial and intellectual mechanisms; it must, like a transport system, be most disciplined, most rational.'[2]

1. William Morris, *The Roots of the Mountains*, 'the best-looking book since the seventeenth century'.

Morison would concede, of course, that a piece of printing could be both functionally right *and* fine, elegant, handsome, beautiful – whatever epithet one likes to use. He was arguing, however, that the 'intellectual element' was paramount. As he wrote in his postscript to the last volume of *The Fleuron:* 'Beauty is desirable – and beauty will come if unsought. There is nothing so disastrous to typography as beauty for the sake of beauty.'

He did not reach this austere point of view by way of abstract theorising or just because he was – and he was – a born rationalist. It came of his own experience and the continual study of the work of other people, in the past and in his own time. Ever since the revival of the eighteen-nineties there had been an ambivalence in regard to book design in Britain and abroad, of which Morris himself provides a prime example. He had first shown an interest in printing in the sixties, when he planned but never brought out an edition of *The Earthly Paradise* with illustrations by Burne-Jones; and in the late eighties he and Emery Walker were engaged with the Chiswick Press in the production of two books, *The House of the Wolfings* and *The Roots of the Mountains*. Morris thought *The Roots* (figure 1) the best-looking book since the seventeenth century. It was his pleasure with this experience, and the inspiration of a lecture by Emery Walker, his companion in many causes, that led him to set up a press of his own. 'I began printing books,' he was to write later, 'with the hope of producing some which would have a definite claim to beauty, while at the same time they should be easy to read and not dazzle the eye, or trouble the intellect of the reader by eccentricity of form in the letters.'[3] The statement is a clue to the way his mind worked – first *beautiful*, second *easy to read;* and the secondary aim could be utterly lost to sight at times. Colin Franklin has pointed out, for instance, that 'title-pages of books of poems could be a nonsense of decoration at the expense of all meaning, a designer's enjoyment with no inhibition.'[4] He cites the double opening of the Kelmscott Keats, 'a solid block of capitals in its thick border, no concession to sense or line division' (figure 2).

Morris's style had its imitators but made little impact on commericial publishing. His importance lies in the way he convinced his contemporaries that the printing of books deserved better workmanship and materials, and greater attention to design, than it had been receiving for a long time. The books of Cobden-Sanderson's Doves Press were altogether different. In the words of Ruari McLean, 'The Doves Press pages are the most devastating criticism ever made of the Kelmscott Press.'[5] His edition of *The Rape of Lucrece* (figure 3) is arresting in its simplicity, enhanced by perfect presswork on fine white paper. By way of contrast, the Vale Press books designed by Charles Ricketts could often be as

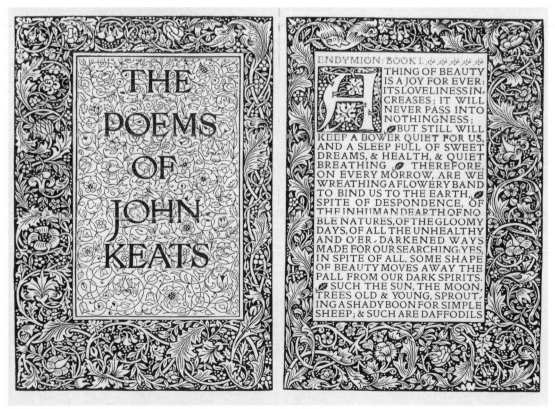

2. The Kelmscott Keats, 'a designer's enjoyment with no inhibition'.

3. The Doves *Lucrece*, 'arresting in its simplicity'.

unreadable, in their own way, as anything of Morris's; witness his version of a Keats title-page (figure 4).

Of the many artists caught up in the printing revival of the nineties, Whistler and Beardsley among them, it was Ricketts who was most active. He was our first freelance typographer, working for several publishers. Just as Morris's earliest efforts, *The House of the Wolfings* and *The Roots*, had been in the true Renaissance tradition, so were the books Ricketts designed for the publishing firm of Osgood, McIlvaine; but later, in commissions for John Lane and in his own Vale Press books, his craving for artistic effect took over. This may have been the cause of Oscar Wilde's aggravation as expressed in a letter to his publishers apropos of *The Portrait of Mr W. H.* 'Mr Lane is quite aware that . . . the manuscript was handed over by me to Mr Ricketts that he might select the type and form and suitable setting for the book, and convey the manuscript to the printers. The manuscript has been in Mr Ricketts's hands for *more than a year.*'[6]

Wilde did not much like Lane (which is why he called the manservant in *The Importance* after him) but it is due to Lane and a few like-minded publishers such as Heinemann, Elkin Mathews, David Nutt and J. M. Dent that the revival in book design in Britain was set on the right path. True, some of their efforts were brashly experimental – one thinks of Whistler's *Gentle Art* and Wilde's *The*

4. Title-page of the Vale Keats, 'as unreadable as anything of Morris's'.

Sphinx – but their more characteristic books were sensibly planned, pleasant to handle, easy to read, with well-proportioned margins and with decoration, if any, properly subservient. The newly invented 'process block' for reproduction of line was much used for illustration or decoration of the pages and on bindings as well (Beardsley was a past master in its exploitation) and the opportunity was often taken to establish an agreeable unity between the inside and outside of the book. This was, of course, before the day of the jacket, that unhappy appendage of the twentieth-century book.[7]

A great deal of the credit for the orderly presentation of the books of Lane and others is undoubtedly due to the printers on whom they largely depended, in particular T. & A. Constable in Edinburgh and the Ballantyne Press in London under their respective managers, Walter Blaikie and Charles McCall. Both men were masters of their craft, with a good sense of design and high standards of composition and presswork. They were the natural successors of Bulmer and Bensley and greatly contributed to the establishment of the style which became more and more accepted in Britain during the first decade of this century and was dominant from then until the sixties, by which time everything had been thrown into the melting-pot by changes in technology and public taste.

What was that once dominant style and how does one identify it? Its roots were in the Renaissance – the classical, ordered format, with type size related to line length for easy reading, headings in ascending sizes and usually centred, well-proportioned margins with facing pages forming a single unit. Such a format persisted with only minor variations and even fewer downright deviations through five centuries. However, the period following the First World War differed from all its predecessors in one important respect – the wide variety of type designs available for book (and other) printing, an outcome of the invention of mechanical composing systems. At first the manufacturers were content to copy the faces in common use at the time – Modern, Old Style, Caslon – but around 1912 they became more adventurous and when Morison was engaged by the then Lanston Monotype Corporation in 1922 he initiated a programme of new faces, some based on designs from past centuries, others by living artists.

In the hands of inexperienced users the result of such abundance could have been disastrous, were it not for the guidance the manufacturers gave – on the special qualities of each face, the amount of interlinear space that suited it best, the most appropriate rules and ornaments, the effects of printing on different classes of paper (and an almost infinite variety of papers was available in those days). The Monotype Corporation was the most prolific, with its *Recorder*, newsletters and other material, edited by the publicity manager, the American Beatrice Warde. Whereas Morison directed his exegeses for the most part to his intellectual peers, Beatrice was out and about, in schools and lunch clubs, preaching the gospel with eloquence and conviction; she also wrote a great deal, one of her recurrent themes being that 'print should be invisible'. Indeed, a characteristic of the prevailing style as seen in English books was an inherent modesty or call it 'good manners', a disinclination to show off. In this they differed from the general run of American books, where too many designers seemed out to draw attention to themselves rather than to the text, disregarding the wise warning of their own Theodore De Vinne: 'The reader does not want to see the printer but to hear the writer.'

Though perhaps the most voluble, Morison and Warde were far from being alone in discoursing on typographical subjects. Indeed, a notable feature of the period was its introspection. Designers thought a great deal about what they were doing; they discussed it with each other and with printers and illustrators in such clubs as the Double Crown, founded in 1924; they wrote about it in various journals and in books produced with specially loving care. The reading public was interested too, a fact recognised by reviewers, who were apt to comment, favourably or not, on a book's physical qualities; a column called 'Book Production Notes' by Bernard Newdigate appeared regularly in *The London Mercury* between 1920 and 1937. The same sort of typographical ferment affected other countries but Britain was the epicentre, thanks to the outstanding talents and enthusiasm of a few individuals and the support of a number of commercial undertakings, either as suppliers of equipment or as patrons of high-class printing.

From the very nature of their work, scholarly and much of it complex, a priority for university presses must be to express the meaning of a text in the most lucid way. Writing of the Oxford Press in the years around 1900, Peter Sutcliffe in his *Informal History* says: 'Oxford printing has been traditionally somewhat austere, not seeking after effect; to hint in any way that the matter is less important than the

Stability of free-surface flows 403

must be included in the analysis. The inclusion of the latter requires that we return to (3.2). Following Yih (1963), we write

$$\left.\begin{aligned} f(y) &= f_0(y) + i\alpha R f_1(y),\\ \hat{m}(y) &= \hat{m}_0(y) + i\alpha R \hat{m}_1(y),\\ c &= c_0 + i\alpha R c_1. \end{aligned}\right\} \tag{6.5}$$

These expressions may be regarded as the leading terms of a power-series expansion in terms of the small parameters αR and α^2, when α^2 is also small compared with αR. Retaining only those terms of (3.2b) which are $O(\alpha R)$, we find that

$$(\overline{m} f_1'' + \overline{u}' \hat{m}_1)'' = (u - c_0) f_0'' - u'' f_0, \tag{6.6}$$

$$\hat{m}_1 = \frac{\overline{m}' f_1}{u - c_0} + \frac{\overline{m}' f_0 c_1}{(u - c_0)^2}. \tag{6.7}$$

First and second integrals of (6.6) are

$$(\overline{m} f_1'' + \overline{u}' \hat{m}_1)' = (u - c_0) f_0' - u' f_0 + C, \tag{6.8}$$

$$\overline{m} f_1'' + \overline{u}' \hat{m}_1 = \int_0^y [(u - c_0) f_0' - u' f_0] \, dy_1 + C y + D, \tag{6.9}$$

where C and D are disposable constants. To the same order of approximation, the boundary conditions (3.6), (3.7) and (3.4) yield

$$(\overline{m} f_1'' + \overline{u}' \hat{m}_1)' = (1 - c_0) f_0' + G \cos\theta + \alpha^2 T \quad (y = 0),$$
$$\overline{m} f_1'' + \overline{u}' \hat{m}_1 = 0 \quad (y = 0),$$
$$f_1 = c_1 \quad (y = 0).$$

The first two of these boundary conditions, together with (6.8) and (6.9), determine C and D to be

$$C = G \cos\theta + \alpha^2 T, \qquad D = 0.$$

On substituting in (6.9) for C, D, $\overline{m}$ and $\hat{m}_1$ we obtain

$$f_1'' + \left\{ \frac{(u'/y) - u''}{u - c_0} \right\} f_1 = -c_1 \left\{ \frac{(u'/y) - u''}{(u - c_0)^2} \right\} f_0 - (u'/y) I - u' (G \cos\theta + \alpha^2 T), \tag{6.10}$$

where

$$I = \int_0^y [(u - c_0) f_0' - u' f_0] \, dy_1 = (u - c_0) f_0 + (1 - c_0)^2 - \frac{u'}{y} \int_0^y u' f_0 \, dy_1, \tag{6.11}$$

on integration by parts. Also, from (6.3),

$$(u - c_0) y f_0'' + (u' - y u'') f_0 = -u' (u - c_0);$$

and this equation may be integrated from 0 to y, to find, after integration by parts, that

$$3 \int_0^y u' f_0 \, dy_1 = (u - c_0 + u' y) f_0 - (u - c_0) y f_0' - \tfrac{1}{2}(u - c_0)^2 + \tfrac{3}{2}(1 - c_0)^2. \tag{6.12}$$

On using results (6.11) and (6.12), equation (6.10) becomes

$$f_1'' + \left\{ \frac{(u'/y) - u''}{u - c_0} \right\} f_1 = -c_1 \left\{ \frac{(u'/y) - u''}{(u - c_0)^2} \right\} f_0 - u' (G \cos\theta + \alpha^2 T) + H(y), \tag{6.13}$$

where $H(y) = -\tfrac{1}{3}(u'/y)[(u - c_0 - 2u' y) f_0 + 2(u - c_0) y f_0' + (u - c_0)^2].$

26-2

5. Typographical mastery in setting mathematics.

form is bad typographical taste.' The books printed by both Oxford and Cambridge in the nineteenth and early twentieth centuries tended to be more indicative of compositors' know-how and technical skill than of the aesthetic sensitivity of those responsible for the overall design. But from about 1920 onwards the two Presses were in the vanguard of the drive to make books as attractive as they were lucid. Walter Lewis, who was appointed Printer at Cambridge in 1923, had at one time been manager of the Ballantyne Press and in his most recent job in Manchester he had worked with Morison, whom he was quick to bring to Cambridge as typographical adviser. With an outstanding craftsman, Frank Gordon Nobbs, in charge of the composing department they established standards of book-production which were universally admired. Nowhere was the typographical mastery of the two Presses better shown than in the way they handled complicated mathematics, and nowhere was the support of flawless presswork so vital (figure 5).

Of course, not everybody was prepared to accept the basic principles which Morison laid down so dogmatically and to which Cambridge was inescapably committed. One such was about what he called the hierarchy of letters. Capitals came first, in time and status; lower-case, to quote again from *First Principles*, was 'a necessary evil which should be avoided when it is at its least rational and least attractive – in large sizes'. Bernard Newdigate contested this; he thought that well-drawn lower-case letters were at their best in large sizes and he could not see that the setting of all displayed proper names in capitals was required either by Logic or Lucidity – those 'twin goddesses whom Mr Morison invokes'.[8] Books published by Faber & Faber mostly followed the accepted style and figured largely in exhibitions, but the partner responsible for production, Richard de la Mare, occasionally broke loose in an effort to be 'modern', as with Herbert Read's *Art Now*, set all in sans serif, and the same author's *Art and Industry*. The design of the latter by Herbert Bayer, former lecturer at the Bauhaus, seemed to Lewis so *outré* that he was hesitant about printing it; set in different sizes and weights of Bodoni, it seems innocuous enough today (figure 6). In Raymond McGrath's *Twentieth Century Houses* the illustrations were bled, a usage which aroused a good deal of controversy at the time and incidentally was a headache to letterpress printers;[9] and the text was set without indentation for paragraph openings. (Morison himself was once guilty of a similar whimsicality in his own *On Printing Types*, published in 1923, in which the text was run on, with marks to indicate new paragraphs; 'an experiment not repeated by S.M.' was how he subsequently referred to it.[10])

Then there was Eric Gill, always provocative, who came out with revolutionary ideas in his *Essay on Typography*. One at least has since become respectable – unjustified lines and ragged right, which he persuaded Robert Gibbings to adopt in the Golden Cockerel *Four Gospels*. The so-called New Typography, introduced into Britain by

6. Herbert Read, *Art and Industry*, 'innocuous enough'.

Jan Tschichold, failed to make any immediate impression so far as books were concerned and Tschichold himself had abandoned it by 1947, when he became responsible for the design of Penguin books. It was not until after the War that asymmetric layouts became at all common.

Francis Meynell and Morison had come together when they were both in their early twenties, first at Burns & Oates, the Catholic publishers, then at the Pelican Press which Meynell had founded for commercial printing. They were an incongruous couple – Meynell with his tweedy clothes and flowing ties, Morison always sombrely dressed; 'a long geezer with a black titfer' was how a publisher's Cockney warehouseman once described him.[11] But so far as their work was concerned, it was hard to tell them apart. Both believed in typography that was orderly, lucid and inviting, the inviting element depending on the use of handsome type faces, well arranged and printed; paper of character; often a decorative use of ornament. So it continued after they had gone their separate ways, Meynell to found the Nonesuch Press, which he ran with one interruption from 1923 to 1968, Morison eventually to supervise design for the Monotype Corporation and serve as typographical adviser to the Cambridge University Press and *The Times*. Daniel Defoe's *Tour* (figure 7), designed by Morison for Peter Davies and printed at Cambridge in 1927, might easily have come from Meynell's hand. In an article 'On Decoration in Printing' which appeared in *The Monotype Recorder*[12] Morison was his usual rationalising self: 'By the disciplined use of decorative borders and flowers, initials, head and tail pieces, charm and distinction may be given to the page without distracting from the main purpose of print – which is to be read.'

From about 1930, however, less and less of Morison's time was being spent on design and those books to which he did turn his hand tended to be of a sort that did not provide scope for fanciful typography. For his part, Meynell continued to expend on Nonesuch books the riches of

7. Daniel Defoe, *Tour through the Whole Isle of Great Britain*, 'might easily have come from Meynell's hand'.

his talent, using decorative schemes when he considered them appropriate but eschewing all preciousness when appealing to a general readership, as in his 'compendious' series of Blake, William Morris, John Donne and others. For all his experimenting – he set out to give each book a different treatment unless it was one of a series – Meynell still regarded Morison as the supreme authority. Morison gave a paper to the Double Crown Club in 1927 on the planning of the preliminary pages of books. No text survives, only some printed pages which accompanied the talk, but *inter alia* Morison referred to half-titles as often redundant and he deplored the shortage of information on title-pages and the use of excessively large type, out of scale with the rest of the book. Meynell's title-page for his Dante, published in the following year, shows that he had taken all this in (figure 8). The page is preceded by a blank leaf and the copy he gave Morison has written under the colophon in Meynell's hand: 'For S.M. who saved it from the peril of a half-title page.'[13]

None of his contemporaries went quite as far as Morison in condemning the deliberate search for beauty as a factor in printing design. Bruce Rogers liked to have it both ways; 'artistic beauty and fitness for purpose' were his declared aims in designing his early, Riverside books and they remained with him throughout his life. The two goals, artistic beauty and fitness for purpose, had for him equal validity, and this involved a balancing act which was the cause of considerable agony both for himself and for those who worked with him; for example, in the present writer's own experience, during the printing of Morison's book on Pacioli for the Grolier Club – the rubbing down of sorts to get a closer fit, the working over line blocks with a tool when they were already on the machine and, after the printing, his painting over solid areas, sheet by sheet, because the ink had too much gloss. Many of his books are commendable by the strictest Morisonian standards; occasionally, however, the scales were tipped to the side of 'artistic beauty', for example the Oxford lectern bible, a consciously beautiful book but not as easy to read as some other folio bibles produced over the centuries.

That other distinguished American printer, D.B. Updike, came closer to Morison when he declared: 'The beauty of any piece of printing is almost always the by-product of its adaptation to its purpose.' As Beatrice Warde spoke of print being invisible, so to Meynell 'elegant invisibility, the Emperor's clothing' was the ideal in the typography of books. Tschichold is on record as saying that a designer of books should start by making them legible, then functionally right, then inviting; and Ruari McLean has said of him: 'Perhaps he has shown, more clearly than anyone else, that the true task of the typographer is not so much in the broad sweep and the dashing effect, which draws the applause, as in the less obvious, infinitely more difficult and painstaking task of getting all the details right – with elegance.'[14] Morison's pronouncements were always emphatic and uncompromising and to many he seems to have overstated his case. But, as these quotations show, he was not isolated but only in his own forceful way expressing views shared with many others and inherent in the actual practice and performance of the mainstream of book-printers since printing began. To take a phrase he used in a letter to Updike it was 'the embodiment of the commonsense of generations'.

The resulting, essentially rational, style proved an excellent basis for the 'economy standards' of the Second World War. Thereafter, as restrictions were relaxed and paper became more freely available, pre-war habits reasserted themselves. In the overall pattern of book production, however, a change was

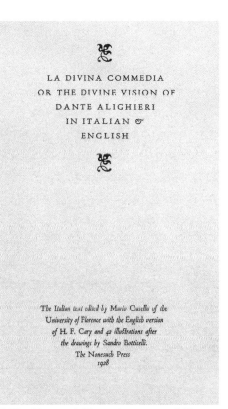

LA DIVINA COMMEDIA
OR THE DIVINE VISION OF
DANTE ALIGHIERI
IN ITALIAN &
ENGLISH

The Italian text edited by Mario Casella of the
University of Florence with the English version
of H. F. Cary and 42 illustrations after
the drawings by Sandro Botticelli.
The Nonesuch Press
1928

8. The Nonesuch Dante; homage to S.M.

soon evident, as more and more space on the booksellers' shelves was taken up by illustrated books in large formats. Such a development had been foreseen by one who was very active in printing and publishing between the wars, James Shand, a Scot with considerable charm, a keen mind and a delight in being controversial, even iconoclastic. His paper to the Double Crown Club on 'Typographical Developments, circa DCCI–DCCX'[15] did not please Morison. Reminded that his subscription was overdue, 'I shall clear out,' Morison replied, 'if there is any more of that Shandy guff'. (Evidently his vexation was not deep-felt, to judge from a letter Shand wrote to Ellic Howe in 1941: 'I had a kindly letter from Stanley Morison this morning. It was generous of him to write after all the hard-boiled impertinences he had had from me in the past.'[16])

Shand deplored the exaggerated deference paid to tradition by the typographic pundits. He also deprecated the current 'book snobbery'; in his view books now occupied a small and comparatively unimportant part of the whole typographic scene. In the first issue of *Typography*, a 'plastoic-bound' quarterly for the appearance and editorial policy of which he was partly responsible, he wrote: 'The future development of typography lies with the more immediate forms of expression for a larger audience uninterested in the cultured refinements of typographical elegance – an audience familiar with daily newspapers, weekly periodicals, monthly magazines; an audience besieged by propaganda enlivened by advertising; an audience quickened in perception by new techniques of presentation in broadcast and talking film; an audience with a camera-eye. Changing social habits will influence typography as surely as they at present influence our architecture.'

The technique of photolithography had progressed slowly during the first half of the century but now the developments in reading taste foreseen by Shand provided a powerful boost. At the same time photocomposing methods were advancing rapidly, as letterpress correspondingly shrank. The task of designing for print was transformed and a degree of professionalism was required which had been unknown before 1939. The objective, of course, remained the same – to convey a message lucidly and economically; but the very profusion of means now available made its achievement not easier but more difficult. In the process it often seemed that the basic principles of legibility were being ignored and, when it came to the peripherals such as the title-pages of books, all restraint could be thrown to the winds. Printing design is a matter of solving problems, not of creating patterns; only when this percept is generally accepted will typography flourish again.

Brooke Crutchley retired from the position of Cambridge University Printer in 1974, after having filled the post for 28 years, during a career at the University Press spanning a total of 44 years. He also played an active part in Cambridge life throughout his term of office at the Press. His influence spread into many fields of endeavour, where he has been recognised as a man of vision and achievement whose career has enriched the worlds of printing and learning.

NOTES

1. This article is based on the Stanley Morison lecture given under the title of 'The Importance of Meaning in Typography' at Manchester Polytechnic in 1984.

2. 'The Art of Printing' in *Proceedings of the British Academy*, vol. XXIII (1938); reprinted in *Stanley Morison: Selected Essays*, vol. 1, edited by David McKitterick (1981).

3. *Note on his aims in founding the Kelmscott Press* (1898).

4. *The Private Presses* (1969), p. 45.

5. *Cobden-Sanderson and the Doves Press* (Wormerveer, 1964).

6. Rupert Hart-Davis (ed.), *The Letters of Oscar Wilde* (1962), p. 367.

7. In the writer's view there was no harm in the old dust-wrapper, to be thrown away before the book was shelved, but with the evolution of the full-blown jacket publishers neglected their bindings, the book as such lost its integrity, and readers were compelled to fork out for an extravagance they did not want.

8. Quoted by Joseph Thorp in *B. H. Newdigate, Scholar-printer* (1950), p. 41.

9. Process blocks were normally fixed to wooden mounts by nails driven through bevels. When blocks abutted in the forme, bevels had to be cut off, making it necessary to remount the blocks on metal. Sometimes the mounts had to be cut so that the blocks rested partly on the rim or crossbar of the chase.

10. In John Carter's *Handlist of the Writings of Stanley Morison*, privately printed at Cambridge in 1950 and superseded by Tony Appleton's *The Writings of Stanley Morison* (1976) which, however, lacks Morison's revealing comments.

11. H. Jones, *Stanley Morison Displayed* (1976), p. 25.

12. XXII, no. 197 (1923).

13. One of Morison's books to survive the raid of 10 May 1941, though not without damage to the binding. Now in the writer's possession. The blank leaf preceding the title is guarded in, suggesting that a half-title had actually been printed and cancelled.

14. *Jan Tschichold, Typographer* (1975), p. 119.

15. Ellic Howe papers (XXIV, 90) in the Morison Room, Cambridge University Library.

16. *Ibid* (XXIV, 27).

1. Jean Garcia, Maximilien Vox and John Dreyfus at Lurs. (*Bernard Mandin*)

2. Maximilien Vox and John Dreyfus, 1972.

The Typographical Importance of Maximilien Vox

BY JOHN DREYFUS

John Dreyfus, the successor to Stanley Morison as typographic advisor to Mono-type, was well positioned to appreciate and convey, in Matrix 17 (1997) *the impor-tance of the seminal French designer, organizer, publisher, and instigator Maximi-lien Vox, founder of the enduring typographic congregation Les Rencontres de Lure.*

His motto was *J'abonde dans l'instant*. It suffers when translated literally as 'I abound in the moment'. So I prefer to condense it both freely and alliteratively to 'I perpetually profuse'. That claim was certainly supported by the extent and variety of his achievements almost until his death in 1974.

He was sixty when I first attended the Rencontres de Lure in August 1955. That was the year when I joined the Monotype Corporation as a typographical adviser. Stanley Morison was still working in that capacity for the Corporation, and he had been friendly with Vox for many years. I believe I first heard about Vox from the staff in the Paris Office of the Corporation. They encouraged me to attend the meeting in August knowing that I could speak French without much difficulty, and being aware that something of unusual interest was going on in Lurs. (I must explain that Vox preferred to use the regional name 'Lure' rather than the village name 'Lurs' when referring to the Rencontres or École. This was because the village had become notorious in 1952 as it was close to the scene of an unsolved triple murder committed in August when Sir James Drummond, his wife and their twelve-year-old daughter were found, shot dead near the bank of the River Durance below the village of Lurs.)

Vox and his wife had come across the village by accident while driving through Provence in 1949. At that time the stone houses were in ruins: there was no water except from a well, and the road was cluttered with debris. A year later Vox came back with two of his friends – Jean Giono, the novelist who lived nearby in Manosque, and Jean Garcia, a graphic designer from Paris. All three were deeply impressed by the sweeping views from the village, and by the extraordinary quali-ty of the light which locals called *le coup de bleu*. So the three friends decided to cre-ate a cultural retreat in the ruined village which would attract talented graphic

3a. Wood-engraving by Vox, c.1917.

3b. *Emma*, designed and illustrated by Vox, 1933–4.

designers from around the world – an idea which had been in their minds for many years. Giono remarked encouragingly, 'Your efforts will succeed because you will be talking shop.'

I was lucky to make my first trip to the École de Lure in 1955 as it had taken several years to get into its swing. Its first manifesto in 1951 clearly restricted its appeal to a few people of proven ability with sufficient leisure and means to enter thoroughly into the spirit of Lure – and get the most out of it. Those who came would, said Vox, need good health as well as good humour if they were to adapt to a communal existence in matters of food, board and work. Vox wanted people who enjoyed the open air and teamwork, and who were devoted to spiritual matters. However in 1952 he became so deeply involved in devising his typeface classification system (of which I will say more below) that he seems to have been unable to organise a session at Lurs in 1952. A year later strikes brought the French railways to a standstill and prevented more than four *compagnons* from reaching Lurs. Only in 1954, according to Vox, did 'more than thirty typographical argonauts' turn up for the summer session. Attendance in 1955 exceeded fifty. Among them were several of my friends, notably Charles Peignot and his son Rémy. Living conditions were far more comfortable than I expected. Like several others I slept in a hotel at Forcalquier, a pleasant little town about nine miles from Lurs; but we took our communal meals at the local bistro in Lurs where the food was almost as good as the view.

Our working sessions were held in the partially restored *chancellerie* and they were dominated by Vox. He cut a short but commanding figure. There was happily something cherubic about his cheeks and fresh complexion which created a benevolent and friendly aura. He spoke with clarity, authority, a quick wit and good humour. Little escaped his attention. Even when he seemed to drop off to sleep on the platform during a boring or confused speech, he was still a good listener. So when the speech came to an end, Vox would suddenly sit up and explain succinctly what the speaker had intended to say. Many a session was saved by Vox's ability to sum up what ought to have been said by the speakers.

His flamboyant names intrigued me, but it was many years later that I learned he had chosen them himself. They suited his personality far better than those given to him by his parents with a lavish use of hyphens: Samuel-William-Théodore Monod. His father became the head of the French Protestant Church. One reason for Vox changing his names was his conversion in 1924 to the Roman Catholic faith, partly through the influence of Jacques Maritain.

It struck me that few men have shown greater originality in choosing such a short and memorable surname, or joining it as euphoniously to a polysyllabic first name. He also exploited the graphic possibilities of the initials MV which he worked into a monogram when signing his correspondence. His stylish appearance as an alert young man in his early twenties can be seen in the photograph of him taken at Aix-les-Bains (figure 4).

His father had intended him to make a career in medicine after taking his *baccalauréat* in philosophy. Instead Vox chose the graphic arts, starting as a cartoonist on the socialist newspaper *L'Humanité* in 1913. In that year he made known his pacifist views. During the First World War he fell seriously ill, but while convalescing he managed to teach himself how to engrave on wood – a skill shared by his wife to whom he was married in 1917. Three of their five sons went into the

graphic arts; the other two became academics, Sylvère Monod making his reputation as a great Dickens specialist at the Sorbonne.

Before their sons were born, Vox and his wife settled at Grasse in the south of France, where he did some wood engraving, and published texts by little-known authors. Then in 1923 he moved to Paris. Within a few years his reputation was established. He worked for three years with the publisher Bernard Grasset whom he greatly liked. A great boost to his career came in 1926 when he was given the Prix Blumenthal for Decorative Art – the first time it was awarded for typographical design. In the same year he set up his own studio, calling it 'Service Typographique'. From this came a succession of publicity pieces for the Deberny &

4. Portrait of Vox, aged twenty.

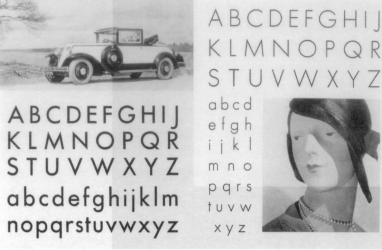

5a. *Les Divertissements Typographiques*, no. 1, 1928.

5b. Opening from *Divertissements*, showing Futura.

Peignot typefoundry. These *Divertissements Typographiques* (figure 5a–b) led to a lasting friendship with Charles Peignot, who persuaded him to take a seat on the foundry's board of directors.

An impressive variety of commissions followed in the 1930s. One came in 1934 from another publisher he greatly admired, Paul Iribe. He needed help from Vox in starting a newspaper called *Le Témoin*. Orders also arrived from leading Parisian shops – the Galeries Lafayette, Le Printemps and Hermès. Yet he still found time during the 1930s to illustrate a great many books, including the complete works of Molière and Beaumarchais, and an English edition of Jane Austen's works. He also supplied eight hundred drawings to illustrate Dumas, *Les Trois Mousquetaires*, and he drew a set of intricate encyclopaedia headings for *Le Grand Larousse*. In addition to his decorative work, he translated several books by G. K. Chesterton into French and was happy to broaden the reputation of an author who had been a strong influence on his own writings.

His literary work continued during the German occupation in the early forties, when he started the Union Bibliophile de France. This small publishing house was very active in those years. Its elaborate limited editions of 500 copies made a sharp contrast with his other ventures during the occupation, during which he published cheap paperbacks in large editions using newsprint.

For his editing of six hundred of Napoleon's letters he was awarded the Prix Saintour by the Académie Française in 1943. With such varied and valuable experience of printing, publishing, editing, writing and book design, he was approached after the Liberation by Grasset, the publisher for whom he had worked in the twenties. But he decided instead to work for another publisher,

Robert Denoël, who was assassinated a year later. Wider scope for Vox's many talents was provided when he was appointed art director of *Air France Revue* in 1948.

It was probably in 1948 that I first heard of Vox from one of his friends during one of my visits to Paris. I saw a good deal of his former colleague Charles Peignot while I was trying to locate John Baskerville's punches. They had been bought by Beaumarchais to print the works of Voltaire in thirty-four volumes from 1783–89. After passing through many hands, the punches had been acquired almost accidentally by Deberny & Peignot. Due to Charles Peignot's generosity, they were presented in 1953 to Cambridge University Press where Baskerville had printed his great Bible and several prayer books.

Looking back now on my friendship with Peignot and Vox, I realise we met frequently from the mid fifties when we became closely involved in three new undertakings intended to advance the progress of typography.

As well as creating the Rencontres Internationales de Lure, Vox had announced in 1952 his new system for the international classification of typefaces. Both these initiatives helped to establish Vox's international reputation, and he made sure that they were given wide and effective publicity. In 1952 the text of his new system was published by the École Estienne in Paris. The following year it was debated at the Graphic Institute in Stockholm, and in 1954 it was taken up at the Paris Printing Exhibition.

Just before the Association Typographique Internationale was founded by Peignot in 1957 at Lausanne, I went there to attend the ninth International Congress of Master Printers. To illustrate my lecture 'On Trends in Type Design' I presented those attending with a 144-page type specimen book which I had arranged in accordance with the Vox Classification. Within a few years it was adopted by many of the leading manufacturers of typefaces, and by several Standards Institutes; it was also adopted by the Association Typographique Internationale in which Vox played an active part. He put a great deal of effort into gaining approval for his system from influential and respected bodies, and he included a discussion of his system in a contribution he made to a survey of *Book Typography 1815–1865 in Europe and the USA* edited by Kenneth Day (London, 1966) pp. 94–5.

He explained that his system classified typefaces into nine families (listed in the table on page 20). These he claimed had 'both a historical past, a personality in the present and the faculty of generation in the future.' They had been given vaguely suggestive poetic names in French, but he asserted vigorously that the names could be freely adapted to the terminology of each language. For example, in English *Réale* was replaced by *Transitional*. His main concern was to have 'common concepts and similar methods of discriminating'.

I remember him telling me why he could not possibly adopt the word *Sanserif* used for *Linéale* by the English. Only they, said Vox, would have thought of describing a typeface by the one feature which it did not possess. He pointed out to me that once we had become familiar with names like *claret* and *hock* to describe certain groups of wine, the names became less important than the distinctions we had made. His system was 'based on the biological concept that each living being (thus each character) has a dual origin and that two family names may be necessary to locate a given character exactly.'

An attractive display of his classification system can be found in a type specimen book he designed and wrote in 1963. Its title *Faisons le Point* (figure 6) may be rendered as 'Let's take our bearings' (which misses the double meaning of point in referring to a compass and to the unit of type measurement). Two editions were handsomely printed by Draeger Frères: one for the Union Bibliophile de France which Vox had set up during the Second World War, and another edition of 1000 copies for friends of the Paris Office of the Monotype Corporation, to which Vox had agreed to act as typographical adviser at my suggestion.

VOX INTERNATIONAL CLASSIFICATION OF TYPEFACES

GROUP	FRENCH	ENGLISH	GERMAN	EXAMPLE
1	Humane	Humanistic	Venezianische Renaissance-Antiqua	Palatino
2	Garalde	Garaldic	Französiche Renaissance-Antiqua	Garamond
3	Réale	Transitional	Barock-Antiqua	Baskerville
4	Didone	Didonic	Klassizistiche-Antiqua	Didot, Bodoni
5	Mécane	Mechanistic	Serifenbetonte Linear-Antiqua	Clarendon
6	Linéale	Lineal	Serifenlose Linear-Antiqua	Gill, Futura
7	Incises	Incised	Antiqua Varianten	Albertus, Optima
8	Scripte	Script	Schreibschriften	Rondo, Mistral
9	Manuaire	Manual	Handschriftliche Antiqua	Libra, Klang

NOTE: for reasons of space, the names proposed for Dutch, Portuguese, Spanish and Latin have been omitted, and fewer examples for each group are cited here.

Vox's text opened with an essay of about 2500 words dedicated to Stanley Morison. This did not deter him from including a gibe at his old friend who had given the Lyell Lectures at Oxford in 1957 under the title: *Aspects of Authority and Freedom in relation to Graeco-Latin Script, Inscription and Type, Sixth Century* BC *to Twentieth Century* AD. As unrevised printed proofs of the six lectures had been circulated, I have no doubt that Vox had Morison in mind in asserting that with due respect to learned writers, the history of letterforms was of minor importance. 'Whether the Graeco-Latin alphabet was born here or there, and whatever its distant and obscure descent may have been, it counts for little compared with the fact that this alphabet EXISTS and is used by hundreds and millions of human beings.' Vox held that too much attention had been paid to historical aspects of letterforms: 'what matters to man is not the history of bread but eating it'.

Elsewhere in his preface, Vox quoted admiringly remarks made to him by Morison about the importance of learning how to select typefaces, and the desirability of them being considered not only by artists but by philosophers. A handwritten note from Vox in 1964 begged me to *read* [emphasised by underlining] some of his text in *Faisons le Point* because I would find there 'the doctrinal heritage of yours affectionately – MV'. I believe he intended me to look closely at his preface. However, he may also have meant me to read some of the aphorisms he put together in a six-page section just before demonstrating his classification system at the end of his book. Most of them are not attributed, and I will give three samples – even though they lose slightly in translation:

> *Typography is a simple craft: as simple as playing the violin.*
> *A type that is friendly to the eye is a Maecenas to the mind.*
> *I put Charlemagne among my saints: he gave us lower-case letters.*

The Monotype Corporation's Paris Office had helped Vox to publicise his classification system long before *Faisons le Point* appeared in late December 1963. For

Caractère Noël 1955 (figure 7), the Office had provided an elaborate twenty-four page insert to explain the system. This was strategically placed after an essay by Vox on 'The biology of typefaces', into which he worked a brief account of the 1955 meeting of *les compagnons de Lure* where they had unanimously adopted his classification system. Since 1950 Vox had worked as editor-in-chief and art director of *Caractère Noël*. It was a bulky annual which became a showcase for French innovation and technical achievement in printing and the graphic arts. Vox used its editorial pages to keep the public informed of his many activities, and in particular of what went on at his Rencontres de Lure. It also served as a sounding

6. Cover of *Faison le Point*, 1963.

7. Dust jacket for *Caractère Noël*, 1957.

board for his ideas. He had a gift for inventing new words and catch-phrases such as *Mort de Gutenberg, La Graphie Latine,* and *graphismes* which he would parade in *Caractère Noël.* Typically the Monotype Office's insert mentioned above was titled in large Perpetua capitals: *Defense & Illustration de la Lettre.*

'Mort de Gutenberg' was the title of a discussion reported in *Caractère Noël 1954* which had taken place at Manosque in April between Garcia, Vox and Giono. Transcribed from a tape recording, it was an extract from a forthcoming book announced by Gallimard. The phrase came to embody the optimism of the mid-fifties on grasping the full implications of the installation of new photo-composing machines as replacements of the old typesetting machines which cast letters in metal, just as Gutenberg had done by hand. It seemed high time to get rid of the restrictive remnants of the invention which Gutenberg had devised *c.* 1440; and it was exciting to look ahead to the new freedoms created by recent changes in printing equipment.

In the issue of *Caractère* for February 1950, Vox had pleaded in the opening article 'Pour une graphie latine'. What he meant by that phrase altered somewhat over the years. In his original article Vox declared that the time had come 'to endow our time and our country with an exact and precise typographic doctrine'. This he believed ought to be *Latin,* but he did not use the word in an ethnic or political sense: he simply wanted to convey a way of being, living, thinking – and writing. He deplored the fact that Latin writing and roman lettering had ceased to be the subject of research in France. He saw it as the task of *Caractère* to give France her place in the international use of Latin letters. In 1954 he proclaimed 'the universality of *la graphie latine* without distinction of country, language or school', thus making it respectable for unanimous adoption by a group as international as *les compagnons de Lure.*

True to his plan, Vox published several excellent historical studies in *Caractère Noël* up to 1964 on various aspects of *la graphie latine.* Among the French writers were Jeanne Veyrin-Forrer, Keeper of La Réserve at the Bibliothèque Nationale; André Jammes, the learned antiquarian bookseller; and Dr René Ponot, teacher and writer. Their contributions had the advantage of being amply illustrated in *Caractère Noël* with reproductions of outstanding quality.

Sadly I must confess that consulting volumes of *Caractère Noël* can be a tiresome affair. Pages are not numbered, and they often spring loose through a combination of poorly constructed bindings, weak adhesives, and the strain of handling such bulky quarto volumes. Omitting page numbers left Vox free to decide on the sequence of contents at a late stage of production, but he still had serious problems to overcome. I sympathise with the wording of a corrigenda slip in the 1955 volume which explained that with a work of 400 pages, involving 120 artists as well as 100 technical contributors and well-meaning suppliers, the result had been some errors, most of which were described as 'benign' (meaning, I suppose, that they were not malignant?)

The final number of *Caractère Noël* featured a valedictory essay by Vox. With dazzling bravura he praised what the annuals had achieved between 1951 and 1964, and also parried some criticisms which could have been levelled against him. He and his production staff had enjoyed their task and they had brought it off, he wrote, 'like a poem, like a fight, like a ballet'. They had resisted the temptation to lean more towards coherence, or to have brought out 'not a *commedia dell'arte* but an orderly work'. Characteristically he worked into his text an English phrase to express his delight at the support given to his annual by contributors from around the world: *Salute to adventurers.* Vox enjoyed taking risks and admired others who were willing to follow him along dangerous or unconventional paths.

As his aims in editing *Caractère Noël* ran parallel with his plans for the Rencontres de Lure, each enterprise helped the other. While events at Lurs from 1953 to 1964 were reported and illustrated in the annual, its editorial pages gained by carrying new and provocative ideas which had first been voiced at Lurs. Yet even with good reporting and excellent photographs and drawings, it has always been hard to convey the magical atmosphere of Lurs. It can be as powerful as that felt by travellers in Greece when they come to Delphi.

The buildings at Lurs are perched about two thousand feet above sea level. The site where they stand was visited *c.* 810 by Charlemagne who gave it to the bishops of Upper Provence. Most of its restored buildings had been built in the seventeenth century as summer retreats for the bishops and their entourage, glad to escape from the heat of their quarters in Sisteron and Digne. Restoration began soon after Vox founded the Rencontres in 1950. The place quickened from 1959 when Shell Oil's French company accepted Vox's proposal to create a Centre Culturel de Haute Provence in Lurs. Winter courses for Shell executives were run for six years to broaden their minds. These courses never overlapped with the Rencontres de Lure.

Shell paid for the renovation of several buildings, notably Le Prieuré; this provided simple but comfortable accommodation on several floors for compagnons who came as speakers, or from abroad. Vox and some of his family moved into the village. Other compagnons settled in the valley, notably a brilliant artist and type designer, Roger Excoffon, who held office from 1963 to 1968 as President of the Rencontres de Lure with Vox attending as Chancellier de Lure. One summer the compagnons cleared a sloping site on the edge of the village to improvise an amphitheatre; the seating and stage were later transformed by professional masons and carpenters to create a permanent space for

8. Promenade des Évêques, Lurs, 1963. (J. Dieuzaide)

the performing arts. Room for a cabaret was made by converting an old oil mill. So there was reasonable space for the compagnons to produce their own entertainment after the daily sessions at La Chancellerie and communal meals at Le Bello Visto.

The spirit of the Rencontres is partly conjured up by the several meanings of the word *compagnon*. It still means companion or associate; formerly it signified membership of a trade guild. When I first joined the compagnons, traditional compositor's songs were sung, led by an elderly master-printer. Visitors from abroad were invited to lead songs in their own language after a communal meal. Food, wine and song helped us to discover new friends and to share, or debate with them, our ideas and opinions. In those early years, the programme left us time to go off together on foot to visit local sites such as the Observatory, or the Monastery at Ganagobie. Of course we talked 'shop' on these excursions; but the exhilarating effect of the mountains and countryside, as well as the clarity of the light and colours, gave our talks quite a different quality from the seated sessions inside La Chancellerie.

Our seated discussions sometimes became heated, partly because few of us sat in comfortable seats. Most sessions, however were good-natured and engrossing. Sometimes they were uproariously funny, as for example when Jean Garcia related with great theatrical skill some of his more ridiculous typographic experiences.

A topic which led to lively debates in the fifties was the choice between visible and so-called invisible typography. The latter was championed by Beatrice Warde in her book of essays *The Crystal Goblet* (London, 1955). Garcia preferred to apply his typographic skill to interpreting a text for his readers. In 1958 he presented the compagnons with his paperback edition of Arthur Rimbaud's *Une Saison en Enfer* of which 12,000 copies were sold. Garcia isolated certain words either by space, or by a change of typeface, or by asterisks. He tried sincerely to give the poem a typographic shape corresponding to what he believed to be the thought which animated the poem. With disarming frankness he admitted that a more traditional setting would have been quite enough for a lot of intelligent readers. His arguments were printed in *Caractère Noël 1950*.

Discussion of this topic led Charles Peignot to argue the need to distinguish between what he called *typovision* and *typolecture*. The first applied to publicity printing whose prime objective was to catch a distracted or unwilling eye; whereas *typolecture* applied to printed texts to be read by people who had already decided that the texts interested them and therefore would resent needless typographical tricks.

Peignot and Vox gave mutual support to each other at Lurs and at meetings of the Association Typographique Internationale. As young men in the twenties (when they were scarcely into *their* thirties) they had a lot of fun with the *Divertissements Typographiques* issued by Deberny & Peignot. In an obituary of Vox published in the Dutch review *Quærendo* vol. 6 (1976) p.8, Fernand Baudin quoted a remark that the twenties were the last great party 'and that mankind has since then been experiencing no more than the hangover'. Baudin added: 'Vox and Peignot were amongst those who threw the party.' By the fifties the pair were older and more serious, both anxious to recover for France some of *la gloire* which it had lost temporarily during the Second World War.

A few years after peace returned, both Vox and Peignot showed great foresight in voicing their views on the new technology which then began to transform the printing and publishing trades. Writing in 1950 for *Caractère*, Vox pointed out the need to work with unknown techniques which had hardly been dreamt of at that time. He asked: 'For example, suppose photo-electric composition becomes widespread, what will be the outcome?' This question led to a continual re-working of his theme 'Mort de Gutenberg'. It also gave a sense of urgency to his conduct of the Rencontres de Lure.

Under his watchful eye and agile mind, the topics discussed at Lurs ranged from letterforms and illustration to layout and design; they also covered printing processes and photography, as well as publishing and publicity. Much else was discussed, sometimes from a philosophical viewpoint and at other times in considerable technical detail.

Vox's involvement with all that happened at Lurs did not prevent him from continuing with his literary career. Apart from many short texts, many of them *jeux d'esprit*, he produced a biography of Napoleon published in 1959 by the Editions de Seuil, and later translated into English. It was followed in 1967 by his *Conversations de Napoléon Bonaparte* for the Club des Amis du Livre. In 1970 he set to work on his memoirs, of which extracts appeared posthumously in Fernand Baudin's *Dossier Vox* (Andenne, 1975). His later years were troubled by differences of opinion with other officers elected to run the Rencontres de Lure. His difficulties were aggravated by failing health which became even harder to bear after his wife died in 1972. Yet even in that year he made plans for creating a new Académie des Artistes Typographiques which he planned to run on the lines of the Académie Goncourt.

Lecturing at Barcelona in 1952 he had described himself as 'a professional graphic artist but also a writer, publisher, journalist, in short if I may say so – a

Maximilien Vox

humanist.' He played with words so often that I do not feel able to define exactly what he meant by the word *humanist*. What I do know from my friendship with him over thirty years is that he had a mind like quicksilver, and a wonderfully generous heart.

John Dreyfus was born in London, 15 April 1918. He joined Cambridge University Press as a graduate trainee in 1939. After six years in the British Army, he returned to Cambridge and was appointed Assistant University Printer (1949–56); he continued as Typographical Adviser at Cambridge until 1982. He was also engaged by the Monotype Corporation as Typographical Adviser from 1956 to 1982. He acted as European Consultant to the Limited Editions Club of New York (1956–77), and was Sandars Reader in Bibliography at Cambridge University (1979–80). Dreyfus helped to organise the Gutenberg Quincentenary Exhibition at the Fitzwilliam Museum in Cambridge in 1940, and also helped to organise the Printing and the Mind of Man exhibition in London in 1963 (he also designed catalogues for both exhibitions). He was Founder Vice-President of the Association Typographique Internationale in 1957, and served as its President from 1968 to 1973. For the Printing Historical Society in London, of which he was President, he organised the Caxton International Congress in 1976. Dreyfus was a Laureate of the American Printing Historical Society (1984), and he received the Frederic W. Goudy Award in 1984 and the Gutenberg Prize at Mainz in 1996. He was the author of many books and articles about printing, and frequently lectured on typographical subjects. With François Richaudeau, he co-edited *La Chose Imprimée* in 1977 (a French encyclopaedia on printing, which was later translated into Spanish). He died on 29 December 2002.

PRINCIPAL SOURCES

Fernand Baudin, *Dossier Vox* (Andenne, Rémy Magermans, 1975) 325 pp.

Frédérique Contini, Joëlle Picard & Marc Renaud, *Maximilien Vox, un homme de lettres* (Paris, 1994) 151 pp. Published by the Agence Culturelle de Paris to coincide with an exhibition in the Mairie du VIème arrondissement, 7 December 1994 to 7 January 1995.

Christine Mazerand, *Le graphisme 'en français' aux Rencontres Internationales de Lurs-en-Provence 1955–1970*. 500 copies printed for the Compagnons de Lure and their friends, August 1973. 171 unnumbered pages.

'Hommages à Maximilien Vox' in *Arts et Métiers du Livre* no. 54 (Paris, January-February 1975) pp. 9–22. With contributions by Charles Peignot, Henri Jonquières, Maurice Robert, Robert Ranc, Robert Naly, Pierre Le Roy, John Dreyfus, Fernand Baudin and Gérard Blanchard; with illustrations.

René Ponot, *Rencontres Internationales de Lure* (Paris, November 1978). Published by the Association des Compagnons de Lure for its members, friends and sympathisers. 40 pp. reproduced from typescript in a paper cover. A record of the Association's activities from 1950 to 1978.

[Also frequent references to Vox and the Rencontres de Lure in the annual numbers of *Caractère Noël* (Paris 1952–64) to which exact references are not given because the annuals were not paginated.]

We are grateful for invaluable help given by Madame Frédérique Contini of the Bibliothèque des Arts Graphiques, and to Dr Sylvère Monod.

Medieval Uncial* (669 AD)	Hammer Unziale 1923	Samson 1931	Pindar 1935	American Uncial 1945
ᚨ	A	a	a	a
B	B	B	B	b
ᚦ	δ	δ	δ	δ
ᵹ	ᵹ	ᵹ	ᵹ	ᵹ
* St Augustine, Homilae decem in epistolae Sancti Joannis, Luxeuil.	w	w	ѡ	ѡ
	y	y	y	y

1. Guide to the identification of Hammer's uncials: If the setting has capital letters, it is either Pindar or American Uncial. If not, it is probably Samson, but for a quick check look at the 'a' to make sure that it is not Hammer Unziale. To distinguish quickly between Pindar and American Uncial, look at 'b' or 'y'.

Victor Hammer

BY SEBASTIAN CARTER

A contemporary of James Joyce and Eric Gill, and a much more private and restrained personality than either Morison or Vox, Victor Hammer followed his own way in type design and cut his own punches, perfecting the little-used uncial style of letter (based on handwriting from the time of Charlemagne) and employing it in brilliantly designed books. The superior quality of his work inspired Sebastian Carter's overview in Matrix 7 *(1987).*

Why should we take note of the work of Victor Hammer? After all, he was a printer who, when it comes to being an anachronism, left William Morris at the starting post. Morris revived printing on a hand-press, on dampened hand-made paper, using types cut to his own design, but Hammer went much further. It was not enough to use hand-presses, but they must ideally be reconstructions of the wooden presses in use before the beginning of the nineteenth century. The model for the design of his types was found not in early printed books but in manuscripts of the period between the fall of the Roman empire and the rise of the Carolingian, on whose uncial script he based first his own handwriting and then his types. And he was not content, as Morris was, to draw over photographic enlargements of his models and hand the sketches to a professional punchcutter, but after his first unhappy experience of this process, he gradually taught himself the craft of punchcutting and cut his own letters. And, finally, he was not an eccentric nineteenth-century contemporary of Morris, but was born in the same year as those other twentieth-century rebels, Eric Gill, James Joyce and Stravinsky, and was only thirteen when Morris died. His best known type, American Uncial, was cut during the Second World War.

The reason is the sheer quality of Hammer's work. Although he printed relatively few books, frequently in editions of under a hundred, they are strange but self-evident masterpieces. On their Magnani or Hosho papers, with their intricately cut and printed two-colour initials, and their dense and rhythmical pages of type, they are magnificent achievements. The quality of their press-work is little short of miraculous. The *Samson Agonistes* and his edition of Hölderlin's poems must rank among the most beautiful books printed this century. Books like these, admirable things in themselves, serve also a functional purpose as objects for other printers to aspire to. Even if one has only a few loose pages, as I have, or a memory of their excellence, they are perpetual spur to do better oneself.

Not many of us, however, would want to copy Hammer's style, nor would he have necessarily wished us to. His adoption of the uncial script was the particular choice of a man of wide culture, well-travelled and familiar with several living European languages other than his native German, as well as with Latin. Above all, he was unusually sensitive as an artist to the appearance of script, and as a linguist to its suitability for conveying a particular language, even through what seem to us the peripheral matters of accents, punctuation and the incidence of capital letters.[1] As John Dreyfus has pointed out,[2] Hammer was brought up in a strong blackletter tradition, and though he reacted against gothic script for Latin, and needed roman for English and French, when he started printing in the early 1920s he found existing German 'romans' such as Behrens Antiqua too bizarre, and those from other countries over-refined. The script he developed, first in his calligraphy and later in his types, was by no means an academic uncial, since it introduced more lower-case forms than its medieval models and, later, founts of roman capitals; it was more of an adaptation of the script's principles to twentieth-century use. It thereupon followed a logic of its own and, through the various refinements Hammer gave it, arrived at its final exposition in American Uncial. When one compares Hammer's uncials with those of other designers – de Roos's Libra for example, or Lange's Solemnis – we must admire the superior flow of

2. Victor Hammer at his workbench. Photograph by Martin Jessee.

Hammer's types, which he likened to 'a string of pearls', and their avoidance of the jumpiness usually associated with the genre. This was achieved by the strong stressing of horizontals, unusually on the base line of the x-height as well as the top. (The conventional wisdom is that since the eye skims along the top of the x-height, the features which lead the eye should be concentrated there.) This sinewy drive forward allows some of the letters, such as the d, the t and the y, to dance with an abandon normally considered impossible.

The difference between Hammer's first and last uncials is quite marked, but to distinguish between the Samson, Pindar and American Uncial takes practice.[3] The diagram in figure 1 aims to clarify the identification.

Hammer designed his types for use in his own work, and only incidentally for other printers. He wrote a note in the first specimen of American Uncial which is more in the nature of an envoi: 'What virtues it has were not achieved magically, but come directly from the love and care with which I have cut it. This requires something from you as a printer. You are requested to use it creatively, that is: not for startling effects, but allowing its virtues a straightforward statement in use.' Every type designer must wish the same, but Hammer must have been saddened by the generally exotic uses to which his type has been put, adorning folksy wine labels and messages in Gaelic.

In writing my *Twentieth century type designers* (1987), I at first assumed that I could ignore Hammer. In no sense, I thought, could he be classed as a man of this century, even though he happened to live in it by accident. And yet on reflection he turned out to be a surprisingly modern figure. The nineteenth-century intelligentsia, when they approached the crafts, did so in a largely theoretical, managerial, *de haut en bas* way. One cannot imagine Ruskin, chisel in hand, actually building a cathedral, although he wrote that 'the workman ought often to be thinking, and the thinker often to be working'; and even Morris actually practised relatively few of the crafts with which his name is connected. He designed for many applied arts, it is true, but only tapestry and calligraphy consistently engaged his hand. It was only in this century that thinking men became practising craftsmen, and completed Ruskin's equation. Hammer is far more like Gill or Mardersteig, men who were rebelling against the tendency of their time towards dehumanised mechanisation but, in their practical response, suited the action to the word.

Victor Hammer was born in Vienna on 9 December 1882, and so was ten months younger than Gill and Joyce, both of whom had been born in February. At the age of fifteen he was apprenticed to the architect and town planner Camillo Sitte, and a year later went to study at the Vienna Akademie der bildenden

Künste (academy of fine arts). His early career was in portraiture, both in a mixed technique of oil and tempera, and also in mezzotint, an intaglio process now little used, which works through the production of highlights by burnishing a plate previously roughened with a mezzotint rocker. Hammer made this medium very much his own, and continued successfully to make portraits both as paintings and prints throughout his life, in a formal, highly realistic style akin to that of the early Renaissance in Germany, as well as painting large Biblical and allegorical subjects. Around 1910 he began experimenting with a quill pen, and this, together with a developing interest in bookbinding, aroused a passion for the arts of the book which consumed the rest of his life.

After the First World War, which he spent first in the army and then as a war artist, Hammer moved to a small house on the estate of Count Ferdinand Arco at St Martin im Innkreis in upper Austria, and there in the winter of 1921 he set about the design and cutting of his first type. He was not technically experienced in punchcutting, and so the punches were cut by a man named Schuricht.[4]

Hammer Unziale (figure 3), also called Hammerschrift, was a single-alphabet type, with a high proportion of capital forms in the 'lower case', but no upper case as such. Hammer himself never used it, though he had a fount in the workshop, but the experience of producing it added to his ambition to cut his own. In 1922 he moved to Florence, though he continued to spend the summer months in St Martin. The following year, during a visit to supervise the casting of his type at Klingspor, he first met the great German type designer Rudolf Koch, who was six years his senior, and was working then, as for most of his life, as Klingspor's house designer, in which he was markedly different from other German type designers, who tended first and foremost to be art school professors. Koch and Hammer formed a friendship which lasted until Koch's death in 1934. They had much in common: a deep religious faith and a conviction that the arts should serve it, a belief in the historic apprenticeship system, and a wayward and original graphic style. Fritz Kredel, the eminent wood-cutter, worked in both workshops, and so did Koch's son Paul, who came to Florence in 1926, fresh from cutting some of the punches for his father's Peter Jessen Schrift. Here he cut the punches and cast the characters of Hammer's second type, called Samson (figure 4) after the book in which it first appeared, Milton's *Samson Agonistes* (1931). This was the first book from Hammer's first press, the Stamperia del Santuccio, 'stamperia' being Italian for a printing works and a 'santuccio' being a little saint: a carved figure of one stood in a niche in the wall of the house in the Via San Leonardo where the press was housed, which was therefore called the Villa Santuccio. With the help of local craftsmen, Hammer built a copy of the wooden

3. Hammer Unziale
(1923)

ABCDEFGHIJKLMNOPQRSTUVWXYZÄŐ
ÚCHFFTT1234567890

4. Samson (1931)

OF DISCOURSE.
OME IN THEIR DISCOURSE DE-
SIRE RATHER COMMENDATION
OF WIT IN BEING ABLE TO HOLDE
ALL ARGUMENTS/THEN OF
IUDGEMENT IN DISCERNING
WHAT IS TRUE/AS IF IT WERE A
PRAISE TO KNOW WHAT MIGHT
BE SAID/AND NOT WHAT SHOULDE BEE
THOUGHT·SOME HAUE CERTAINE COM-
MON PLACES AND THEAMES WHEREIN
THEY ARE GOOD/AND WANT VARIETIE/
WHICH KINDE OF POUERTIE IS FOR THE
MOST PART TEDIOUS/AND NOWE AND
THEN RIDICULOUS·§THE HONOURABLEST
PART OF TALKE/IS TO GUIDE THE OCCASION/
AND AGAINE TO MODERATE AND PASSE
TO SOMEWHAT ELSE·§IT IS GOOD TO VARIE

press housed in the Biblioteca Medicea Laurenziana in the city, the only common press in Italy,[5] built in 1818 but believed in the 1920s to be much older. On it, and later another copy, Hammer began to print, assisted by his son Jacob, Fritz Arnold from Klingspor, and Edgar Kaufman, an American disciple whose father generously subsidised the Stamperia. (He also commissioned Frank Lloyd Wright to design his epoch-making house, Falling Water.) Later a student from the Bauhaus at Dessau joined the workshop for a brief period. This must be one of the strangest cross-fertilisations in cultural history, for the Bauhaus's ruthlessly doctrinal drive towards single-alphabet printing began from a quite different starting point, and occured when Hammer was abandoning his.

The Samson type was the first of Hammer's mature uncials, and the two which followed were subtle rather than radical improvements on it. For the first time, the uncial form appears rhythmical and natural, and the letters flow into each other. Hammer's improved design, and Paul Koch's superlative engraving, make it a wonderful achievement. Although trial capitals were cut, the type was used without them, and enough capital forms remained in it to make this tolerable. Hammer himself often used paragraph marks at the beginning of each sentence as a signal – in Bacon's *Essayes* (1933), which was the last book printed in Florence, they were printed in a second colour. Anyone who has ever struggled with a wooden hand-press will appreciate the astounding quality of the work which Victor Hammer did on his. In the event, the three first books were the only ones for many years to be printed in this way. In 1933 he moved away from Florence, put the presses into store in Vienna, and went to London for two years. It was not until he moved to Kolbsheim in Alsace, where he was engaged in designing, building and decorating a private chapel for his friend and patron Alexandre de Grunelius, that he began to print again, and this time it was on an iron hand-press. For his next book, Hölderlin's *Fragmente des Pindar* (1935), Hammer used a new type, called Pindar (figure 5), and for this type he had cut the punches himself.

It is not quite accurate to say that either Rudolf Koch or Victor Hammer was a self-taught punchcutter: Koch had watched the craftsmen at Klingspor, and Hammer had watched Schuricht and Paul Koch. But they did not serve the gruelling apprenticeship of the trade punchcutters, and in each case the act of cutting was subservient to the idea: they were not interpreting a design, as most punchcutters did, but creating as they went along. What is interesting is to compare the first efforts of the two men. Koch's first type for which he cut the punches himself was Neuland (1923), best known in the English-speaking design world through its use by Francis Meynell in the Nonesuch Press *Genesis* (1924). It is no criticism of Koch to say that it was a cautious choice of letter for a beginner, for it was a bold, irregular sanserif design in which it would be difficult to go wrong. But Pindar is quite another story, a delicate 12-point type cut as though its maker had decades of experience behind him. It was the first of Hammer's types to have a set of capitals, and so marks his relinquishing of the doctrinaire single-alphabet uncial, though several capital forms survive in the 'lower case'.

A working fount was cast at the Stamperia, and a later casting was made in 1937 by Klingspor, though they never issued the type commercially. Paul Koch had a fount at his workshop in the Haus zum Fürsteneck in Frankfurt, and here in 1938 the young Hermann Zapf used it to set his first piece of printing, a business card.

In 1936, after the completion of Hammer's work at Kolbsheim, he moved his workshop and the Stamperia to Grundlsee in Austria, where he had a teaching post, and two years later back to Vienna, where he was appointed professor at the school where he had studied, the Akademie der bildenden Künste. Finally, in the autumn of 1939, political opposition from the Nazis forced him to leave Vienna for the safety of the United States, abandoning most of his possessions,

5. Pindar (1935)

ʋon West-Canaɒa/unɒ um ɒie kolossalen
Trümmer ɒes Azteken Pallastes/ɒer/ein amerikanisches Palmyra/sich ʋerlassen in ɒer
Einöɒe am Gyla-Flusse erhebt·Der langhör-
nige Mouflon/ɒer Stammʋater ɒes Schaa-
fes/schwärmt auf ɒen ɒürren unɒ nackten
Kalkfelsen ʋon Californien umher·Der süɒ-
lichen Halbinsel sinɒ ɒie kamelartigen Vicun-
nas/ɒie Alpacas unɒ Lamas eigenthümlich·
Aber alle ɒiese nuzbaren Thiere haben/ɒas
Lama abgerechnet/Jahrtausenɒe lang ihre
natürliche Freiheit bewahrt·Denn Genuss
ʋon Milch unɒ Käse ist/wie ɒer Besitz unɒ ɒie

6. American Uncial
(1945)

SAPIENTIA FILIIS SUIS VITAM IN-
Wisdom breathes life into her children
spirat et suscipit inquirentes se
and shelters those who seek her and she
et præibit in via justitiæ: et qui
will go before them in the way of justice: and he
illam diligit diligit vitam: et qui
who loves her loves life: and those
vigilaverint ad illam complec-
who watch for her will embrace

including all of his printing equipment. In America, through the intercession of his friend Nicholas Nabokov, cousin of Vladimir, he took up a teaching post at Wells College in Aurora, New York State, and here he began printing again under two new imprints, the Wells College Press, used for teaching purposes, and the Hammer Press, for his own work. His uncial types having been left behind in Vienna, he used roman faces designed by others, his favourite being Joseph Blumenthal's Emerson. But he quickly began to work on a new uncial. In 1940–1 he was asked by American Type Founders to cut some punches, for a type to be known as Aurora Uncial; but though some trial sorts were cast, the fount was left incomplete, possibly because ATF's usual practice was to cast from engraved matrices, not from strikes made from hand-cut punches, and the technical problems were insuperable. But at the same time he was working on

7. Two examples of Hammer's two-colour initials. The metal letters were made in two parts, inked separately, and printed together, in the manner of the Mainz Psalter.

another set of punches which became American Uncial (figure 6), his final refinement of the conventional uncial form. The 14-point was finished in 1943, and to have it cast Hammer went to the Dearborn Type Foundry in Chicago, one of the few independent plants outside the ATF consortium. This casting was supported financially by the Society of Typographic Arts of Chicago through the encouragement of Robert Hunter Middleton, head of design at Ludlow and the secretary of the Society, who had met Hammer in 1941 at the Newberry Library, studied punchcutting with him, and was later to complete some of his founts. Middleton tirelessly supervised Nussbaumer's casting, and enough of the type was delivered in January 1945 to print a keepsake for the STA, Hammer's *A dialogue on the uncial*.[6]

The first major use of American Uncial was in Hammer's great edition of Hölderlin's *Gedichte*, printed in an edition of fifty-one copies on Magnani paper. It was begun at Aurora as technically a Hammer Press book, but completed as a Stamperia del Santuccio one in 1949 at Lexington, Kentucky, where Hammer moved in 1948 after his statutory retirement from Wells College at the age of sixty-five. The Hammer Press continued as Jacob Hammer's imprint until about 1958.

After his retirement, Hammer became artist-in-residence at the charmingly-named Transylvania College in Lexington. Here he revived the Santuccio imprint and brought what survived of his equipment from Vienna, including one of the wooden presses, which is now in the King Library of the University of Kentucky at Lexington. In 1952 a group of friends and students, including Joseph Graves of the Gravesend Press and Carolyn Reading, formed the Anvil Press for the purpose of carrying out projects with Hammer as designer and advisor. After the death of Hammer's first wife Rosl in 1954, Hammer married Carolyn Reading, and she continued the Anvil Press imprint until her death in 2001. Apart from a few broadsides, the Stamperia produced no more books after Victor Hammer's *Concern for the art of civilized man* in 1963. Hammer retired from Transylvania in 1953, but continued to work until his death on 10 July 1967. In 1953 he cut a magnificent set of 30-point initials for American Uncial, which were cast by Klingspor, who also cast the later founts of the 14-point after Nussbaumer's retirement, and the 18-point which Hammer cut in 1954–5. Just after this, Klingspor was absorbed by Stempel, who had had a controlling interest in the smaller foundry since 1918: Karl Klingspor, the moving spirit behind it, had died in 1950, and the business had been carried on by his nephew Karl Hermann, but it could not long survive the exile of the Klingspor family in South America during the war or the bombing of Offenbach. Shortly before Hammer's death, to his great distress, Stempel reissued a full range of sizes of American Uncial with mechanically engraved matrices, calling it Neue Hammer Unziale, and returned the punches to Lexington.

Because of these difficulties, Hammer turned to another foundry for his last type. In 1959, Deberny & Peignot of Paris cast, though they did not issue, his extraordinary cursive uncial Andromaque (figure 8), which he had cut the year before for an edition of Racine's tragedy of that name. You have to give Andromaque a second look to realise that it is not Greek. Although Hammer had cut some Greek founts already, to accompany Samson and American Uncial, they blended well with the 'romans' they were designed for. But Andromaque was developed as a face on its own, from some inscriptional lettering Hammer had done for the back panel of a painted triptych, and though undoubtedly attractive, cannot be said to be legible enough to make a serviceable typeface. It does however have the dubious virtue of making the other uncials seem easy to read by comparison, and also works well in harness with them.

Victor Hammer stands apart from many who seem to resemble him, in the total integrity with which he carried out Ruskin's precepts. He could perform all the handiworks and physical operations relating to typography, in Moxon's phrase, and more: for he could write the texts and bind the finished books as well. His purpose in all this was not an ostentatious display of talent, but the

8. Andromaque
(1959)

ONE light, ONE ray and it will be the angels' spring;
ONE flash, ONE glance upon the shiny pond, and then
asperges me! sweet wilderness, and lo! we are redeemed!

das maedchen: vorueber! ach, vorueber!
geh, wilder knochenmann!
Jch bin noch jung! geh, lieber!

reduction of the printing process to its simplest level, so that he could exercise the maximum control at all times to the best possible effect. As he wrote himself,[7] 'The secret of the craftsman's procedure is always to see details and distinctions in connection with the whole form he works upon. He does not know beforehand exactly what his work will look like – he will only know when he has finished it. No drawn or lettered "design" can do else than anticipate what the punchcutter's hand and eye will produce. A punchcutter must be alive to calligraphy. He must be aware of the task of reconciling changing forms of language with the unalterable forms of the Roman capital letters by blending new letter combinations into a legible stream, the line. Then he will be able to cut his punches in as straightforward a manner as he would write a love letter or invoke the name of a god in an inscription – and his work will be alive.' These last words were written about his punchcutting, but they apply to everything he did.

Sebastian Carter was born in 1941, and studied English literature and the history of art at King's College, Cambridge. After university he worked for a number of publishers and designers in London and Paris before joining his father Will Carter at the Rampant Lions Press in Cambridge, which he now runs from his house outside the town. Here he has produced a long series of fine editions, often in rare typefaces such as Eric Gill's Golden Cockerel Roman and Hermann Zapf's Hunt Roman. Highlights have included Milton's *Areopagitica*, Samuel Beckett's *As the story was told*, and T. S. Eliot's *Four Quartets*, as well as a number of typographical display pieces such as *A printer's dozen* and most recently *In praise of letterpress*. He writes extensively on printing and typography, reviewing regularly for the *Times Literary Supplement* and the British Printing Historical Society's *Bulletin* and *Journal*. He guest-edited the 1990 Eric Gill number of the *Monotype Recorder*, and wrote the section on 'The Morison years' in the centenary number in 1997. His *Twentieth century type designers* (1987; new edition 1995; now out in paperback) has become a standard work. With only two exceptions, he has contributed to every number of *Matrix*.

NOTES

1. English speakers can afford to take a light view of these problems, since we are hardly encumbered with accents at all, and although what one might call 'Winnie-The-Pooh' capitalisation lingers, it is becoming more and more of a joke. The French and the Germans, however, are seriously burdened with accents, and the Germans with obligatory capitals for all nouns, a rule which has survived several attempts at reform.

2. John Dreyfus, 'Printing as industry and craft: Victor Hammer's example', *The Kentucky Review*, v, 2, Winter 1984.

3. Characteristic of the confusion is the reference to Hammer's types in *The encyclopaedia of typefaces*. The first edition (1953) correctly illustrated and identified just his first type, usually called plain Hammer Unziale, which was cut around 1921 and issued by Klingspor in 1923. But by the fourth edition edition (1970), the type illustrated has become American Uncial, and the text reads, 'Designed by Victor Hammer in 1923 for Klingspor together with a set of initials. In 1953 a NEW HAMMER UNCIAL, also known as AMERICAN UNCIAL, was issued, which stems from the version cut by Nussbaumer in 1945. The characters go back to letter forms practised before black letter or roman were evolved.' Almost everything here is wrong, or misleading.
American Uncial is an enormous improvement on Hammer Unziale, and better even than the two designs which came in between. It was *cut* by Hammer and *cast* in 1945 by Charles Nussbaumer

of the Dearborn Type Foundry in Chicago, and the 'set of initials' was designed for it in 1953. Neue Hammer Unziale was the name given by Stempel to the engraved-matrix version of American Uncial which they issued after they had absorbed Klingspor, who had cast some of the type privately for Hammer after Nussbaumer's retirement.

4. Schuricht is a shadowy figure, and the roundabout difficulties I experienced in confirming who he was for the purposes of *Twentieth century type designers* are a cautionary tale of the problems of writing potted biographies with insufficient time for research. The first source I naturally consulted was the *Chapters on writing and printing*, published by the Anvil Press in 1958. (The Anvil Press, as its name suggests, was the imprint used by Hammer's pupils under his supervision. The distribution of titles between the various Hammer imprints is somewhat complicated, but I hope it will be clarified in the course of this article.) In her 'Notes on the Stamperia del Santuccio', the artist's second wife Carolyn Hammer wrote that N. Schuricht, 'a type-cutter from the Staatsdruckerei in Vienna', came out to St Martin to cut the punches under Hammer's supervision. The Klingspor foundry cast and issued the type a few years later, but Hammer was dissatisfied with it. However, in the more recent Anvil Press publication, *Victor Hammer, artist and printer* (1981: not printed at the Hammer studio, but by Martino Mardersteig at the Stamperia Valdonega), Mrs Hammer's nephew, W. Gay Reading Jr, wrote a valuable and well-illustrated survey of the Hammer types in which he said that Hammer Unziale was cut by 'the punch-maker A. Schuricht of the Klingspor foundry in 1925'. To check which of the references was correct, I wrote to Mrs Hammer, and she answered that 'Victor could never remember his first name, so said "just call him A. for Anonymous". Gay is right, *Chapters* is wrong.' On the strength of the caveat printed at the end of *Chapters*, that it agreed with the polite Chinese custom of leaving errors in a book so that the reader, on finding them, might feel superior, I omitted Schuricht's initial altogether in my *Type designers* book, and had him working for Klingspor. Doubts lingered, however: Gay Reading dated the cutting of Hammer Unziale as 1925, whereas Hammer himself, in *Chapters*, had said that it was cut, but not cast, when he went to live in Florence in 1922, and all the printed sources had the type being issued by Klingspor in 1923. Finally, Walter Wilkes has confirmed that Arthur Schuricht was born in Leipzig in 1882, worked in Vienna, and died there in 1945.

5. Illustrated and described as Number II in Philip Gaskell's 'A census of wooden presses', *Journal of the Printing Historical Society*, 6, 1970.

6. Victor Hammer, *A dialogue on the uncial*, Aurora, Hammer Press, 1946.

7. Victor Hammer, 'Digressions on the roman letter' *Chapters on writing and printing*, Lexington, Anvil Press, 1958.

Several people have given me much help with Victor Hammer. Mrs Carolyn Hammer and Gay Reading entertained me with great hospitality in Lexington, and showed me round the press, as well as answering many points of detail, and giving me some Hammer material to work with. William Hesterberg of Chicago gave me a copy of his dissertation on American Uncial, and provided the photograph of Hammer by Martin Jessee. James Birchfield of the University of Kentucky Library sent additional material. John Lane of Reading and Leiden answered my questions with grace and industry. I am most grateful to them all.

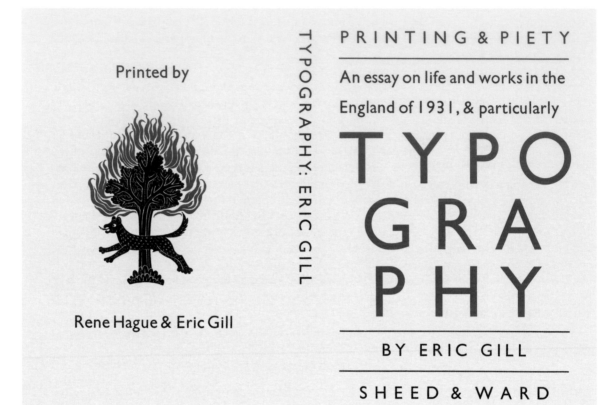

Printed by

Rene Hague & Eric Gill

TYPOGRAPHY: ERIC GILL

PRINTING & PIETY

An essay on life and works in the

England of 1931, & particularly

TYPO
GRA
PHY

BY ERIC GILL

SHEED & WARD

1. Dust-jacket from the first edition.

Eric Gill's *Typography* Examined

BY CHRISTOPHER SKELTON

Eric Gill was famously talented and famously cantankerous. His Essay on Typography, *first published in 1931, reflected his attitude toward work and society while attempting to be a practical handbook at the same time. In* Matrix 7 *(1987) Christopher Skelton looked at both the book itself and its impact – an impact that's renewed today, with the book back in print again.*

Eric Gill was highly regarded as a teacher in the workshop by his associates and assistants. His work, however, left him little time for formal teaching. The *Essay on Typography* is the one book that he devoted to any practical aspect of his work with letters. For this reason alone it is worth our continued attention, even though in the thirty-three years since it was last reprinted the revolution in the techniques of the reproduction of letters has been immense. But the letters themselves, including Gill's, are still the same as they were in 1931.

Gill himself defines typography as 'the reproduction of letters by means of movable types', a definition that can include all forms of typesetting and printing, although in Gill's context he takes typography as being synonymous with letterpress printing.

The book was first published by Sheed & Ward in 1931, titled on the front of the jacket 'Printing & Piety' and simply 'Typography' on the spine. 'An Essay on Typography' appears on the contents page, which also serves as a title-page. 'Essay' is a misleading description for a work of over 140 pages divided into nine chapters. (It may have been originally intended as a shorter work as René Hague's estimate was for eighty pages of composition.) It was the first substantial piece of Gill's writing to be published. His previously printed works are all small pamphlets, short essays and lectures – mostly collected in *Art Nonsense* in 1929.

Gill began designing typefaces in 1925. Gill Sans was first shown by the Monotype Corporation in 1929, and the first book printed in Perpetua also appeared in that year. Gill's collaboration with Robert Gibbings, begun four years earlier, was at its most active with the drawings for the Golden Cockerel type in 1929 and with *The Four Gospels*, published in 1931. The drawings for the Joanna typeface were started in April 1930. This was the period, too, of Gill's closest association with

Stanley Morison, whose *First Principles of Typography* was published in 1930 in *Fleuron* no. 7. A large part of that volume is devoted to Gill's work. By 1931 he had become a considerable figure in the typographical world.

Gill had moved to Pigotts in Buckinghamshire from Capel-y-ffin in South Wales in 1928. In April 1930 he and his future son-in-law, René Hague, set about buying the equipment for the printing business, Hague & Gill, which was to share the farm buildings with the stone-carving workshop and the engraving studio. One of the objects of the new press was to make use of Gill's types, and Joanna was designed specifically and exclusively for it. René Hague, a somewhat wayward Irishman, had met the Gill family in Wales in 1924 and married Gill's daughter, Joanna, after whom the type was named, in November 1930. How he came by his printing knowledge is somewhat obscure although there is no doubting his competence. It may well be that Gill's establishment of this new venture had a lot to do with giving his son-in-law employment within the workshop milieu.

With the years of his type designing coming to fruition, and the establishment of the printing business, it was natural for Gill to set down his ideas on typography in a way that was characteristic of him. The *Essay* can be seen partly as an attempt to explain his excursion into the industrial activity so alien to his often stated principles.

Gill's diary records that he began writing *Typography* in October 1930 while he was in hospital. The writing continued throughout October and November, sometimes being dictated to René Hague. He notes several periods of discussion with him and it is probable that in the more technical sections the book is partly Hague's. Hague himself wrote very little on the subject. His provocative essay 'Reason and Typography'[1] is full of phrases that echo Gill, and there is no doubt that in typographical matters the two men thought alike.

As we have seen, this was a period of concentrated activity for Gill. Besides the work mentioned he was busy with drawing the variations of Perpetua and Gill Sans, the BBC carvings and the *Four Gospels* engravings. He seems to have induced activity in others as well: there was barely six months between finishing the drawings for Joanna Roman in June 1930, and his record of correcting the proofs of *Typography* on 4 January 1931. In this time the typefounder, H. W. Caslon, had cut the punches and cast the type, and Hague & Gill had set it up by hand for its first use in the book.

The first edition of 500 copies is noted as number four of the publications of Hague & Gill and is dated in the colophon, June 1931, although Gill's diary records their being signed in September. The whole edition is signed by both Gill and Hague (Hague first). It is printed on the specially watermarked Hague and Gill hand-made paper in a format of 7½ x 5 ins, almost certainly on an Albion hand-press.

The second edition was published in 1936, also by Sheed & Ward, in a smaller format. It has additions to the introductory paragraphs, a new chapter at the end, and other revisions. It is basically the same typesetting as the earlier printing with several significant differences. Joanna Italic became available in 1931 and is used for the captions and running headlines. A third edition was published by J. M. Dent & Son in 1941 from the same typesetting (Dents were part owners of Hague & Gill from 1936). The book was reissued by Dents in 1953, but set in the 11-point version of the type that was cut by the Monotype Corporation in 1937.

Sheed & Ward, the book's first publishers, normally handled work of specifically Roman Catholic interest; and from its inception Gill must have regarded the book as something far different from a mere treatise on typography. Underneath the heading 'PRINTING AND PIETY' on the jacket of the first edition is the subtitle 'An essay on life and works in the England of 1931, & particularly TYPOGRAPHY', the last word dominating the cover in large red capitals split into three lines. Clearly, it was never intended to be all typography. Although this theme is restated in the opening sentence of the book, the tone and hectoring style of the first chapter must have come as a surprise to those seeking instruction on typographical matters and unfamiliar with Gill's brand of Christian socialism, particularly without the jacket of the first edition to sound a warning.

In the expanded introduction to the 1936 edition Gill wrote, referring to the earlier issue, 'It was one of the author's chief objects to describe two worlds – that of industrialism and that of the human workman – & to define their limits'. It is with the application of his 'two worlds' theory to the trade of printing that the first chapter is especially concerned. 'On the one hand is the world of mechanised industry claiming to be able to give happiness to men and all the delights of human life – provided we are content to have them in our spare time and do not demand such things in the work by which we earn our livings', and 'On the other . . . a world in which the notion of spare time hardly exists, for the thing is hardly known and very little desired; a world wherein the work is the life & love accompanies it.' Gill, himself, in the same 1936 introduction considered that these 'chief objects' had been 'imperfectly remembered' and faulted the book on that account, although the theme recurs frequently in succeeding chapters.

It is from this world of mechanised industry or bureaucratised commerce that many readers of *Matrix* must have sought to escape to what Gill called 'the indestructible world of the small workshop', if only in their 'spare time'. It is to the 'humane craftsman' that the book largely speaks and its teaching is particularly relevant to today's 'fine printers' who for many reasons of their own have decided to avoid the mechanised way of doing things. 'There will always be many,' Gill writes 'who will choose to be masters of their own work and in their own workshops'.

He had earlier written essays on stone-carving and wood-engraving.[2] Those, unlike *Typography*, were solely concerned with assessing the position of the practitioner of those arts in twentieth-century society. There is no practical advice in either. In the typography essay he is ever willing to leave the practical point to draw a social or religious moral. Perhaps under the influence of René Hague he was persuaded to devote more space than he intended to the chapters on the sound common sense of the practice of typography, for which the work is chiefly remembered.

The chapter on lettering is by far the longest in the book. A historical survey is followed by a discussion of legibility and letter forms, plain and fancy. The world of machinery and standardised production 'can only decently turn out the plainest of plain things', and 'Fancifulness is therefore within the competence of a smaller and smaller number of workmen.' Thus it should be with letters. In 1929 Gill himself had designed a fanciful letter, a floriated initial N for Stanley Morison's *Fleuron*. Morison wanted him to design a whole alphabet, but Gill declined, taking the position outlined above that the mechanical methods employed by the Monotype Corporation were in contradiction to the nature of his design. He must have changed his mind by 1936 when Monotype Gill Floriated was made as a complete alphabet.

The section headed 'Typography' opens with a practical explanation of the application of lettering to printing, roman and italic alphabets, etc. and their uses. His advice on the use of italics would find little support today, least of all his suggestion that for emphasis letter-spaced lower case might be used as a substitute for italics. Nothing is said about the use of small capitals and Gill did not design any for Joanna. He did, however, provide two sets of roman capitals for the face and their use is well demonstrated in the book's pages, the smaller being used generally and the larger for paragraph openings and chapter titles. The height of these 'smaller' capitals is one of the distinguishing and distinguished features of the Caslon cutting of Joanna and contributes to its even appearance on the page.

The 'two worlds' theme then reasserts itself – 'The typography of industrialism' and 'humane typography'. The latter is 'comparatively rough & even uncouth; but while a certain uncouthness does not seriously matter in humane works, uncouthness has no excuse whatsoever in the productions of the machine'. The best hand-press printers would not agree. One wonders if Gill had in mind the St Dominic's Press and their early printing of his pamphlets and engravings; the word 'humane' then becomes very apposite.

The colophon to the first edition reads: 'Printed by René Hague and Eric Gill'. Was Eric Gill ever a printer? In the sense that he set type and fed sheets of paper into a machine the answer is certainly 'No'. Neither his diary nor his account sheets show any evidence of time spent in this way except briefly with Hilary Pepler at Ditchling in the early years. He certainly printed his own editions of engravings on both wood and metal, using the hand-press in his own workshop. His contribution to the books of Hague & Gill was as typographical advisor; occasional author (the fee he asked for *Typography* was £35); and, as existing records show, financial supporter until 1936.

In Gill's account of machine punch-cutting he is at pains to point out how many different people are involved, another of his habitual disparagements of the industrial system. The earlier essay on wood-engraving makes the same point, about mechanical engraving, 'degradation is inevitable when one man draws, another touches up the drawing, another photographs, another touches up the negative,' and so on, until 'to crown all, another takes the profits.'

The short chapter on paper and ink reads strangely in the printing world of today yet still has relevance for the fine printing enthusiast, although Gill's recommendation that the 'hand-press printer should make his own ink' will have few supporters. There are though, nuggets of sound advice and guiding principles for today's 'humane' printers.

It is perhaps for Gill's advocacy of 'unjustified' setting that *Typography* is best known – that is, pages of typesetting in which the space between the words are all even so that as a consequence the lines themselves are of slightly different lengths, resulting in a 'ragged' right-hand margin. The case for close word-spacing has long since been recognised but even today Gill's words are relevant, when the 'tyrannical insistence upon equal lengths of lines' is as much in evidence and when the designer's grid has taken the place of what Gill's chapter heading calls, 'The Procrustean Bed' of the composing stick. Although Gill's remarks are mainly aimed at book designers it is, perhaps, newspaper and advertising typesetters who would most benefit from his advice. The pages of *Typography* itself are, of course, witness to Gill's principles. The first two pages of the chapter are in normal 'justified' setting to demonstrate the argument.

The frequent use of ampersands and the occasional contractions such as 'tho' and 'sh'ld' may jar, though not as much as one practice abandoned in the 1936 printing. In the first edition the final few letters of some words were set in a smaller size in order to fit them into the line, a very time-consuming practice when hand-setting. Although technically feasible using Monotype hot-metal machine composition and now easily achieved with film-setting, it remains a distracting way to achieve equal word spacing. The use of paragraph marks instead of indented lines, although idiosyncratic today, has distinguished precedents and adds to the evenness and consistency of the colour of the pages.

Much unjustified typesetting today is ruined by the unwillingness of the typesetter to break words, resulting in the ugliness of excessively uneven lines. In the use of word breaks and slight adjustments of spacing to achieve not too disparate line lengths Gill's pages are exemplary. This effect, it must be admitted, has been achieved at a cost. Excessively uneven word-spacing is bad, of course, and Gill's cure is effective; but there are just as many word breaks as in normal setting, some of them very dubious. If Gill had used the same treatment with justified setting, one wonders whether any unevenness of word spacing would be noticeable. It was surely under Gill's influence that the pages of the Golden Cockerel *Four Gospels* were set with ragged right-hand edges in 1930. The first specimens, which Robert Gibbings favoured, are set normally.

Towards the end of the discussion of typesetting, spacing and readability comes this typical Gill passage:

> The responsible artist, the printer who elects to stand outside industrialism, and who regards the job of printing as a sculptor regards the job of stone-carving, or a village blacksmith the job of working iron, regards himself & his customer as sharing a joint enterprise, namely the production of good books; and the terms good, lovely, pleasant, beautiful, mean for them not merely what will sell, or what can, by cunning advertisement, be made to sell, but what the widest culture & the strictest discipline can make them mean.

Gibbings and Gill, in their notable collaboration over the *Four Gospels* must have frequently discussed typographical matters. Of the other influences on Gill's and Hague's typographical ideas it is hard to be certain. There was little in the way of style books and works on typographical design available at the time. De Vinne's volume on composition in the four-volume *The Practise of Typography*, full of sound detail, was probably known to them. Morison regarded it highly. His *First Principles of Typography* must have been well known to Gill.

'The workman should not have to watch his instrument, his whole attention should be given to the work.' Thus, under the heading of 'The Instrument' Gill

116   there is no occasion to go to extremes in this matter, & it is as foolish to make a thick book of a short story as it is, by small type & cramped margins, to make one volume of a book which is properly two. ¶ As to binding: the Continental practice of issuing books in sheets, or simply sewn with a paper wrapper, is much to be praised. The English book buyer's insistence on a stiff cover, even for the cheapest books, has been met by the invention or development of the 'case', i.e. a stiff cover which may be applied after the sheets are sewn, & is designed for making in large quantities. The only objection to such cases is that they nearly always retain certain conventional ornamentations which are derived from the 'binding' of former times & are not appropriate to machine-made things. For sixpenny novels the work is done from end to end by machine —including the ornaments on the sides and back. For more expensive books some parts of the work are still done by hand, e.g. the pasting of the endsheets & the insertion of head bands of parti-coloured cloth. But except for individual private customers 'binding', i.e. the sewing of the sheets and the lacing of the whole thing to the cover so that book & cover are one thing, is not done at all. Doubtless

the ordinary products of commercial printing are   117
not suitable for any other treatment, & while the cry is for cheaper and cheaper books anything but what can be done by machine is out of the question. Printing done by machinery on machine-made paper may well be cased in machine-made casing, but printing done by human beings on paper made by human beings ought to be bound by human beings. ¶ The question arises: how many copies of a book should be printed? There are several appropriate answers to this question. The first is: as many as can be sold; and this is the only answer we shall consider here. But there are two primary considerations in the selling of anything: (a) the number of people who can be supposed to desire a thing because it is desirable in itself; and (b) the number who can afford to buy it. If all those to whom a book is desirable can afford to buy it, then the edition is properly limited to 'all those'; but if only a few can afford to buy it the edition is properly limited to that few. What is this book? How ought it to be printed? These things being determined the ground is clear for the consideration of the problem of the number of possible buyers. ¶ It is obvious that the number of possible buyers of expensive

2 Double-page spread from the first edition.

chooses a hand-press for the 'humane printer'. He acknowledges the world of the 'automatically fed power presses' and is content to grant each of the two worlds its place. Like much of the rest of the book the pages where Gill writes of printing machines are a kind of charter for his own printing and, incidentally, for the 'fine printer' and small press of today.

He can be scornful too, both of the commercial printer with higher aspirations, 'Printers who give themselves the status of poets or painters are to be condemned', and of those who indulge in 'the artificial limitation of numbers in order to capture a "collectors" market'. 'Properly understood,' Gill says, 'this is purely a "business" matter, and the printer whose first concern is quality is not a man of business.'

What was originally the final section is headed 'The Book'. Gill's logical common sense and practical instruction are to the front as he discusses type sizes, book sizes and margins. There is much good stuff for the book designer and especially healthy advice for those tempted into the current fashion for overdesign and bogus refinement:

The title of a book is merely the thing to know it by; we have made of the title-page a showing-off ground for the printers and publishers. A smart title-page will not redeem a dully printed book any more than a smart cinema will redeem a slum.

The first edition of *Typography* faithfully reflects Gill's tenets. The title and author's name are no more than a heading to a few lines listing the contents on the opening page. The publisher's name appears on the jacket only.

The final chapter, a substantial addition to the first edition, is really an appendix, in which Gill gives full rein to a hobby horse mounted briefly in the opening paragraph of the 'Typography' section. It is a typical Gill polemic in support of shorthand or what he calls 'phonography', full of sweeping statements, question-begging arguments and pretended naivety; ('although the saying "time is money" is too difficult for me to understand'). He calls for abolition of lettering as we know it and for the substitution of phonographic symbols. So the essay subsides into a thought-provoking and interesting note of crankiness, seeing phonography as a way to start again and rid ourselves of the world of fancy lettering.

An Essay on Typography is quintessential Gill. It epitomises his idealism, his pragmatism and his Christian view of the world of everyday work. Practical advice is shot through with moral precept and maxims of wisdom. Parallels are drawn between plain and ornamental lettering and the vicissitudes of Christian marriage, mention of the grinding of ink leads to an extolling of the virtues of pain and suffering. He hardly ever resists an aside critical of commercial activity, often unfair ('designers who for some inscrutable reasons must live'). It is thus, however, that the reader is stimulated in all sorts of ways other than typographical.

Christopher Skelton, whose mother was Eric Gill's sister, was bitten by the printing bug when he went to work for Hague and Gill after leaving Oxford (as described in *Matrix 2*). He worked there for two years until 1951, and then for 12 years worked in commercial printing. In 1968 he started up on his own as Skelton's Press, which rapidly gained a well-deserved reputation for high-quality commercial work, and in 1984 he printed and published *The Engravings of Eric Gill*, as described in *Matrix 4*. From 1984 to 1989 he ran the September Press with Alan Bultitude (described in *Matrix 11*), until motor neurone disease cut short his life in 1992.

NOTES

1. *Typography* no. 1, November 1936.

2. Essays 9 and 10 in *Art nonsense and other essays*, Cassell and Walterson, 1929.

Based on the introduction to the facsimile of the second edition of *An Essay on Typography*, issued by Lund Humphries.

The wisdom of a learned man cometh by opportunity of leisure: and he that hath little business shall become wise. How can he get wisdom that holdeth the plough, and that glorieth in the goad, that driveth oxen, and is occupied in their labours, and whose talk is of bullocks? He giveth his mind to make furrows; and is

1. Romulus roman and sloped roman, with Chancellersca Bastarda, 1932-1936

The wisdom of a learned man cometh by opportunity of leisure: and he that hath little business shall become wise. How can he get wisdom that holdeth the plough, and that glorieth in the goad, that driveth oxen, and is occupied furrows; and is diligent to give the kine fodder. So every carpenter and workmaster, that laboureth

2. Romanée roman, 1928, and italic, 1949

SAPIENTIA SCRIBAE IN TEMPORE VACUITATIS

3. Open capitals, 1928

The Types of Jan van Krimpen

BY SEBASTIAN CARTER

In contrast to Gill, Jan van Krimpen wanted control over every aspect of the type-faces he designed, and he resisted all compromise in their manufacture. The nobili-ty of Van Krimpen's types set a high standard, though they were never best-sellers. Sebastian Carter's survey in Matrix 12 (1992) accompanied a specimen of Van Krimpen's typefaces that Carter hand-set and printed just before the closing of the original Enschedé foundry in 1990.

Dutch type designer Jan van Krimpen's best-known roman types are Lutetia, Romanée, Romulus and Spectrum. Romulus is not shown here in its entirety (figure 1): it proliferated into a large family, with not only a separate italic called, at Morison's suggestion, Cancelleresca Bastarda (the regular roman was accom-panied by a sloped roman, again at Morison's suggestion), but also a related bold, a sans serif and a Greek. The last three are omitted here, as are small capi-tals where they were cut, and figures.

These four types were first cut by a hand-punchcutter, P. H. Rädisch, who was resident at the foundry of Joh. Enschedé en Zonen in Haarlem, where Van Krimpen was house designer from 1925 up to his retirement shortly before his death in 1958. They were cast at the Enschedé foundry, for use in their own print-ing works and for outside sale. The English Monotype Corporation, where Mori-son was typographical adviser, subsequently cut Lutetia and Spectrum, and worked very closely with Van Krimpen and Enschedé in the development and cutting of Romulus roman and sloped roman, but not the rest of the family. Romanée roman was designed in 1928 as the companion to an original seven-teenth-century italic, possibly by Christoffel van Dijck, which had survived among the magnificent historic material in Enschedé's collection. Although it is a handsome face, it was never happy in this arranged marriage, and in 1949 Van Krimpen designed the extremely condensed and upright italic lower-case shown here (figure 2), for use with the roman capitals. Partly because of its two-decades' deprivation of a true italic, and partly because of Morison's oddly lukewarm feel-ings towards the type, it was never cut by Monotype.

In addition, three open titling founts were produced at Enschedé. The Open

SAPIENTIA SCRIBAE IN TEMPORE VACUITATIS

4. Lutetia Open Capitals, c 1930

SAPIENTIA SCRIBAE IN TEMPORE VACUITATIS

5. Romulus Open capitals, early 1950's

Capitals (figure 3) were designed with additional Greek characters in 1928 to accompany Antigone. The inline Lutetia capitals (figure 4) were made by Rädisch working with a graver on cast sorts of regular Lutetia capitals, under Van Krimpen's supervision, around 1930. Matrices were than made electrolytically from the incised sorts. The same process was employed for the Romulus Open Capitals in the early 1950s (figure 5).

Two further types were cut by Monotype, but not by Rädisch and Enschedé. Haarlemmer was designed in 1939 for a Bible project of Van Krimpen's, and briefly taken up by the Dutch publishing house Het Spectrum for their own Bible. The war intervened, and during it Van Krimpen designed Spectrum (figure 6) for the same purpose. For reasons of speed and economy, Haarlemmer was designed to fit an existing Monotype keyboard arrangement, which meant that the widths of the letters were preordained and Van Krimpen had to tailor his design to them. This clearly did not work too well, though it is the relative weights of the roman and italic which are the type's chief drawbacks. Van Krimpen was unhappy with the type. Although technically it was issued, no sets of matrices were ever sold until John Randle and I jointly bought one in 1991. The Haarlemmer shown here (figure 7) was cast at Whittington.

The wisdom of a learned man cometh by opportunity of leisure: and he that hath little business shall become wise. How can he get wisdom that holdeth the plough, and that glorieth in the goad, that driveth oxen, and is occupied in their labours, and whose talk is of bullocks? *He giveth his mind to make furrows; and is diligent to give the kine fodder. So every*

6. Spectrum roman and italic, 1949-1956

The wisdom of a learned man cometh by opportunity of leisure: and he that hath little business shall become wise. How can he get wisdom that holdeth the plough, and that glorieth in the goad, that driveth oxen, and is occupied in their labours, and whose talk is of bullocks? He *giveth his mind to make furrows; and is diligent to give the kine fodder.*

7. Haarlemmer roman and italic, 1939

The other Monotype face is another Bible type, Sheldon, designed for the Oxford University Press in 1947 (figure 8). It is a 7-point type with a deceptively large x-height, and was used at Oxford for an octavo Bible. The present whereabouts of the unique die-case is unknown, and the original of the specimen was printed from a line-block made from this Bible.

With one exception, the rest of the type in the specimen was set at Enschedé's on 26 February 1990. The firm was due to move from its historic buildings in the Klokhuisplein in the centre of Haarlem, where it had been since the eighteenth century, and the future of the foundry was uncertain. (Events have shown this uncertainty to have been justified: since the move, although all the punches and other material, together with sample founts, have been preserved, no further Enschedé type is available.) I decided to act swiftly, and wrote to Maurits Enschedé, then the head of the firm, for permission to come and set the type I needed; he gave it, and as he had to be away when I was coming, put me in the care of his cousin Just Enschedé.

I drove out from Amsterdam in one of the storms which was battering northern Europe that winter, which nearly lifted my little Citröen 2cv into the Haarlemmer Trekvaart canal which runs alongside the road. In the Klokhuisplein I was introduced to Jan Willem Enschedé, another cousin who had been brought in from retirement to sort out the firm's massive typographical archive in preparation for the move. (The wonderful Enschedé collection had been left in some disorder since the museum had been closed after the tragically early death of its curator Gonne Flipse.) Jan Willem and Just then handed me over to Henk Drost, head of the foundry since the retirement of Rädisch in 1957, who was himself about to take early retirement. The composition room was completely deserted, and the wind howled mournfully around the old building. Drost showed me the whereabouts of the cases, and explained the layout of the Dutch lowercase, and left me to get on with it.

The text I had chosen to set was from the thirty-eighth chapter of *Ecclesiasticus*. Van Krimpen had the opening words, in the Vulgate Latin, cut in his fireplace, according to John Dreyfus's beguiling description of his study at the beginning of the handsome book Enschedé produced for Van Krimpen's sixtieth birthday. That is the text of the three display types shown here. The King James version is used for the text setting. It is an interesting reflection of Van Krimpen's views about craftsmen: although they keep the world going, they should not get above themselves. That was certainly the attitude he took towards Rädisch, whom he never mentioned by name in his correspondence with Morison.

I soon discovered that despite Van Krimpen's censorious attitude towards Monotype, and his assertion of the superiority of hand-cut punches, in practice Enschedé used the Monotype version of his type, cast on a Thompson, in preference to the Rädisch-cut version, whenever there was a choice. My time was

---

8.   Sheldon,
1947-1950

24 The wisdom of a learned man cometh by opportunity of leisure: and he that hath little business shall become wise. 25 How can he get wisdom that holdeth the plough, and that glorieth in the goad, that driveth oxen, and is occupied in their labours, and whose talk is of bullocks? 26 He giveth his mind to make furrows; and is diligent to give the kine fodder. 27 So every carpenter and workmaster, that laboureth night and day: and they that cut and grave seals, and are diligent to make great variety, and give themselves to counterfeit imagery, and watch to finish a work: 28 The smith also sitting by the anvil, and considering the iron work, the vapour of the fire wasteth his flesh, and he fighteth with the heat of the furnace: the noise of the hammer and the anvil is ever in his ears, and his eyes look still upon the pattern of the thing that he maketh; he setteth his mind to finish his work, and watcheth to polish it perfectly: · 29 So doth the potter sitting at his work, and turning the wheel about with his feet, who is alway carefully set at his work, and maketh all his work by number; 30 He fashioneth the clay with his arm, and boweth down his strength before his feet; he applieth himself to lead it over; and he is diligent to make clean the furnace: 31 All these trust to their hands: and every one is wise in his work. 32 Without these cannot a city be inhabited: and they shall not dwell where they will, nor go up and down: 33 They shall not be sought for in publick counsel, nor sit high in the congregation: they shall not sit on the judges' seat, nor understand the sentence of judgment: they cannot declare justice and judgment; and they shall not be found where parables are spoken. 34 But they will maintain the state of the world, and [all] their desire is in the work of their craft.

The wisdom of a learned man cometh by opportunity of leisure: and he that hath little business shall become wise. How can he get wisdom that holdeth the plough, and that glorieth in the goad, that driveth oxen, and is occupied in their labours, and whose talk is of bullocks? He giveth his mind to make *furrows; and is diligent to give the kine fodder. So every carpenter and*

9. Lutetia roman and italic, 1925-1930

limited, so I contented myself with cajoling Drost into laying some foundry Lutetia roman into case, and that is what is shown in figure 9. The Romanée, of course, is hand-cut, and so is the Cancelleresca Bastarda. One peculiarity of the Enschedé cases was that the upper-case boxes for Romanée italic contained small capitals rather than the full roman capitals intended by Van Krimpen. This was because Bram de Does's design for the great folio English edition of Charles Enschedé's *Typefoundries in the Netherlands*, published in 1978, which was entirely hand-set in Romanée, specified small capitals with italic. Although De Does's preference has considerable merit, I reverted to that of the type's author.

The exception mentioned above is the Lutetia italic. The Enschedé case was extremely depleted, and time was running out, so the type shown in figure 9 is the Monotype cutting, which we have had at the Rampant Lions Press for many years.

Drost's initial distrust of an amateur intruder imposed on him by the management had softened somewhat when he saw I could set type, even though the Dutch lay of the case was a handicap. When I had finished, and finally mastered the powered proof press, he explained there was a problem. I had assumed that Dutch type would be the same height-to-paper as French or German, that is, a point or so higher than Anglo-American. Although Stempel and other German foundries would plane their exported type down, the French were not so amenable, yet I was able to use my Fonderie Olive type with Anglo-American founts by packing them up with thin card. It turned out that Dutch height is about three points above ours: a fact which I should have known, since Van Krimpen advised Morison about it in a letter of 27 May 1933. This difference is too great for such makeshifts, so Drost offered to plane down the type I had set, and we arranged that John Miles, Enschedé's design consultant, who had learned punchcutting with Rädisch and is now an internationally known designer, would bring it over. John very decently fell in with this plan.

One final problem remained. In my haste at Haarlem I had failed to spot a few Spectrum sorts which had crept into the Romanée case and thence into my setting. By the time the error was noticed, Enschedé had moved and closed its foundry. The correct sorts have been inserted thanks to the nuns of Stanbrook Abbey, who have Romanée amongst their splendid collection of Van Krimpen types.

I hope that the illustrations in this essay will show the nobility and beauty of Van Krimpen's designs. Although they are rooted in classical letterforms, they owe little to other typefaces and are freshly thought-out responses to the broadly-defined needs of type categories. Lutetia roman has dated most: it was the first to be designed, and reflects the Jenson-inspired family of faces commissioned by Morris and the English and Continental private presses which followed his lead. But Lutetia italic and the three major designs which followed are timeless creations.

For all this, the limited marketing of the Enschedé foundry made the foundry types a specialist interest, while even the Monotype versions did not sell particularly well. Van Krimpen did not hesitate to express his dissatisfaction with Monotype, so it is regrettable that he never gave the Corporation due credit for investing so much time and money in founts of which even the most successful, Romulus, sold only 220 sets of matrices (compared with nearly 40,000 of Morison's Times New Roman). Spectrum and Lutetia came immediately after, with 147 and 118 sets respectively. Without Morison's advocacy, it is doubtful whether any of the three would have been cut at all.

Ironically, in view of Van Krimpen's often-expressed disapproval of historical recuttings, Van Dijck, for which he lent his reluctant help, proved more profitable, and has been adapted for the Monophoto and digital composition. It is only now that Enschedé are issuing the other designs in digital form.

It is hard to explain this neglect. Walter Tracy, in *Letters of Credit*, attributed it in part to the flaws in some of the founts – Van Krimpen's generally poorly designed numerals, the imbalance between Lutetia roman and italic, the eccentric use of a sloped roman in Romulus – but more seriously to the lack of a specific utilitarian purpose in their design: they were idealised forms, not responses to the needs of printers. 'In short, Van Krimpen thought like an artist, not like a designer.' Van Krimpen himself admitted this, though he did not see it as a fault. He wrote: 'I do not believe it is possible to sit down and design a type to order, as it is attempted in Germany. The type which originates in such a manner may be tolerable in advertisements, but it cannot satisfy the requirements which experience demands for book printing. A satisfactory book type must be present in the mind and at the fingertips of the designer before he sits down to draw. Such a type does not require any added "personality" – either it is essentially personal or it is not.'

This austerity may have delayed the acceptance of Van Krimpen's types, but I am sure that it will ultimately guarantee their survival. Of letters, he wrote, 'they have fascinated me from the very first time I saw a picture of a Roman inscription. And I can only explain this because of their being nothing but meaning'. 'Nothing but meaning' – what better definition of the ideal type could there be?

Sebastian Carter was born in 1941, and studied English literature and the history of art at King's College, Cambridge. After university he worked for a number of publishers and designers in London and Paris before joining his father Will Carter at the Rampant Lions Press in Cambridge, which he now runs from his house outside the town. Here he has produced a long series of fine editions, often in rare typefaces such as Eric Gill's Golden Cockerel Roman and Hermann Zapf's Hunt Roman. Highlights have included Milton's *Areopagitica*, Samuel Beckett's *As the story was told*, and T. S. Eliot's *Four Quartets*, as well as a number of typographical display pieces such as *A printer's dozen* and most recently *In praise of letter-press*. He writes extensively on printing and typography, reviewing regularly for the *Times Literary Supplement* and the British Printing Historical Society's *Bulletin* and *Journal*. He guest-edited the 1990 Eric Gill number of the *Monotype Recorder*, and wrote the section on 'The Morison years' in the centenary number in 1997. His *Twentieth century type designers* (1987; new edition 1995; now out in paperback) has become a standard work. With only two exceptions, he has contributed to every number of *Matrix*

1 2 3 4 5 6 7 8 9 0

¶ Aa Bb Cc Dd
Ee Ff Gg Hh Ii
Kk Ll Mm Nn
Oo Pp Qq Rr Ss
Tt Uu Vv Ww
& Xx Yy Zz §
1 2 3 4 5 6 7 8 9 0

Jan van Krimpen's Spectrum Roman typeface, the digitized version from Monotype

On Preparing Designs for Monotype Faces

SO AS TO PREVENT ARBITRARY ENCROACHMENTS FROM THE SIDE OF THE DRAWING OFFICE ON THE DESIGNER'S WORK AND INTENTIONS AND OTHERWISE INEVITABLE DISAPPOINTMENTS AT THE DESIGNER'S END

BY JAN VAN KRIMPEN

One of the most austere and uncompromising of type designers, Van Krimpen took a very critical look at the process of converting foundry type to machine composition. He helped Monotype create a revival of the classic Dutch types of Van Dijck, but he later decided that it had been a bad idea, and in this essay, originally published in the 1950s and reprinted in Matrix 11 *(1991), he explains why.*

Ever since the beginning of my co-operation with the Monotype Works on the production of certain type faces, which has been early in 1928 when a rendering of foundry Lutetia was taken in hand, I have admired a number of the Corporation's achievements and, at the same time, not felt fully satisfied with what we had been able to perform together. When we started our co-operation I had but vague notions about the Monotype system and, astonishing as it may sound now, I was of opinion that the system was and should be the Corporation's concern while mine could only be the making of designs as good as I should be able to do. It now seems obvious to me that my error was that I only thought of foundry type and that I disregarded the additional limitations the Monotype system and Monotype machine involve. And, on top of that, my idea, rightly or wrongly, was that foundry type was the real thing and, therefore, that bringing composing machine type nearer to foundry type would mean improving the former; only many years later I have formed the opinion that, at least, they can be two fundamentally different things and that they should be thought of and treated as such. Another point that in those days had not yet come into my reasoning was the difference between hand- and mechanically-cut punches. One may still think, as I for one do, that the best hand-cut punches are superior to any machine-cut ones; but one has to realise and to admit that as soon as a composing machine is accepted hand-cut punches are no longer possible.

I have, at the request of Mr Morison, a few years before the war written a short memorandum on the same subject I am dealing with now. It seems to have disappeared. If it has I can only be glad for it. And I have to ask that if it should turn up again it should be disregarded. My aim was then to narrow, or if possible close, the gap between foundry type (then still not seldom made by means of hand-cut punches) and Monotype type. Now, when talking of the latter, I want completely to forget hand-cut punches and designs in which only the age old limitations of foundry type are taken into account.

At present it is my aim to point out how, in my opinion, a Monotype face can and should be made within the limitations of the Monotype system itself; and that such a face can, again within these limitations, be quite as good as a foundry face provided that the characteristics of mechanically-cut punches, in as far as they differ from those of hand-cut punches, are accepted.

To begin with a few things should be said regarding the reasons for my far from entirely being satisfied by the joint performances of the Monotype and myself. They are partly due to certain human shortcomings, which it may or may not be possible to remedy, to which I will revert later on; and for another part not so much to the Monotype system itself but rather to too easily found and followed practical ways of applying the system to, both, existing type faces and designs not in some other way executed before. If I have formerly devised means to improve the attempts of the Corporation to copy existing faces – in the first place my own on which we have been working together – I have now found that this is essentially a hopeless enterprise. What can be done is, with the help of the designer if he is available, make a Monotype version after what originally has been a face produced by a type-foundry which is, at the very least, unlikely to have taken the Monotype limitations – if only the limited number of possible widths imposed by the system of unit arrangements – into account. Now, contrary to before the war, it is my firm belief that no better Monotype face can be produced than after a design, and drawings, made specially for the purpose along the lines I will set forth presently. If, for some reason or other, an already existing face has to be adapted for use on the Monotype this will have to be done largely along the same lines. In most cases severe modifications will prove to be necessary; and people will have to prepare themselves on finding that the Monotype version does not have overmuch to do with the original fount.

Before I proceed to dealing with my subject properly speaking I want to say a few words on so-called copies of historical type faces which the Corporation has produced in considerable numbers.

I need hardly say here once more that I am no friend of copying or even adapting historical type faces. Not, may this be well understood, because I should see, not to say fear, in them competitors of designs of our own day; but for no other reason than that they are neither flesh nor fish: they are not, nor can they be, the thing they pretend to be; they only have a mock flavour of antiquity because of the many violations of the nature of the machine – the punch-cutting machine, that is, in this instance – and the many concessions made to the limitations of the Monotype composing machine; all of these violations and concessions being unavoidable in the process of making them fit for modern use. And, on the other hand, they are not actually products of our time because of the mock flavour of antiquity that has to be aimed at and retained or there could not be spoken of copies or adaptations; nor could they be named, as it is done, after their models. I will not further deal with them and only say that if what I have to suggest might prove to be useful for the future production of similar type faces, which I doubt, I should almost be sorry to have at all written this memorandum. What I am after in the first place is a system to get the best possible machine made face, for use on a certain composing machine (Monotype), and this system must tend to shake the producers of such a face free from the tyranny of their model in type, if such a model there is, in order to get a machine made machine face that is closely enough related to the model to be virtually identical with it and, at the same time, an independent face that answers completely the requirements of the machine. In the second place, and I think most important of all, I want to set forth how a designer and the works' drawing office can and should co-operate in producing a set of satisfactory drawings for a type face that has no model in type; in other words a type face that entirely originates with the Monotype though possibly according to the ideas of a designer who is not directly connected with it. In many respects the methods to be followed will be found to be nearly identical.

I have repeatedly professed the highest possible regard and admiration for Mr Morison's achievements, now during nearly thirty-five years, as a producer of type faces – if I am allowed to call him thus – and I want to repeat them here once more. But still I differ with him and certain of his convictions so fundamentally that it seems to me that what, in *A Tally of Types*, he relates to have been 'the convictions with which the Monotype Corporation's new programme was drafted in January 1922' may well have led, unintentionally, to a number of the errors I am now trying to remedy.

On page 21 he says 'The way to learn to go forward was to make a step backward'. This is put as an axiom and no attempt to give a proof or a justification is made. On the one hand I should like to say to this that, particularly in Great Britain, so many steps backward had already been made, by William Morris and his disciples, that I take the liberty to doubt whether any more of such steps were really necessary. On the other hand, though quite as convinced of the use and necessity to study the past as Mr Morison, that this conviction does not in the least mean to me that our investigations should lead us to a more or less slavishly copying or following the productions of the past.

The errors I have hinted at are caused by the type drawing office having been taught to copy the models they get – historical type faces or, in fact, prints from them – as closely as possible in order to make it, as Mr Morison says on page 38 of *A Tally of Types*, 'possible, in fact, to compose, according to the correct dimensions of the original, a page of the Monotype version [of Poliphilus], place it side by side with the original, and find no difference except in paper. This test was in fact made, and, naturally, it gave the greatest satisfaction to the works'. If this should be entirely true, which in my opinion it is certainly not, still an objection, and a very serious one, could, and would have to, be raised. I have called these pretending copies of ancient type faces neither flesh nor fish. And in no instance they would be more fundamentally such bastards as in this. Not only that they pretend to be, or are hoped to look, old while in fact they are new; but over and above this ambiguity they are given a look of being handiwork, in as much they follow painstakingly the engraver's and even the typefounder's irregularities – of the one due to his using by hand simple tools under a none too strong magnifying glass and of the other due to his hand mould – while, in fact, they are made by machine. And this I do not hesitate to call – but may it be well understood: philosophically speaking – dishonesty. No talk about 'the man behind the machine' is able to disguise this fact. The dishonesty may not be intentional; and I am sure that here it is not; but dishonesty there is and remains.

I should be very surprised if anybody of those who are daily trying to imitate hand-cut type by mechanical means would be prepared to accept, say, a frying pan with so-called hammer marks if the hammer marks came out of a mould and the pan were forced on some machine. Why do people here notice and reject the obvious dishonesty and in the other instance, where it is quite as obvious, accept and submit to it?

The fundamental error, of imitating hand-cut type by mechanical means, has not stopped at the producing or rendering of ancient type faces. I will mention here two series with which, in slightly different ways, the same sins have been committed.

It just seems rightful to begin with my own (Monotype) Lutetia. I think it was early in 1928 when the late W. I. Burch and Mr Morison suggested that my (foundry) Lutetia should be copied for use on the Monotype machine. I doubted, though I very much admired and was impressed by the Monotype achievements and the Monotype ways of working which had been extensively shown to me, that the Corporation would be able to produce a rendering of Lutetia that might satisfy me; and I said so. This was taken as a challenge and W. I. Burch said to me that, if I would only take into account the Monotype limitations regarding bevel and width, he was prepared to give me the right of disapproving anything that I might think not to be fully satisfactory. This counter-challenge was accepted by me and the work started.

I knew, in those days, something of cutting type by hand; but there could hardly be spoken of real and full understanding which only can be the fruit of a long practice and much thinking. I knew next to nothing of cutting punches by machine; and if, already then, I should have condemned and refused the 'hand made' frying pan produced by machine it had not yet occurred to me that hand-cut type imitated by mechanical means was quite as objectionable because of its equal dishonesty. And if I knew in my heart of hearts that what had been done with Poliphilus, and which gave 'the greatest satisfaction to the works', was wrong, and should therefore not have been done, I had not yet formulated in my mind *why* it was wrong. It was exactly on that greatest satisfaction to the works that the Corporation's counter-challenge could be and was based. The Corporation have won; and Monotype Lutetia, as a consequence, is one more unsatisfactory machine made type face because it is only one more imitation of a fount typically made by hand.

(When, not long afterwards, work on the series Romulus started my understanding of this side of the job had in so far developed that I could at least prevent that the same mistake should be made. I then had, otherwise than a few years a fair understanding of the Monotype unit system; but I had not yet conceived the idea that not the unit system should be applied to a given design but, rather, that a rudimentary design should be gradually adapted to the unit system.)

The other series I am thinking of is Mr Bruce Rogers' Centaur. Here too a fount of foundry type has been the original model after which the Corporation was supposed to work, not a more [redrawn] design was accepted after which it was undertaken to produce matrices to be used on Monotype machines. If I am right Mr Rogers resided in London when Centaur was being cut – I met him there, in those days, several times in his room in Sir Emery Walker's office in Cliffords Inn – and so had an opportunity of much more closely supervising the production of Centaur than I had with Lutetia; and, to be sure, he did so. (I have learned from a paper which Mrs Warde has read on Mr Bruce Rogers, at St Bride's Foundation in the autumn of 1955, that Mr Rogers was by far the most difficult designer the works had ever had to deal with 'until', she added when she realised that I was in her audience, 'until, of course, Mr Van Krimpen turned up'. I should like to say to this, firstly, that if we, Mr Rogers and myself, have reason, regarding this remark of Mrs Warde's, for anything it is a feeling of pride for having taken the matter more seriously than other designers had or have done; and, secondly, that there can be little reason for Mrs Warde to insert the word 'until' since the two founts were produced at about the same time – the series number of Centaur being 252 and that of Lutetia 255 – or she must have been thinking of Romulus during the cutting of which I have certainly been more difficult than on the former occasion.)

D. B. Updike, in a passage in *Printing Types* on the production of type faces, starting on page 10 of the first volume, quotes from a letter from Mr Rogers to him: 'Even with strict instructions and with best intentions it is difficult for the habitual user of a very accurate machine *not* to insensibly smooth out what he has always been taught to be "imperfections" and to make as mechanically perfect a letter as is possible. . . . I have come to believe that perhaps only hand-cut punches, *cut by the designer of the type*, can preserve the real feeling of the design.' I have wanted to give Updike's quotation from Mr Rogers' letter in full. I do not agree with his last point, in as far as hand-cut punches are concerned, but it would be beyond the scope of this memorandum to expatiate on my reasons for it.

My first reaction when reading this passage is that it reveals a surprising and queer enough attitude with one who gives a design of his for use on a composing machine; a composing machine, at that, which can only properly be worked with matrices driven from punches that have been cut mechanically. As, however, Updike's book is nearly ten years older than Monotype Centaur it is possible enough that Mr Rogers had changed his mind in the meantime. On the other hand Monotype Centaur does not look as though this should have happened.

I even think that Mr Rogers has, undoubtedly 'with best intentions' – so without as much as dreaming that he might be doing something he should rather not do – given 'strict instructions' for the introduction of 'imperfections' or irregularities in the cutting of his design in order to have the printed type look closely like type cut by hand; this should, I think, be taken for an objectionably arbitrary piece of conduct [given] the size of the drawings and the great flexibility of the punch-cutting machine; a cheap proceeding of arbitrarily determining one's own chosen 'imperfections' while, when punches are being cut by hand, one has to wait and see how the punchcutter's genuine imperfections will look whether he be his own punchcutter or working with another man. In Lutetia the punchcutter's imperfections have, as far as it went, slavishly been copied. What exactly has happened with Monotype Centaur I am unable to say; I understand, however, (from *The Centaur Types* by Bruce Rogers, Chicago, October House, 1949) that Centaur has never really been cut by hand but, originally, by Robert Wiebking of Chicago 'on his machines', the working drawings reproduced in the little book mentioned clearly show[ing] that Mr Rogers does not have what I would call the right ideas of what should or should not be asked from a machine. So, reasoning further from my point of view, I may say, or even have to say, that what has happened, in different ways, to both Centaur and Lutetia, in the course of their production by the Corporation, is wrong and therefore objectionable. These and similar methods, caused by a certain lack of understanding, have, in their turn, caused a lot of wrong to be done indeed. And still they are the least of my troubles since one simple decree can stop their being followed any longer.

The methods I am going to suggest for the production of a fount that is to have its origin on the Monotype can *mutatis mutandis* be applied to the re-production or adaptation of one that is already in existence. That is to say that I think it may be found to be most simple and efficacious to start from the design, if it is still there, or, if it is not, to replace it by an enlargement of a rough impression from the (foundry) type or a reduction of the first drawings the drawing office normally makes in similar cases.

My main points are (1.) that a (*rudimentary*) design should be adapted to the unit system and (2.) how, in my opinion, this can and should be done.

Some designers – I am thinking of Dr Giovanni Mardersteig and myself – have tried to adapt, sometime, a design to an existing unit arrangement and have failed in as much as neither of us has finally been able to get himself to approve the type face thus produced. There remains to be seen what is worse: to admit the necessity of having a, theoretically at least, unlimited number of unit arrangements and good type or a limited number of standard arrangements and type that fits one of them as good, or rather as bad, as ready made clothes fit even the most normally built people. (I wonder how many of the prophets of the last named system, who defend it because of its economy, may wear ready made suits themselves!) My argumentation would be superfluous and useless when standard arrangements were to become the rule. An observation I should like to make by the way is that, generally speaking, every designer has a certain rhythm, largely of his own, that is apt to change much less thoroughly than, for instance, his treatment of detail. The consequence of this fact might well be that a unit arrangement that has once served him to his satisfaction will serve him again for a subsequent fount; unless, of course, it should be a fount designed for a very special purpose.

What normally happens at present is this: a ready design is given to the drawing office which, guided by a number of general rules – which, I am afraid, few of the people present and working now know the reason of – and a lot of practical experience, arranges it thus that it fits into an existing or new arrangement – the latter may be quite near several existing ones – and which, the drawing office, proceeds to make fit what does not fit exactly by, arbitrarily, making certain characters wider and others narrower. I need hardly say that this may well upset many intentions of the designer. Such inconsistencies as different widths of the counters in the several f-ligatures, here to mention only one class of them, are not seldom the result of this initial operation; and it should be obvious that such inconsistencies are unacceptable, even intolerable, to the conscientious designer. By the time the designer is called in, and shown anything (normally 'Trial number one' or a later one), so much work has already been done that he must be a cruel and most uneconomical monster to reject all of it; at the same time so much harm may have been done, too, that the drawing office's version has very little to do, indeed, with the original design.

The process I have just described may be the fate befalling a rendering of an existent fount and a completed original design alike. For the latter there is a remedy, if applied in due time, but for the former I fail to see any. The rendering of an existing fount can never be very closely related to its model. Hence the recipe I have given before in case such a fount *has* to be adapted; and also my advice to accept the inevitable modifications resignedly. For all these reasons I have at long last formed the opinion that Monotype and foundry type are and have to be looked upon as two essentially different things and that this truth should be accepted by all those concerned: type designers, typefounders, and Monotype rulers.

The consequence is that I am convinced that the best result can be obtained for a fount to be used *on* the Monotype, by having a design originally made *for* the Monotype. I have already said that no designer should try to make it on an existing unit arrangement that does not correspond with his own particular rhythm. I must now add that he should not complete his design without the Monotype people, and with them the Monotype restrictions, coming in long before; it is for this reason that I have, twice already, been using the term 'a rudimentary design'. I mean by this that the designer, when he knows himself what he wants, should make a sketch in which his intentions as to form are of no importance whatever but which clearly shows the suggested widths of all of the characters in his projected fount. It depends on the size of his sketch whether he should take one millimeter, a sixteenth or an eighth or even a quarter of an inch, a pica, or any other unit he likes or that suits him, as representing one unit – of which set is nor should be, certainly for the time being, a concern of his – in what the drawing office is going to do next.

A few things the designer has to keep in mind when working on this first step of his part of the job: (1.) everyone of his characters should fit in a whole number of his units; fit, that is, as the face of a letter fits on the body on which it is cast; (2.) no character should be narrower than the narrowest (measured in as yet undetermined units) in the Monotype system nor wider than the widest; (3.) that he should try to avoid as much as possible that an awkward number of characters has the same width; by this I mean an awkward number with regard to the number of characters in one row of the matrix case: if, for instance, he has seven or eight characters of say fourteen units he should understand that either they will all have to be made wider or narrower or that about an equal number of other ones will have to be sought to complete his row that is filled only by half.

He should, on the other hand, not be over scrupulous in this respect since taking into account too many technicalities, which are not primarily his concern, might hamper his designing abilities nearly as severely as his trying to work on a given arrangement would. It seems obvious that, in case a prospective designer were found entirely unacquainted with the unit system or nearly so, a little theoretical instruction would not only be useful but quite indispensable.

This sketch or rudimentary design   which has to be complete with ligatures, punctuation marks, signs, figures, and maybe special and accented sorts – has to be studied by the drawing office which should suggest, but by no means dictate yet, a unit arrangement. This provisional arrangement is likely to include suggestions for making certain characters wider and other ones narrower. Counter-suggestions from the side of the designer may follow.

A designer who understands his job (which is only a part of knowing it) will, for example, not accept that certain f-ligatures have a counter width differing from that in other f-ligatures or from those in M or n (whichever of these two, if they are not equal, he may have chosen); nor will be accepted that h and n have different unit values or certain capitals which, in a sound design, have equal width. Tampering with the once accepted set width should not be tolerated either. Rules like these should be known and respected by the designer and the works alike. They are part and parcel of the 'rare discipline' advocated by Mr Morison.

It is, however, quite possible if a and e were of equal width in the sketch, that one of the two has to be made wider or one wider and the other one narrower, that the works' suggestion will not cover the designer's preference. There is no need to mention all the possible modifications in the works' suggestions which the designer in his turn may prefer.

In the sketch there is, of course, a certain relation settled of the unit value and the body size. If it should be necessary, which is quite possible, to change this relation, if only by a trifle, this should be made known to the designer at the same time with the suggestions I have just been dealing with. It seems quite possible to me that I am overlooking some other point.

Two things I want to emphasize here. The first is that, at the drawing office, it should be kept in mind that during this stage their work is strictly advisory: if it went further the designer would be tied or restricted at a moment when he still has to be entirely free. The second is that the consultations described so far will involve no extra work on the side of the works since what is being done has to be done in any case.

After the two parties have reached an agreement on the unit arrangement the designer can proceed to make his design in considerably more than a rudimentary but not more than a preliminary stage. It should consist of a set of drawings in pencil and in outline – for I take it that the designer will, later on, want to elaborate on this same set – and, moreover, 'readable' and not, as is the actual practice of the works, reversed; nobody in the world is able to judge a letter or a character from a reversed drawing: is there anything sharper and more distinct than a steel punch? and is there any punchcutter working by hand who does not make smoke proofs finally to judge of his work or, incidentally, to have it judged by the designer with whom he is working? These drawings, now, need not be too accurate except in places where there may be risk of fouling [i.e. kerns clashing]. And with these drawings in hand works and designer should, between them, settle the matter of avoiding fouling.

I am unable to see a reason why anyone could, from now on, go wrong, provided that both parties keep strictly to what they have agreed upon. So now the designer can complete his drawings which should be done in black on white; for, again, there is nobody in the world able to judge a drawing for printing type from a mere outline in greyish pencil.

From the drawings so completed the works may start on their job. They must have a right to smooth out imperfections and irregularities – even if the designer should think, like Mr Rogers, that they are an asset to the fount – for, in the first place, studied and intentional imperfections are not real and therefore objectionable; in the second place they are opposed to the nature of the machine and they should, as a consequence, not be introduced into the machine's work; in the third place they will not look the same in the type as they did in the drawing and, so, they are no good and of no use; and, finally, even the most carefully handled precision machine will yield its own imperfections which, having to be accepted at all events, will, for imperfections, have to do at the same time.

I want to repeat that it should not be forgotten that foundry type and Monotype type are different things just as hand-cut and machine-cut punches are. The properties and peculiarities of the one cannot be combined with those of the other; and who tries to do so does it at the risk of producing a hybrid or a bastard. Both will reveal their failure: and both, in the end, are bound to be unable of giving satisfaction.

I am now coming back to the 'certain human shortcomings' I have hinted at earlier in this memorandum. To remedy them I cannot give a recipe but only a recommendation. It is that the people who actually make the working drawings learn to see the subtleties in a design they have to prepare for the machine and, which is equally important, to respect them. I will mention only a few of the kind of subtleties I am thinking of: serifs that are hollowed out ever so slightly or next to nothing of a shoulder in such characters as N. It may be true that the hollowing out of the serifs or the deviation from the smooth curve are so slight that a line of that thickness, supposed it could be drawn, *on itself* cannot be seen by the naked eye. This does not mean, however, that this same thickness, or even less, added to or deducted from a considerably thicker line cannot be seen or noticed either. For it can and it is seen by a keen and trained eye as I have had the satisfaction of proving to the late F. H. Pierpont. It seems to me that the soul, so to say, of any design lies in its subtleties. If this be true it applies first of all to designs which, as those for type, largely consist of subtleties.

I have found it not to be understood by the works that, for instance, a serif may have been made concave not in order that it may show concave but just to prevent it from showing convex. I have an infinite respect for the works' ability to measure. But I am absolutely certain that a keen ability to see, if only with a limited number of people, is of equal or even greater importance for the making of type. As long as some people are not trained and have [not] learned to see and appreciate essential subtleties they will go on to sin against the rightful intentions of designers and to spoil their designs by vulgarizing the fine touches from which they derive their value and charm. There is nothing against the use of french curves in the drawing office's work, for they give a clear and unequivocal line, on condition that the curve is changed as soon as the merest deviation from the original design can be noticed. A subtle and careful design deserves to be followed with the utmost exactitude: 'it is about right' will never do.

I do not expect that the necessity of re-designing a number of characters, and re-cutting the corresponding punches, will entirely belong to the past when my system draughted here, should be adopted and followed. It is more than possible that even an experienced designer will be disappointed and not satisfied by the reduction in print of certain ones of his characters. But, then, I have never heard of any fount of type that has been approved in its entirety at once. I am, however, confident that the number of necessary re-cuttings will be considerably reduced. And, and this is of infinitely greater importance, that a type face produced according to my suggestions will be nearer the intentions of the designer and as a consequence be better than it could have been when made along the lines now followed.

The Dutch designer **Jan van Krimpen** (1892–1958) spent his career at the printing house of Joh. Enschedé en Zonen in Haarlem. His work demonstrates finely proportioned classical typography. Influenced by the work and writings of Edward Johnston, Van Krimpen created elegant Roman types such as Lutetia (1925), Romanée (1928), Romulus (1931) and Spectrum (1952). Although Van Krimpen became famous because of his typeface designs, he was also an influential calligrapher and book designer, and was responsible for the lettering and design of many Dutch stamps.

1. Regulus: The punches

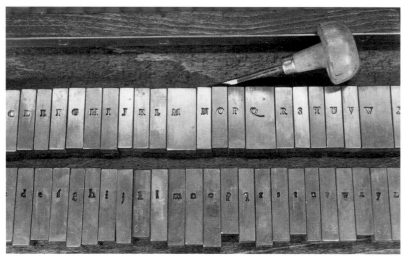

2. Regulus: The matrices

Making a Visible Spirit: Cutting the Regulus Punches by Hand

BY DAN CARR

Dan Carr works in the tradition of type designers who cut their own punches, and he is one of the craftsmen learning and preserving this tradition today. In this essay from Matrix 16 *(1996), he has a bone to pick with digital type that is artificially 'antiqued' to look old; the irregularities of a hand-made type, he feels, should grow naturally out of the process itself.*

In 1996 a new metal typeface, made from punches cut by hand, was finished in the small village of Ashuelot, New Hampshire. A decade earlier in 1986, at Golgonooza Letter Foundry & Press, my partner Julia Ferrari and I saw a need for a new metal type. For two years I had been experimenting with punchcutting and had made some successful punches. I was deeply involved in the history of type and typefaces, and sought out and studied many of the accessible stones cut by Eric Gill, during a trip to England. Simultaneously I was studying calligraphy with the contemporary calligrapher, Suzanne Moore. There was no reason to delay. After a decade of work done whenever I could find time outside the operation of the foundry and press I can now set type with a voice that is my own. Now that the capital and lower case alphabets are done we have begun setting our first book with the type, *Gifts of the Leaves*, an exploration of the seasons of the year through the symbolic alphabet of trees. The type is called Regulus for the star rising in the constellation Leo when the first alphabet was finished in 1989. The name doubly evokes a beautifully formed Regulus of Antimony I had seen pictured in a book on Alchemy. At the time I was studying the properties of type metal and hoped that, like Antimony in type metal, the cutting of a new type would help metal typography endure. Making this type required that I learn to cut punches well, to strike and justify matrices accurately and make or acquire all the necessary tools. In this process I gained fresh insights into the history of making type. Though the professional need for punchcutting has disappeared, it can still offer a valuable and unique means of expression as an art form.

It is generally accepted that punchcutting was an art adapted to printing. Punchcutting is in its widest sense a toolmaker's art. A typographic punchcutter cuts a set of letters in steel while at the same time adapting these letters to make a fount of type that will compose words legibly with style. A reductive view, that the alphabet is a system of symbols or that it is simply a graphic palette, will miss the voice of intellectual expression contained in an alphabet's design. Punchcutters like calligraphers tend to express the age they live in. The expression in their letters is like music, informing us with subtlety and clarity, without self-conscious imitation. It is part of their hand, a part of how they see. An original Bodoni type has the contrast and nuance of a concerto by Beethoven. In an original Caslon type the unique shapes of the letters form words with a repose that lets me see Caslon, after a Thursday night full moon concert, singing Purcell's songs in his home and foundry. Harry Carter in his notes to Moxon points out that two skills are essential to successful punchcutting: the punchcutter must have 'the aptitude and inclination for minute metalwork combined with a sufficient capacity for drawing the alphabet.'[1] To the degree to which a punchcutter achieves excellence in both these skills there is a separation between the need to reproduce letters and the desire to create the splendid qualities of letters cut in steel. Punchcutting no longer has much to do with the need to reproduce letters but it still offers as much as it ever did to the desire for refinement and personal expression.

Cutting punches by hand is an occasion to experience the passage of time from a pre-industrial perspective. Unlike even hand-bookbinding or printing, the results of one's efforts are appreciable only after work carried out over a long period of time. When I set Regulus types side by side, hours and entire days of the experience of cutting the letters are remembered and they compose a deepening appreciation of this effort. It's worth every trial and struggle. Even broken letters are worth a moment's pause as they are pitched into the hell-box. Anaïs Nin said of setting type by hand: 'Each letter has a weight. I can weigh each word again, to see if it is the right one.'[2] Weighing words with letters that have come from your own hand is a way to dance the dance of language itself.

Cutting a single punch would not be too hard for most of us, but cutting a set of punches that will form legible and pleasing words is more difficult. A typeface is a house for ideas – about form, proportion, rhythm, colour or contrast, as well as emotional and intellectual expression. Cutting a typeface is like building your house with stones, you must hold each stone in your hands. Finding the shape and weight of each part of every letter and placing it where it fits involves choices that reveal the taste a punchcutter has for letters. And as with a stone wall, after the roof holds and wind is turned away, we come to admire features which aren't apparent, a repose of diversity and balance. The formation of a word, the legibility of the line, the attractiveness of the page, will stand or fall with the placement of each part of each letter. Minute variations in the forms of letters reveal the depth of the culture of this enclosure of thought. Warren Chappell noted, 'It is an essential virtue of the punchcutting method that the design is constantly in flux.'[3] An imperceptible amount of steel can be removed by a file or graver. Cutting punches by hand, in steel, offers the control and spontaneity which breathes life into an alphabet.

I have also made letters with a pen and with digital fount editors. Each medium is distinctly different. Calligraphy has just as much freedom and the speed of writing determines detail. Digital type, like phototype and pantographically produced type before it, depends heavily on drawing, advance planning, and comparative measurement. The simple desire to bring a drawing to perfection tends to deaden the letterforms and only a few designers overcome this without exaggeration. The current explosion in display type created with computers shows a capacity to represent the sketchier elements of drawing. If you approach digital design like punchcutting you will spend a lot of time removing subtleties so that the computer won't make unintended changes to the letters. To return to a metaphor, making digital type is more like making your house with plywood and studs supplied in common lengths, it works to its own end.

There are two primary reasons for practising punchcutting, the aesthetic and the philosophical. I have spoken about aspects of these ideas above. Bruce Rogers notes separately and succinctly: 'Whereas in a really fine type there are perpetual variations, within narrow limits it is true, but still enough to give a living quality to the type when combined in words.'[4] 'I have come to believe that perhaps only hand-cut punches, cut by the designer of the type, can preserve the real feeling of the design.'[5] He came to this conclusion partly because of the failure of drawn types either to include desirable variations or to conceal the imitation of hand-cut qualities. Of the hundred or so types designed by Goudy, for example, very few conceal their conscious imitation of a hand-cut look. In contrast Jan van Krimpen's Lutetia cut in close collaboration with punchcutter P. H. Rädisch shows subtle variations in the shape of curves, stems and serifs which are vivifying. Yet in no way do these variations include the imitation rough edges which show an uninformed expectation of a hand-cut type. In learning to cut punches I certainly had my share of slips. In fact some of my letters retain the influence of unplanned cuts. At the same time, every impulse in me as a cutter sought first of all the effective realisation of a well-designed type. These desirable variations are subtle refinements that grow out of a spontaneity in the appreciation of the design. It is only incidental that accidents may suggest a new variation in a letter.

3. Regulus in composing stick with punches and graver.

The second motive for cutting punches, the philosophical, is perhaps best seen in the life and career of Victor Hammer. His dedication to a less popular letterform, the uncial, bears witness to a philosophical aim as much as an aesthetic aim. Hammer cut his letters so that the words would form like strings of pearls – pearls of meaning. He thought of type as organic. He felt that craft could open the spirit to wider horizons and believed in the holiness of work. When I am cutting punches I experience a relaxation and clarity never achieved except in traditional meditation. Part of the discipline becomes getting up to refocus my eyes on something far away to preserve my eyesight. The challenge and reward of dealing with a tough physical substance like steel opens my experience to something outside myself. When I am cutting steel anything is possible.

Giovanni Mardersteig tells us that Charles Malin never tired of recutting a punch. I do not think this was simply grace but rather enthusiasm. Malin, apparently, would divert any attempt to talk about himself to the typographic work at hand. Mardersteig credits Malin with developing a perfect expression of his (Mardersteig's) concepts of type.[6] The value of letting the cutting move towards its own pace can be seen in Malin's example. Indeed this is the lesson that has been the hardest to learn. Through the loup at about 4x magnification, the sculptural world of the punch becomes completely engaging. The punchcutter enters into the scale of a world where a sense of time is gauged by the cutting of small chips of steel.

Punches are cut in a finished state at the size they will be used. Because of this the cutter's own hands and tools aid in the adjustments of the proportion of that size. To cut a small counter for a letter a small counter punch or a small graver must be made. The tool must be held in a punchcutter's hand, and fashioning this tool influences the shape of the letter. Tools can be allowed to encourage the swelling of stems or to develop a concave curve in serifs to compensate for the tendency of the serifs at the baseline to appear convex. Sometimes the curve cut in a serif is no more than a single pass with the file to lighten where the main stem joins at the baseline. In an opposite way a darkness at a joint of a stem and a hairline can be lightened by actually trimming out the curve quite abruptly without losing the apparent curve. The weight of stems and hairlines can be varied slightly from letter to letter to balance them together. In drawn letters these subtleties must be added on with premeditation. They are often overdone or become lost in scaling from size to size. In mechanically scaling the drawings, optical effects must be anticipated and odd constructions are used to simulate the effect of a letter that obeys the proportion of its size. So far none of the attempts to overcome this problem can be called a true success, despite inventive solutions like averaging between two extremes. The problem with letters mechanically or electronically scaled from a set of drawings is that the result is mechanical and it always will look stiff in several of the sizes.

Of course the argument that cutting punches by hand is no longer practical for commercial markets is true beyond doubt. And because of this controversy people who could truly be rewarded by cutting a typeface resort to a reproducing technology and remain unsatisfied. The aesthetic and philosophical satisfactions take some practice to achieve. You realise the spontaneous possibilities when you see vitality arise in a typeface as you minutely adjust the length and shape of serifs to promote the rhythm of the letters. This is possible in other mediums but by creating a physical object and not just an image of an object, a different relationship is found. A physical object informs me in ways that images never do. Using a graver to refine the ductus of a letter I rest the graver on the beard of the letter. The beard guides the graver as I scrape a few tenths of thousandths of an inch away. In this way I can repeatedly adjust the ductus of the letter without losing the essential shape. Drawing-derived tools excel at production. Making physical letters, as calligraphers, stonecutters and punchcutters do, promotes the discovery and refinement of creative ideas. A punchcutter becomes the source of letters.

I began the cutting of Regulus as an exploration that would have a useful final result. It was my premise to study how lettering evolved by posing myself as a sixteenth-century punchcutter in North America, who wanted to emulate the latest printing of Italy and France, much as we suppose happened with Augereau, Garamond and De Colines. To begin, I looked at the types of Jenson, but I used as my exemplar a Garamond type from his early period. Though I continually referred to my exemplar I did not intend to copy it. Variations came into the letters to satisfy my personal sense of typographic style. For example, I wanted to create a typeface that used space in a unique way, I wanted the sense of time in my lower case letters to reach up a little out of the moment. I wanted the capitals to be rich in colour when set together but not stand out in composition. Therefore as a concentration and formalisation of the time and space of the typeface, they would have a horizontal expansion in contrast to the lower case. The type would have long ascenders and descenders and short capitals that were slightly expanded. I made the eye of the **e** introspective and let the **c** show more of the distinction. I often feel the lower case **w** has not fully evolved and may be too wide in other types and I have also let the **w** retain its first cut look to heighten its sense of immediacy. In one critique of the type the lower case **a** has been noted for its tapered bow, which though daring, works in this size. The idea was that the **a** would begin from an infinitesimal point. As each letter developed, I found and accepted or accentuated features that would express a typographic style that was not simply imposed but also grew out of the typeface itself. Another source of variation was an effort on my part to try to hold an image of a letter in my mind. I soon found that the image was changing to reflect my personal understanding of the letter. In fact as I cut each letter my mental image of the letter evolved. A third source of variation was begun by error, which I accepted as a starting point. I did not, however, accept an error as a final form, and as a result a few letters were faced down (reground to become bolder) and recut. Regulus developed as an independent typeface following a calligraphic model, using an exemplar while encouraging variation.

From my experience with punchcutting I can say that the evolution of a typeface is the result of the growth of a sense of typographic style in individual punchcutters, calligraphers or designers. In most typefaces which have the qualities to serve as text types, contemporary fashion has only general or peripheral influence, it governs the overall style. The strength of the design however is in the detail, and the detail is developed within the context of the typeface not outside of it. It is the development of an overall style into a coherent and functional typeface that matters most. An individual, facing the need to make useful and

A QUESTION OF APPLES

The letter of query, Q is an apple
a globe spun from a stem, a seed.
Cut an apple in two
and five seeds make a star,
to begin a spiral purse your lips.

In the small valley the orchard
is chattering with people
like a flock of birds
not even the lonely seem alone
trading in apples.

Women and men, children,
hidden and seen,
laughing, calling through the trees,
feeling good in their flesh,
gather up the apples
like spirits for a soul.

From where I sit on the cemetery wall
there's no after life,
the dead at my back giggle
when lovers walk by
leaning into their armpits.

Love's no apple in a market,
it's that old tree you find each fall,
the apples bearing yellow-jackets,
blemishes and worms,
our flesh sweet with change.

Dan Carr

4. Poem set in Regulus

tasteful letters, advances the history of the design of type. A good type is not defined by its age, though it may help define an age.

The technique used in cutting Regulus was likewise exploratory. The lower case was cut traditionally with counterpunches using only the exemplar as a source. The capitals were cut entirely with gravers. Drawings two inches high were made as a guide. Part way through cutting the capitals I had the good fortune to study with the professional punchcutters in Paris at the Imprimerie Nationale (Christian Paput and Nelly Gable), and there I learned the basics of just this method of cutting. The technique they use for cutting steel bears the marks of a long continuous tradition. Four years earlier, after about my third year of my punchcutting, there's a note in my journal noticing that an even and smooth beard helps control the engraving by supporting the graver. I didn't make too much of this idea and used it only slightly in my work. In Paris I found that an amplification of this idea was the cornerstone of both their engraving and their filing technique. These masters practise a technique which allows for such precision that they can make exact duplicates of existing punches. In addition while there I learned to use my existing f, i, and l punches to create a smoke proof image on steel for ligature punches. In cutting the figures I had no exemplar and have instead followed the example of Rudolf Koch, writing out figures with a pen, choosing the best forms and transferring the images to the steel. While I have come to understand how the peculiarities of certain letters of Kis, Caslon and Bodoni could develop, in the end I have found that a skilled punchcutter can do anything with steel. Steel allows qualities to be realised that are remarkable.

Punchcutting is still alive in the skills of punchcutters active today, an astonishing statement for the end of the twentieth century. The punchcutters that I know, Stan Nelson, Christian Paput, Nelly Gable and one or two cutters in India (and I hope to hear of others elsewhere) could each conserve and pass on these skills to enthusiasts and artists of future generations. The techniques of punchcutting were hidden in the past and there were few cutters. I think the skills could be developed by greater numbers of people than history leads us to believe. My enthusiasm comes from learning to make letters that are real things, not just images of letters, a distinction valued by Eric Gill. A student will need to be aware that it may take the patience of building a house with stone, as did the poet Robinson Jeffers or the philosophers Helen and Scott Nearing (*Living the Good Life*). Punchcutting is for me a way that my words can be shared in a voice which expresses my tastes and thoughts, an expression of my discovery of meaning in life. At the rate of change in our culture at the end of

ABCDEFGHIJKLMNOPQRSTUVWXYZ

abcdefghijklmnopqrstuvwxyzfiflff,.'

5. Specimen of Regulus

this century, I can no longer see the need to speed up to become that much more quickly part of the past. Punchcutting is part of a culture I am proud to maintain. It is part of the past and the present and I have no doubt, a part of the future.

Dan Carr is a typographer and poet who writes about type and type history. His articles have appeared in *Matrix*, *Serif*, the *Book Club of California Quarterly Newsletter*, and elsewhere. Carr and partner Julia Ferrari operate Golgonooza Letter Foundry & Press, where they design and print fine press books, both for themselves and on commission, printing exclusively with metal types. Carr designs metal and digital type and cuts steel punches by hand at the foundry. He has taught typography for the past seven years. In 1999 he was elected a Master Typographic Punchcutter of France for his metal typeface Regulus. Carr's digital type, Châneau, won a Judge's Choice award in the 2000 Type Directors Club type design competition. Carr has lectured at ATypI, Leipzig, Germany; the Department of Typography, University of Reading, England; the Colophon Club, San Francisco; the Typophiles, New York City; the Society of Printers, Boston; the San Francisco Public Library; the San Francisco Center for the Book; and elsewhere. In the 2001 bukva:raz competition held by ATypI, he was awarded a Certificate of Excellence in Type Design for his new metal typeface, an Archaic Greek type called Parmenides (cut by hand in steel).

NOTES

1. Joseph Moxon, *Mechanick Exercises on the Whole Art of Printing*, ed. Herbert and Harry Carter (London: Oxford University, 1962), p. 376.

2. Anaïs Nin, *The Diary of Anaïs Nin*, III, ed. Gunther Stuhlman (New York: Swallow Press and Harcourt Brace Jovanovich, 1969), p. 186.

3. Warren Chappell, *A Short History of the Printed Word*, (Boston: Nonpareil Books, 1970), p. 46.

4. Bruce Rogers, *Bye-Ways of Book-making, or Random Notes of a Tramp Printer*, (New York: unpublished manuscript in Carl H. Pforzheimer Library).

5. D.B. Updike, *Printing Types*, Vol. 1, (Cambridge: Harvard University Press, 1937), pp. 11–12.

6. Giovanni Mardersteig, *The Officina Bodoni*, ed. and trans. Hans Schmoller (Verona: Edizioni Valdonega, 1980), pp. 230–31.

ABCDEFGHIJKLMNOPQRST
UVWXY&Z
abcdefghijklmnopqrstuvwxyz
ff fi fl ffi ffl ſt ſ ſſ ſſi ſl ſſi ſſl ſb ſh ſk ſt
ABCDEFGHIJKLMNOPQRST
UVWXY&Z
abcdefghhijkklmnopqrstuvvwwxyz
ff fi fl ffi ffl ſt ſ ſſ ſſi ſl ſſi ſſl ſb ſh ſh ſk ſt
ABCDEGFKMNPQuRTUY
1234567890£1234567890

OTHER VERSIONS OF CASLON

Monotype Caslon Old Face	*old face type*
ATF Caslon Oldstyle	*old face type*
Linotype Caslon Old Face	*old face type*
Ludlow True-Cut Caslon	*old face type*
Haas Caslon Antiqua	*old face type*
Газетный заголовок	*барочный шрифт*

ADDITIONAL SWASHES AND LIGATURES

CEFHKLMOSW&

[AMERICAN TYPEFOUNDERS]

f f,f.f-fafefofrfsftfufyff ff,ff.ff-ffaffeffoffrffsffuffy
f f,f.f-fafefofrfsftfufyff ff,ff.ff-ffaffeffoffrffsffuffy

[LINOTYPE]

1. Founders Caslon complete showing (see caption on facing page)

A Type for All Seasons

BY ALAN DODSON

The types of William Caslon have been in almost continuous use since the 18th century, and they have practically defined straightforward, workmanlike printing in England. In Matrix 13 (1993) *Alan Dodson explains the history of this typeface and its many variants and revivals up to that time.*

For me, as for the printer of *Matrix*, the historic Caslon types have been an important part of life for many years. When I first made my acquaintance with print in 1940, at Kingston School of Art, most work was still printed by letterpress, and Caslon Old Face, at least in the display sizes, was standard equipment in most book houses, to be seen on the title-pages of works of every kind.

The history of the face has been recounted many times in scholarly detail; suffice it to say here that for some sixty years after its inception in the 1720s it was used all over England for both book and job printing, and indeed in an early private press, that of Horace Walpole at Strawberry Hill; it likewise found a secure place across the Atlantic in the work put out by Benjamin Franklin and others. After a period of eclipse in favour of the 'modern' face, the publisher Pickering initiated the use of Caslon on his title-pages. When his printer, Charles Whittingham of the Chiswick Press, was commissioned in 1841 to print *Lady Willoughby's Diary* (see page 94), (describing life during the seventeenth century English Civil War) in the typographical style of that period, he prevailed on the firm of H. W. Caslon to cast a sufficient supply of Caslon Old Face for setting the book. Once more available, Chiswick proceeded to use the type for a variety of work, and it was slowly taken up by a few other enlightened firms, amongst them Unwin Brothers and the Leadenhall Press, though it still tended to be used mostly for display, while the 'old style' that was derived from it took over from 'modern' as the standard text face.

---

1. Alphabets of Caslon at left show all the characters currently available, including the archaic long-s and its ligatures, but omit the diphthongs, which are now no longer cast, and accented characters. All the alphabets here were proofed from Stephenson Blake's Caslon, except for the roman capitals, which are Monotype, as being closer in respect of certain 24-point letters to those formerly supplied with foundry founts, and superior to the founder's version sold today. This latter appears to have had its origin as a titling fount, cast on two-line brevier (16-point) body, and as 36-point small capitals. 24-point small capitals are identical with the normal 18-point capitals.

Due to the virtual impossibility of obtaining type or slugs of the ATF, Linotype and Ludlow versions of Caslon, these have had to be made up from lines in specimen books, some of them lithographed on coated paper, hardly

Continued on page 82

About the same time as the old face revival in England, the typefounder Laurence Johnson of Philadelphia came to an arrangement with H. W. Caslon for the production of the original Caslon designs in the United States. Just how they were reproduced, whether electrotyped from cast types, or from locally finished matrices struck from the original punches, is not known, but the latter method seems probable; because the 14-, 18- and 24-point roman, whilst of the original design, were cast on over-wide bodies, giving a letterspaced effect. This persisted even when the face was ultimately taken over by American Typefounders in 1892, though later reissued, on the correct set, under a different series number.

Another development was the establishment by Caslons of an office and small foundry in Paris, from which they sold the type used in many French *éditions de luxe* of the twenties and thirties of the present century.

Most users of the Caslon types in the late 1800s tended to look backwards, and whilst much of their work was a relief from the incredible mixtures of badly designed display faces which characterised most work of that period, it frequently took the form of a pastiche of seventeenth- and eighteenth-century layout, including the frequent use of the archaic 'long-s'. Even the magnificent Caslon specimen produced by George W. Jones at the Sign of the Dolphin, Gough Square, in 1924, consists entirely of resettings of work from the seventeenth century onwards, mostly quite unrelated to the kind of job the average printer might expect to encounter.

With the turn of the present century came a growing consciousness of design in every field, including printing, culminating in the formation of the Design & Industries Association in 1915. Whilst Art Nouveau contributed a few contorted horrors to the printers' repertoire, a kind of contemporary vernacular tradition gradually emerged, parallel to the achievements of C. F. A. Voysey in architecture, and quite early on we find Caslon being used, sometimes in new ways, for the

---

the most appropriate way to display this particular face. However, they serve to demonstrate variations in set, the extreme regularity of the Swiss Haas founts, and the differing slopes and fitting of the various italics; the wording was chosen to show these latter modifications.

The cyrillic version was produced in Russia, and as far as can be ascertained, in display sizes only, with the 'common' characters closely following the corresponding sizes of the Caslon original. The reproduction of the 42-point (English) size in Shitsgal's Ruskii grazhdanskii shrift is captioned as 'Newspaper headline type', and indeed this has been an important use of the Caslon founts in England, for the mastheads, amongst others, of the historic Berrow's Worcester Journal and the official London Gazette.

Reference is made in the text of the article to the ATF italic swash capitals and the Linotype f-ligatures shown at the foot of the page.

The 'other versions' have partly been assembled by means of a combination of photocopying and pasting up, with some missing letters in the cyrillic being drawn in. But I am grateful to those who generously supplied material from which the reconstructions could be made: George R. Gasparik of Kingsley/ATF Type Corporation; Frank Bryant of L & M Limited (Linotype and Ludlow); James Mosley of St Bride Printing Library (ATF and cyrillic); Ian Mortimer for his kind assistance with the Caslon Italic long-s ligatures.

titles and texts of Bernard Shaw's works and those of Kipling, whilst more enlightened publishers, such as Burns & Oates, Basil Blackwell and the University Presses, aided by such printers as the Arden and Shakespeare Head Presses, used the face extensively. The Favil Press of Church Street, Kensington, was one of the few smaller firms aiming at quality work, and used almost exclusively Caslon Old Face for jobbing.

The earlier private presses tended to commission their own type faces, but later on Caslon became a favourite of such as the Cuala Press in Ireland, staffed entirely by women under the direction of Elizabeth Yeats, sister of the famous poet, the Stanbrook Abbey Press, Worcester, the Welsh Gregynog Press near Newtown, and Robert Gibbings' Golden Cockerel Press. At the time when these presses commenced operations, early this century, Caslon was in fact the only readily obtainable book face, outside the 'proprietary' faces, which offered the colour, strength and character appropriate to fine book printing, and this position did not change until the end of the First World War when, starting with Baskerville and Garamond, the Monotype Corporation began to introduce other suitable faces.

Actually, Caslon became available for Monotype composition in 1915, though many of the presses continued to use founder's type, and even for those larger printers like R. & R. Clark, printers of Shaw's and Kipling's works, Monotype Caslon represented quite a heavy capital investment. In a virtually facsimile recutting, following all the variations in the different sizes of the original face, it was impossible to establish a standard unit arrangement in the Monotype matrix case, so that a fresh set of keybars had to be bought for every size. However, this did not put off those printers who were design conscious and determined to raise their standards, as witness the wholesale clearance of Victorian types from the Curwen Press in 1915 (helped by the high price of lead in wartime) and their replacement, initially, by only a handful of faces amongst which both Monotype and founder's Caslon were the most prominent, and thereafter imaginatively used in much of Harold Curwen's own promotional material.

It could hardly be expected that Monotype would add such an important face to their repertoire without Linotype following suit, and this in fact happened on both sides of the Atlantic. As one might imagine, the extreme slope of Caslon Italic and the many kerned letters were something of a complication on the Linotype, especially in the larger sizes, and a number of adjustments were needed, not only on the double-letter matrices of the composition sizes, but even more on the single-letter display matrices, where the angle and form of many letters had to be drastically altered to accommodate them within the confines of a rectangular matrix, to that extent the Linotype version could not compete in quality with the freely kerning italics available from Monotype, though a range of f-ligatures was made available in the smaller sizes of Linotype Caslon, in which a kerned f was combined with a number of other letters and punctuation marks.

Ludlow also entered the fray with 'True-Cut' Caslon and Italic, cut in 1922 and 1928 respectively. This is a close copy of the original apart from a non-kerned f, and the kerns and slope of the italic were taken care of by the use of angled matrices, though not without retaining a slight stiffness of appearance by comparison with the original and Monotype versions of the face. Lining figures were usually supplied as standard.

A further version of Caslon, not so often seen in England, and only available on Didot bodies, is that cut by Haas in Switzerland about 1944. Some sizes, such as the 20-point Didot are fairly close copies of the original, particularly in the roman, but no small capitals are available, and most sizes of the italic are bolder, at less of an angle, and more regular than the original cutting. Many of the display sizes are also cast on too small a body – the worst is the erstwhile 22-point cast on a 16-point Didot body – resulting in shortened descenders and a somewhat truncated appearance. Figures tend to be rather closely fitted, with clumsy alternative lining version, and the capital Q, like that offered by ATF, varies from the original Q in both roman and italic. No matrices for this alternative form appear to exist in the Sheffield Foundry of Stephenson Blake, who took the face over from H. W. Caslon in 1937, so it is difficult to know what caused its introduction in the other versions, or in the Monotype composition sizes, where it also occurs.

Indeed, many of the versions of Caslon have been offered in an alternative form, incorporating deliberately shortened descenders, sometimes to conform to the ill-conceived point lining system which was temporarily in vogue in the early years of this century, and from which some faces, like founder's Baskerville, still suffer. The standard lining system put out by H. W. Caslon is one of the worst, with each face cast on a body one size smaller than normal. This not only looked hideous, but called for such wide leading to compensate for the close fit of the lines as to cancel out any saving of space.

A more favourable innovation, which has added to the attractiveness of the italic, was the introduction, about 1887, of a range of swash capitals and a few lower case. In the words of *Caslon's Circular* no. 54, 1890, these 'peculiar italic sorts do not belong to the original founts; the first Caslon, deeming them superfluous, discarded them. They have recently been engraved in obedience to the modern demand for imitations of the old Dutch printing.' As originally designed and shown on Caslon's 1734 specimen sheet, *J*, *Q*, *T* and *Y*, and lower case **b** were only cut in the swash form, but normal versions of these letters were later substituted and became standard, though the swash *J* and *Y* remain in Monotype composition sizes. The additional letters were drawn and cut by unknown hands – typefounders are notoriously bad at keeping records – and are now supplied by Stephenson Blake as normal components of their italic founts. The long tails of *K* and *R* tend to be rather at risk in smaller sizes up to 18 point, but most of the larger sizes were recut in the fifties, and are now cast from doubledepth matrices, making even the longest kerns robust enough to stand up to continued use without breakage.

A further range of swash letters was designed about 1920 by Thomas M. Cleland to accompany ATF Caslon Italic, and by 1923 these had been augmented, possibly by another designer, so that practically every capital letter had its swash alternative, some of them, it is only fair to say, over extravagant and better ignored; many of the letters betray the spirit of the time when they were introduced, definitely *not* the eighteenth century!

There is a tendency amongst amateur printers – and others – to be rather carried away in the use of swash capitals; in fact, they should be used very sparingly, and never in the middle of a word. Mostly they will be combined with lower case; the extreme and irregular slope of Caslon Italic capitals makes them generally unsuited to combination in words, or at very least, only in the smaller sizes and with adequate letterspacing.

Many other variants of Caslon exist, both in founder's type and in machine composition systems, including a Caslon Heavy and Heavy Compressed, introduced by H. W. Caslon, probably early this century, and a number of other semibold and inline variants, principally of American origin. Most of them have little resemblance to the original other than the name, and should be avoided.

There are, as far as I know, only two versions of Caslon for photo-composition which have even the slightest authenticity: one is based on the great primer or 18-point size, the other on French cannon or 48-point, but understandably when one of these is enlarged or reduced it just does not 'work' apart from having little relation to the original outside the body size from which it was derived. In any case, Caslon was originally hand-cut and conceived for letterpress printing, i.e. for being impressed into the paper, so a highly finished, mechanical representation, coupled with two-dimensional offset printing, is really a contradiction, and frequently unsatisfactory.

But having learnt something of the history of the face, it is time to find out why

HENRI - MATISSE

Messrs. ERNEST BROWN & PHILLIPS have the honour of inviting you to the Private View of an Exhibition of Drawings, Etchings and Lithographs by HENRI - MATISSE, on Saturday, 14th January, 1928, from 10 till 6.

THE LEICESTER GALLERIES
Leicester Square, London

EASTER SUNDAY 1870

T HE happiest, brightest, most beautiful Easter I have ever spent. I woke early and looked out. As I had hoped the day was cloudless, a glorious morning. My first thought was 'Christ is Risen'. It is not well to lie in bed on Easter morning, indeed it is thought very un-lucky. I got up between five and six and was out soon after six. There had been a frost and the air was rimy with a heavy thick white dew on hedge, bank and turf, but the morning was not cold. There was a heavy white dew with a touch of hoar frost on the meadows, and as I leaned over the wicket gate by the mill pond looking to see if there were any primroses in the banks but not liking to venture into the dripping grass suddenly I heard the cuckoo for the first time this year. He was near Peter's Pool and he called three times quickly one after another. It is very well to hear the cuckoo for the first time on Easter Sunday morning. I loitered up the lane again gathering primroses.

Androcles and the Lion, Overruled, Pygmalion. By Bernard Shaw.

Constable and Company Ltd. London: 1916.

2. Since the time of the Old Face Revival in the latter half of the nineteenth century, the use of Caslon was popular amongst booksellers and art dealers as conferring a certain cachet on their stationery and announcements. However, as the Matisse card of 1928 demonstrates, most printers still had little idea how Caslon should be used. By contrast, the Easter greeting card of 1990 shows careful letter-spacing of the italic capitals, with the use of roman numerals in the same line adding a certain sparkle. The text is close spaced, and the decorative initial T is made up from one of the original Caslon fleurons.

3. For many years Bernard Shaw insisted that his books be set in Caslon, initially by hand and later in Monotype Caslon 128. He pioneered the introduction of the asymmetrical title-page from as early as 1898, and though the example shown looks crude by comparison with later work, particularly by Continental designers, it was really revolutionary in its day. Astonishingly, as late as 1916 the printers, R. & R. Clark, were still using pre-point system types, and this title-page is set in two-line English!

A SPECIMEN BOOK OF
PATTERN PAPERS
DESIGNED FOR AND IN USE AT
THE CURWEN PRESS
WITH AN INTRODUCTION BY PAUL NASH

PUBLISHED FOR THE CURWEN PRESS BY
THE FLEURON LIMITED
101 GREAT RUSSELL STREET, LONDON, W.C.

IDYLLE

I.

Bedelaar. SLAAP WEL, MIJN OUDSTE BROE-
der Zon, slaap wel.
Wij hebben beide onze plicht gedaan;
Gij wandelt zonder doel den hemel langs
En ik de aarde. — In tevredenheid
Willen wij beide van dit wijze werk
Rusten op welverdiende lauweren —
Gij in de zee en ik bij deze bron.
Vriendlijk daalt schemering in 't moede dorp.
Daar komt een meisje dat zich heeft verlaat
Zich wiegend als een jonge wilgeboom
Met slanke heupen; op het donkre hoofd
De roode waterkruik. Nu schrik maar niet,
Ik ben geen faun al is mijn wang behaard.
Mijn voet is ongespleten en geen hoorn
Versiert mijn menschelijken zwerverskop.
Meisje. De steen is hard. Aan de ingang van het dorp
Honderd schrêe verder staat een herberg. Bed. Duifje,
Ik zag er veel maar nergens zoo gastvrij
Als deze vrije nacht. Mei. De wijn is goed!
Bed. Een verre wijn is altijd minder goed
Dan water in de buurt. Mei. De koele lucht....
Bed. Zoo is uw vader dan de herbergier?

4

4. The title-page of the Curwen Press specimen of pattern papers, c. 1930, exemplifies a style of display popularised by J. H. Mason at the Central School of Arts and Crafts around 1910, characterised by the use of different sizes of type and varying degrees of letterspacing to achieve a rectangular panel of display lines. The version of the Curwen Press unicorn trade mark was designed by Lovat Fraser.

5. The former Enschedé Typefoundry in Haarlem, Holland, held matrices derived from the original Caslon, and type cast from them was used in some of Jan van Krimpen's early essays in book design. This example, 1924, is in great primer on 16-point Didot body, to a wider set than the original. The drawn lettering has the characteristics of his Lutetia type face, which appeared the following year.

it still retains so much popularity in certain circles, in spite of all its imperfections and inconsistencies. Perhaps the key lies in these two very qualities. Just look at human beings: what is it that makes them so interesting, even if at times so exasperating? Simply the fact that they are all different, can never be entirely categorised or pinned down, and yet are withal amazingly adapted to life. The same goes for Caslon types: their individually imperfect forms yet have in mass a practical, workaday quality about them when it is needed, yet most of the larger sizes, particularly, have an almost monumental dignity, especially in a line of carefully letterspaced capitals, whilst one can be positively frivolous and carefree with the italic. While, as mentioned above, it is essentially a letterpress type, with due allowance made for a slight thickening of the smaller sizes in printing, yet from 18-point upwards the alphabets grow proportionately heavier, so that without recourse to a bold face the 72-point can hold its own even on an outdoor poster.

Working with the face over the years, as I have done, one comes to know every letter in every size quite intimately, and to know that certain features can be exploited whilst others are better avoided. Some sizes were not cut by William Caslon I at all: the two-line pica and two-line double pica – 24- and 42-point respectively – were cut by Caslon's son, and lack some of the mastery displayed by his father; the French cannon, or 48-point lower case is probably from the hand of Moxon and was just taken over by the Caslon Foundry, and the figures show the characteristics of the previous century. Caslon I cut a new and very fine set of capitals to replace the rather poor ones which came with the fount, and added a closely fitted, slightly condensed italic.

Originally the range of sizes included, in addition to those currently cast, 5-, 7-, 9- and 11-point (the two latter still available as Monotype matrices), variants of 8-, 9-, 10-, 11- and 12-point, exhibiting minute differences of lower case x-height and fitting, and a rather handsome paragon (approximately 19-point), but none of these is any longer cast.

Caslon is usually thought of as a book type, but some of the examples displayed show that this is far from being the case, and its versatility makes it ideal as a jobbing type, though equally it can be employed to make a superbly readable page in any format from a pocket paperback, set in 10- or 11-point, to a fine folio, for which the 18-point is just the right weight for text composition. But in the days following its inception Caslon was used for a variety of jobbing work, and nowadays, in spite of lacking a related bold – though I find Imprint Bold 310 on occasion a useful adjunct – its variations of weight between sizes, the existence of small capitals and generally satisfactory italics, make it of far greater utility than one might expect. A further extension, should one wish to strike a festive note, though a purist might object, is found in the use of Imprint Shadow capitals. Whilst slightly rigid and mechanical, they are after all derived from Caslon, and in some sizes are of just the right weight to combine well with smaller sizes of the parent face.

Certain variations in set have taken place over the years: early this century the 14-, 22- and 24-point sizes were cast on a slightly wider set than originally, and this is perpetuated in the Monotype versions, which were cut about that time. The founder's type has since reverted to its former close fitting, and indeed, some lower case letter combinations, such as 'ea' in 18-point, are better for the insertion of a half-point space, and certain letters in 24-point and larger also call for some adjustment. But generally justification is regular, and even letter-spacing of capitals can be carried out quite easily.

The recutting of a face when the original punches wear out needs to be carried out with the utmost care if variations are not to creep in, and in fact new matrices are nowadays more often made by growing a new copper shell on a good cast from the original matrix. This is then backed up, and plated with nickel or chromium to lengthen its life in the casting machine. Most sizes of Caslon have been expertly recut over the years, but odd letters here and there have deteriorated, including many of the 24-point roman capitals; the Monotype version of these is now far nearer the original than that purveyed by Stephenson Blake. The 12-point lower case n unaccountably diminished in size in successive recuts until it finally looked like a wrong fount in the line. I prevailed on the founders to make a new matrix – by whatever means – and the n is now closer to the original than for many years. The 24-point o, which had become thinner and thinner until it no longer matched its fellows, was corrected by the ingenious expedient of casting from an accented letter matrix, made many years ago and struck from the original punches, and then shaving the accent off after casting. One cannot but wonder at the lack of supervision or awareness which allows these obvious faults to remain unchecked and uncorrected through to the production stage.

A description of the Caslon types would be incomplete without a mention of the related range of fleurons, a few of which are still sold by Stephenson Blake, whilst others were revived and cut in different sizes by Monotype. Some appear at the foot of the 1734 specimen broadsheet, but these were later vastly augmented, and specimen books of 1766 and 1785 contain many pages displaying ornaments from 5- to 24-point, for use in straightforward borders, and combined to make up typographical initials, 'pictures', cartouches and panels, reminiscent of those in Fournier's *Modèles*, for use as head pieces.

My own present range of Caslon – and I once ran a small shop for three years with nothing but Caslon and a couple of sizes of blackletter – consists of Mono-type founts in 8-, 10-, 11-, 12-, 14- and 60-point, sufficient to set most of the work I undertake, though it is comforting to know that at least one trade typesetter can handle any large work I might attempt in those sizes, and that all the common – and some uncommon – accents are easily obtained. My founder's Caslon runs from 10- to 48-point, including the now rare 22-point, recently recast, and I have also been fortunate enough to find some Caslon woodletter. Not so many years ago sales of Caslon were tailing off, and many sizes had become unobtainable in founder's type, until a sudden surge in demand, from the United States of all places, justified fresh castings, but at the time of writing, though most sizes from 10- to 60-point are still in stock, there are again some gaps in the range available, including the 36-point, one of Caslon's best founts. Hopefully sufficient orders will be forthcoming to justify a fresh casting of this important size.

I must confess, I am myself sometimes surprised at the adaptability of Caslon in use. My own production over the past few years, using Caslon almost exclusively, has ranged through visiting cards, personal and commercial stationery, handbills, advertising folders, a publisher's catalogues, certificates, devotional and quotation cards, broadsheet versions of poetry for framing, museum captions and notices, and a museum guide booklet – one could hardly have a more varied list. Of course, like any typeface, Caslon depends not only on its own intrinsic qualities, but equally on *how* it is used, and even today one has to admit that a lot of printers are very good technicians but have singularly little idea how to make the best use of their typographical material.

Generally speaking I favour a centred style of layout as being, for most purposes, straightforward and expedient, and far less likely to 'go wrong' than sophisticated asymmetrical arrangements. It also works best when a design incorporates traditional material in the form of printers' fleurons. But Caslon will perform equally well in off-centre designs where these are appropriate, and the only real criterion is that the result shall be readable, elegant and effective, and refute the ugliness which nowadays so often passes for novelty. Normally I make only the roughest pencil sketch to guide me in setting display work, and then make final adjustments to spacing, sometimes even to the size of a headline, in the light of what is revealed by the first proof.

The accompanying illustrations are too few to give more than the barest outline of the ways Caslon has been used, but will perhaps serve to awaken fresh interest in this important face, and encourage other letterpress *aficionados* to explore its potentialities in contemporary printing.

6. Synopsis
of 22-point
Caslon

A RARE FOUNT

The 22 point size of William Caslon I's old face type has been judged as one of his best designs. It was in use as early as 1732 and appeared in the 1734 broadsheet specimen as 'Double Pica Roman'. Effectively filling the gap between 18 and 24 point, its colour is such as to fit it equally for large-scale text matter or for display in chapter heads and the like. Noticeably close fitted, most of its matrices derive from the original punches.

The italic has the customary exuberance of the Caslon italics, with sufficient weight to hold its own when used with the roman.

A B C D E G J K M N P Qu R T V & Y

Alan Dodson was born 1924 in New Malden, Surrey. He attended Kingston School of Art to study architecture, but was seduced by presses and type in the graphic art department, and decided to make a career in print. He was mainly self-taught, developing a small press at home. After four years in Royal Air Force as landscape model maker, he spent an instructive few months working in Lausanne and St Gallen, Switzerland. Following posts in designing and teaching, Dodson spent five years, 1954–58, as Head of H.M. Stationery Office Layout Section. He immigrated to South Africa and took a post as chief typographer at Hortors, then the leading printers in Johannesburg; this was followed by a period, 1964–68, of planning and conducting a postgraduate diploma course in typographical design at the University of the Witwatersrand. After a year in Canada (too cold!), he returned to teaching at the Johannesburg College of Art, then set up a freelance design and repro business. In 1978 Dodson moved to Grahamstown, where he met his wife, and in 1985 returned to England to live in Malvern, Worcestershire. Here he continued to practise book design and specialised repro and short-run printing by letterpress, using mainly Caslon types, until a stroke put an end to his activities in 1999.

8· ABCDEFGHIJKLMNOPQRSTUVWXYZ & ÆŒ ABCDEFGHIJKL
MNOPQRSTUVWXYZæœabcdefghijklmnopqrsßtuvwxyzæœ ctffffffffi
ffbfhfifkflffffiffiflftﬅﬆ $£# 1234567890%*+.,:;''!?-/[]()} <> @ § ¶ † ‡
©®πχ ABCDEFGHIJKLMNOPQRSTUVWXYZ ÆŒ abcdefghij
klmnopqrsßtuvwxyzæœ :;!?()cffffffffiffbfhfifkflffffiﬄﬆ ABC DEGI

10· ABCDEFGHIJKLMNOPQRSTUVWXYZ&ÆŒabcdefg
HIJKLMNOPQRSTUVWXYZæœabcdefghijklmnopqrsßtuvwxy
zæœctffffiflfifbfhfifkflffffiffiflftﬅﬆ $£#1234567890%*+.,:;''
!?-/[]()}} <> @ § ¶ † ‡ © ® π χ ABCDEFGHIJKLMNOPQR
STUVWXYZÆŒ abcdefghijklmnopqrsßtuvwxyzæœ :;!?
()ctffffiffififlﬄﬆﬄﬅﬄﬆﬄﬆﬆﬅABC DEGJKMNPQRTU Yh

12· ABCDEFGHIJKLMNOPQRSTUVWXYZ
&ÆŒ ABCDEFGHIJKLMNOPQRSTUVWXYZæœabc
defghijklmnopqrsßtuvwxyzæœ ctffffffffiﬄfifﬅfbfh
fifkflffffiﬄﬆﬅ $£#1234567890%*+.,:;''!?-/[]()
}} <> @ § ¶ † ‡ © ® π χ ABCDEFGHIJKLMNOP
QRSTUVWXYZÆŒ abcdefghijklmnopqrsßtuv
wxyzæœ:;!?()ctffffffffifiﬄﬆﬅﬅﬄﬆﬅﬆﬅ ABC DE

14· ABCDEFGHIJKLMNOPQRSTUVWXY
Z&ÆŒ ABCDEFGHIJKLMNOPQRSTUVWXYZÆ
Œ abcdefghijklmnopqrsßtuvwxyzæœ ctffffi
fffiflfifbfhfifkflffffiﬄﬆﬅ $£#1234567890%*+
.,:;''!?-/[]()}} <> @ § ¶ † ‡ © ® π χ ABCDEF
GHIJKLMNOPQRSTUVWXYZÆŒ abc
defghijklmnopqrsßtuvwxyzæœ :;!?()ctffffﬄ
fiﬄﬅﬆﬄﬄﬅﬄﬆﬅ ABC DEGJKMNPQR

18· ABCDEFGHIJKLMNOPQRSTUV
WXYZ&ÆŒ ABCDEFGHIJKLMNOPQRST
UVWXYZÆŒabcdefghijklmnopqrsßtuv
wxyzæœctffffffffiﬄfiflﬅfbfhfifkflffffiﬄﬆﬅ $
£#1234567890%*+.,:;''!?-/[]()}}
<> @ § ¶ † ‡ © ® π χ ABCDEFGHIJKL
MNOPQRSTUVWXYZÆŒ abcdefghij
klmnopqrsßtuvwxyzæœ:;!?()ctffffffﬄfiﬄﬅ
ﬄﬆﬄﬅﬄﬆﬅﬆﬅ ABC DEGJKMNPQRT

22· ABCDEFGHIJKLMNOPQRS
TUVWXYZ&ÆŒ ABCDEFGHI
JKLMNOPQRSTUVWXYZÆŒabcde
fghijklmnopqrsßtuvwxyzæœct
ffffffffiﬄfifﬅfbfhfifkflffffiﬄﬆﬅ $£#1
234567890%*+.,:;''!?-/[]()
}}<> @ § ¶ † ‡ © ® π χ ABCDEFG
HIJKLMNOPQRSTUVW
XYZÆŒ abcdefghijklmnopqr

24· ABCDEFGHIJKLMNO
PQRSTUVWXYZ&Æ
ŒABCDEFGHIJKLMNOPQR
STUVWXYZÆŒabcdefghijkl
mnopqrsßtuvwxyzæœctffffi
fffiflfifﬅfbfhfifkflffffiﬄﬆﬅ $£# 1
234567890%*+.,:;''!?-/
[]()}}<> @ § ¶ † ‡ © ® π χ ABC
DEFGHIJKLMNOPQR
STUVWXYZÆŒ abcdefg
hijklmnopqrsßtuvwxyzæœ : ;
!?( )ctffffffffiﬄﬅfbfhfifkflﬄﬆﬅﬆ

30· ABCDEFGHIJKLMN
OPQRSTUVWXYZ&
ÆŒABCDEFGHIJKLMN
OPQRSTUVWXYZÆŒabc
defghijklmnopqrsßtuv
wxyzæœctffffﬄﬄfiflﬅfbfh
fifkflffffiﬄﬆﬅ $£ # 1 2 3 4
567890%*+.,:;''!?-/[]
()}}<> @ § ¶ † ‡ © ® π χ AB
CDEFGHIJKLM
NOPQRSTUVWX
YZÆŒabcdefghijkl
mnopqrsßtuvwxyzæœ
:;!?( )ctffffﬄﬄfiﬄﬅfbfhfi

Founder's Caslon, 8-point through to 30-point

The Compleat Caslon

BY JUSTIN HOWES

By the time of Matrix 17 *(1997), Justin Howes was well on his way to delivering a complete revival of Caslon's typefaces, taken directly from printed specimens of each individual size of type, as a family of digital fonts. He explains the genesis of this project, originally called Ligature Caslon but later released as Founder's Caslon, which puts the original Caslon typefaces back into the hands of book designers as a digital tool.*

In 1998 International Typeface Corporation (ITC) released the first four sizes in what was eventually to become a series of thirteen digital types based on the eighteenth-century designs of William Caslon I. A couple of years earlier John Randle had asked me to write about the project for *Matrix* readers, when I promised the imminent revival of just about everything Caslon had ever done. In the event, the revival took far longer – three years longer – than I'd ever thought possible, and the complete series was only released in 2001, when (after another six months spent struggling with the website design and the complexities of e-commerce), I launched the fonts at http://www.hwcaslon.com.

Founder's Caslon comprises twelve sizes of Caslon Old Face, from 8- to 72-point, with an additional Poster size and an assortment of flowers. As a reconstruction in digital form of the best part of the leading eighteenth-century English type foundry it offers seasoned typographers an enjoyable alternative to the commercial 'type libraries' available on CD-ROM; and gives students a second chance (now that the art schools have nearly all scrapped their metal type) to explore the expressive range possible when using a single family of related typefaces.

My own enthusiasm for Caslon was fired by the acquisition at a Whittington Press Open Day *c.* 1983 of John Randle's splendid broadside, set in twelve sizes of Caslon Old Face, of Eric Gill's letter to the Dominicans of Hawkesyard Priory. Gill was writing at a time when Caslon could still be described as 'the best on the market,'[1] but by the time I started assembling my own composing room – partly to get away from the PC – Caslon Old Face had become the best *not* on the market and I realised that the only way of ensuring myself a constant supply of

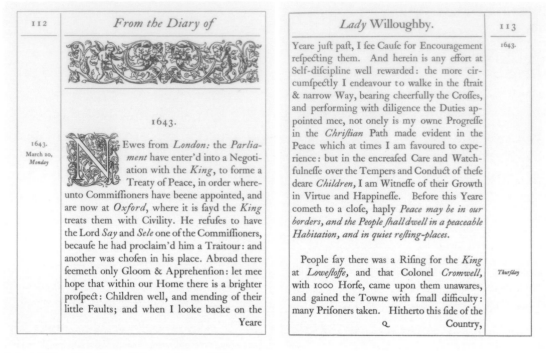

2. *Lady Willoughby's Diary*, Chiswick Press, 1841

freshly cast founder's type would have to be a digital reconstruction. And so, with mixed feelings, I went back to the keyboard.

In the same year that Gill wrote his letter to the Dominicans of Hawkesyard, 1917, Monotype released the last three text sizes of their series 128, the version of Caslon in which *Matrix* is set and which I have 'laid in', together with caster, supercaster and a bewildering assortment of spares.[2] The 31 volumes of Bernard Shaw's collected limited edition formed another bulky purchase, justified at the time as 'an important example . . .' – and irresistible, anyhow, at a ridiculous £20. The story of how Shaw came to be set in series 128 has given my own project a useful focus. William Maxwell, of the Edinburgh firm of R. & R. Clark, recalled that

> [Shaw] insisted on hand-setting throughout. I told him this would be impossible, and we argued loud and long. I then took a risk. I told Shaw I would show him a hand-set page and a machine-set one side by side, and let him choose. I showed him these without, of course, indicating which was which.

Shaw, who 'produced a magnifying glass and various other gadgets and retired into another room to scrutinise the two specimens closely' chose the Monotype-set page and, though even then 'not fully convinced' eventually gave way 'after referring the pages to Emery Walker.'[3] I think that Founder's Caslon would have got past G.B.S. – perhaps even past E.W. – and the story has suggested a straightforward way of evaluating a digital revival: it should be good enough (or bad enough) to deceive.

There have been a number of attempts to produce a digital Caslon; none to *reproduce* Caslon as exactly and comprehensively as modern scanning and printing technology now allow. On one level this is perhaps because type revivals tend to be done by a 'designer', and designers are warier than they really need be of Gill's (or Morison's, or Van Krimpen's) argument that 'modern machinery should be employed to make letters whose virtue is compatible with their mechanical manufacture, rather than exact and scholarly resuscitations of letters whose virtue is bound up with their derivation from humane craftsmanship.'[4] Digital Caslons are 'better designed' than Caslon's originals and cannot help sharing some of the faults associated with the regularised 'Old Style' types of the 1860s and 70s. The Victorian description of these as 'wiry and attenuated in character'[5] holds true of most redrawn founts, even discounting the entirely different (and easily resolved) problem of 'ink squash'. There *is* a temptation to 'improve' on the original (as I found when trying to redraw the 14-point at 20x original size), but even if that can be resisted every generation has surprisingly precise expectations of 'normal' letterforms through which an individual's perceptions of printing types are filtered. In our own time the result of redrawing is, unavoidably, type design which edges ever closer to this period's dominant letterform, Times New Roman.

The example of the only completely successful Caslon imitation may prove the point: Joseph Fry's 'imitations' of Caslon, cut in the 1780s when Old Face was still the dominant letterform, remain almost indistinguishable from the originals.[6] And of course Fry, or his punch cutter, would at no stage have had either to draw a letter in outline, or to work at anything other than 'same size' – bypassing the dangers of the type drawing office.

The less rationalist revivals often seem to work best: Monotype Poliphilus, for instance, cut in 1922 without Morison's guidance, has withstood the transfer to digital format better than most of Monotype's more careful revivals. Most recently, Jonathan Hoefler has produced highly successful – and, to anyone who has ever hankered after the originals, highly *desirable* – digitisations of the Fell types. These have, like Founder's Caslon, been traced algorithmically to form 'a set of digital fonts which preserves the eccentricities of its metal forebears, for better or worse', with what their designer (if that is still the right word in this context) calls 'a warmly arrhythmic pace' and 'agreeably (and ironically) *un-digital*' feel.[7]

Founder's Caslon offers a further demonstration that re-drawing is unnecessary when all that is sought is an 'exact and scholarly resuscitation'. Such

3. Optical differences from one size to the next are illustrated here in the design chosen for a Caslon commemorative T-shirt, produced in 2002.

reconstructions, if offensive to Gill, Morison and Van Krimpen, at least sidestep the conceptual and problems associated with re-interpreting punch-cut letters in terms of pencil outlines and computer curve points. The founts have been reproduced, whenever possible, from high-resolution scans of new proofs of the founder's type, printed either from material in my own collection of pre-war castings from the Caslon foundry or (with exemplary care) by Alan Dodson (see p. 81). The digitisation process captures both the face of the type – and its fit – rather accurately; and, with these, the qualities of the original founts.

The process (or, almost, *lack* of process) works 'well enough', even if it means accepting the limitations of the original founts. The overweight T of Caslon's 14-point, for instance, is visible in his Specimen of 1734; a century later in the 1845 edition of the *Diary of Lady Willoughby* (figure 2); and in every fount of the founder's type since – despite being cast, until recently, from a matrix made, probably, more recently than Monotype series 128 and itself struck from a punch that can be no older than 1845. Why change it?

I have gratefully taken advantage of recent typographic research, much of it by James Mosley whose writings on Caslon have transformed knowledge of Caslon's achievement. Only the availability of this new research has made it possible – as it was not when series 128 was made – to construct a Caslon more authentic in detail than most castings of the types since the 1890s. The rediscovery of the matrices for Moxon's capitals to the 'Caslon' 48-point Roman by another active and diligent researcher in this specialist field, John Lane, has allowed these to be supplied in an 'alternate caps' fount for the first time since they were replaced (by William Caslon I's superb 36-point Titling) in the mid-nineteenth century.

My own researches into Caslon have concentrated on documenting the more recent castings of the founder's type. The result of several weeks' work in Stephenson Blake's fabled 'Tomb' has been the first comprehensive listings of the surviving punches and matrixes for Caslon Old Face. These notes have made it possible to be very clear about why, when selecting versions of Caslon for digitisation, some characters can legitimately be restored to earlier versions whilst others cannot. Founder's Caslon has placed the unauthentic characters added to the metal type since Caslon's time in alternate fonts. This leaves the base fonts unencumbered by fake swash italic capitals (only the *J T Q Y* are authentic), by italic figures, and by the truncated roman Q – characters which have disfigured less academic versions of Caslon, including Monotype series 128 and, surprisingly, Adobe Caslon. Similarly, the 24-point founder's capitals (on which see Alan Dodson) are replaced by those supplied with the fount in the 1890s and include a particularly fine and (in metal, extremely fragile) Q.

The irregularities of letterpress printing are also faithfully captured by the process of digitisation. I see no reason to remove them, since they become troublesome only under high magnification and, at normal size, make an important but virtually invisible contribution to the texture of the page. Much has been written about the problems of ink squash and impression[8], and of the best ways of eliminating them, but I suspect that that debate should now move on to think in terms of the 'diversity' of surface described by David Pye in *The Nature and Art of Workmanship* – a book every hand-printer should possess. Pye demonstrates that in hand workmanship (which he calls the workmanship of risk) it is the differing qualities of surface finish that define an object's appearance and visual quality. He also suggests that machines 'can do nearly everything well except produce diversity.'[9] Founder's Caslon, if it cannot *produce* diversity, makes an attempt to *reproduce* it.

Caslon brewed his own, excellent ale[10] and support for a 'real' Caslon, as for a

4. Mark van Bronkhorst's design for ITC's *U&lc* magazine launched ITC Founder's Caslon in 1998.

real ale, has been widely expressed: on the Internet, in *Serif* and, intriguingly, in a lengthy article in *Emigré* magazine which (whilst introducing Mark Andreson's Not Caslon type, a collection of initials made by rubbing down 'bits and pieces of dry transfer lettering: flakes, nicks and all') offered a careful criticism of Adobe Caslon, regretting that of the twenty-one founts which make up Carol Twombly's 'careful revival' not one 'is true to any particular font by Caslon.'[11]

There has also been an upsurge of interest in 'real' types: a result of both 'font overload' and designers' realisations that of the tens of thousands of faces available on the 'desktop' few possess integrity or authenticity. Perhaps also there is a feeling that in a world 'crowded with essential rubbish'[12], as Norman Potter has it, 'there is a case for seeing what you can do with the cheapest, most simple, and most ordinary materials'; and that Caslon (whilst none of these) remains versatile across a range of jobs. 'Job satisfaction' is certainly an issue since graphic designers, like anyone else, tire of trickery.

Justin Howes is a typographer, type designer, and historian. He has been a contributor to *Matrix* since 1983, when still a student at Christ Church, Oxford. He co-edited Edward Johnston's *Lessons in Formal Writing* (1986) with Heather Child. Other publications include *Typefounder's London A–Z* (1998), *Edward Johnston's Cat*, and the definitive account of Edward Johnston's type designs for the London Underground, *Edward Johnston's Underground Type* (2000). He is currently working on a bicentenary history of the Stanhope Press. Recent book-design projects have included the British Library's new studies of *The Doves Press* by Marianne Tidcombe and *The Golden Cockerel Press* by Rod Cave and Sarah Manson, an edition of William Tyndale's New Testament, and bibliophile editions for the Roxburghe Club. He is Chairman of the Friends of St Bride Printing Library, and a member of the Double Crown Club. In 1998 the International Typeface Corporation released his ITC Founder's Caslon, and he has since completed the series with an additional eleven sizes, marketed exclusively through H.W. Caslon & Company Limited.

NOTES

1. See Adrian Cunningham, 'Eric Gill and *The Hawkesyard Review*', *Matrix* 2, pp. 5-9.

2. The first sizes of Monotype series 128 were cut as a 'faithful copy of [the] original Caslon types' at the behest of R. & R. Clark of Edinburgh. The 11- and 12-point were the first sizes to appear, in 1915, followed by the 13½ point ('English') in 1916, and by the 8-, 9- and 10-point in 1917. The larger sizes appeared in the 1920s and '30s: 18-, 24-, 30- and 36-point between 1922 and 1924; 42- and 48-point between 1927 and 1929; 60 point between 1929 and 1934; 22-point (described as '24-point small face') in 1930; and 72-point between 1930 and 1934. Monotype also released a series of Caslon's Titling (series 209), in the 18-, 24-, 30-, 36- and 72-point sizes, betweeen 1927 and 1932. The 18-, 24- and 30-point sizes are pantographic reductions from the 36-point design. I am grateful to Duncan Avery of Monotype Hot-Metal for these dates.

3. Quoted in *Monotype News Letter*, 65 (March 1962), p. 7. See also James Shand, 'Author and Printer: G.B.S. and R. & R. C.: 1898-1948' in *Alphabet and Image*, 3 (December 1948), pp. 3-38.

4. Eric Gill, *An Essay on Typography* (London, Lund Humphries, 1988), pp. 37-8.

5. [T. W. Smith], 'Old Style Founts', in *Caslon's Circular*, I, 3 (July 1875), pp. [1]-[2].

6. Philip Gaskell, 'Photographic Enlargements of Type Forms', *Journal of the Printing Historical Society*, 7 (1972), pp. 51-3, reproduces Caslon's Long Primer No. 2 and Fry's Long Primer No. 3 for comparison as plate VIIb and VIIIb

7. *The Hoefler Type Foundry Catalogue of Typefaces*, 1 (May 1997), p. 4.

8. See Beatrice Warde, 'Typography means more than layout', *The Bowater Papers*, 3 (1954), pp. 46-52.

9. David Pye, *The Nature and Art of Workmanship* (Cambridge, Cambridge University Press, 1968), p. 73.

10. Johnson Ball, *William Caslon* (Kineton, The Roundwood Press, 1973), p. 445.

11. John Downer, untitled article in *Emigré* 36 (1995). Other recent articles have included D. A. Hosek, 'Which Caslon', *Serif* 3 (Fall 1995), pp. 14-20, 62; and Rich Hopkins, 'Dispelling Caslon Myths', *ATF Newsletter* 19 (January 1996), pp. 19-29.

12. Norman Potter, *What is a Designer: things · places · messages* (London, Hyphen Press, 1989), p. [193].

A B C D E F G H I J K L

a b c d e f g h i j k l m n o p q r s t u v w x y z

M N O P Q R S T U V W

a b c d e f g h i j k l m n o p q r s t u v w x y z

X Y Z & 1 2 3 4 5 6 7 8 9 0

a b c d e f g h i j k l m n o p q r s t u v w x y z

A B C D E F G H I J K L

abcdefghijklmnopqrstuvwxyz

M N O P Q R S T U V W

a b c d e f g h i j k l m n o p q r s t u v w x y z

X Y Z & 1 2 3 4 5 6 7 8 9 0

Imprint, the digitized version from Monotype

Type for Books, and Books for Type

BY SEBASTIAN CARTER

On the centenary of the Monotype Corporation in 1997, Sebastian Carter wrote this account in Matrix 18 *(1998) of the unique period when, under Stanley Morison's influence, Monotype brought out an unprecedented series of new and revived typefaces for machine composition, and partnered with some of the leading presses and publishers of the day to get those typefaces immediately into the public eye.*

The year 1997 saw the centenary of the establishment of the Lanston Monotype Corporation, the British company set up to exploit the invention by the American engineer Tolbert Lanston of a system of mechanical hot-metal typesetting of separate letters.

The event itself was emblematic of what now seems to us a far-off period of romantic capitalism. Two colleagues of Lanston's, J. Maury Dove and Harold Duncan (who were to become respectively the president of American Monotype and the managing director of the British company), were travelling by liner to England in search of additional venture capital: the Monotype machine was proving slower to perfect than had been thought. They fell into conversation with an Anglo-Irish peer, Lord Dunraven, who offered to buy the British and Colonial rights to the Monotype, which we must remember at that time included India, Australia and New Zealand, and most of Africa, though not Canada, since the Lanston company based in Philadelphia retained North American rights. Dunraven became the first chairman of the British company until his death in 1926.

The Monotype hot-metal typesetting system represents a peak in the history of precise heavy engineering. The casters were so robust that many printers were still running their original machines up to the end of the hot-metal era, and they were accurate to within a fraction of a thousandth of an inch. You do not have to be old to remember when a substantial majority of books published in Britain were set on Monotype equipment and printed from metal type. At the same time, we need to remind ourselves how very brief was the dominance of hot metal, well within the life-span of one person. The period of Monotype's most celebrated achievements coincided with the career of Stanley Morison, typographical adviser to the Corporation between 1923 and 1956, who was born in 1889; this was a year before Tolbert Lanston filed his patent for a hot-metal typesetting machine. Two years before Morison's death at the age of seventy-eight, Dr Rudolf Hell announced the Digiset, the first of the digital typesetting machines which were to make redundant even the photosetters which had already ousted hot metal.

In 1900, not long after the British Monotype company was formed, it opened a factory at Salfords, between London and Brighton. Initially Salfords repaired and modified American machines, but before long the works began manufacturing their own machines; and from the beginning British Monotype had its own type programme. The American engineer Frank Hinman Pierpont was appointed as works manager, and he brought with him a German, Fritz Max Steltzer, as head of the Type Drawing Office. In the same year that Salfords opened, Series 1, a modern face, was issued.

The Type Drawing Office under Fritz Steltzer became immensely skilled at the sensitive adaptation of existing foundry faces for Monotype composition. On the caster, the die-case which carried the assembled matrices was arranged in a grid, each row of which was assigned to letters of the same width. The allocation of letters in a given row could vary, but not the identical-unit-width principle. A great deal of skill went into planning the die-case layout, and inconspicuously squeezing or widening some letters to make them fit, and this skill was needed whether the drawing office was adapting an existing design or preparing a new one.

The first few years of production at Salfords were given over to the conversion of existing foundries' faces for machine setting, in such a way that very few people would notice. This was what the printers and their customers demanded. The most celebrated example of this took place in 1916 with Caslon. The Edinburgh printing house of R. & R. Clark were printing a big *History of the British Army*, in foundry Caslon, and had run out of type. The Caslon foundry could not produce more because the country was in the middle of the First World War and they were given over to armaments manufacture. Although Monotype too were doing war work they managed to cut quickly a facsimile of Caslon good enough to complete the book without the publisher's objecting to the change half way through. The fidelity of the facsimile was tested again a few years later: George Bernard Shaw, a very type-conscious writer, was insisting on hand-set Caslon for his plays. Clarks, who wanted to use Monotype setting for reasons of cost, showed him specimen pages set by both methods, and Shaw had to admit that he couldn't tell them apart.

Some years before Caslon, however, Monotype had begun a new programme of considerably modifying existing faces for new printing needs. The first notable example of this was a type made at great speed for a pioneering printing journal, *The Imprint*. The editor in charge of design, J. H. Mason, who had been a compositor at the Doves Press and had strong Arts-and-Crafts principles, wanted to use Caslon. Another editor, the printer Gerard Meynell of the Westminster Press, wanted to use his Monotype equipment, both for economy and to emphasise the forward-looking aims of the journal. They also wanted a stronger-looking face than the composition sizes of Caslon. Imprint, a cleaned-up but darker version of Caslon with increased x-height, was rushed through at the end of 1912 ready for the first issue of the journal in January 1913. Although *The Imprint* barely lasted the year, the type went on to become one of Monotype's best selling series.[1]

Around the same time, an even more innovative design was introduced. The managing director Harold Duncan suggested to Pierpont that a version of one of the types used by the sixteenth-century Antwerp printer Christophe Plantin, made bolder for printing on smooth or coated papers, should be cut. Pierpont acquired some examples of printing from the original type, which had been cut by Robert Granjon, from the Plantin-Moretus Museum in Antwerp, and the drawing office produced Plantin, a highly modernised redrawing, with greatly enlarged x-height and reduced ascenders and descenders, which to a greater extent even than Imprint has been in continuous use ever since.

Thus two approaches to type had already been demonstrated which were to be greatly developed in the decades between the World Wars. There were the facsimiles of earlier faces, as faithful as the drawing office could make them, and the free reworkings of existing designs for modern conditions. A third strand, that of completely new designs, was to appear only in the 1920s. In fact, the first two major designs after the First World War were both in the middle category, though they were closer to their originals than Plantin. Bodoni was a regularised version of a face cut by the great eighteenth century Parma printer Giambattista Bodoni, and Garamond a recutting of some types in the collection of the Imprimerie Nationale in Paris, which were thought at the time to be by the sixteenth-century punchcutter Claude Garamont, though they were later shown to be copies. The Monotype recuttings of both faces had been anticipated by American Type Founders (ATF), and American Monotype had produced a version of Garamond, redrawn by Frederic W. Goudy, the year before Salfords issued theirs. Goudy had also been made 'artistic adviser' to the Philadelphia company, a position which was mirrored a couple of years later in England, with the creation of the post of typographical adviser to British Monotype. The man who was to fill this position for a third of a century was Stanley Morison.

Morison was then in his early thirties and beginning to make a name for himself as a designer and type historian. From humble beginnings, largely self-taught, he was to become the most powerful force in the British typographical scene of his time. His dominant position at Monotype in the 1920s and 1930s, the period of the Corporation's major programme of typeface production, has led over the years to varying views of his achievements. His strong personality and decided opinions persuaded his friends and admirers sometimes to claim for him achievements which were not his, or only partly his, and he did not always put them right. On the other hand, his detractors were often objecting as much to the commercial domination of Monotype, and the way typographical history of the period became at least partly identified with the history of Monotype, as they were to Morison personally. He himself, particularly in his 1953 book *A Tally of Types*, his account of the Monotype programme, put insufficient emphasis on the collective nature of type production and the contribution of the staff at Salfords. Indeed, he went so far as to refer slightingly to 'the mechanic ... with his pantograph and the rest of the gear',[2] seeming to forget that it was these mechanics who were behind the success of the Monotype programme. Yet for all this, as the Dutch type designer Jan van Krimpen put it in a letter to Morison himself, writing about his own book on type design, 'Yes: S.M. has been mentioned over freely. How could it be otherwise? . . . How could, in our days, anybody, in a more or less dogmatical way, say or write anything about typography without finding S.M. on his path?'[3]

Morison's achievements have been, and doubtless will continue to be, exhaustively discussed. But at the risk of adding further to the Morison myth, my purpose here is to show how he and a small circle of colleagues, working for their own different purposes, subtly changed the Monotype repertoire of faces and the nature of fine printing.

When he became typographical adviser, Monotype setting was used for trade book work and for magazines. The private presses of the previous generation, Kelmscott and Doves, continuing with Ashendene through to the Golden Cockerel

Press in the 1920s, used hand-set type, usually a special design for their exclusive use. Morison and his colleagues were to show that the Monotype could produce fine work, but also were to initiate a new intermediate kind of fine printing, aimed at a wider public, and produced by commercial printers.

In 1924, in the third number of *The Fleuron*, the sumptuous journal of typography edited by Oliver Simon of the Curwen Press, together with Morison, the anonymous reviewer of the latest *Monotype Recorder* wrote, 'The Lanston Monotype Corporation needs watching; we are inclined to suspect it of having at heart the interests of fine printing. This is a serious statement to make, since nobody who has seen the Corporation's complete "specimen" would imagine that it was capable of rising by a jump to a high standard of typography, for apart from copies of faces for which the type founders had created a demand, the Monotype in its whole career had not contributed more than two or three types not to be found elsewhere.'

The Monotype Recorder was the trade journal of the British company, and the number under review was the January-February 1924 one in which Morison had announced the Corporation's intention to issue Fournier, which was indeed cut that year, Van Dijck, which had to wait another decade, and 'a late Georgian letter of wider, and perhaps universal application', which was almost certainly Bell, a face which came out half way between the other two. Morison also announced the intention to cut 'at least one fine original design'. The *Fleuron* reviewer went on to observe that this number of the *Recorder* was 'a very decent piece of printing' and that the review copy was one of a bound edition limited to 150 copies. It had been printed by Cambridge University Press in Poliphilus, and represents a transformation of the usual idea of a trade journal.

Morison is not credited with this review; it was probably by Simon, but it certainly represented the combined view of their circle. To show how this circle developed, we need to go back a few years.

Stanley Morison had become interested in the form as well as the content of books at an early age, and managed to get a job as an assistant on *The Imprint*. Gerard Meynell then got him a position at the firm of Burns and Oates, a Catholic publisher part-owned by Gerard's uncle Wilfrid. (It must have helped that Morison had become a Roman Catholic in 1908.) There he found himself working on design and production with Wilfrid Meynell's son Francis, who was two years his junior. Both men had an interest in typography, both had left-wing sympathies, and both were pacifists. During the First World War both were interned. It was during this period that Francis Meynell set up the Pelican Press, at least in part to print anti-war propaganda, and Morison was brought in to help with the design. After the War this became briefly a full-time position, while Francis worked at George Lansbury's newspaper *The Daily Herald*; but then there was a splendidly cloak-and-dagger escapade in which Francis was involved in the smuggling of diamonds out of Russia to sell on behalf of the Soviet government. He had to resign from the *Herald*, and so had more time for the Pelican Press. This meant that Morison had to look elsewhere for employment, and found it at the Cloister Press, a new printing works being set up near Manchester by Charles Hobson, an advertising agent. As his works manager Hobson had brought in a man who was to become one of the last great master-printers of the letterpress era, Walter Lewis; and as designer Lewis had recommended Morison. Morison and Hobson began an enterprising policy of buying new types, many from America, and showing them off in handsome specimens which Morison wrote and designed.

Soon, however, the Cloister Press ran into financial difficulties, and Morison began to look elsewhere. It was at this time, during 1922, that he established his habit of never serving one master if three were available. He spent as much time as he could at Cloister's London office where, besides working for his employer, he undertook a number of freelance commissions. One of these was the design of the printing trade yearbook, *The Penrose Annual*, which was to be set in Garamond. He may well therefore have been partly instrumental in persuading Monotype to cut the face; he certainly went on to advise the Corporation on many aspects of the design, which led to his formal advisory appointment early the following year. He also became involved with a new typographical journal called *The Fleuron*.

His partner in this venture was the designer at the Curwen Press in east London, Oliver Simon. Simon was six years younger than Morison, and had little experience, but with the temerity of youth he had suggested in the middle of 1922 the setting up of a publishing society of like-minded enthusiasts, with the purpose of producing 'one book a year to demonstrate to collectors, and anyone else who was interested, that books set by machines could be as beautiful as the books of the Private Hand-presses which, aesthetically, still dominated the scene immediately after the 1914–1918 war.'[4] The people who attended the first meeting were Francis Meynell, Morison and Simon, and two more senior book people, the writer Holbrook Jackson and the printer Bernard Newdigate. Newdigate was then writing an influential monthly column of news and opinion on book production for *The London Mercury*.

At this first meeting, Francis Meynell suggested 'The Fleuron Society' as a name for the group, which turned out to be the only thing the members could agree on. According to Simon's later account, the main point of contention was Newdigate's refusal to concede that machine setting could rival hand-setting. This does not tally with Newdigate's open-minded view of the question as expressed in his 'Book Production Notes' in *The London Mercury*, where he sympathetically reviewed the Monotype faces as they appeared, and even predicted a future for photocomposition. According to Meynell, in his autobiography, 'Oliver was, I think, depressed by the number of strongly opinionated people who had come together (he could never adjust to a committee of more than one).'[5] Whatever the reason, the Fleuron Society disbanded after a couple of meetings; but two important publishing ventures grew from it, which were to have a strong influence on the perception of Monotype's ability to produce work of high quality.

To us today Simon's belief in the ability of the printing trade to rival the work of the private presses seems incomprehensible. The gulf which exists now between modern 'fine' printing, and run-of-the-mill book production is not simply one of quality, but of completely different methods. In the early 1920s, however, there existed a number of general trade book houses capable of printing by letterpress on hand-made or mould-made papers, in large editions of between one and two thousand, and printing well. There were the two university presses, Oxford under John Johnson, and Cambridge under Walter Lewis, who had moved there after the closure of the Cloister Press. Morison was shortly to be made typographical adviser to Cambridge as well as to Monotype, and was able to help create at Cambridge a market for Monotype faces which greatly helped his bargaining power at the Corporation. There was Curwen, under Harold Curwen, a fine designer himself as well as Oliver Simon's employer. There were the Westminster and Chiswick Presses in London, and R. & R. Clark in Edinburgh, and the Kynoch Press in Birmingham, where Oliver Simon's brother Herbert became designer. Outside Britain, there was the ancient house of Enschedé in Holland, where the resident typographer, Jan van Krimpen, was to have a long association with Morison and Monotype. And there were a number of others who emerged as the typographical renaissance grew.

Simon and Morison met after the collapse of the Fleuron Society and resolved to publish a journal of typography, and to call it *The Fleuron*. The first four numbers were edited by Simon and printed by Curwen; then Morison took over for the last three, and moved the printing to the Cambridge University Press. *The Fleuron* was in handsome book form, a quarto stoutly bound, and there was a hand-made paper edition of most of the seven numbers. There were numerous type reviews, often with elaborate specimen booklets bound in. All the numbers were Monotype set, the first in Garamond, the second in Baskerville, the next two reverting to Caslon. The last three were set in Barbou, the slightly bolder trial cutting of Fournier which Morison always preferred: he had rescued the unique die-case from Salfords and installed it at Cambridge. *The Fleuron* also published several of Morison's most significant essays, including 'Towards an ideal italic', with its suggestion of replacing the chancery italic as an accompaniment to roman with a sloped roman – which was to have a considerable influence on Eric Gill and Van Krimpen – and in the last number in 1930 his much reprinted 'First principles of typography'.

The other result of the Fleuron Society was Francis Meynell's Nonesuch Press. Oliver Simon's manifesto for the Society, that it was to prove the ability of machine production to rival the hand-made book, might stand equally for the Nonesuch Press, except that the volume of production was very much greater than one book a year. In the first five years after 1923, the Press averaged over nine titles a year, several of them in more than one volume. Editions, though technically limited, were often between one and two thousand, and some, like *The Week-end Book* and the 'compendious' series, were unlimited. Yet while Nonesuch, using the printers listed above, pioneered a more democratised kind of fine printing in which economies of production and scale meant that their books were more easily affordable than those of the private presses, to modern eyes many of the books, such as the Dante, the Shakespeare, the *Bible* and the Herodotus still look superbly grand.

The Nonesuch list reflected more modern literary interests than the output of most of the private presses, and some of the illustrators too were quite progressive. Edward McKnight Kauffer and Paul Nash both illustrated for the Press, and the German George Grosz had his first work in Britain published by Nonesuch. This, together with Meynell's highly eclectic style of design, primarily modelled on that of Bruce Rogers though with references to others, meant that the look of Nonesuch books was very different from the stylistic homogeneity of the big three earlier private presses. Even Robert Gibbings, who took over at the Golden

Cockerel Press around the same time as Nonesuch began publishing in 1923, gave his books more of a cohesive feel than Meynell did to his.

Much of the variety was achieved with adventurous binding styles, illustration, and imaginative choice of foundry display types. In the first years, Monotype's introduction of new faces had scarcely begun, and so the text setting was still from a small range of designs. Of the first twelve Nonesuch titles published in 1923, half were in Garamond; three were in Caslon, two were hand-set at Oxford in their Fell type, and one was set in Plantin. Meynell was later to have Monotype cut a variant of Plantin with lengthened ascenders and descenders. This 'Nonesuch Plantin' was used first for the *Bible* at the end of the following year. Another face he tinkered with was Fournier: for the first Nonesuch Shakespeare of 1929–33 he ordered a fount of capitals slightly reduced in height, to align them below the tips of the lower-case ascenders.

In the second year of publication, eight titles appeared. The new Monotype Baskerville made its first appearance. To the types already listed in the first year was added another hand-set type, the bold irregular sans-serif Neuland, which was used in one of the most outstanding and forward-looking Nonesuch books, the *Genesis*, to accompany Paul Nash's striking wood-engravings. Neuland had been issued the previous year by the enterprising small German foundry Klingspor, and was the work of their resident designer Rudolf Koch. In fact it was the first of his designs for which he himself had cut the punches: he was one of the very few twentieth-century designers who practised this demanding craft, although a number of trade punch-cutters still survived. The Curwen Press had bought Neuland, and printed *Genesis*, and it became a popular advertising face; so much so that Monotype issued a close copy in 1928, called Othello.

That year of 1928 saw the introduction of the Monotype Super Caster, an adapted caster which could produce sizes of type up to 72-point, for hand-setting. Up until then, the regular composition caster could manage only sizes up to 24-point and, with a special display attachment, 36-point. For larger display sizes, printers had used foundry type of some related – or completely contrasting – design. With Caslon there was no problem, since the Caslon foundry was still producing the original types. In the case of Plantin, there is evidence that an outside foundry, possibly Stephenson Blake, was commissioned by Monotype to make larger sizes. But elsewhere the choice was limited, although the more type-conscious printers built up collections of display founts, many of them from overseas foundries. The Kynoch Press, for example, printed the charming Nonesuch edition of *The Pilgrim's Progress* in Caslon, for which Meynell chose Rudolf Koch's cross-hatched blackletter Deutsche Zierschrift as a display face. But with the introduction of the Super Caster, printers acquired what was in effect an inhouse type foundry, and Monotype embarked on an ambitious programme of designs for display use, as well as extending existing ranges of types into larger sizes. They also operated a system of matrix rental so that printers did not have to make a huge investment in founts. Othello was an early fruit of this programme, and was followed by well-known faces such as Berthold Wolpe's Albertus and many of the variants of Eric Gill's hugely successful Gill Sans family.

Neuland was not the only type bought by Curwen and then cut by Monotype: far more significant was Walbaum, a kind of warm-blooded Bodoni made by the Berthold foundry of Berlin. Curwen had a full range of this face in both composition and display sizes, and used it extensively. It looks especially handsome in the Nonesuch *Benito Cereno* of 1926, where it was hand-set. Monotype issued it for machine setting nearly a decade later, and one of its first uses was in Oliver Simon's journal *Signature*, which began publication in 1935: this was intended to fill the gap left by the end of *The Fleuron*, although its format was more modest and its interests were far wider and more progressive.

Study of the next few years of the Nonesuch output shows it slowly keeping pace with the enlargement of the Monotype repertoire. The first face for which Morison could claim to be wholly responsible, in that he had not been anticipated by another manufacturer or, as in the case of Poliphilus, the impetus had not come from an outside source, was Fournier. This type was a version of an eighteenth-century proto-modern face by Pierre-Simon Fournier, and was prompted by Morison's admiration for it, backed up by that of the great Boston printer and type historian Daniel Berkeley Updike, whose ground-breaking book *Printing Types, their History, Forms and Use*, had appeared in 1922. Fournier, it will be remembered, was one of the types Morison mentioned in his list of plans in the *Monotype Recorder* quoted above, and would seem to be tailor-made for Nonesuch: it is surprising that it was four years before Meynell used it, for North's Plutarch in 1929. It is more surprising still that he never used Bell, a recutting of another favourite face of Morison's and an impeccably 'period' design.

Fournier was the last of the significant Monotype recuttings planned by Harold Duncan, the first managing director of the British company, who died in 1924. He was succeeded by his deputy, the Englishman William Isaac Burch, who too was to prove a staunch ally of Morison's. The next few years saw an important advance into another of the fields mentioned in Morison's plans, the producing of new designs by living designers. The first of these, Goudy Modern, had already been issued in America by Goudy's own Village Letter Foundery in 1918 and was released by Monotype in 1928. Nonesuch quickly took this face up and used it in the handsome *Don Quixote* of 1930, with illustrations by Kauffer. The text was printed at Cambridge, and according to Brooke Crutchley[6] Meynell criticised the loose word spacing in the galley proofs. Lewis agreed with him and the book, two volumes of over five hundred pages each, was respaced by hand.

However, Morison had in mind a more ambitious plan than the purchase of new faces from other manufacturers, and soon began to try to persuade Eric Gill to turn his hand to type design. Gill was by then a well-known sculptor, letter-carver in stone, and wood-engraver. Morison had first met him when working with Francis Meynell at Burns and Oates, where they had used some of his wood-engravings in their books. Although Gill as an ardent Catholic convert became increasingly cool in later years towards Meynell the lapsed Catholic playboy, he and Morison kept up a long, argumentative and creative friendship.

Gill had little experience of working at type scale, but had the advantage of being a carver and not a calligrapher: Morison fought long and hard against what he saw as the undue influence of calligraphers on type design. For Gill's first type, Perpetua, Morison took the unusual step of sending Gill's drawings to a hand punch-cutter, Charles Malin of Paris, for a trial cutting. Morison was more or less permanently at loggerheads with Pierpont at Salfords, and he needed to prove that designs by an outsider such as Gill could work as type before he approached Monotype. Armed with the Malin cutting, he successfully got Burch's approval to go ahead. Perpetua first appeared in 1929 in a book printed at Cambridge, Gill's book of essays called *Art-Nonsense*, but without an italic: words which needed emphasis were underlined. Gill was under the influence of Morison's sloped roman theories, and the italic was giving him trouble. A version was shown the following year in the last number of *The Fleuron*, but this was later superseded by the more familiar fatter design. As Morison put it in a letter to Van Krimpen, 'The sloped roman idea does not go down so well in this office [Monotype] as it does outside. The reason for this is that when the doctrine was applied to Perpetua, we did not give enough slope to it. When we added more slope, it seemed the fount required a little more cursive in it. The result was rather a compromise.' Nevertheless, in Gill's later roman face cut by Monotype, Joanna, a very narrow and upright hybrid sloped roman was quite successfully used. Joanna, though it was a development of a Monotype face Gill had designed called Solus, was in fact first produced privately by the Caslon foundry for Gill's own printing business Hague and Gill, set up with his son-in-law René Hague. It was first used in 1931 for Gill's exasperatingly written but deliciously produced *Essay on Typography*. It was only later when Hague and Gill was taken over by the publisher J.M. Dent that Monotype cut Joanna for hot-metal composition.

The next designer Morison brought on board was the Dutchman Jan van Krimpen. Van Krimpen, slightly younger than Morison, was the house typographer of the printing firm of Johannes Enschedé en Zonen in Haarlem, founded early in the eighteenth century and still under the control of the same family. Enschedé were most unusual in maintaining a foundry as part of the business, including a resident punchcutter, the superlative craftsman Paul Rädisch, and Van Krimpen's first task on joining the firm in 1924 was the design of a new typeface, Lutetia. In 1928 he agreed that Monotype should cut the face, though with reservations about the drawing office practice already mentioned of adapting the widths of letters to fit the die-case arrangement. Indeed, Van Krimpen took some pride in being the scourge of Monotype: he criticised the programme of recutting historic faces, and he criticised many drawing office procedures. Once when Beatrice Warde, Monotype's publicity manager and editor of *The Monotype Recorder*, was giving a talk she described Bruce Rogers as the most difficult designer the Corporation had had to deal with; then, seeing Van Krimpen in the audience she added, 'That is, until Mr Van Krimpen turned up!' Van Krimpen himself told this story as a point in his favour.

Despite this, he and Morison kept up a long and fascinating correspondence, and Monotype cut most of his major designs. This was in spite of relatively low sales of matrices: given the length of time and the care taken over cutting them the Van Krimpen types can never have made money for Monotype, and they must have been thought of as successes *d'estime* only. Lutetia was followed by Romulus, with its Morisonian sloped roman, and after the war by the beautiful Spectrum.

The Nonesuch Press occasionally used Enschedé as a printer: the two extremely handsome Homer titles published in 1931 were both set in Van Krimpen's Greek type Antigone, although the facing translations were in Monotype Cochin, based on an eighteenth-century French original. Meynell used Lutetia later, in example ninety-nine of the *Nonesuch Century*, *The Greek Portrait*, and after the Second World War he set a handsome edition of Hilaire Belloc's poems in Romulus.

In the meantime, shortly after the publication of *The Nonesuch Century* in 1936, Meynell was forced by financial difficulties brought on by the Depression to relinquish control of Nonesuch to the American George Macy, owner of the Limited Editions Club. In one of the ironies of type history, it was only now that the Nonesuch Press engaged Monotype to cut a face for them: Bulmer, based on an ATF recutting of William Bulmer's late-eighteenth-century original, was made for the Nonesuch Dickens, which began appearing in 1937. After the War Macy handed Nonesuch back to Meynell, but production in post-War conditions could never rival that of the earlier books.

One final Nonesuch surprise is that it was only once, before the War, that Meynell used the type designed by his hero Bruce Rogers, Centaur. Monotype had cut this in 1928 under Rogers's eye, which led to Beatrice Warde's remark already quoted. The type had first been made as a foundry type in the United States; Rogers had been approached by Harvey Best of American Monotype to have it cut for mechanical composition, but preferred to entrust the work to Salfords. The foundry type had no italic, and so a much redrawn version of Arrighi was made by Frederic Warde, Beatrice's husband. Since Frederic blamed his wife's relationship with Morison for the break-up of their marriage, and accompanied Rogers to England, it is most unlikely that Morison was directly involved in the recutting of Centaur.

Centaur was most famously put on display in Rogers's magnificent Oxford Lectern *Bible* of 1935, but at the time of its cutting Monotype produced one of the finest of their specimens, superbly designed by Rogers, reprinting an essay 'The trained printer and the amateur' by A. W. Pollard. The printer is not credited, but the booklet is a shining example of the kind of nearly-fine printing which some of the better printing houses were doing at the time.

In the period after the Second World War, shortages of personnel and materials, as well as the need to cut non-roman faces for the newly independent members of the Commonwealth, meant that Monotype were no longer able to produce new book types at the same rate as before. In some ways the need had already been satisfied, and book printers had an unprecedented range of faces to choose from. Nevertheless, some excellent designs appeared: Van Krimpen's Spectrum, Jan Tschichold's Sabon, and Giovanni Mardersteig's Dante. But by the time Dante came out in 1957, the great age of hot-metal typesetting was drawing to a close. In that year the first Monophoto machine went into commercial service, and the new technology of typesetting evolved from exposure through photographic negatives to digital storage with prodigious speed.

These new methods of typesetting are capable of marvellous things, but they presuppose the shift of printing technology from letterpress to offset lithography. What characterised the period between the Wars was the uniquely seductive alliance of new typesetting technology with the craft skills of traditional letterpress. *The Fleuron* and the books of the Nonesuch Press were not just fine productions, they were showpieces of what was possible with what were then new typesetting methods. It is this that gives them their special allure.

And yet, those of us who are interested in type and printing probably estimate the importance of all this more highly than the rest of the world. In Lord Dunraven's *Who's Who* entry, his titles, his military service and diplomatic positions, his association with the turf and his clubs are all dutifully listed. There is no mention at all of his chairmanship of Monotype.

Sebastian Carter was born in 1941, and studied English literature and the history of art at King's College, Cambridge. After university he worked for a number of publishers and designers in London and Paris before joining his father Will Carter at the Rampant Lions Press in Cambridge, which he now runs from his house outside the town. Here he has produced a long series of fine editions, often in rare typefaces such as Eric Gill's Golden Cockerel Roman and Hermann Zapf's Hunt Roman. Highlights have included Milton's *Areopagitica*, Samuel Beckett's *As the story was told*, and T. S. Eliot's *Four Quartets*, as well as a number of typographical display pieces such as *A printer's dozen* and most recently *In praise of letterpress*. He writes extensively on printing and typography, reviewing regularly for the *Times Literary Supplement* and the British Printing Historical Society's *Bulletin* and *Journal*. He guest-edited the 1990 Eric Gill number of the *Monotype Recorder*, and wrote the section on 'The Morison years' in the centenary number in 1997. His *Twentieth century type designers* (1987; new edition 1995; now out in paperback) has become a standard work. With only two exceptions, he has contributed to every number of *Matrix*.

NOTES

1. See the league table printed in John Randle's article 'The Development of the Monotype Machine' in *Matrix 4*.

2. Stanley Morison, *A Tally of Types, cut for machine composition and introduced at the University Press, Cambridge*, 1922–32, Cambridge University Press, 1953. A second edition 'with additions by several hands, edited by Brooke Crutchley', 1973.

3. Van Krimpen letter of 24 May 1957, printed in 'Stanley Morison and Jan van Krimpen, a survey of their correspondence, Part 4', edited by Sebastian Carter, in *Matrix 11*.

4. Oliver Simon, *Printer and Playground*, London, Faber, 1956.

5. Francis Meynell, *My Lives*, London, Bodley Head, 1971.

6. Brooke Crutchley, *Two Men*, Cambridge University Press, 1968.

This article is an edited version of the 1998 Gryphon Lecture given at the Thomas Fisher Rare Book Library in the University of Toronto, and is printed with the kind permission of the Library.

ABC
DEFGHIJK
LMNOPQRS
TUVW&
XYZ

[*]

abcdefghijklmn
opqrstuvwxyz
1234567890

Bell type, the digitized version from Monotype

Types for Books at Cambridge, 1923–45

BY BROOKE CRUTCHLEY

One of the historic spurs to the development of new typefaces was the desire of university presses to put them to use. Brooke Crutchley's careful look, in Matrix 8 (1988), at the role of the Cambridge University Press in the typographic renaissance that began in the 1920s details the complementary relationship between Cambridge and Monotype, and the books that were the fruit of that union.

In 1923 Walter Lewis became the forty-seventh holder of the post of Printer to the University of Cambridge. Six years earlier Bruce Rogers, brought in to advise on the typography of the University Press, had confided to Lewis's predecessor: 'I cannot believe that any other printing-house of equal standing can have gone on for so many years with such an inferior equipment of types and particularly of display types. They are, in my opinion, bad beyond belief.' The situation had improved by the time Lewis arrived, with the discarding of a lot of old foundry type and the introduction of Imprint, Plantin and Caslon to supplement the dreary range of Monotype's old style, modern and old face types. The next ten years, however, were to see a quite remarkable expansion, thanks primarily to the enterprise of Stanley Morison, who had been associated with Lewis at the Cloister Press in Manchester and was quick to link up with him again at Cambridge. In 1922 the Lanston Monotype Corporation in London, with Morison as consultant, launched its enlightened programme of type face production and an informal liaison was set up by which Cambridge would install faces as they became available and demonstrate their qualities in books designed under Morison's guidance.[1]

So far as the publishing side of the University Press was concerned, its mainly academic output might have been adequately served by half a dozen faces or so, with due regard to the need for mixing with mathematical symbols and exotic founts. For the Printer, however, commissions from other publishers were necessary to keep the order book full and Lewis's mind went to those more progressive houses with whom he had contact in his pre-Cloister, Ballantyne Press days. To win and maintain their custom the possession of fashionable new types was essential; Morison would have had little difficulty in persuading him of that.

Actually, the only face introduced by Lewis during his first year at the Press was not from Monotype but from Shortts of High Holborn, acting as agents for American Type Founders. This was Goudy Old Style, one of the more successful of the, literally, scores of designs produced by the American Frederic Goudy. In *A Tally of Types* (1953) Morison wrote: 'It is not so easy today to realise the paucity of new types, books or jobbing, literary or commercial, in the 1920s.' Goudy Old Style was 'one of the best designs available and has its use today. Cambridge acquired a full range of it and employed it for every kind of advertising and propaganda.'

Setting by hand was still being used occasionally for books as well as for jobbing work throughout the twenties and thirties. Despite the acknowledged benefits of Monotype composition, it was not in the character of the Press to make redundant men who had been with it since apprenticeship. Further, the nationally agreed restriction on apprentice numbers was ignored and the relevant union was too sparsely represented to enforce it. There was therefore a pool of hand-compositors to be kept busy over and above those required for the make-up and correction of books keyboarded and cast by Monotype. There was still plenty of old founder's type around and occasionally a new importation, such as Ancien Romain from Deberny of Paris used in a very limited edition (115 copies) of Maurice Baring's *Hildesheim* (1924), one of the rare books claiming to have been 'printed by Stanley Morison'. Then there was Stephenson Blake's Bell, used in Morison's monograph on its originator and also in *The Art of Carving* (1931), the second in that series of Christmas presentation books which was to achieve such renown and one of the few to be given a separate trade publication. Mostly, however, hand-compositors worked from cases filled with Monotype-cast founts, replenished as necessary so that whole books could be set without recourse to the old process of 'set, print and diss'.

In 1924, the year after his arrival, Lewis introduced three Monotype faces – Poliphilus, Baskerville and Garamond. Garamond had in fact been the first of these on the market; the decision to proceed with it had been taken before Morison's engagement by Monotype but he was responsible for the choice of models for both the roman and the italic. The excitement aroused by the appearance of this type, and of its precursor produced in 1918 by American Type Founders, was intense. Here was a design that was altogether different from anything else available. It had a sort of delicate grace which made it most suitable for *belles lettres*, as well as for such items as menus and concert programmes. Of the twelve books published by Francis Meynell in 1923, the year in which he launched the Nonesuch Press, six were in Garamond. In the same year the first volume of *The Fleuron* appeared; that was in Garamond too.

But first – Poliphilus. When the decision was made to reproduce the type of the *Hypnerotomachia Poliphili*, nobody involved appreciated the extent to which faults in casting and printing had obscured the true character of the original design. Morison atoned for this lapse some six years later with the production of Bembo, altogether a more sensitive reproduction of an Aldine alphabet. Meanwhile, however, and somewhat ironically, Poliphilus was to be used at Cambridge in two of his most impressive works – his own *Four Centuries of Fine Printing* (1924) and the three-volume double-column Royal Quarto *Catalogue of the Portuguese Books in the Library of King Manoel* (1929–35). The italic, based on the chancery hand of Antonio Blado, was shown off beautifully in the Nonesuch two-volume edition of Milton's *Poems in English* (1926).

The fact that for some time roman and italic were only available in 16-point accounts for the use of Garamond for the footnotes, and Caslon for the dropped initials, in J. L. Shear's volume on terracottas printed for the American Society for the Excavation of Sardis (1926). (The preface states that 'the typographical arrangement of the book has been designed by Frederique [*sic*] Warde of London, whose intelligent assistance is gratefully acknowledged'.) Garamond was similarly used for the dedicatory letter to George Moore and Moore's reply in C. K. Moncrieff's *Letters of Abelard and Heloise* (1925), a particularly handsome book printed for the short-lived publishing firm of Guy Chapman. Other books printed in Poliphilus in its early years were *The Examples of San Bernardino*, translated by Ada Harrison and illustrated by Robert Austin (Gerald Howe, 1926); a narrative poem, *Lucy Harvington*, printed in a small edition for the author, Herbert Sleigh (1928); and John Marplet's *A Green Forest* (Hesperides Press, 1930). As time went on it was used only occasionally, one loyal supporter being the Royal Geographical Society, whose secretary, A. R. Hinks, was a typographical enthusiast.

It was to be expected that the Monotype cutting of Baskerville would have an enthusiastic reception at Cambridge. After all, its originator had been Printer to the University for a few years in the eighteenth century, when he produced his magnificent folio Bible and four editions of *The Book of Common Prayer*. A number of admirers in the University had formed a Baskerville Club in the early years of the present century and a memoir of Baskerville by R. Straus and R. K. Dent had been printed for Chatto & Windus in 1907. Bruce Rogers, during his time at Cambridge, had correctly surmised that some type on sale from Fonderie Bertrand in Paris was cast from genuine Baskerville matrices. He suggested that, if this could be proved to be the case, Cambridge should seek to acquire the matrices and, if still in existence, the punches as well, with a view to adopting the design for exclusive Cambridge use.[2] At his suggestion a small fount of type in imitation of Baskerville had been obtained from Stephenson Blake.

The design was, therefore, familiar (as Poliphilus and Garamond were not) and was soon being used with understanding of its possibilities and its limitations. Properly handled, that is with plenty of space, Baskerville makes an attractive page, even if it lacks the charm of old face types. This may be because it is too perfect. There had always been in old face types a fundamental lack of homogeneity between the capitals, based as they were on carved letters, and the lower case with its obvious calligraphical background. Some of its charm can be seen as coming from this slight disorder. With Baskerville no such dichotomy was apparent; the engraver had taken over the lower case along with the capitals. Character might be infused into a page, however, by the judicious use of rules (particularly thick-and-thins) and of Baskerville's own favourite ornaments, lozenge and star. The choice of paper was important – smooth and as white as possible without dazzling. And the inking firm and even.

Baskerville was soon being used in a variety of CUP publications and in books for Harrap, Heinemann, John Lane, Constable and Cobden-Sanderson.[3] The last-named was particularly successful with *The New Forget-me-not: a Calendar*, amusingly 'decorated' by Rex Whistler and containing short contributions by some forty well-known authors. Five thousand copies printed in September 1929 in good time for Christmas proved insufficient and repeats of 3000 and 5000 were hurriedly put through. Morison adopted Baskerville for three books published over the imprint of *The Fleuron* – Milton's *Paradise Regained* (1924) and his own *Type Designs, Past and Present* (1926) and *A Review of Recent Typography* (1927). He was also responsible for the design of *The Devil in Love* by J. Cazotte, with engravings by J. E. Laboureur, published by Heinemann in 1925, and of Ambrose Heal's *English Writing Masters* (CUP, 1931), enhanced by some fine calligraphic flourishes by H. K. Wolfenden. Wolfenden was one of a number of craftsmen from whom Morison often commissioned work; another was R. J. Beedham, who almost certainly engraved the block for Lewis's 1929 Christmas card (figure 1).

Garamond, the third type to be acquired in 1924, was not to figure as often in the CUP's own publications as Baskerville but it proved popular with other publishers, notably Harrap. Faber chose it for Geoffrey Keynes's six-volume edition of *The Works of Sir Thomas Browne* and it was deployed with spectacular effect in a book for Benn's Julian Editions – Lady Wilde's translation of Wilhelm Meinhold's *Sidonia the Sorceress* (1926), with illustrations by Thomas Lowinsky. It was also used for a poem by Pierre Jean Jouve, *Les Mystérieuses Noces*, printed

for Librairie Stock of Paris (1925) and referred to in the colophon as 'une édition originale établie par les soins de J. Holroyd-Reece'. Among CUP publications Garamond was used for a new edition of E. G. Browne's *Year among the Persians* (1926), perhaps because it seemed to have just that element of the exotic appropriate to an oriental subject. Additional matrices were obtained for letters with the diacritical marks conventionally used for transliteration of Arabic words, incidentally ensuring that the face would continue to be employed at Cambridge for works in this field. Some arabesque ornaments, a fine laid paper and handsome binding all helped to make the appearance of Browne's book worthy of its reputation as one of the great records of travel.

The next face to be added to the Cambridge repertory was Fournier and this was Meynell's choice for his seven-volume *Shakespeare* – the *chef d'oeuvre* of the Nonesuch Press, as he called it. The preparatory work that was involved is described in John Dreyfus's *History of the Nonesuch Press;* it included the cutting of smaller capitals, which were widely used thereafter as an alternative to the originals. (The CUP records show that Fournier was also used for what appears to have been a trial setting for the Nonesuch *Plutarch*, consisting of thirty-six pages and a label, presumably for a wrapper. There is no reference to it in Dreyfus's *History;* was it ever sent out? The eventual edition was printed elsewhere.) In the *Tally* Morison tells how a misunderstanding led to a design being followed for the type which was not the one he had intended, but it proved nevertheless to be extremely popular. Lewis's first use of it was in another book for Julian Editions, Milton's *Comus* (1926), followed by Sacheverell Sitwell's *Dr Johnson and Gargantua* for Duckworth (1930), Edmund Blunden's *Leigh-Hunt* for Cobden-Sanderson (1930), and William Rothenstein's *Men and Memories* for Faber (1931–32).

Like Garamond (and Caslon) Fournier was light in colour and for comfortable reading did not need as much interlinear space as did bolder types such as Baskerville. This, along with its narrow set, made it ideal for long books where it was important to get as many words as possible on to the page. Two such books published by CUP were D. S. Robertson's *Handbook of Greek and Roman Architecture* (1929) and F. J. Harvey Darton's *Children's Books in England* (1932). There was no such reason, however, for the choice of Fournier for Edith Sitwell's *Five Poems* (1928), lavishly set out on a quarto page and printed in 275 copies for Duckworth; nor for Maurois' *Aspects of Biography* (CUP, 1929), translated by S. C. Roberts, a small octavo with large margins. Roberts was Secretary to the Syndics of the Press and head of the publishing arm. He was also author or editor of several books published by the Press and with his interest in typography (he was an early member of the Double Crown Club) he is likely to have expressed a preference so far as type face was concerned. Variety seems to be the keynote; successive books of his were set in Caslon, Baskerville, Imprint, Fournier, Scotch Roman and Bell. His assistant, R. J. L. Kingsford, also a member of the Double Crown, was responsible for the design of a series of announcement lists of coming publications, each in a different type face and most elegantly produced.

Morison was not to be denied a sight of the heavier version of Fournier which he had preferred. Accordingly it was cut in one size, 13½-point, and the only set of matrices conveyed to Cambridge. Named Barbou, it was used in volumes V-VII of *The Fleuron*, Morison having taken over the editing from Oliver Simon and brought the printing to Cambridge. Its only other appearances at the time were in Arthur Clutton-Brock's *The Miracle of Love* (1926), published in Julian Editions, and a privately printed posthumous book of poems by Charles Walston, former director of the Fitzwilliam Museum.[4] Several years later two books were printed at Cambridge using the original matrices, Flaubert's *Salammbô* for the Limited Editions Club of New York (1960) and a Cambridge Christmas book, *Two Men: Walter Lewis and Stanley Morison at Cambridge* (1968).[5]

For all the attractions of the new types introduced by Lewis, Caslon continued to be used on a substantial scale and in many of the best designed and printed books of the inter-war years. Any exhibition of British book production of that period would be likely to include Vita Sackville-West's *The Land* (1926), printed for Heinemann, Defoe's *Tour through Great Britain* (1927) for Peter Davies, John Sparrow's edition of the poems of Henry King for Nonesuch (1925) and Geoffrey Keynes's bibliography of William Harvey (CUP, 1928). (Actually, the typography closely followed that of the same author's bibliography of John Donne, printed at the Press for the Baskerville Club in 1914, an unusually good-looking production for that time).[6] Caslon was also used in the Cambridge *New Shakespeare* which appeared at an average rate of a volume a year from 1921 onwards. The fact that the type had been in almost continuous use in Britain since the eighteenth century, despite the competition of the moderns, means that publishers and printers must have been fond of it. Compositors knew just how to handle it – text, prelims, notes, index and all.

Other Monotype faces which had been introduced before Lewis's arrival and were still in frequent use were Imprint, Plantin, Scotch Roman and the varieties of modern regularly employed in scientific books and journals. Imprint was chosen for Adrian Fortescue's edition of the *De consolatione philosophiae* of Boethius (1925), which Morison designed for Burns & Oates. A type face of marked character can be used on a straightforward text without interfering with the reader's comprehension; may, indeed, by its 'congeniality' assist it.[7] But for an intricate work of scholarship, with all apparatus of footnotes, marginal notes, alternative readings and so on, the more neutral and self-effacing the type, the better. For such books Imprint became a natural choice.

Plantin had been seen by Rogers as only acceptable as a Clarendon and (apart from two small books printed for a local bookseller-publisher, Deighton Bell) it was not otherwise used by Lewis until Meynell prescribed it for his catalogue 'Prospectus and Retrospectus of the Nonesuch Press 1932'. Meynell was much addicted to Plantin and used it in many of his books, including two of very different character printed at Cambridge – *The Week-end Problems Book* (1932) and the monumental *Herodotus* (1935), for which lengthened ascenders and descenders had to be cut. The first CUP book to be set in Plantin in Lewis's time was one known to many generations of law students, H. J. Jolowicz's *Historical Introduction to Roman Law* (1932).[8]

Scotch Roman was used occasionally in CUP publications, for instance in *The Eighteen Seventies* (1929), essays by Fellows of the Royal Society of Literature edited by H. Granville Barker. (By way of variety *The Eighteen Sixties* (1932) was in Bembo and *The Eighteen Eighties* (1930) in Caslon.) A period piece of great charm was the reprint in small octavo of *The Book of Ranks and Dignities of British Society*, attributed to Charles Lamb and edited by Michael Sadleir for Cape (1924). Other notable books in Scotch were Disraeli's *Dunciad of Today* printed for Ingpen & Grant (1928); Le Fanu's *In a Glass Darkly* (Peter Davies, 1929), the first book to be illustrated by Edward Ardizzone; and Elizabeth Ann Hart's *The Runaway* with engravings by Gwen Raverat (Macmillan, 1936).

In the last two cases the aim was obviously to use a type which would match the illustrations in colour. For the same reason the rarely used Bodoni was picked for another book illustrated by Gwen Raverat, R. P. Keigwin's translation of four tales by Hans Andersen (CUP, 1935). Bodoni had been introduced piece-meal by Lewis. Its production by Monotype was itself piecemeal, extending over eight years from 1921–28, the delay apparently due to difficulties in obtaining satisfactory models of the original types. Besides the Hans Andersen book the type was used in three CUP publications, G. L. Bickersteth's edition of Dante's *Paradiso* (1932), E. E. Phare's *Poetry of Gerard Manley Hopkins* (1933) and F. L. Lucas's *Poems 1935*. The Dante is interesting because the type seems to suit the Italian text but to be less happy in the facing English translation; the relation of type face to language needs more study. Geoffrey Grigson's poetry magazine, *New Verse*, was in Bodoni and Meynell chose the 16-point italic, well leaded, for James Laver's *Love's Progress or the Education of Araminta*.

The more types from which to pick, the more important was the specimen customarily set for each new book if not one of a series. The practice at Cambridge was to set two facing pages, the verso usually illustrating a chapter opening, the recto including some quoted matter and footnotes when relevant. Thus the general appearance and readability could be judged. Comfortable reading depends on nothing so much as the interlinear space; to get this right, neither too little nor too much, might be a matter of a half-point adjustment. A cast-off of the typescript (or manuscript, as it was in many cases) was prepared at the same time and this too might prompt some modification such as enlarging the type area to contain more words and altering the margins accordingly.

So long as there had been virtually only three type faces for books – old face, old style and modern – instructions given by publishers tended to be minimal and printers could safely be left to handle the detail such as chapter and page headings, title-page and contents list, along conventional lines. Now, with the increase in available faces, publishers were finding themselves faced with more and more decisions on points of design.[9] Whether the whole or only part of the typography fell to Cambridge, the responsibility there rested mainly with Frank Gordon Nobbs, overseer of the Monotype department and later in charge of all composing, a man of quite remarkable talent. No detail was too small for him and the orderly presentation and graceful appearance of books printed at Cambridge owed more to him than to anyone else. Presswork was the responsibility of the machine-room overseer, Harry Franklin, whose standards were hardly less stringent. The larger machines in his care were mostly engaged on long-run reprints of school and university textbooks, bibles and prayer books. New books were printed on single-side Quad Crown or Double Demy Miehles or Wharfedales, the latter in particular when hand-made paper made pointing necessary. Runs being often no more than 1000 or 1500, machines were down most of the time while minders 'made ready', including the finicky process of cutting paper overlays for pasting on the cylinder.

Six more Monotype faces were installed in the years 1928–32, of which three – Bembo, Bell and Times New Roman – were to find frequent use, while Goudy Modern, Centaur and Perpetua, being less versatile, made comparatively few appearances. Of Goudy Modern Morison wrote in the *Tally*: 'While not, strictly speaking, a book-type, it can be used for texts, even of great length, as may be seen in the Nonesuch *Don Quixote*. . . . But while it is admirably serviceable for limited editions, it finds its best general employment in certain kinds of extra-literary composition as, for example, catalogues and prospectuses.' It was indeed used in the Nonesuch prospectus for 1931, printed on a limp, grey paper which had originally been delivered to Cambridge for the printing of *Herodotus* but rejected after trials had demonstrated its unsuitability. This *papier d' Auvergne à la main*, to quote its flowery watermark, was discovered by Meynell on his travels; its proper use was as a filter in the brewing of beer.

The first book to be set in Goudy Modern at Cambridge was the *Don Quixote* referred to by Morison, illustrated by McKnight Kauffer (1930). Neither Meynell nor Lewis was satisfied with the word-spacing as seen on the proof and the whole was put through the stick. The expense must have been considerable but Lewis took a certain pride in the incident, demonstrating as it did his insistence on the highest standards and his determination to satisfy his customers. The type was used in a few CUP books including *Dean Swift's Library* by Harold Williams (1932) and another book with Raverat engravings, Frances Cornford's *Mountains and Molehills* (1934).

In the mind of Bruce Rogers when he agreed to the cutting of his Centaur by

Monotype was no doubt his plan to print T. E. Lawrence's translation of *The Odyssey*. The text was set at Cambridge and the type delivered to Emery Walker's works in London, to be made up and printed and eventually published over the imprint of 'Sir Emery Walker, Wilfred Merton and Bruce Rogers'. As Morison said in the *Tally*, Centaur 'bore itself with an aristocratic air which made it apt for the making of non-commercial editions'. Such were Sacheverell Sitwell's *Beckford and Beckfordism* printed for Duckworth (1930) and *The Magic Horse,* translated from *The Arabian Nights* by E. W. Lane, with illustrations in colour by Ceri Richards (Gollancz, 1930). Others were Morison's *Fra Luca de Pacioli,* designed by Rogers for the Grolier Club of New York (1933), and the Nonesuch *George Chapman* by Havelock Ellis (1934). In contrast with *Herodotus*, which was four and a half years in the press, this book of 160 pages was composed, printed, bound and published all within seven weeks of the receipt of copy despite difficulties with the Van Gelder hand-made paper which, like the Auvergne, had originally been intended for Herodotus and varied in thickness, according to Lewis's calculation, by as much as fifty per cent. Somewhat surprisingly, for it was not designed as a monumental book, though it may well be so regarded for its content, Centaur was used for Charles Sherrington's *Man on his Nature,* published by CUP in 1940.

Perpetua was, so to speak, the climax of Morison's Monotype programme – a new design by a living artist but profiting from all the experience gained in the recutting of designs from the past. Endless trouble had been taken to get it right. The italic, initially known as Felicity, was a sloping roman in accordance with Morison's current theory, though with certain deviations; but it was not yet ready for the first book to show the roman – Gill's own *Art Nonsense* (1929), printed at Cambridge for Cassell. Instead, underlining was used. Another book by Gill and illustrated with his engravings, *Clothes,* was printed for Cape (1931), and the type was successfully used in a novel, Susan Prior's *Awake* (1932), printed for Pharos Editions of Bedford Square. Thereafter Perpetua was used from time to time in CUP publications but more, it would seem, for the sake of a change and to give it an airing than from any feeling that it was right for the particular work. Gill's own view was that the face retained 'that commonplaceness and normality which is essential to a good book-type', but Morison, writing some twenty years later in the *Tally*, thought it 'expressed a note of particularity and self-consciousness not universally acceptable'. It appeared in two books of poetry published by CUP, F. L. Lucas's *Ariadne* (1932) and E. H. R. Altounyan's *Ornament of Honour* (1937); indeed, Beatrice Warde found that it was a favourite among poets.

Perpetua might have made more mark if Morison had chosen it for some major production such as the Coronation Service of King George VI (it is the practice for the three privileged presses – Oxford, Cambridge and the King's Printer – each to produce its own version) or for the 'swagger edition' (his words) of the *Order of Solemn Entrance in Time of War* for Liverpool Cathedral. But he chose Bembo instead. However, he liked to use Perpetua capitals for displayed lines in books set in other types, particularly Baskerville and Bembo, and this became a common Cambridge practice.

As with so many of the new Monotype faces, Bembo made its first appearance in a book printed at Cambridge, the catalogue of a British Museum exhibition of British and foreign printing, 1919–28. It was set in the only size then available, 16-point, and 'in its absolute simplicity', writes Nicolas Barker, 'it is one of the finest Morison designed'. Bembo was soon being used in a wide variety of books and miscellaneous printing for the University and colleges. The narrow italic of Alfred Fairbank was seen in the British Museum catalogue but then gave way to the Tagliente design. Several books printed at Cambridge in Bembo were to figure in the exhibitions of the National Book League in the following years.

With Bembo Morison was happy to have revived what he considered the prototype of all old face types. Bell he regarded as the first of the moderns. The tracking down of John Bell himself and of his types was pursued with characteristic gusto and it was fitting that the first use of the Monotype cutting should be in Morison's own work, *The English Newspaper* (1932). There is about this type a solid quality which seems to add to the stature of any book that is set in it. Frank Kendon, one of the CUP editors, was particularly fond of Bell and prescribed it for books of such varied subjects as F. M. Cornford's *Before and After Socrates* (1932), Thomas Hennell's *Change on the Farm* (1934), Charles Ffoulkes's *Gunfounders of England* (1937) and Helen Morris's *Portrait of a Chef* (1938); and it does well by them all. Sidgwick & Jackson specified it for their new editions of J. C. Stobart's popular works, *The Glory that was Greece* (1933) and *The Grandeur that was Rome* (1934).

The success of Times New Roman as a book fount was not foreseen by Morison. However, Meynell had quickly appreciated such aesthetic merit as it possessed and used it in three Nonesuch books in 1934, the year after its release. He was also to choose it for *The Nonesuch Century* (1936) celebrating the first hundred books his Press had published. The handling of this volume, and of its parcels of type and ornaments and ninety-six insets sent in by printers from all over the country, was a nightmare, well chronicled in Dreyfus's *History*. Lewis had been supplied with Times matrices ahead of general release for the printing of a special number of *The Monotype Recorder* devoted to the type. He also undertook the printing of the first two volumes of the special hand-made paper edition of *The History of The Times*; owing to other pressures subsequent volumes had to be printed elsewhere. A semi-bold version of the face was cut in 7-point for a Cambridge edition of the Bible, the 'Pitt Minion', first issued in 1936, and a few books were printed in Times around that date – M. W. Childs's *Sweden, the Middle Way* (1936) for Faber (Richard de la Mare was always one for trying out new types), Maurice Baring's *Have You Anything to Declare* for Heinemann (1936), probably suggested by Morison but not a success typographically, and a series of 'English Institutions' for CUP.

The BBC switched to Times from the previously favoured Fournier for its series of green-paper-bound 'Broadcast National Lectures'. (The BBC was one national institution which habitually ordered printing from Cambridge; the National Trust was another.) The type's suitability for publications of an official character was first recognised in the *List of Current Periodicals* for the University Library, soon followed by an address list of members of Magdalene College. For literary works, however, it did not seem to have any particular quality to make it preferable to the many other faces by then in the Cambridge repertory. It was wartime economy, and the need to squeeze as many words as possible on to a page, that gave Times its great fillip.

The typographical renaissance had reached its climax in the mid-1920s, when the zest of so many of its protagonists was at its keenest. During the succeeding decade the excitement was dying down a little and the world economic slump was inevitably affecting book publishers. Some of the smaller and most adventurous disappeared, while all were looking for economies in production. Despite Lewis's launching of his series of attractive Christmas books 'for friends in printing and publishing' (the first appeared in 1930), orders from outside publishers were harder to get and even the Press's own publishing arm was finding trade conditions difficult. With the Second World War new problems arose. When it was over, and Lewis had retired, some rationalisation of the composing department seemed to be called for. Was it necessary now, or commercially sensible, to hold so many type faces? Would not (say) eight, with their associated bolds if any, meet all foreseeable needs? Despite such merits as they might individually possess, could one not manage without Poliphilus, Centaur, Bodoni, Goudy Modern, even Perpetua? But they all survived, and were used in some of the best books printed in the post-war years.

Brooke Crutchley retired from the position of Cambridge University Printer in 1974, after having filled the post for 28 years, during a career at the University Press spanning a total of 44 years. He also played an active part in Cambridge life throughout his term of office at the Press. His influence spread into many fields of endeavour, where he has been recognised as a man of vision and achievement whose career has enriched the worlds of printing and learning.

NOTES

1. Understanding was not always perfect between Morison and the Monotype works in Surrey, where the drawing office and matrix-making department were housed. There is no doubt, however, that his task would have been far more difficult but for the skill of the technicians there, in particular four Germans whom the manager, F. H. Pierpont, had brought with him from his previous post with Typograph AG. See the article 'Monotype matrix making and type design' by John Dreyfus in *Typos* No. 1 (1980), published by the London College of Printing.

2. The punches were, in fact, acquired by Cambridge in 1953 through the generosity of Charles Peignot of the Paris firm of Deberny & Peignot, into whose possession they had passed.

3. When installing a new typeface the practice was to order the equipment (diecase keybars, etc.) for a few point-sizes in the first instance and then add to the sizes, and duplicate the equipment, as the demand occurred.

4. In his handlist of Stanley Morison's writings Tony Appleton states that the Julian Edition *Comus* mentioned above was set in Barbou. The text type is, in fact, 18-point Fournier.

5. By that time a smaller size (12-point) had been cut at the behest of Yale University Press for use in *The Papers of Benjamin Franklin* (1960) and rechristened Franklin.

6. In his autobiography, *The Gates of Memory*, Keynes states that it was at his insistence that the book was set in Caslon Old Face, with a liberal use of swash letters. Probably he was mainly responsible for the design of the book as a whole.

7. See the present writer's article on this subject in *Matrix* 6, pp. 134–9.

8. Despite Rogers' opinion of it Plantin had been used occasionally as a text type before Lewis's time. Morison mentions one such book with approbation in the *Tally* – S. A. McDowall's *Beauty and the Beast* (1920).

9. A challenge which some of them took up with relish and flair, notably Wren Howard of Cape, Richard de la Mare of Faber and Charles Prentice of Chatto. Increasingly the appearance of a book gave the clue to who had published it rather than to where it had been printed.

I am grateful to Nicolas Barker for pointing out that the design of the panel in the 1929 Christmas card is taken from Morison's favourite Yciar and follows, in rather simplified form, the second of the two panels of 'letra formada' in the 1550 edition of the *Arte subtilissima*. He suggests that Morison probably did a pencil rough and handed this with a photograph of a page from Yciar to Beedham who did the rest, straightening out the slightly irregular lines of the fifteenth-century engraver and notably tidying up the flowers, which are a bit different in the original.

Specimen of types designed by Eric Gill for the
GOLDEN COCKEREL PRESS

A B C D E F G H I J K L M
N O P R S T U V W X Y Z Æ Qu
❋ 1 2 3 4 5 6 7 8 9 0 ✷

ABCDEFGHIJKLMNOPQRSTUVWXYZ
abcdefghijklmnopqrstuvwxyz
£1234567890&ÆŒæœ([.,:;'-!?fiffiflfflff
abcdefghijklmnopqrstuvwxyz

St Bride Printing Library, January 1996

1. A specimen of types designed in 1930 by Eric Gill for the Golden Cockerel Press set and printed in a small number of copies on a hand press at the St Bride Printing Library. It shows the 18-point capitals, and the full character set of the 14-point roman and italic, and was printed from the only surviving fount which is at the Library. The Golden Cockerel italic was made for the 14-point size only, and like the original version of Gill's Joanna type (and following the model of some early italics) it has no sloped italic capitals.

Eric Gill and the Golden Cockerel Type

BY JAMES MOSLEY

One of the earliest subjects covered in Matrix, *in the second issue (1982), was the elegant typeface that the protean Englishman Eric Gill created for the Golden Cockerel Press. In the first of two articles about the Golden Cockerel type from that issue, James Mosley describes how Gill came to create this uniquely 'robust' typeface for the press's proprietor, Robert Gibbings.*

The Golden Cockerel Press, which in its name commemorates the exotic glories of the *Ballets Russes*, had been intended by its founder Harold Midgeley Taylor as a co-operative venture for young authors who would set and print their own work. For Robert Gibbings, who took over the press in January 1924, it provided the opportunity for using the work of the new school of wood engravers of which he was himself a member. 'Strangely enough, in view of later events,' wrote Gibbings, 'the only one to reject my invitation was Eric Gill. He wrote a very nice letter but he gave several reasons for refusal, the chief of which appeared to be that I was not a Catholic.'[1] Gill did, of course, capitulate. He engraved illustrations and initials for the *Sonnets and Verses* of his sister Enid Clay, printed by the Golden Cockerel Press and issued in April 1925. This was the beginning of an association that was to produce some of the most remarkable illustrated books of the years between the wars. Gill's illustrations or decorations were a feature of a dozen of the seventy books that were printed before Gibbings gave up the direction of the Press in 1933.

The type that Gibbings inherited from Taylor was Caslon Old Face. When the Press was established, there was a certain inevitability about the choice of this type for hand-printers who had neither the inclination nor the means to have their own private type designed for them. It was sanctified by tradition as the type of 'special' commercial houses, such as the Chiswick Press for whom it had been revived in the eighteen-forties. George Bernard Shaw, under the influence of Emery Walker, had insisted on its use in each volume of his plays since 1898, and it was for the printers of these, R. & R. Clark of Edinburgh, that a Monotype cutting of the face was begun in 1916. Elizabeth Corbett Yeats at the Cuala Press, Hilary Pepler at the St Dominic's Press, and A. H. Bullen at the Shakespeare Head Press were all users of the Caslon types.

Our father who hallowed be thy dom come. Th earth as it is in

The drawings for the Golden Cockerel Press types, including the sketches and enlargements reproduced here, form part of the Gill Collection of the St Bride Printing Library. The punches and matrices, together with the Caslon drawings and brass patterns, are housed at the University Printing House, Cambridge. The surviving

When he took over the Golden Cockerel Press, Gibbings was, in his own words, 'almost completely ignorant of typography'.[2] Gill had the advantage, even at the start of their association, of the experience of having worked over a period of twenty years on the projects of Graf Harry Kessler, first at the Insel Verlag, and then for Kessler's Cranach Presse. He had been involved in the work of the St Dominic's Press, for which so many of his engravings had been made. Lately, moreover, he had embarked on another association, of which he could hardly have foreseen the full consequences. Early in 1924, the Monotype Corporation, which had shown outstanding skill in adapting historic types for mechanical composition, promised a programme for the future that would include 'other distinguished faces of the past and in addition at least one original design'. Stanley Morison, Monotype's new adviser on typographical matters, may have already had Gill in mind as a designer who would help them fulfil this promise. Given Gill's view on the reproduction of his work by mechanical means (he had given up drawing for photographic reproduction as 'beastly in itself') his co-operation was by no means to be taken for granted. But by November 1925 he was already, by his own account, drawing 'alphabets for Stanley Morison'.[3]

rt in heaven
iame. Thy king-
will be done on
eaven.

3 prints to S. M.

Reduce 2" to 1/7"

founts of the 18-point roman and the titling are at the Rampant Lions Press, Cambridge, and the 14-point, roman and italic, is at the St Bride Printing Library. Gill's letters are reprinted by courtesy of the Syndics of the Cambridge University Library.

The Perpetua type, for which these alphabets would form the model, was to have a protracted gestation: it was not formally released to the printing trade until 1932. In 1927, however, Gill drew another alphabet for Morison from which Monotype made Gills Sans, a type that was given his name because it came out, in 1928, before the new roman. It was to make him more widely known as a type designer than he would ever be as an engraver or sculptor.

Following the *Sonnets and Verses*, Gill had continued his work for the Golden Cockerel Press with the *Song of Songs* (1925), *The Passion of the Lord Jesus Christ* (1926), and Chaucer's *Troilus and Criseyde* (1927), for which he made sixty engravings. For these, Gibbings supplied galley proofs for Gill to paste in the illustrations and initials that he had engraved. But the 'ideal partnership', as Gibbings described it, came with the close collaboration, page by page, between the two of them in *The Four Gospels*, the most ambitious work made by the press, which was only completed in 1931; and for this a new type was used, designed by Gill for the use of the Golden Cockerel Press.

Three letters from Gill to Morison, written during the summer of 1928 when Gill was already contemplating the move from Capel-y-ffin to his last home Pigotts, near High Wycombe, throw some light on the making of this fount.[4] The immediate occasion for the correspondence was that difficulties had arisen in producing a satisfactory italic for Perpetua. From Gill's point of view this was embarrassing because he was now enmeshed in an agreement with the Golden Cockerel Press which seemed to debar him from making new designs for Monotype. On 16 June he wrote to Morison:

> Re *Italic:* Yes, I agree & I think the right step wd. be to make an italic fount which, while being an improvement on existing forms, would not jump out at the reader as a novelty. This must be done & 'England' shd. do it. But my agreement with G.C.P. specially bars me from designing new founts of type except for the G.C.P. and they are particularly anxious that I shd. do a new italic to go with the Caslon l.c. & yet be an improvement on the existing Caslon italic. My agreement with the Monotype Corpn. does not touch the designing of new type by me – it relates simply to advice & criticism of types brought out by them & of which other people are the designers. (n.b. the Sans Serif & this new Roman l.c. are not an infringement as they were designed before the G.C.P. agreement.) You'll see the point of all this. I think it's fair and square. G.C.P. wants me to do for them various types. I agree. So they say Well give us the bloody things then & don't go spreading yourself on other people till you've done ours. So I agree. I don't quite see why the Monotype shd.n't come into it & make the type & give G.C.P. exclusive rights for say 5 years – but that's not feasible perhaps.

The exact terms of this agreement are unknown, but the end in view was clearly not so much a new italic for Caslon as a wholly new type for the Golden Cockerel Press. This would require from Gill more responsibility for the final result than anything he had done for Morison. As he put it to Morison on 23 June:

> . . . you will remember that when I made you these drawings of alphabets I expressly disclaimed the suggestion that I was type designing. I did not & do not even now profess to know enough about it – (i.e. typographical exigencies). The same applies to the Sans Serif alphabet I drew. You remember my surprize when you showed me the pages of the Sans-Serif. I was v. pleased because I thought such a good thing had been made & it was an honour to me.

This was a view that Gill expressed publicly in the prefatory note to *The Passion of Perpetua and Felicity,* printed in 1929 and incorporated in the seventh and final volume of *The Fleuron* as a specimen of the Perpetua roman: 'These drawings were not made with special reference to typography – they were simply letters, drawn with brush and ink. For the typographical quality of the fount, as also for the remarkably fine and precise cutting of the punches, the Monotype Corporation is to be praised'. 'However,' Gill concluded his second letter, 'I am coming round by degrees to consider myself capable of designing a fount of type'.

A month later, he had already embarked on the design of his new fount. His letter to Morison of 22 July shows both his diffidence and the ingenuity with which he tackled the problems posed by this, his first independent type design:

> *Re Gibbings Type* I am now working on this – but am at a loss how to proceed.
>
> (1) I have made drawings of 5 Caps & 5 l c & numerals to large scale, but how am I to tell what they'll look like small?
>
> (2) I have made a drawing of part of Lords Prayer actual size of 18 point (body). But neither my hand nor my eye is capable of working so small. Still the general effect is what I want – colour character etc.
>
> What I need now is a photographic enlargement of (2). I wd. then work on it and have it photographically reduced again. I wd. like to do this before showing it to Gibbings.
>
> This is not a Monotype business – leastways you know how the matter stands & nothing has yet been arranged between Monotype & G.C.P. Under the circumstances can you help me by getting the photo-enlargement made? Even if you think it improper at this stage to get the Monotype people to do it, you probably know a photographer who would.* May I trouble you thus far? Presuming I may, *I send my sketch herewith.* I hope this will not horrify you. My terms of reference are: *a heavy, closely massing type* suitable for use with modern wood engravings. Therefore I plump for an almost *even line* letter & *short ascenders & descenders*. The sketch enclosed (Our Father etc) is practically a 24 pt. letter on one [?] 18 pt. body. Doubtless this is too big a letter for R.G.'s purpose. But I propose to have the enlargement made & then, when I have worked it up neatly, to have it photographically reduced to 18 pt. (letter) size – or perhaps several sizes. I'm sorry my sketch is so rough. I hope you'll see possibilities in it.
>
> * at *my* expense of course.

The sketch of the five capitals and five lower case characters and numerals, to which reference is made in the letter, no longer seems to survive, but the second item does, and so do two related pieces. Here is Gill's sketch of part of the Lord's Prayer that he sent to Morison, reproduced from the original at the same scale:

Our father who art in heaven
hallowed be thy name. Thy kingdom come. Thy will be done on
earth as it is in heaven.

This reproduces, not at full scale, the photographic enlargement that Morison supplied in response to this letter, showing Gill's extensive reworking of the design. Below, finally, is the retouched enlargement, brought down to the intended size of the new type:

Our father who art in heaven
hallowed be thy name. Thy kingdom come. Thy will be done on
earth as it is in heaven.

Enlargements on a similar scale were made of the 18-point Caslon roman and of the 16-point Jenson roman that had been made for Kessler's Cranach Presse, with the object, apparently, of observing how such letter forms looked in different sizes. Being now more certain of the relationship between the letters that he had drawn in the intended size of the type and those on the larger scale on which he was accustomed to work in stone, Gill drew finished drawings of capitals, lower case and figures, making the capitals 1½ in. high. These are dated 2 April 1929. They were passed to the typefounders H. W. Caslon & Co, who made their own enlarged drawings of each character from which brass pattern letters were cut. These, in turn, were used with a Benton-style punchcutting machine to make punches, from which the matrices were struck. This work was done during the period October to December 1929 under the supervision of Caslon's chief punchcutter, J. Collinge,[5] and delivery of the type, according to the Golden Cockerel Press prospectus for October 1929, was promised for January 1930.

A 24-point titling fount was made from the 18-point roman, and this, as Gibbings explains, was to give Gill a further lesson in type design: 'But when this arrived, we found that it lacked something of the distinction of the 18-point. The thicks and thins had lost a little of their balance in the larger size. And yet the work was mathematically correct. It was an interesting demonstration to us both that mathematics and aesthetics do not always agree, and that one of the greatest changes you can make in a design is to alter its scale. For the 36-point titling which I commissioned soon afterwards, Eric worked again on his designs, reducing the weight of the horizontals in proportion to that of the verticals, and so retrieved the lost elegance of the design.' A 14-point roman was also made, presumably using the patterns that had served to make the 18-point, and this was provided with an italic lower case modelled closely on Gill's early (and rejected) italic for Perpetua. It is a 'sloped roman' with a minimal slant, designed to work with the upright capitals of the roman. Although the 14-point type was the last to be made, it was the first to appear, being used for *The hundredth story of A. E. Coppard*, issued in January 1931. The 18-point and the two sizes of titling had been used during 1930 and 1931 for the composition of *The Four Gospels*, which was issued in November 1931.

The Golden Cockerel Press fount is a big type, big on its body, and looking, as Gill remarked to Morison, a couple of sizes larger than it is. This suited Gibbings whose preference was for large books (while Gill, as he was soon to show at his own press, preferred small ones). It is, moreover, a wide letter, suiting a broad page better than a narrow one. I have some sympathy with the judgement of Colin Franklin, who finds that this is not Gill's most sensitive invention. It does indeed appear graceless by comparison with the type that Gill made for himself, the exquisite Joanna, and judged by the brief that Gill set before Morison, for 'a heavy closely massing type suitable for use with modern wood-engravings', it may be criticised for a looseness of fitting (which is almost certainly to be laid at the door of the typefounder – the 14-point is better). But its stout scrifs, robust modelling and generous proportions seem admirably suited to the requirements of its owner, Robert Gibbings, a man built on similarly generous lines and one of the most likeable figures of the whole private press movement.

James Mosley is Visiting Professor in the Department of Typography and Graphic Communication at the University of Reading, where he has lectured on the history of letterforms and related subjects since 1964. In 1999, he retired as Librarian of the St Bride Printing Library (London), a post he had held since 1958. During that time he was a founding member of the Printing Historical Society and the first editor of its *Journal*. He is currently a faculty member in the Rare Book School, University of Virginia, Charlottesville, and in the Ecole de l'Institut d'histoire du livre, Lyon. He is a Senior Research Fellow in the Institute of English Studies, University of London. Mosley's research interests broadly follow several lines that include Italian inscriptional lettering 1400–1600, traditional letterforms in England from 1700, and the history of typefounding.

NOTES

1. Robert Gibbings, 'Memories of Eric Gill', *The Book Collector*, vol. 2 (1953), p. 95.

2. 'The Golden Cockerel Press', *The Colophon*, no. 7 (September 1931).

3. Nicolas Barker, *Stanley Morison* (1972), p. 197. On the progress of the Perpetua type, see also *Fine Print*, vol. 8, no. 3 (July 1982), pp. 90–95.

4. The first two are quoted in full in Barker, *Stanley Morison*, pp. 233–35. The originals are at the University Library, Cambridge.

5. H. W. Caslon & Co. Ltd., Inventory of punches (St Bride Printing Library).

ABCD abcdef

ghijklm EFGH

HIKL nopqrst

vwxyz MNOP

QRST *abcdefghi*

jklmnopq UVW

XYZ *rstvwxyz*

Eric Gill's Golden Cockerel type, the digitized version from ITC

A Note on the Golden Cockerel Type

BY CHRISTOPHER SANDFORD

Christopher Sandford took over the Golden Cockerel Press from Robert Gibbings in 1932. This first-hand account of the press's later years, also from Matrix 2 (1982), *complements the previous essay by James Mosley. It also serves to set the scene for the following essay, about the digital revival of the press's proprietary type.*

The Golden Cockerel Press, which took its name from the Ballet '*Le Coq d'Or*', was founded in 1920 by Harold Taylor, as a Co-operative Society for the benefit of young authors seeking publication for their early work. In the words of its first prospectus, 'The Press is a Co-operative Society for the printing and publishing of books. Its members are their own craftsmen, and will produce their books themselves in their own communal workshops without recourse to paid and irresponsive labour.' (Shades of William Morris!)

Authors printing under Taylor's direction appear to have included A. E. Coppard, H. T. Wade Grey, J. D. Beresford, Havelock Ellis, Martin Armstrong, Richard Hughes and Peter Quennell. In its initial form the Co-operative was short-lived. 'Scribblers' do not take kindly to the slow process of setting type by hand; and the attempted sale by an unknown press of unknown works by unknown authors is not an economic proposition. Nevertheless some of their books were reprinted two or three times; any stock remaining at a certain time was taken over for sale by Jonathan Cape; and the foundation stones of several successful literary careers had been laid.

By 1922 the Press announced its ability to undertake 'fine letterpress printing of all kinds . . . and the complete production of all kinds of privately issued books and booklets generally'.

In 1924 the Golden Cockerel was taken over by the engraver Robert Gibbings, and the co-operative spirit was continued, but with changed emphasis. A prospectus from 1925 explains that, 'The members of the Golden Cockerel Press would like to point out that they are a group of artists and craftsman more interested in the aesthetic than the commercial aspect of book production'.

A friend and neighbour of Robert Gibbings was Eric Gill. Together they formulated their conception of a book beautifully printed in a limited edition on hand-made paper and illustrated by the imaginative young engravers of their day.

As it had previously done with young authors, the Press was then able to provide up-and-coming fellow-artists with the means to develop their techniques.

During the first seven years that Gibbings ran the Press, all the books were hand-set in Caslon's Old Face type, but in 1931 the new 'Golden Cockerel' type, designed for the Press by Eric Gill, was ready and used in many books, of which two of the greatest were *The Four Gospels* (1931) using the new type in its 18-point size, illustrated with sixty-five engravings by Eric Gill, and *Twelfth Night* (1932) in 14-point with twenty-nine wood-engravings, printed in colour, by Eric Ravilious.

All Gill's types – Perpetua, the Golden Cockerel, Felicity, Joanna, or Gill Sans – are variants of Eric Gill's own very lovely, very personal hand-lettering. Following the precepts of William Morris, the illustrations favoured by the Press were wood-engravings, in the medium which was presumed to combine best with the kindred surface-printing of type. Indeed, given a sympathetic paper, a skilled pressman could print even the finest wood-engravings at one impression with the type. While it is important that type in combination with finely cut engravings should not be so 'bold' as to 'kill' the artists' work, it is also important that it should not be too light to make a comfortable combination. While Gill's Perpetua is probably better suited to combine with line-engravings in copper, etchings, mezzotints, or watercolour paintings, the 'Golden Cockerel' type undoubtedly fulfilled Gill's intention for it to combine most charmingly with surface printing from wood-blocks.

Reverting to the history of the Golden Cockerel Press, 1932 was at the end of the hey-day of the so-called private presses and even the most successful of their 'masters', under-capitalised and finding themselves unable to sell books during the sales-stagnation of the great depression, which at the time we called 'the Slump', sought to extricate themselves from their current and future liabilities by selling out.

I was then a partner in the old Chiswick Press, founded by Charles Whittingham in the eighteenth century and then still going strong. My desire to choose, design and print books similar to the limited editions of the private presses brought me, post haste, to the rescue. It has been recorded that I offered to take over both the Gregynog Press and the Nonesuch, but without result. In the latter case I remember having studied Meynell's accounts and submitted an offer, but I was presumably out-bid by George Macy of the Limited Editions Club of New York. On the other hand, Robert Gibbings was happy to accept my offer for the Golden Cockerel Press, which I brought to London, lock, stock and barrel, and housed in the premises of the Chiswick Press.

Uninhibited by the strictures of some die-hard arts and crafts purists, I did not hesitate to use mechanical composition for a large proportion of the six score books I published during the quarter century that I ran the Press. The wide range of typefaces adapted for Monotype Composition by Stanley Morison gave me the variety of typographic effect that I so much desired. Of the 120 'Golden Cockerels' that I designed and printed during the twenty-five years that I ran the Press, fifteen were hand-set in Golden Cockerel type; four in 18-point Perpetua (too large for Monotype composition), and the rest set by Monotype, viz: forty-five in Perpetua; thirty-three in Caslon's Old Face (including many in the 18-point which I was able to set mechanically); seven each in Bembo and Poliphilus, and Gill Sans; and one each in Blado, Cochin, Bodoni, and Bell. The operator would, as far as possible, maintain close, even spacing, but I always read all the galley proofs myself and marked all the paragraphs which required to be 'put through the stick' to achieve a standard of composition equal to that of hand-setting.

With special reference to the 'Golden Cockerel' type, the Press paid Gill a fee of £500 or £600 to design it. The mats and punches were cut by Caslon's free on the understanding that the type should always be cast by them. At first they kept the mats and punches, but, about 1935, the Press discovered that Caslon's were proposing to cast a fount of the type for a third party. So that this should not happen, we removed the mats and punches (with Caslon's agreement) and lodged them in a bank. With the kind permission of Mr H. Myers, they are now being housed and cared for on behalf of the Golden Cockerel Press by the Cambridge University Press.

For hand-composition the type is available in two sizes – the 'English' (roughly 14-point) roman caps and lower case with italic lower case only (for use with roman caps) and the 'Great Primer' (roughly 18-point) roman caps and lower case (no italics). These types being rather large and bold on their body, the Press used to 2-point lead the 18-point and 1-point lead the 14-point. There is also titling in 24-point and 36-point.

While it was possible to use the 14-point very satisfactorily on page sizes varying from 12½ x 7½ in. right down to 9 x 4½ in., the 18-point (which corresponds in appearance to 24-point in other faces) seemed to require a page at least 13½ x 9½ in. or 13½ x 9 in. – *The Four Gospels* size, for which it had been designed. Another, more recent, very satisfctory, example of its use was in *Songs and Poems of John Dryden* (1957), page 14½ x 10 in. Both sizes also called for adequate margins. (Very roughly, I used to divide the page laterally into six and devote 1/6 to the inner margin, 3/6 to the type measure, and 2/6 to the foredge margin – similarly 'up and down', the head would be 1/6 (after trim) and the tail 2/6 – though sometimes more, according to the shape of the page.)

It may be useful just to record that the history of the Golden Cockerel Press is largely recorded in four Bibliographies: *Chanticleer* for April 1921 – August 1936; *Pertelote* for October 1936 to April 1943; *Cockalorum* for June 1943 to December 1949; and *Cock-a-Hoop* for December 1949 to December 1961. The first three I compiled and published at the Golden Cockerel Press. The fourth volume (compiled by David Chambers and myself) was published in 1976 by the Private Libraries Association for the Golden Cockerel Press.

Christopher Sanford ran the Golden Cockerel Press from 1932 to 1959.

ROMAN

abcdefghijklmnopqrstuvwxyz
ABCDEFGHIJKLMNOPQRSTUVW&XYZ
1234567890

ITALIC

abcdefghijklmnopqrstuvwxyz
ABCDEFGHIJKLMNOPQRSTUVW&XYZ
1234567890

Saving Face: the ITC Golden Cockerel Type

BY RODERICK CAVE

The creation of ITC Golden Cockerel was an important project in the digital revival of typefaces originally created by hand in metal. In Matrix 17 (1997), Roderick Cave describes how Eric Gill's well-known but rarely available typeface was converted into a new medium.

My first contact with Christopher Sandford came in the late 1950s, when I wrote to him with an enquiry about the post-war use of the proprietary type designed for Golden Cockerel by Eric Gill. His kindly and informative reply set me off on a lifetime of interest in the Press, so when I recently saw an announcement of its revival as a digital design for the International Typeface Corporation, I naturally decided to indulge myself and buy the font. It was, after all (I persuaded myself) the first time any private press typeface had been digitised and made available commercially, apart from William Morris's Troy type.[1]

To be sure, Gill's proprietary design was not the first typeface used by Golden Cockerel; nor was it the most extensively used after the face was cut by the Caslon foundry. Before Robert Gibbings bought the Press at Waltham St Lawrence from Hal and Gay Taylor in 1924, all the books had been printed in original Caslon Old Face, and the publicity (advertisements, dust-jackets, and some spine labels) in Caslon and Forum Titling. In the earliest books, much of the setting was in 11-point or even 9-point Caslon, though from 1922 onwards much more was set in 14-point and 18-point type, and the Press ceased using the 11-point for several years. In 1927, needing further supplies of Caslon type, Gibbings went back to H. W. Caslon & Co. and ill-advisedly bought more: of Lining Caslon type, just on the market. This modification greatly shortened the length of the descenders in the original Caslon Old Face, so that what was in effect a type the same size as 14-point Old Face could be cast on a 12-point body. In addition it was provided with modern style numerals which would align better with capitals in place of the non-aligning old style numerals of the original Old Face. The arguments which the Caslon Foundry had put forward at its introduction were also advanced by Golden Cockerel (in its Spring 1927 List) as a reason for preferring to use it for the *Psalms* of David: 'one of the chief aims of this volume is to use as large a face of type as is possible within the limited proportions of the book. For this reason the type selected is Messrs. Caslon's recent modification of their famous "Old Face" type, in which the descenders have been shortened, thus allowing a much larger face to the same size type body. This new 12-point is as readable as the old 14-point while taking considerably less space' – an argument persuasive enough for publishers of cheap series of textbooks, no doubt, but a very odd one from a private press.

A reviewer of that book[2] commented on the ugliness of the type, but several other Golden Cockerel volumes were also disfigured by its use. *The Twelve Moneths,* for instance, showed a clumsy mixture of a smaller size of the Old Face (for the Glossary) with the Lining Type; and the old style numerals would certainly have been preferable in that volume. Lining numerals were also used in *The Chester Play of the Deluge* and in *Micro-Cosmographie.* Coppard's *Count Stefan* was also spoiled by the use of the Caslon Lining type. Eric Gill's ideas on type had a lot of influence with both Moira and Robert Gibbings at the time, but whether he had persuaded them the Lining Caslon was a good idea is uncertain – probably not, since in the books he commissioned them to print for him, he stuck with the original Caslon Old Face in 12-point. As far as I know, Gill never had any of his own work printed in this debased version of Caslon.

Rather than lose face, accept that its purchase had been a wrong decision, and abandon its use, or perhaps because Gibbings could not actually afford to replace it by Old Face at a time when the preparation of the proprietary Golden Cockerel type was in process, he also used Caslon Lining type in *Utopia* and in the *Phaedo.* In these, Gill's superb engraved lettering, and the masterly use of several sizes of Caslon capitals, plus the device of putting 2-point leading between the lines, effectually disguised the essential weakness of the design. But this expedient also made it no more economical in use than 14-point Caslon Old Face, set solid, would have been. Caslon Lining type was silently abandoned; it had always been a poor choice for a private press.

While Robert Gibbings ran the Press, Golden Cockerel used no other founts than the two versions of Caslon, and the face designed for him by Eric Gill which has now been revived by the International Typeface Corporation. But once printing for the Press had been transferred to the Chiswick Press premises, Christopher Sandford and his partners were more experimental. To gain the use of the proprietary face had been one reason to buy Golden Cockerel, of course, but in the hard days of the thirties they could not afford hand-setting alone; the Chiswick Press needed work for its Monotype men too. Nor was the proprietary Golden Cockerel type the only contemporary design by Eric Gill they could use. For Gill's *The Lord's Song* which they issued in January 1934, it was entirely appropriate that they should choose to set it in the 14-point Perpetua face which had just been acquired by the Chiswick Press. Sandford really preferred

Perpetua to the Golden Cockerel design, and thereafter made much more frequent use of Perpetua in the books he designed. From time to time he still continued to specify the use of Caslon – but normally in the Monotype version, no longer the beautiful foundry type. Had the repertoire of the Chiswick Press been larger, he would certainly have employed other faces, but even within their limited range he specified many other types – Scholderer's New Hellenic whenever Greek was called for; Garamond, Poliphilus, Bembo, Baskerville.

In the later years when running Golden Cockerel alone, and not necessarily limited by the rather conservative range of faces held at the Chiswick Press, at a time his need to match the colour of wood-engravings had gone because he was now using different illustrations often printed by collotype, Sandford's style changed. On the one hand, he made more use of the Golden Cockerel typeface once more, with some very successful books. And for others he became more playful, more experimental; particularly in his use of titling founts. One finds the use of faces such as Imprint Shadow, or Pharos Titling, or Goudy Open. The effect of these, and of the composition faces (such as Pastonchi, or Perpetua or Poliphilus) on the soft-sized papers the Press was using in the early fifties clearly was not to everybody's taste, but was an effect he liked.

Overall, when one analyses the typography of Golden Cockerel books, three type designs dominate. Caslon was used in 110 books (in original Old Face, the 'bad' Caslon Lining and in the Monotype version); a little more than half its output. Gill's designs (Golden Cockerel, Perpetua, and Gill Sans) were used in eighty-two, with the Monotype versions of Francesco Griffo's classic old faces (Poliphilus and Bembo) used in seventeen. These were the mainstays of the Press; other old face or transitional designs were used in but five books; modern faces in only two. In this, Golden Cockerel was characteristic of its time and the class of work it produced.

Used well, Gill's design for Golden Cockerel was one which could look magnificent, printed on the papers and by the methods for which it was designed. James Mosley's article[3] in *Matrix 2*, and the study of the production of *The Four Gospels* by John Dreyfus[4] say all that really needs to be said about it. I had been sad when the type dropped out of use; I was concerned that during the years Thomas Yoseloff had it in store at Bentalls (and rather clearly had no idea what to do with it) it would be destroyed before anyone who knew what they were about was aware of it. There was a sense of relief when the Rampant Lions Press took over the founts, and the punches, mats and drawings also passed into better care. And Will and Sebastian Carter had shown again just how good the face could look.

However much one appreciates the chance to experiment personally with a version of this august type, one rather wishes that the International Typeface Corporation had done a little more preparatory work than the account[5] in *U&lc* suggests was in fact the case. Or perhaps what I seek is a more accurate and informative account of what the new designers actually did once they had consulted James Mosley, Sebastian Carter and John Dreyfus, and looked at the original drawings and patterns at Cambridge. For there is little doubt that what is being made available owes more to Gill than to Golden Cockerel, and that the designs have been modified in many ways. The most obvious are both the results of very sensible marketing decisions. The first was to provide a set of ornaments and an initial alphabet which *U&lc* says 'represents Gill's style of wood letters, including the exuberant flourished serifs and splendid lombardic stresses found in commissions from the Golden Cockerel, St Dominic's and Curwen Presses and simple bookplates and devices developed through his life with letters.' Some of them I find charming. Others rapidly become tiresome, as I suspect Mr Gill found himself, but no doubt they will fill a niche and we shall encounter sub-Chaucerian motifs in all sorts of unlikely places.

The second addition to the fount was entirely predictable. In the twenties, it was entirely acceptable for a private press to adopt a face with the conceit of using upright roman caps married to lower case italic *à la* Aldus, but that's not a way to commercial success today, so the designers have provided italic caps 'devised by studying Gill's other types and alphabets, along with his numerous lettering projects, including stone engravings, to ensure that the set of capitals would complement the lowercase and relate well to the existing roman' as *U&lc* put it. Quite so; a look at the face will indicate how successful they have been in this.

The more I look at Gill's work, the more I come to think that he completely misunderstood the true nature of italic, and though the new caps are very much in the spirit of Gill's own lettering, I don't feel that the revised italic fount is a fount of enormous importance; one I will want to use regularly or even frequently. The initials have more attraction, and no doubt a good many of us will play with these, and establish that it's a lot harder to get the superb effects possessed by the books produced through the hands of Cooper, Gibbings and Gill. The dangers present in playing with some of Gill's ornaments were demonstrated when a set of flowers was marketed in the fifties; will we do better today? I rather doubt it.

On the other hand, in some sizes, the Golden Cockerel type was a splendid, majestic fount; whether printed on smooth Basingwerk or on a rough paper with a lot of ink-spread. In both cases it could look good, but when used for scholarly books (like Owen Rutter's *John Fryer*, printed but not published by the

Press) its lack of a range of sizes often caused difficulties. Even in such bread-and-butter work as the title-page for *The Hansom Cab & the Pigeons,* or the advertising booklet printed for *The Cumberland Hotel* one can see some of the shifts to which Christopher Sandford (or the Chiswick Press compositors) were reduced. Even though the face looks much better in larger sizes than small, there are occasions when it is necessary to use both large and small, and we now have the opportunity. Now, when will someone issue a digitised version of the Doves Press type?[6]

Roderick Cave is perhaps the most frequent contributor to *Matrix,* with articles in every issue since 1983. His career as a Professor of Library and Information Studies has taken him for long spells to the West Indies, West Africa, New Zealand, and Singapore as well as Britain and the United States. Now retired, he lives in England. Founder-editor of the annual *Private Press Books* in 1959, Cave maintained close contacts with the fine printing world throughout his travels, and has written extensively about private press history (particularly the Golden Cockerel Press) in other American, British, and German journals as well as *Matrix.* A selection of these was published by the British Library as *Fine Printing and Private Presses* in 2001. His book *The Private Press* (1971, 2nd ed 1983) remains a standard reference in the field. Cave's other books include *Typographia Naturalis, a History of Nature Printing* (jointly with Geoffrey Wakeman, 1968), *Printing and the Book Trade in the West Indies* (1987), *Chinese Paper Offerings* (1998), and a *History of the Golden Cockerel Press,* written jointly with Sarah Manson and published in 2003.

NOTES

1. At the time I was ignorant of the digitization of another of Gill's faces: the Aries type which he designed for the Stourton Press, available from an American source.

2. A reviewer wrote that the book was printed in a large type 'apparently Caslon, though with deformity of shortened descenders' in the *Saturday Review of Literature,* 12 May 1928.

3. James Mosley, 'Eric Gill and the Golden Cockerel Type' (p. 131); supplemented on pp. 139 by 'A Note on the Golden Cockerel Type' by Christopher Sandford.

4. *A Typographical Masterpiece; an account by John Dreyfus of Eric Gill's collaboration with Robert Gibbings in producing the Golden Cockerel Press edition of 'The Four Gospels' in 1931.* San Francisco: Book Club of California, 1990, especially Chapter 2, pp. 12–29.

5. 'ITC Golden Cockerel' by Joyce Rutter Kaye, James Mosley and Dave Farey *U&lc* v. 23 no. 2, Fall 1996, pp. 24–27. The article provides a good conspectus of the faces available in the four Title, Roman, Italic and Initials founts.

6. At the time I first wrote this article for *Matrix,* I had not seen the splendid specimen which was published by ITC and gives the best showing of their new type: *Golden Cockerel Type: A Collection of Essays on Eric Gill and his Type for the Golden Cockerel Press in Celebration of the Launch of ITC Golden Cockerel* New York: International Typeface Corporation, 1996.

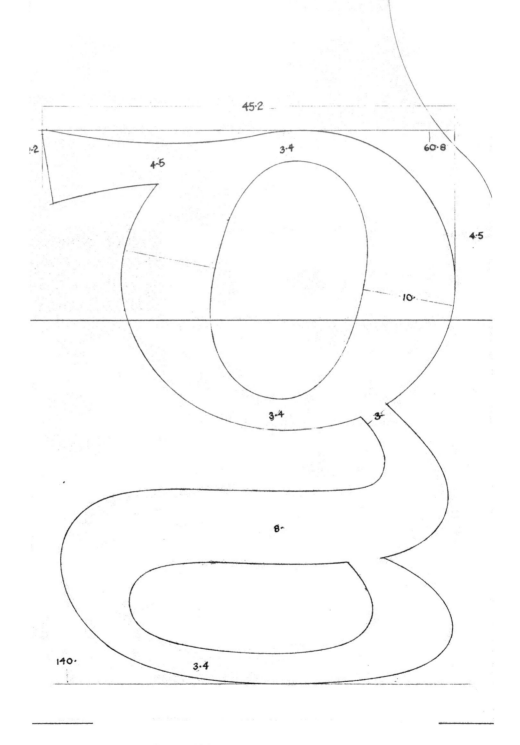

1. Final type drawing for Series 610 lower-case g

Two Oxford Bible Types

BY PAUL LUNA

Creating a readable type for a Bible is an exacting task, rarely appreciated by the book's students and readers. Paul Luna, in Matrix 17 *(1997), contrasts Jan van Krimpen's demanding but idiosyncratic Bible type and Harry Carter's bolder attempt, both for the Oxford University Press in the 1950s; both, eventually, left in the dust of technology.*

Van Krimpen and Oxford's White Elephant

In 1939 John Johnson, Printer to the University, asked Charles Batey, then Assistant Printer, to draft a request to Jan van Krimpen, the distinguished Dutch designer, to suggest type designs for setting Bibles. The starting point was that for setting Bible text, standard Monotype faces (Plantin, Imprint, Times are mentioned) had not always been successful, and were not specifically designed for Bible work. (The fact that Collins, a rival publisher of the Authorised Version, had a proprietary design in the Fontana Bible Face was also noted.) Sizes were explicitly stated: 4½-, 5½-, 6-, 7½-, 8½- point – 'a complete series of Bible founts.' Van Krimpen replied immediately and seized upon Batey's criticism of existing founts: 'the small sizes [are] mere adaptation of founts designed for some other purpose.' (This was hardly fair to Monotype – their efforts in optical scaling of Bembo, Plantin, Garamond and Times New Roman were exemplary.)

Van Krimpen then expounded on an idea which was to have a profound effect on the whole project:

> a large 'x' height can only be obtained by sacrificing much of the ascenders and descenders. By adapting standard founts, however, too much of the descenders is being sacrificed since sacrificing equal parts on both sides would involve the cutting of new capitals, etc. Nothing is being gained on the width of the capitals which, exactly for a Bible face, could easily be done.[1]

Van Krimpen went on to request that OUP make up its mind in respect of the set width for each body size, knowing that this ratio determined the relative widths of letters as they fitted into the matrix-case arrangement. Batey conferred with Geoffrey Cumberlege (Deputy Publisher in OUP's London office), who expressed support.[2] An elegant dance ensued with Batey requesting that Van

CHAPTER 8

T HESE are now the chief of their fathers,
and this is the genealogy of them that
went up with me from Babylon, in the
reign of Artaxerxes the king.
2 Of the sons of Phinehas; Gershom: of
the sons of Ithamar; Daniel: of the sons
of David; Hattush.

2. 8/7-pt. Plantin 110

CHAPTER 8

T HESE are now the chief of their fathers,
and this is the genealogy of them that
went up with me from Babylon, in the reign
of Artaxerxes the king.
2 Of the sons of Phinehas; Gershom: of the sons of Ithamar; DANIEL: OF THE SONS? .   Ezra 8, 1–2

3. Photographic print, October 1947,
reduced from an original drawing by Van
Krimpen now in the University Library,
Amsterdam

CHAPTER 8

THESE are now the chief of their
fathers, and this is the genealogy
of them that went up with me from
Babylon, in the reign of Artaxerxes
the king.

4. The same passage in type from the first
trial page

Krimpen suggest his fee, evincing the lofty reply that he had no idea (being on a salary from the printing firm of Enschedé of Haarlem), and the suggestion that Stanley Morison be called on to propose a sum.

Van Krimpen interestingly sent Batey proofs of the Haarlemmer Bible type which he was then working on (this was a 14-point Didot typeface, (figure 5 on page 152). The proof was produced by drawing lines of characters four times over-size, and then photographically reducing the drawing. Because of Van Krimpen's perfectionist style of drawing, this mimics a typeset page won-derfully.[3]

The war put the project into abeyance. Some six years later it resumed, and when in 1947 Van Krimpen visited Oxford and the subject of Bible types arose again, he expressed further interest and Batey had a breakdown of the exact number of matrices required for each size (now 4½-, 5-, 6-, 7-point) costed. A formal proposal to have the face designed and manufactured was made to the Finance Committee on 8 July 1947: the four founts would cost £3500, and approval was forthcoming.[4] One month later Batey (now Printer) confirmed the sizes required, and enclosed a page of a school Bible set in 8/7-point Plantin 110 (figure 2). 'It is essential', he wrote, 'that the design shall permit us to achieve an extent of exactly 896 pages.' The 8/7-point Plantin is a pleasant page, with good overall colour. The descenders, one imagines Van Krimpen noting with disapproval, were horribly cropped, while the capitals were large relative to the lower case. A second sample was sent in September 1947, set in Times Semibold 421.

Meanwhile Batey had discussed production possibilities with both Morison and Silcock, Monotype's General Manager at Salfords. Morison, he reported, 'was most pessimistic . . . the matrix department of Monotype is overwhelmed . . . mak[ing] good the war losses and [replacing] the worn-out matrices of the whole of Europe.' An appalling five-year delay in production was envisaged, confirmed by Silcock: 'when this can be done is almost impossible to foresee' – Monotype having in hand a whole range of Arabic and other faces for the Near East and for Indian dialects. Van Krimpen, undeterred by the delay, proposed that he should design the face and accept payment as and when OUP could get it manufactured. 'Van Krimpen is obviously a great man', exclaimed a delighted (or relieved) Cumberlege.

The great man moved fast. On 22 October 1947 he sent 'two little prints' – photographic reproductions, to a type size of 7-point, of 'my first drawings for your Bible face' (figure 3). This 'little print' shows how precise Van Krimpen's working method was. Here is, almost completely formed, the typeface that was eventually called Sheldon. Everything that is right – and wrong – with the face is already present.

The preciseness of cut, the sharp contrast between the thick and thin strokes, the equally truncated ascenders and descenders – Van Krimpen's first thoughts about a Bible face, expressed five years earlier, have come to pass. Unlike his earlier Haarlemmer type, which was sturdy and bold, and unlike the Plantin and Times Semibold specimens he had been sent, this face has a preciousness and flimsiness about it that seem to run counter to its intended use in small sizes for compact setting. Van Krimpen might not have produced drawings for so small a point size before; his working method for Lutetia, described by Dreyfus, was to draw trial lines for the 12-point fount at about five times the intended size, relying on the skill of his punch-cutter to provide the necessary optical scaling for smaller sizes.

In short, it can be argued that Sheldon represents, as Walter Tracy has implied, yet another manifestation of a perfect typeface that somehow existed within Van Krimpen, and which all his designs – Lutetia, Spectrum, Romulus, Sheldon – seem to be endowing with physical presence.[5] This was a Van Krimpen typeface first and foremost, in the squat proportions of an OUP Bible face.

'He left me with some very nice drawings', wrote Cumberlege to Batey on 13 November 1947. The Printer asked his technical staff what they thought of the proposals. Mr Smith, Mr Stewart, Mr Fathers and Mr Ayres duly commented.[6] Their remarks show a wonderful grasp of what makes a typeface tick. They selected preferred letters from the variants in Van Krimpen's drawing: 'The italic seems over-condensed.' 'Crossbar of A just a shade too high.' 'In italic, does the lower-case s appear to stop the flow of the line?' 'I do not myself like the abrupt finish to the tail of figure 2.'

Ken Stewart singled out the lower case f a g r for particular comment: 'f: top curve too flat. a: beginning a little uncertain. g: top of the g in reign and tail of first g in genealogy would seem to be the combination. r: arm appears too cramped.'

Ayres criticised the light weight of line – 'it would be better strengthened to accomodate the colour for 6-point and below' – and suggests the weight of 7-point Times 327.

There is no indication that Van Krimpen ever received these comments direct. Batey instead asked Vivian Ridler, shortly to join the Press from Faber & Faber as Assistant Printer, to comment on the drawings. (Batey delegated this to Ridler in much the way Johnson had to Batey.) 'I have already submitted it to one or two of the people here. But most of all I would value your own opinion,' he wrote. Ridler replied, perceptively but more circumspectly than the craftsmen at Oxford. In particular he 'hesitate[d] before asking Van Krimpen to increase the weight of the line.' Ridler felt Times 'errs a bit on the dazzle side, whereas this seems very good for general colour.'

Yet this discussion on colour ignored the heavy appearance of the stalwarts of OUP Bible publishing, the Bold Face Prayer Book and the Clarendon Reference Bible, set in an Antique Old Style – and the fact that at this time both Cambridge and the King's Printer were setting excellent Bible pages in 6½-point Times New Roman. All of these were strong without being at all dazzling.

Finally, in April 1948 a fee was agreed – '2 guineas per letter character drawn and approved'. Van Krimpen expressed the hope in November that the drawings would be complete by 'the end of the year.' By February 1949 Monotype were proposing to produce the typeface within a year of receipt of the drawings, but by 30 May 1949 Van Krimpen was still in the process of drawing, and rather grumpily rejected a proposal that drawings for roman caps and lower case be submitted ahead of the italic. In August 1949 he announced completion, and stated that he would bring the drawings himself. They were delivered on 21 October, and on 26 October Ridler and Van Krimpen discussed the project at Salfords with John Tarr of Monotype.

5. Layout by Van Krimpen. The setting appears in Dreyfus, *The Work of Jan van Krimpen*

Silence then descended: three months passed without word from Monotype. Van Krimpen was paid part of his fee in the form of a Bruce Rogers Lectern Bible.[7] The rest was paid in suits – Van Krimpen had these made by his tailor in London and OUP paid the bills   or in cash passed direct to Van Krimpen in London to avoid exchange-control regulations.

Another three months passed. Finally, a tiny photographic proof of some 38 characters appeared.[8] Drawings had in fact begun on 17 March 1950 and had been completed in a fortnight. The results elicited a 'complaint' from Harry Knight of Monotype's Matrix Factory, which was reworked by Silcock and forwarded to Batey. These were the comments, not of a craftsman who used type, but of a skilled engineer who knew how to make type. They were concerned with widths, kerns, and the avoidance of shapes which demanded extraordinarily fine tolerances in punch-cutting and casting. Tollingly, Knight points out that

> the so-called 'hollow' on otherwise flat tops and bottoms of some letters is so small that it will probably disappear in manufacture, and not be visible in print. It is recommended that this 'hollow' be eliminated and so make easier any adjustment to the punches.

Also of concern were the narrow unit widths of f j : ; ? ! which necessitated considerable kerns. Increasing unit widths would speed punch-cutting because standard 0.053-inch mill tools could be used rather than the special, smaller 0.040-inch.

Presumably because of the prestige of both client and designer, it was Morison himself who passed these comments on to Oxford. Rather disingenuously he remarks: 'I don't know if my rather casual observations are of any use to you'.

---

28 Hitherto is the end of the matter. As for me Daniel, my cogitations much troubled me, and my countenance changed in me: but I kept the matter in my heart.

CHAPTER 8

IN the third year of the reign of king Belshazzar a vision appeared unto me, even unto me Daniel, after that which appeared unto me at the first.
2 And I saw in a vision; and it came to pass, when I saw, that I was at Shushan in the palace, which is in the province of Elam;

concerning the daily sacrifice, and the transgression of desolation, to give both the sanctuary and the host to be trodden under foot?
14 And he said unto me, Unto two thousand and three hundred days; then shall the sanctuary be cleansed.
15 ¶ And it came to pass, when I, even I Daniel, had seen the vision, and sought for the meaning, then, behold, there stood before me as the appearance of a man.
16 And I heard a man's voice between the banks of Ulai, which called, and said, Gabriel, make this man to understand the

6. Trial page for the Sheldon Bible. 7-pt. Sheldon set solid

---

17 THESE were the words of the Lord GOD to me: "O Man, speak to the Israelites in allegory and **3** parable. Tell them that these are the words of the Lord GOD:
'A great eagle[1] broad of wing and with long pinions,
In full plumage, and richly patterned, came to Lebanon.
4 He took the very top of a cedar tree; he plucked the highest of its twigs, And carrying it off to a land of trade,

you not know what this means? The king of Babylon came to Jerusalem, took its king and its officers and had them brought to him at Babylon. He **13** took a prince of the royal line and made a covenant with him, exacting from him a solemn oath. He took away the chief men of the country so that it should become a lowly kingdom unable **14** to rise again, but should keep the covenant and ⁷stand by it.⁷ But the prince **15** rebelled against him, and sent messen-

7. Trial page, November 1951, for a new translation of the Bible. 7-pt. Sheldon on 8-pt.

But he rallies and encourages Batey to 'instruct the Corporation to get on with the job.' Interestingly, he comments on avoiding kerns, but 'not because the machine cannot do it . . . but because kerns in small sizes . . . tend to compromise legibility.' The photographic proofs elicited comments from Ayres and his men at Oxford similar to the reaction to the drawings. Monotype's 'remarks from the works' were endorsed by the OUP technicians: lower case c a r f p y g and capital C were criticised. Ayres wondered if a slight thickening of weight would occur when electros were made.

Batey seems to have wanted to make light of these comments. Only the bulbous p, tail of y, and lower case g were commented on, rather vaguely, in a letter to Silcock. By September 1950 trial matrices were ready for casting some ten characters (Knight did not like the resulting g, and demanded that the punch be remeasured). Ayres at Oxford still objected to the 'ugly cap C, design of g and p' on sight of this specimen, and was worried about the width of a fount that had a 7-point body and 7½-point set width. Finally, in October Van Krimpen visited Salfords and saw the proof. He did not like the lower case g either.

It is at this point that a certain antipathy to the whole production method surfaces in Van Krimpen's comments, when he proposed having some punches recut by hand at Enschedé:

> I should like to direct our punch-cutter on the g and on the f as well. So if you could let me have either the matrices or a dozen castings I could see what could be done. I think S.M. agrees less than ever before whereas I more than ever before am of the opinion that shortcomings of this kind can best be corrected by hand . . .

He then defends the curiously squashed f by referring to his 'generally speaking, good system of having equal height above and under the l.c. x. This system leaves little room for the fully developed f' And later, more forcibly:

> I meant to offer . . . to have them put in order, under my own eyes, by my own punch-cutter. . . . When we talk of punches cut by hand we use terms like 'a hair or even less' or 'the tiniest little trifle' &c. I am sure they could not convey or mean anything to the people of the Pierpontion [sic] workshop who use brobdingnagian drawings and conjurors' wands and then talk of 'tens' and 'thous'.[9]

Van Krimpen here glides over the difference between the punch-cutter working as an artist-craftsman under his direct supervision and the sequence of manufacturing at Monotype, where a worn or damaged matrix would have to be replaced with an exact duplicate. The type drawing was the master, and all subsequent operations in the Matrix Factory were mechanical, controlled by its dimensions. This definitive style of drawing was distrusted by Van Krimpen: in *A letter to Philip Hofer on certain problems connected with the mechanical cutting of punches* he explains how the designer's initial sketch 'being nearest the conception and in fact part and parcel of the conception itself, is the best.'[10] 'Tens' are presumably tenths of a thousandth of an inch – showing the fine engineering tolerances to which Monotype worked. The characters Van Krimpen criticises are exactly the f and g that had attracted most criticism earlier – none of which seems to have been reported back to the designer.

By March 1951 proof pages were available, which Morison had seen and commented on, his only criticism being the roman and italic cap W. This was indeed amended by Van Krimpen, and reamended by the Monotype Type Drawing Office to avoid a clearance of less than six thousandths of an inch between serifs. Ayres was happier with f and g, but spotted the imbalance between the wide h u n d, and narrow r t s. He also indicates that Van Krimpen's system might not be working by suggesting casting on a 7¼- or 7½- point body – and was still unhappy about the strength of line, hoping that when set and printed 'a little more "colour" would be achieved.'

Ridler was now more forthcoming in his own comments on the face. Morison's comments on italic W were of course agreed with, and Z c r and italic f criticised. Ironically, the italic fount, used only for occasional words in Bible setting, was deemed 'the most satisfactory'.

By April 1951 Batey was putting a brave face on things: 'on the whole I think the fount is very promising, although a certain amount of tidying up will have to be done.' This tidying up was discussed by Morison – armed with Van Krimpen's comments – Silcock, Ridler and Batey at Salfords in mid-April 1951. Alternatives to the Van Krimpen design had already been discussed (as early as May 1949), including a 7¼-point version of Monotype Bembo Semibold 509, but these plans did not materialise. It must have been with considerable relief that trial Bible pages were set in the new typeface in April 1951 (at Monotype, for matrices were not yet available for release). These were cast as electros and printed on lightweight paper to provide a better guide to final appearance.

With hindsight the type looks precise but cramped – far less appealing than the more open 6½-point Times that Cambridge and the King's Printer were using for Bibles of similar size. Ayres was still unhappy about W and Z and lower-case s, but a sense of fatigue seems to have finally overtaken Ridler and Batey. 'We feel there is little to be gained by further adjustments', he wrote to Monotype in August. 'Will you now proceed on the assumption that the fount is in its final state?'

Monotype did so, and matrices and equipment were delivered by the end of 1951, its Monotype designation being OUP Bible Face Series 552. The name Sheldon (an early benefactor of the Press) had been settled on by Batey and Ridler (without consulting Van Krimpen, which peeved him).[11] The Sheldon Bible was set in 1953 and published in 1954. It made exactly 896 pages, as specified by Batey seven years earlier. An interesting sideline was the experiments carried out in variant styles of paragraphing for prose and poetry, which predate the style of the New English Bible and Good News Bible. The final Sheldon Bible had the then conventional style of paragraphing, however. For such a protracted effort, the final results were disappointing. When set solid, as the extent dictated, Sheldon had insufficient white between the lines of type because the x-height is so large relative to the ascender height. Its appearance is both precious and crowded. In 1952 there was a desultory attempt to investigate a 9-point, but when it became clear that the 7-point drawings would produce an overlarge and 'contrasty' 9-point the plan was abandoned.

Even before publication in 1954, Batey admitted that the fount was 'a little disappointing.'[12] This was putting it mildly: no further sizes were cut, and no other book ever set in Sheldon.[13] As it was a proprietary fount, for OUP's exclusive use, no other customer was supplied: Van Krimpen reacted vigorously when Monotype proposed to recoup some of its development costs by making the typeface generally available.[14] Perhaps a witty correspondent to the *Bookseller* (R.W. David, of CUP) was right when he observed: 'Nor am I impressed by the fact that Sheldon is to be reserved for Bible printing. Because Oxford's elephant is to be kept for ceremonial and never let out to the workaday world, are we to deduce that it is white?'[15]

Sheldon shows the pitfalls of commissioning a typeface design. All the right ingredients somehow got into the wrong mix: the intended use of the type as a practical, utilitarian face and the designer's philosophy seemed at odds; there was a failure of briefing, and most significantly a failure to recognise that Van Krimpen's design came from inside his head rather than springing from the use to which the design would be put. It did not quite end in tears – but it did not end in glory either.

Harry Carter's typeface: a bolder approach

The development of another typeface for Bible setting later in the 1950s followed a quite different course from that of Sheldon. Importantly, all the design work was carried out within OUP, by Harry Carter (Archivist, Librarian and 'Type Founder'), encouraged by Vivian Ridler (who was to succeed Batey as Printer to the University in 1958). In the year in which the Sheldon Bible was published, Ridler had proposed using a version of Monotype Plantin (Old Face No. 2, Series 281) which had greater stroke contrast than the normal Series 110.[16] Ridler was

17 So all Israel went to their homes, and Rehoboam ruled over those Israelites who lived in the cities of Judah.

18   Then King Rehoboam sent out Hadoram, the commander of the forced levies, but the Israelites stoned him to death; whereupon King Rehoboam mounted his chariot in haste and fled to 19 Jerusalem. From that day to this, Israel has been in rebellion against the house of David.

11 1   When Rehoboam reached Jerusalem, he assembled the tribes of Judah and Benjamin, a hundred and eighty thousand chosen 2 warriors, to fight against Israel and recover his kingdom. But 3 the word of the LORD came to Shemaiah the man of God: 'Say to Rehoboam son of Solomon, king of Judah, and to all the 4 Israelites in Judah and Benjamin, "This is the word of the LORD: You shall not go up to make war on your kinsmen. Return to your homes, for this is my will."' So they listened to the word of the LORD and abandoned their campaign against Jeroboam.

5   Rehoboam resided in Jerusalem and built up the defences of 6 certain cities in Judah. The cities in Judah and Benjamin which 7 he fortified were Bethlehem, Etam, Tekoa, Beth-zur, Soco, 8 9 Adullam, Gath, Mareshah, Ziph, Adoraim, Lachish, Azekah, 10 11 Zorah, Aijalon, and Hebron. He strengthened the fortifications of these fortified cities, and put governors in them, as well as 12 supplies of food, oil, and wine. Also he stored shields and spears in every one of the cities, and strengthened their fortifications. Thus he retained possession of Judah and Benjamin.

13   Now the priests and the Levites throughout the whole of 14 Israel resorted to Rehoboam from all their territories; for the Levites had left all their common land and their own patrimony

8. Trial page for a proposed pocket Old Testament (Revised English Bible). 61/2-pt. Series 610 on 7-pt.

seeking a typeface that could compete on equal terms with the Times Semibold 421 that Cambridge University Press was using so successfully. He felt that Cambridge, advised by Stanley Morison, had stolen a march on Oxford in the area of Bible typography, and sought a solution in a distinctive Oxford production.   Although   trial matrices of Series 281 characters were cut in 6½-point and proofed at Monotype, OUP did not approve development of the fount.[17]

Harry Carter had been employed by Batey as a kind of project manager to move forward Morison's Fell book and other volumes of typographic history: he was to undertake research in Antwerp and act as Batey's confidant. But his talents were also turned to other areas of the Press's activities and, probably in early 1956, Carter began work on the typeface which later became known simply as Series 610 (although the terms New Emerald Bible Face and Carter Type appear in internal OUP documents). No eminent designers or advisers were called upon. This was to be an Oxford production in its entirety. Carter's aim seems to have been to match the robustness of Times Semibold without imitating its regularity. Goudy Catalogue (Monotype Series 364), excellent at 5½- and 6-point, would also have been in Ridler's and Carter's minds. A page of a Collins Bible set in Fontana Bible Face (Monotype Series 437) is still with the drawings in OUP's files.

2 CHRONICLES 1   *Solemn offering of Solomon at Gibeon*

thousand rams, *and* a thousand lambs, with their 'drink offerings, and sacrifices in abundance for all Israel:

22 And did eat and drink before the LORD on that day with great gladness. And they made Solomon the son of David king 'the second time, and 'anointed *him* unto the LORD *to be* the chief governor, and 'Zadok *to be* priest.

23 'Then Solomon sat on 'the throne of the LORD as king instead of David his father, and prospered; and all Israel obeyed him.

24 And all the princes, and the mighty men, and all the sons likewise of king David, 'submitted themselves unto Solomon the king.

25 And the LORD 'magnified Solomon exceedingly in the sight of all Israel, and 'bestowed upon him *such* royal

21 Gen. 35. 14
22 Cp. ch. 23. 1
22 1 K. 1. 33–39
23 1 K. 2. 12
23 2 Chr. 9. 8
24 Heb. *gave the hand under Solomon*
25 2 Chr. 1. 1
25 1 K. 3. 13
27 2 S. 5. 4
27 2 S. 5. 5
28 Gen. 15. 15
28 ch. 23. 1
29 2 Chr. 9. 29
29 Or, *history* Heb. *words*
29 1 S. 9. 9
29 2 S. 12. 1
29 1 S. 22. 5
29 2 Chr. 19. 2
30 Dan 4. 23

majesty as had not been on any king before him in Israel.

26 ¶ Thus David the son of Jesse reigned over all Israel.

27 And the time that he reigned over Israel *was* 'forty years; 'seven years reigned he in Hebron, and thirty and three *years* reigned he in Jerusalem.

28 And he died 'in a good old age, 'full of days, riches, and honour: and Solomon his son reigned in his stead.

29 Now the acts of David the king, 'first and last, behold, they *are* written in the 'book of 'Samuel the seer, and in the 'book of 'Nathan the prophet, and in the 'book of 'Gad the 'seer,

30 With all his reign and his might, and 'the times that went over him, and over Israel, and over all the kingdoms of the countries.

9. Trial page for the New Emerald Bible, November 1959. 61/2-pt. Series 610 set solid

10. States of Series 610 lower-case a: the first on a cancelled type drawing; the final type drawing with modifications still visible.

Carter was an expert critic of type, but had only designed one typeface for text composition, a Cyrillic version of Monotype Baskerville.[18] Series 610 is a synthesis of other type designs that are effective at small sizes. Carter had laid down firm opinions about the qualities necessary for a small-text typeface some twenty years earlier in his essay on 'Optical scale in typefounding': 'legibility is all that matters in 6- to 10-point types; so that their successful design is a technical, and not in the ordinary sense an artistic, achievement.'[19] He emphasised that a typeface should be judged on performance and readability at small size, but on elegance in display sizes. Van Krimpen deliberately reduced both ascenders and descenders in Sheldon, and used flattened curves at the top on n h b d: he regarded a strong 'tram-line' effect at the head and foot of lower case letters an important aid to legibility. Carter's study of sixteenth- to eighteenth-century punch-cutters had led him to a different conclusion:

> Fleischman was the only one who studied the newspaper market: he was a superb cutter of small types. . . . Fleischman made very beautiful junctions of thick and thin strokes: in h m n the join comes down low in the letter and the effect is clearer than that of the joins in the Times fount or Plantin.[20]

Although Carter seems to have followed Fleischman's example by using low joins and by lowering the bowl of d and b relative to the x-height in early drawings, these features are less pronounced in the finished alphabets, and they were further modified, with Carter's apparent approval, in redrawing at Monotype.

The first tentative drawings were by Harry Carter himself, executed freehand in pencil and blue fountain-pen ink on graph paper. They have an x-height of about 30 mm. There is a pronounced Old Face feeling to the early alphabets, but all have heavy, bracketed serifs. In the various drawings, details characteristic of Monotype Plantin, Monotype Garamond, and even the Walpergen Fell types emerge. Each stage of drawing seems to have increased the overall weight of the face. Carter by now suffered from a shaky hand, and could not draw well in the technical sense. For the next stage of drawing he turned to his son Matthew, then eighteen, who had gone to work at Enschedé as a trainee in September 1955. Matthew Carter returned to Oxford for a short break in early 1956, and worked at the Press in a room adjoining Harry's, redrawing the roman alphabets in black ink, so they could be photographed, and giving them a better edge. These were the first formal type drawings done by Matthew Carter, whose year at Enschedé was spent in the type-foundry working in metal, not on paper. The drawings were used to print dozens of alphabet sheets, with an x-height of about 25 mm, which allowed paste-ups of words for photographic reduction. Two weights were tested: the heavier, which was clearly preferred, being made by thickening up the drawings of the lighter. Only the printed sheets survive in OUP's archives.

The roman was redrawn and an italic added, both with an x-height of about 30 mm, in black ink on board. The italic capitals are smaller and lighter than those of the roman, the lower case has a looping, rounded feel. The proportions of 6½-point letterforms were more normal in Carter's typeface than in Van Krimpen's, of which he was 'pretty scathing'.[21] The x-height was given due prominence, and instead of being centred on the body, descenders were shorter than ascenders. In the drawings sent to Monotype the x-height is fifty-eight per cent of the k-p height, and it was further increased by Monotype.

The drawings were dispatched to Monotype in April 1957 for 'investigation' and establishment of a provisional matrix-case arrangement. John Goulding of the Type Drawing Office (TDO) examined them, and in an internal Monotype memo was critical: 'many letters are extremely poor in design and have little or no merit ... many of the letters are extremely ragged in outline – one presumes that a smooth outline will be required.'

It is unclear how much of this criticism was relayed back to OUP. Nevertheless, new drawings to a much higher standard of finish were supplied by mid-October 1957. These were basically tidied-up enlargements of the previous drawings, with an x-height of 45 mm, and were probably done by a technical draughtsman within OUP. Straight lines and curves were regularised, outlines made precise, but there were still small discrepancies in character alignments and heights, and in details of curves and junctions, which required interpretation by the TDO. In July Carter had requested a scale of units at drawing size;

Monotype provided a table of widths in thousandths of an inch for unit values of 5 to 20 units at the set size of 7½-point. The October 1957 drawings have the expected unit widths pencilled in above the characters. This may explain the rather odd proportions of some characters, H for example being extremely wide. Perhaps too much effort was being put into designing for certain unit values, instead of allowing the characters to have 'natural' widths at this stage, and leaving the TDO to make the necessary adjustments.[22]

Goulding's first reply was that the 'standard of these drawings is greatly improved [but] we find that the kerns . . . will be impracticable unless appreciably modified. The unit widths are not proving satisfactory . . . there are inconsistencies in some features of design which we consider may be unintentional on the part of the designer.'

By January 1958, a more detailed report included the following:

> 1. Owing to the large x-height and small descenders, the problem of 'kerns' is very great. The kerns at top will require modification to the italic lower-case f. The kerns at bottom will be quite impracticable, unless the ball type terminal is altered. The drawings of italic capital I J show how impracticable the bottom kerns are.

> 2. The above has made defining of unit widths rather a matter of guess-work. Certainly some of the units allocated will not make for satisfactory fitting – see italic lower-case j being wider than i and l; also compare units of roman capital I J with italic capitals I J.

> 3. The finial strokes of lower-case a, m, n, etc. vary in length, shape and thickness, which can also affect unit variation – see u and n.

> 4. There are variations in basic design shape which could be regularised; shape of italic lower-case letters b, d, h, k, l, vary . . . Roman lower-case b, d, h, k, l have different shape to italic and also vary in height – see b and d. In italic lower-case the position of angled ends of strokes varies in relation to the curved ends of strokes; also what relationship should these have to square or round alignment. In italic lower-case the x-height characters are not always consistent in height.

> 5. Some portions of characters have two strokes very close together. These are nearly impracticable for satisfactory printing in roman capitals E, F, K, W, Æ, Œ; roman lower-case k, m, s, x, ffi, ff; italic capitals E, W, Æ, Œ: whilst it is quite impracticable in roman capital F.

Harry Carter responded:

> I have amended the drawings to meet your criticisms so far as I could do so without sacrificing features that I would specially like to keep. It is quite understood that you will have to adapt them farther to suit your system of working. . . .

1. I have reduced top kerns somewhat; but the reduction of those at the bottom is a necessary evil that I think I had better leave to you to do as little as you can.

2. I would like to keep the existing j at any rate as far as an experimental cutting. Our operators do not mind the departure from customary fitting.

3. The characters have been regularised.

4. These also I have altered with the aim of making them uniform, and the difference in alignment of round and square characters is deliberate.

5. I agree that in making enlarged drawings it will be necessary to enlarge the intervals between certain strokes to the 0.006 in. that you require. I think it is best left to you, because on the scale of my drawings it is difficult to measure the intervals exactly. . . .

It would always be a pleasure to come and see you, probably best reserved until we have clear-cut issues to discuss.

A 'specification for new fount' was prepared by Goulding in April 1958, with the note:

> It is obvious we may well have to modify the design regarding kerns and allowances, but I don't think we should depart too far from the general design. Certainly OUP are not going to be able to be as dogmatic as, say, Van Krimpen about any changes we make so we are allowed a fair amount of latitude in interpretation.

He also suggested that 'planning to be done for 6½-point only as 10 in. drawings at normal scale' – i.e. no allowance would be made on the drawings for the inclusion at a later date of any further sizes, and manufacturing tolerances for smaller sizes would not be considered. The next set of instructions for the draughtsman was the 'pre-planning investigation' by Dora Laing which includes a note on 'peculiarities of original design'. This concerns the quality of the originals and specific characters:

> Set machine by It l/c *f* to 10 in. If reduced further Caps come very small indeed, although at this setting many asc. as h *h* have to be shortened after T[ype]. D[rawin]gs.

> Actually R[oun]d Rom Caps come 5˙ [i.e. 0.005 in.] shorter than *f*.f, with It Rd Caps 5˙ shorter than Roman Rd Caps – i.e. It Rd Caps 10° *shorter than* *f* f h h etc. . . .

> *v w* are generally termed the *initial* shapes – [plain] *v w* not among originals. Spacing is not easy for clearance. *f*w is a necessity for Welsh –

> M *M* are unusual, but if 'design', can be!

> T *T* cross bar 1˙5 below square, tips to full R[oun]d.

i j oval dots, *i j* round dots.

The K point of contact *is* just a point – how should it be interpreted?

When proof goes for approval – The size of [] () () † to be mentioned, also if the kerned R. Cap Q is required as special. . . . For the other peculiarities we make as originals, except K *K* at point of contact make 1· gap and pointed tip as see 552–7.[23]

Ten-inch type drawings of the trial characters were prepared in June 1958, and in July matrices were ready of the letters C H M O a e f g h i n o p in both roman and italic to allow the standard Monotype proofing to be done. The proofs raised comments in the Matrix Factory about italic i j ('too "italic" ') and f ('too much space at std. [right]),' and there is evidence that patterns and matrices were measured and checked against the drawings, but were passed by John Goulding 'as design' and within tolerance. (Goulding would have been the only one concerned who was aware of the design criteria.) The proofs were sent to OUP, who promptly requested the trial matrices so they could do their own tests. The outcome of these trials was that Carter supplied new drawings for roman a e g, adjusting the unit values. The a was made narrower, and the e wider, to give a more even flow to words containing these characters. Carter added:

> Apart from narrowing a and widening e the drawings are meant to indicate a tilt to the main stroke of a, a lightening of the shading on the right-hand side of e and lengthening of its tail, and a very slight enlargement of the lower counter of g, which at present tends to fill up.

The adjustment to the g was noted at Monotype as 'not pract.' because it would create an ink trap between the two bowls, and the counter-suggestion made to reduce the top bowl and to thin the top stroke of the bottom bowl. This was agreed by Ridler, and the go-ahead for manufacture was given on 28 October 1958. Two days latter the formal order was passed by Monotype's London office to the works at Salfords. By mid-November the works confirmed that delivery of the complete fount would take place by mid-February 1959.

In fact drawing work resumed in mid-January. The ten-inch type drawings show how the design was interpreted by the Type Drawing Office. The originals were projected by epidiascope, enlarged so that ascender to descender height of f was 10 ins, and traced letter by letter on to the drawing sheets. This freehand outline was then scribed, so that it would remain as a guide when the pencil marks were erased. The definitive drawing was first sketched in with a 3H lead pencil, using a straight-edge but with all curves drawn freehand. After approval by a supervisor, a hard 7H lead was used to finish the drawing: ship's curves were uscd to guide the pencil over the 3H drawing, biting into the paper and rendering the outline permanent.

å b c d e f g h i j

q r s t u v w x y

11. Printed alphabet sheets (second version) used for paste-ups (reduced from original size).

a b c d e f g h

o p q r s t u v

A B C D E F G

N O P Q R S T

12. The redrawn ink alphabets sent to Monotype in April 1957 (reduced from original size).

The roman lower case required the most adjustment – the final outlines show
that the weight of thick strokes was retained but that thin strokes were reduced
to be about half the width of thick strokes; serif brackets were made consistent
and less heavy. Ascenders and descenders were shortened, and kerns on f and j
were made less extreme. Following normal practice, as little deviation from the
supplied drawings as possible was done within these constraints, even if this
meant reproducing 'flat' curves or unconventional character shapes, as noted in

the 'peculiarities of original design'. However, horizontal alignment was regularised, and this eliminated what remained of the dropped bowl of b and d, making them match the 'round overlap' of e.g. o n p. Capitals were in general a little wide for their allocated widths and were adjusted by reducing the length of horizontal serifs. Side walls were made as small as manufacturing tolerances would allow.[24]

On 23 March a full setting was proofed at Salfords – and this included the rejected forms of a e g. Three days later proofs with the corrected characters were pulled, and sent to Oxford for approval in the first week of April. OUP immediately requested the actual matrices so that trial setting of a complete Bible page could be done in Oxford.

By early June 1959 Harry Carter had annotated the sample page, and identified nine characters for further amendment:

> a leaves an awkward gap after it, especially before l, t, u. I suggest making it lean forward more. Drawing supplied.

> c is pleasant but rather wide and leaves a gap after e. Try it on a narrower set. Drawing supplied. But keep the old one in case it proves to be better.

> o is rather light. Put a little more on the shading, especially inside.

> s is slightly high for line. Lower it a little.

> t appears to lean backwards. Slope it in the Italic direction a little and thicken the crossbar slightly. Drawing supplied.

> w leaves awkward gaps. Try it on a narrower set. Drawing supplied.

> w is ugly. Try one of the same width from the drawing supplied.

> v Alter to suit w. Drawing supplied.

> ' Please make it like a turned comma.[25]

The amendments were incorporated into a new proof dated 22 July 1959, but it was not until 5 October that Monotype had an answer from OUP. Although the narrower c was chosen, the a was still not approved – it was now felt by Carter to 'lean too much to the right – redesign for the same unit row, moving the base of the upright stroke a little to the right.' In the fourth trial proof, dated 8 October, the a had reverted to being more upright, and at last the fount had reached its final state. The status of Series 610, along with Sheldon 552 and Treyford 226, as 'for the exclusive use of Oxford University Press' was confirmed in a memo from Typographical Committee, to C. A. Poore, the Salfords works manager, dated 9 December 1964.

The typeface was used in the New Emerald Reference Bible. Its brief required an extent of 960 pages, and the use of a new cueing system to relate words and phrases to the text in the 'references', the list of chapter and verse numbers set in a centre column, which refer the reader to other relevant instances of the same word or phrase in other parts of the Bible. Conventionally this was done by a superior italic letter. It was a suggestion from an OUP proof-reader that a simple mark (both a degree sign and a prime were considered and trialled – the prime was chosen) should precede the word or phrase to be referenced. The first specimen page, dated June 1958, is actually set in Times Semibold. Carter's fount appeared in specimens dated May 1959.

Further specimens of the new Reference Bible were set in February 1960, and composition began in May 1960. Proofreading was complete by August 1963, and the New Emerald Reference Bible was published in 1964. The new face was regarded by Harry Carter and Vivian Ridler as a success – certainly far superior to the embarrassment of Sheldon. Its overall weight and the ratio of x-height to body size were well-judged, which overcame the effect of some uncomfortable character shapes (g and H for example) and a certain looseness of fit, apparent in sample settings to wider measures. In 1965 it was used for the smallest ('vest pocket') edition of the New English Bible (NEB). Specimens dated March and August 1964 include an elegant one where it was cast on a 7-point body across a measure of 17½ picas.

Events and technology conspired to limit further use of the typeface. Availability in only one size, 6½-point, that was already appearing small to a public growing accustomed to larger type in newspapers and paperbacks, rendered it inflexible in use. New translations of the Bible, particularly the standard editions of the NEB, which was set single rather than double column, required larger sizes, 7-point and above. Although by December 1963 trials were being conducted with Monophoto Plantin 110 for an illustrated Old Testament, photocomposition ('filmset' in OUP terminology) was not used for Bible composition. Vivian Ridler and Ken Stewart (in charge of the Layout Department until 1979) continued to use hot-metal Goudy Catalogue, Plantin, and even Times Semibold for a variety of Bibles produced for OUP itself and for various Bible societies throughout the 1960s and early 1970s. The existence of these typefaces in a range of sizes and the transfer of investment into photocomposition ensured that Carter's face was never revived.

Paul Luna was born in London in 1952. His interest in printing began at school, and he studied typography at Reading under Michael Twyman and Ernest Hoch. After working for Ruari McLean Associates in Scotland, he joined Oxford University Press as a designer in 1976. Initially designing book jackets, he moved on to complex typography, taking over the design of the Oxford Shakespeare volumes, and designing the second edition of the *Oxford English Dictionary* and the Revised English Bible. These projects involved computer-assisted typesetting and started Luna's interest in the electronic structuring of text. While head of design for OUP's academic division, he directed the design of Oxford dictionaries, introducing new typefaces and more accessible designs, culminating in the Oxford Starter series for learners of foreign languages in 1997. He was closely involved with Colin Banks in developing a new corporate identity for OUP. In 1998 he joined the staff of the Department of Typography and Graphic Communication at the University of Reading as Professor.

Luna's research interests are complex text typography, especially dictionaries, and typeface design; recent publications include 'Clearly defined: continuity and innovation in the typography of English dictionaries' in *Typography papers* no. 4 (2002), pp. 1–56.

NOTES

1. Van Krimpen further rationalised his approach in John Dreyfus's 1952 volume *The Works of Jan van Krimpen*. An idealised Bible setting in Sheldon was shown, set by Monotype to Van Krimpen's own layout. The claim is also made that 'stressing the horizontal strokes at the head and foot of lower-case letters' (h n b d) was an 'extremely important aid to legibility'.

2. Cumberlege and Van Krimpen were later to correspond on a personal basis, exchanging notes about Leonardo Walsh's hotel on Lake Garda (see John Lewis, *Such Things Happen*, 1994, p. 154). In 1955 Cumberlege returned to business matters, quizzing Van Krimpen for information on Dutch printers and binders who might cope with long-run work from the Overseas Education (later English Language Teaching) department of the Press.

3. Haarlemmer is discussed in Walter Tracy, *Letters of Credit*, 1986, pp. 114–15.

4. It was later agreed that General Fund (the 'holding company' of OUP) should contribute £1000, leaving the Publisher (Cumberlege) to pay Van Krimpen's design fees; while the Printer paid Monotype for matrices etc. Batey had succeeded Johnson in 1945, having been Assistant Printer for seventeen years.

5. Tracy, *op. cit.*, pp. 116–20.

6. Tom Smith was in charge of jobbing founts, Ken Stewart of the Layout Department. Mr Fathers was responsible for copy preparation, and Joe Ayres for the Monotype composing room.

7. Cumberlege wrote to Van Krimpen: 'I think it is appropriate that you, who have done so much in designing typefaces suitable for Bibles, should possess what I believe you and I agree to be the finest Bible that has ever been produced, namely the Bruce Rogers Bible. I am therefore making over to you this copy so that you may take it back with you to your own country to enjoy and become perhaps an heirloom.'

8. The use of a photographic proof hints at the pressure on matrix production. It was normal Monotype practice to take trial characters through the complete manufacturing process to type, so that every stage of production was tested.

9. On 6 November he complained that Monotype's 10-inch type drawings were 'about one hundred and fourteen times that of the actual size of the type'.

10. Jan van Krimpen, *A letter to Philip Hofer . . .*, ed. John Dreyfus, 1972.

11. Ridler and Batey chose the name without consulting either Cumberlege or Van Krimpen.

12. Batey to Cumberlege, 11 September 1953; Cumberlege was blunter in his reply: 'I am considerably disappointed in the type.' The total fee paid in cash to Van Krimpen was £417. 18s. 0d., Monotype charged 15s. per character for a total of 209 characters, the standard rate being 2s. per character. There was also a charge of £78 6s. 7d. for ancilliary equipment. The costs were divided equally between Publisher and Printer.

13. The Sheldon Bible was still in print at the time of writing (1996), and the setting is also in use, photographically reduced, in OUP's Wedding Bible. In November 1951 specimen pages were prepared for a 'new translation' of the Bible. For these, the Sheldon type was cast on an 8-point body: the improvement in appearance because of the extra interlinear white is considerable.

14. Morison had a personal resistance to 'exclusive' typefaces, although Monotype had twenty such series as late as 1964. Batey regarded OUP's ownership as of the design, not the type, to ensure that OUP retained its rights in the design even if Monotype delayed manufacture. Monotype proposed, and Batey agreed, that the type be put on the open market in October 1957. Van

Krimpen exploded on seeing the announcement in the *Monotype News Letter* of October 1957, and an acrimonious exchange of letters followed, culminating in Monotype withdrawing Sheldon from general sale on 28 November 1957. (Of course, no other printers had been supplied.) Van Krimpen's drawings were returned to him in January 1958 at his request to 'complete [Enschedé's] collection'; some nine sheets of drawings are now in the University Library, Amsterdam.

15. *Bookseller*, 30 October 1954. David, CUP's Bible manager, had first contested OUP's promotional claim that Sheldon was 'the only modern type designed solely for Bible setting' by citing Times Semibold: 'Mr Morison's type-face was planned exactly for [CUP's] Pitt Bible'.

16. Plantin 281 was designed in 1929 in 9- and 11-point to work as the companion roman to a Fraktur typeface.

17. The earliest trial was a photographic reduction of 9-point 281. In October 1954 6½-point trial characters H d e g i n p were drawn and matrices made. Proofs were sent to both Ridler and Morison on 4 November 1954. The drawings for Plantin 281 have completely smooth outlines; those of Plantin 110 were 'rough cut', being drawn with deliberate irregularities to mimic hand-cut punches.

18. In the 1930s Carter had also designed the condensed version of Johnston's sans serif for use on London Transport bus destination blinds, type for Underground railway tickets, and special figures for use in LT timetables.

19. 'Optical scale in typefounding', *Typography*, 4, 1937.

20. *ibid.* David Saunders has pointed out that low joins can cause ink traps, because in machine-cut punches counter depth is controlled by the followers on the pantograph and the shape of the cutting tool, whereas with hand-cut punches crotches can be made deeper.

21. Matthew Carter recalls that Van Krimpen visited OUP in 1957, and commented on work then in progress on the new typeface to his father, apparently without any awkwardness about the implied criticism of Sheldon. Information from Matthew Carter to author, 1996.

22. The TDO had established procedures for producing smaller sizes of existing typefaces, without requiring an outside designer's drawings. The small sizes of Times New Roman and Bembo show how effective these were in producing readable (and manufacturable) type.

23. The redoubtable Dora Laing, whose position in the TDO has been likened by David Saunders to that of a solicitor's chief clerk, 'all the knowledge and little standing', was originally taken on by Fritz Max Steltzer. She had worked on Eric Gill's typefaces in the late 1920s, and was meticulous in recording her work and the procedures of the TDO and matrix manufacture. See David Saunders, 'The Type Drawing Office', *Monotype Recorder*, new series 8, Autumn 1990.

24. Trial characters were drawn in the TDO by Frank L. Clarke in June 1958. The remaining drawings (January-February 1959) were by Patricia Mullet (later, as Patricia Saunders, the designer of Monotype Columbus) and Ann Lowder. David Saunders supervised the drawings.

25. The opening quote mark had originally been drawn as a mirror image of the closing quote, with the ball terminal at the top.

All correspondence cited is from OUP and Monotype archives. I am grateful to the Secretary to the Delegates of Oxford University Press and Peter Foden, OUP's archivist, and Robin Nicholas of Monotype Typography for access to, and permission to reproduce, this material. My thanks are also owed to Vivian Ridler, Ken Stewart, Matthew Carter, David Saunders, and John Lane for their kindness in answering my many questions, and to Michael Johnson for his useful criticisms.

তুমি এক রজ্জুতে আমার গলা রুদ্ধন করিয়া আমাকে সশরীরে সেই রাজার নিকট লইয়া যাও এরং তাহাকে কহ যে তুমি যে রক্তের মস্তকের জন্য করিয়াছিলা তাহাকে আনিয়াছি তোমার সাক্ষাতে তাহার মস্তক ছেদন করিয়া দির।

অ ই ঈ উ ঊ ঋ এ ঐ ও ঔ আ অং অঃ

ক খ গ ঘ ঙ চ ছ জ ঝ ঞ ট ঠ ড ঢ ণ

ন ধ ন্ত ন্ত্র দ দ্ব ত্ত প্র ব্র ত্র ল্ল ক্র গ্র ক্ষ

ড্ঢ জ্জ ঙ্গ হ্ণ ল্ল ব্ব ব শ্চ শ্ব শুু শ্র শ্রী ক্ষ স্ত

ষ্ট স্ত্র স্ম স্ম স্তু স্ত্র স্তু ষ্ণ ক্ণ ক্র ক্ল ক্ষ্ম হ হৃ য ব

ত থ দ ধ ন প ফ র ভ ম য র ল ড় ঢ়

স শ ষ হ া ি ী ে ৈ ো ৌ ৃ ু ূ ্

ক্র ক্ক ত্ত ক্ষ্ম ক্ষ দ্ম দ্ধ দ দ্র ন্ত ন্ত ন্ন ন্দ ঙ্ক ন্ধ

ঞ জ ভ ৎ ং ঃ দ ন ৭ ৬ ভ স ল ৰ শ ঋ ঃ

৺ ৺ ৺ ৬ ২ ৫ ৪ ৪ ৭ ৯ ৩ ০

1. The Bengali and Modi types

An Unexpected Legacy, and its Contribution to Early Indian Typography

BY FIONA ROSS AND GRAHAM SHAW

The discovery of the pattern drawings and castings of the Bengali and Modi types of Sir Charles Wilkins, of the East India Company, throws new light on the challenges of turning Indian scripts into movable type in the early 19th century. (Matrix 7, 1987)

(Dedicated to the memory of Miss Mary Lloyd, Assistant Keeper in charge of the European Printed Books at the India Office Library from 1968 to 1984, who first drew attention to Wilkins' materials.)

Among the more curious and unexpected items still preserved in the India Office Library and Records, London, besides prototype pistols and muskets, ceremonial chairs and model ships, is a small collection of typographical materials – letter drawings, punches, matrices and types – which give a new and fascinating insight into the development of certain Indian typefaces in England during the early nineteenth century. These materials originally belonged to Sir Charles Wilkins, the first librarian to the East India Company, friend of the first Governor-General of India Warren Hastings and of the supreme orientalist Sir William Jones. Wilkins was one of the earliest European scholars of Sanskrit, the classical language of India, and a founder-member of the Asiatic Society of Bengal.

European attempts to design and manufacture types in Indian scripts date back to the 1570s when Portuguese blacksmiths at Goa and Quilon cast founts of Tamil to print Christian texts for the use of converts in south India. But in England the primary motive for the development of Indian typography was commerce, not conversion, centred on the ever-expanding needs of the East India Company with its lucrative monopoly on trade with the Orient. By the end of the eighteenth century very little progress had yet been made. The London type-founder Joseph Jackson had cut and cast founts of Bengali and Devanagari (the script commonly used for printing Sanskrit as well as Hindi) for Willem Bolts, a Dutch adventurer dismissed from the Company's service, and William Kirkpatrick, an officer in the Company's army. The Bengali was apparently never satisfactory enough to have been used but the Devanagari, with its distinctively calligraphic style, was exported to Calcutta for the printing of several works in the 1790s. More successfully, Vincent Figgins, Jackson's former apprentice, had been commissioned by the East India Company itself to prepare a Telugu fount for the printing of regulations by its Madras administration, and the printed specimen delivered in February 1802 was a superb achievement of the day.

The materials described below relate to Wilkins' later years in London but in the course of his career he undertook typographical experiments with oriental scripts in two continents – Asia as well as Europe. He was born in 1749 at Frome in Somerset into a family of clothiers. At the age of twenty he was appointed a writer (junior clerk) of the East India Company and sailed for Calcutta early in 1770. His career as a Company servant made steady if unspectacular progress but he soon displayed a talent rare among Company men – an aptitude for oriental languages (Hindustani, Bengali and above all Sanskrit). This brought Wilkins to the attention of Warren Hastings who commissioned him to design and manufacture a set of Bengali types for the publication of Nathaniel Halhed's *A grammar of the Bengal language*, urgently required to make the Company's servants better acquainted with the language of the people among whom they worked. The book was printed at Hooghly, north of Calcutta, in 1778 and is famous today as the first work containing Bengali words printed in their own character. Discounting Jackson's earlier efforts, Wilkins had produced the first *usable* fount of Bengali types, and Halhed's introduction to his work did much to establish Wilkins' reputation as the 'Caxton of Bengal': 'In a country so remote from all connection with European artists, he has been obliged to charge himself with all the various occupations of the Metallurgist, the Engraver, the Founder, and the Printer'. Other contemporary sources, however, suggest that he was aided in this venture by Joseph Shepherd, a Calcutta gem-engraver, and Panchanan Karmakar, a Bengali blacksmith. A proposal by Wilkins for the establishment of a Company press in Bengal was soon approved and he was appointed its first superintendent, the printing of official documents, regulations, etc. to be undertaken not only in English and Bengali but also in Persian (the language of taxes and justice) for which he designed and had cast an elegant fount of Nastaliq.

In 1786 Wilkins returned home to England for reasons of ill-health. Before leaving India he had compiled a grammar of Sanskrit but this had remained unpublished for 'the want of Sanskreet types, to design and superintend the execution of which I have not yet found leisure', as he explained in the preface to his English translation of the *Hitopadesa*, a collection of Sanskrit fables (distant cousins to those of Aesop and La Fontaine), which he published at Bath in 1787. This lack of Sanskrit (Devanagari) types Wilkins had finally made good by

1795 when in May the next year his house at Hawkhurst in Kent was burnt to the ground. His types, matrices, and punches were saved, 'thrown out upon the grass in heaps', but further work on perfecting a Sanskrit fount was halted. New duties came to preoccupy him. In February 1801 he was appointed Librarian to the Oriental Repository of the East India Company, the ancestor of today's India Office Library and Records. His typographical interest took another turn with the preparation of a fount of Arabic (Naskh) types to publish his new revised and enlarged edition of John Richardson's *A dictionary, Persian, Arabic, and English*: 'The punches were gratuitously designed by myself, and executed, under my superintendence, by that ingenious mechanic, Mr. William Martin'. Naskh was preferred to Nastaliq by Wilkins because of 'its superior regularity and plainness over all other hands, . . . in my humble opinion, the only form which should be used for printing, whose object is not only to multiply and disseminate with superior expedition, but to facilitate study by plainness and uniformity of character'. Wilkins was no doubt remembering here the difficulties he had himself encountered when designing a Nastaliq fount in Bengal in the late 1770s. The two massive quarto volumes of Richardson's work were published in 1806 and 1810 and had consumed of Wilkins 'every disposable moment, and a very large proportion of those hours commonly dedicated to recreation or to rest'.

The stimulus to resume work on his Sanskrit grammar and the types needed for its publication was his appointment in May 1805 as Visitor in the Oriental Department at the East India Company's newly-opened College at Hertford (moved to Haileybury, also in Hertfordshire, in 1809). There new recruits undertook two years' study of oriental languages and other subjects before being posted to India. From 1810 onwards Wilkins also acted as Public Examiner at the Company's Military Seminary at Addiscombe, near Croydon. Apart from examining the students themselves, he was responsible for appointing Professors and other teachers of oriental languages, for inspecting new grammars and textbooks submitted for possible use in the Colleges, and (in his other capacity as the Company's librarian) for supplying all class-books, some to be imported from India, for arranging their printing and binding, and for the loan of books and manuscripts to the tutors and for general use. As no suitable grammar of Sanskrit was then available, Wilkins was commissioned by the Company to complete his own and this was published in 1808 using types cast from his own matrices. In the preface he apologised for the large number of misprints due to 'the Devanagari character, as well as the language, being entirely new to the compositor'. By this time Wilkins was already fifty-nine and it was believed (until the

India Office Library material was unearthed) that the remaining twenty-eight years of his life did not see any further typographical experiments. Apart from his commitments to Haileybury and Addiscombe, there is ample evidence of his generous assistance to other scholars in the oriental field such as the historian Charles Stewart and the linguist John Shakespear. Above all there was his preoccupation with the Oriental Repository which led one contemporary to describe him in 1835, rather unkindly as the Company's venerable but 'superannuated' librarian. He died, aged eighty-seven, still in office, on 13 May 1836.

Sixteen months later, in September 1837, the Repository's 'day book' (the detailed log of all items received or borrowed) recorded that 'the printing press, types and appurtenances belonging to the estate of the late Sir Charles Wilkins' had been delivered to the Company's official printers, Messrs Cox of 75 Great Queen Street. But, due probably to a porter's negligence rather than official design, a wooden box curiously inscribed 'Miss Wilkins' (Sir Charles had three daughters, Elizabeth, Maria and Lucy) and two smaller wooden cases were overlooked and left behind in East India House. When opened some 140 years later their contents revealed new and unsuspected evidence of the range of Wilkins' typographical experiments. The two wooden cases were both neatly packed with matrices in almost pristine condition. In one were Bengali matrices, enough for the preparation of a working fount, still in their original paper wrap-

2. Wilkins' Bengali matrices in their case.

3.General view of the contents of Wilkins' box

pers on each of which the appropriate Bengali character had been carefully written, along with its transliteration, in Wilkins' own hand. The other case contained an equally large set (but without any wrappers) of Modi matrices, 'Modi' being a cursive script used for writing Marathi, the language of the Maharashtra region of western India. The contents of the larger wooden box were undoubtedly the most interesting of all. There were five small oval medicine boxes (one labelled 'Ipecacuanha lozenges') and one rectangular box containing Modi punches. When tried, they fitted perfectly into their respective matrices in the Modi case and were obviously the work of professional craftsmen. A small canvas bag held a number of types of Modi and Gujarati (another western Indian script). These had been hand-cast and were presumably more or less contemporary with the punches and matrices since there is no evidence that the contents of Wilkins' boxes had ever been disturbed since his death. Four small round tins held printers' spaces and a larger tin some additional Bengali matrices.

Most spectacularly, the box contained a set of some sixty pattern drawings of Modi characters, from the handwritten transliterations evidently the work of Wilkins himself. Such drawings are extremely rare and, to our knowledge, no similar set for an early Indian typeface has ever previously come to light. The drawings were on pieces of card 3 ins in height. The width of the card varied according to the relative width of the character portrayed. Some of the drawings are unfinished and thus indicate Wilkins' method of letter-drawing. Rules were first drawn on the card in pencil to position the headline and any vertical strokes, and a baseline 1 in. below the headline to set the height for the basic characters. The principal elements of the character were then completed in pencil outlines prior to being filled in with ink. On several cards it can be seen how Wilkins corrected the angle or thickness of a stroke by scraping away with a scalpel. These Modi letter drawings are unquestionably of a very high standard which evidently contributed to the superb quality of the punches (which are remarkably faithful to the drawings), and consequently that of the matrices and types. We can therefore trace the evolution of Wilkins' Modi fount from the original design in his drawings through the punches and matrices, no doubt prepared under his close supervision, to the small number of types preserved, perhaps the result of a trial casting. Unfortunately the precise models on which Wilkins based his drawings are not known but we can tentatively suggest one source. The India Office Library today possesses just one Marathi manuscript that originally belonged

4. End-on and side view of Modi punches.

to Wilkins. It is typical of the kind of miscellany prepared by an Indian scribe for a European wishing to learn the local languages of the region in which he was serving, in this case western India. It contains alphabets, vocabularies, and short poems for reading practice in three scripts: Devanagari, Konkani (i.e. Kannada) and Modi. The alphabets are very detailed: not only are the basic vowel and consonant forms given but also each consonant in every combination with a vowel, and almost every conceivable conjunct consonant form. The transliterations which have been provided appear to be in Wilkins' hand, and it is not difficult to imagine this manuscript open on his desk as he meticulously prepared his drawings of the Modi characters.

The relevance of the new material to Wilkins' typographical activities could not be established merely by inspecting the contents of the boxes. The exact identity of the Bengali and Modi founts could only be ascertained by casting types from the matrices which had remained in excellent condition. In 1980, upon advice from the St Bride Printing Library, an arrangement was made with Eric Buckley, then Printer to the University of Oxford, for types to be cast by Don

Turner at the Oxford University Press, and in May that year the Bengali and Modi matrices were taken to Oxford. The Bengali matrices, which had evidently seen some use, appeared to predate the Modi but Don Turner was convinced that both sets were of English origin and of professional workmanship, probably manufactured during the first quarter of the nineteenth century – independent corroboration that they did indeed belong to Wilkins' era. The Bengali were less skilfully executed than the Modi, the rounded ends of which – unlike the squared ends of the Bengali – were similar in style to the matrices produced by the Figgins foundry during this period. The types were cast using a Banaman Pivotal Caster on a 13½-point body at the special OUP height. Turner filed them down to the standard type height after the customary processes of breaking-off, dressing, and rubbing the types. Twenty of each sort were selected and tied up into pages for transfer to the St Bride Printing Library. There the lengthy process of sorting the types and composing the specimen was undertaken by Fiona Ross with the guidance and assistance of James Mosley. The task was made more difficult by the larger character set to be handled in a Bengali compared to an English fount. Finally the galley proofs and the initial 'pull' of the specimen were printed off (figure 1).

The galley proofs of the Bengali types soon revealed the typeface to correspond to Wilkins' fourth and last Bengali fount (the other three having been produced while in India). The earliest known use of this fount is to be seen in the *Mahārāja Kṛṣṇacandrarāyasyacaritram* by Rajivalocana Mukhopādhyāya, a biography of the Maharaja of Nadia who sided with the British at the Battle of Plassey, published at London in 1811, the first Bengali book printed in Europe in Bengali characters. One copy of this book, held in the Library of the Indian Institute at Oxford, has a note on the fly-leaf which mentions that 'the types were cut by the late Dr (after Sir Charles) Wilkins. Several of them being large and uncouth, were thrown away, and others smaller and neater substituted in their place'. The note bears the signature of F[rancis] Johnson, Professor at Haileybury College. This explains why some of the letterforms share the same design as those of Wilkins' earlier (third) Bengali fount used in India by the Honorable Company's Press for printing regulations and *inter alia* the earliest known work printed in Sanskrit, *Rtusamhāra*, Kālidāsa's poem on the Indian seasons. It seems reasonable to suppose that Wilkins brought some Bengali punches with him on his return to England in 1786 and that these, supplemented by the revised versions, were evidently used to strike the matrices found in the India Office Library. Another work printed with this typeface was G. C. Haughton's *Rudiments of Bengali grammar* (London, 1821) which became the standard

Bengali grammar in use at Haileybury College until the 1860s. It was from Haughton's work that a text, followed by a fount synopsis, was chosen to be set with the new types cast at OUP. No true facsimile of Haughton's original text could be made, since any peculiarities due to each matrix were unknown before the types were cast at OUP. Consequently, the reduced forms of certain characters were cast on the same body size as the rest of the types, as were any subscripts or superscripts. Thus it was not possible to reproduce combinations of consonants – conjuncts – made up of two reduced elements, nor correctly position floating vowel signs. In Wilkins' system of composition, a floating vowel sign was cast on a separate piece of metal, normally a quarter or a third of the body height, and positioned over, or under, the character it affected. Letterforms which were designed to kern with another character clearly required painstaking and skilful filing in order to produce the desired results. Similarly, dots and connecting strokes would have been removed from some types to create other forms. Moreover, the collection of matrices does not contain all the characters employed in Haughton's text, and the fount synopsis also shows some numerals to be missing. The specimen produced unequivocally demonstrates the common origin of both founts and, although it cannot be said that the Bengali matrices found in the India Office Library are those which produced the types for Haughton's *Rudiments of Bengali grammar*, the same punches must have created both founts of type. With their original paper wrappers intact, the India Office Library matrices have the appearance of a reserve, almost archival, set.

Wilkins' fourth Bengali typeface represents the culmination of his skills in the design of Bengali types, perfected over a period of more than thirty years. In this face more conjuncts have been included than in his earlier founts in order to overcome combinations of sorts which were aesthetically unpleasing. In so doing Wilkins was able to maintain a fairly uniform character height and depth, thereby obviating the need for copious leading, and at the same time providing a homogeneity lacking in his previous designs. The oblique downstrokes of the basic characters lend a liveliness to the face, but it should be said that the types lack the dynamism of those produced by indigenous Indian foundries towards the end of the nineteenth century, and the design is far removed from Bengali calligraphy. The construction of the characters does not follow the stroke sequence of the penned hand – a characteristic introduced by Wilkins and adopted by European designers of Bengali founts – and some of the letterforms appear ill-proportioned and the weight distribution uneven. However, the typeface is very readable and possesses an elegance which appeals more perhaps to a European reading public, the public for whom the fount was after all intended.

5. Wilkins' Modi matrices in their case.

But what was the specific impetus for Wilkins to prepare this last Bengali fount? The same as that which prompted him to resume work on his Sanskrit grammar and Devanagari types – the urgent need for textbooks for the teaching of Indian languages in the East India Company's Colleges at Haileybury and Addiscombe. In February 1809 the College Committee accepted his proposal (first mooted in 1798) that a press equipped with oriental types should be set up in East India House to print these works locally, avoiding 'the expense of print-ing books in Bengal, with the delay and uncertainty of obtaining them from thence'. Wilkins was to superintend the press and prepare the necessary type-faces. According to the 'day book', on 24 February 1809 four type-moulds were received from Wilkins and a printing-press from Moorman about 3 March, fol-lowed by five bundles of paper and a box of letters on 5 April, again received from Wilkins himself. A room in East India House was obviously set aside specifically to house the press as the 'day book' contains several references to material being taken up to the 'Printing Room'. Only four works are known to have been printed on the Company's premises, two in Sanskrit and two in Ben-gali, in the space of four years 1809–12. The first was a quarto edition of the *Hitopadesa* in 'about 500 copies' and notable, as the advertisement pointed out, for being 'the first Sanskrit book ever printed in Europe'. The editor was Alexan-der Hamilton, Professor of Sanskrit and Bengali at Haileybury and a close friend of Wilkins. Printing had probably begun in May 1809, for on 7 June twenty-four copies of the second sheet were sent off to Hamilton at Haileybury. The edition was completed by 28 August 1810 when 'the whole of the Sansk. Hitopadesa B excepted; which sheet had been pressed' was sent out to Mr Cox 'to be pressed' i.e. presumably for the sheets to be flattened in a press before being sent on for binding. The first consignment of twenty-five complete copies went by waggon to Haileybury on 17 December 1810. Next were printed 'about 250 copies' of a *Grammatical analysis of the Sanskrita Hitopadesa*, composed by Hamilton as class-notes for his students, which again went to Cox 'to be pressed & beaten' on 14 May and 2 July 1811. In both works Wilkins' Devanagari types were used, and his Bengali fount must have been cast by the spring of 1811, for in the summer months the biography of Maharaja Krishna Chandra of Nadia was printed in an edition of 500 copies octavo. We can perhaps speculate that William Martin, who had earned Wilkins' praise for his cutting of the Naskh punches for Richardson's dictionary, may have collaborated in the Bengali fount's preparation. On the fly-leaf of the India Office Library's copy of the Bengali biography is a manuscript note 'Printed in Library 1811' which corroborates the evidence from the 'day book'. Mr Cox was again sent the entire edition for pressing on 27 August 1811. The last work known to have been printed in East India House is an octavo edition of the *Totaitihāsa*, a Bengali version of the Persian 'Tales told by a parrot'. 500 copies were printed during 1812, the first batch of twenty-six for Haileybury's use being sent off on 2 September.

The press in East India House was comparatively short-lived and the evident collaboration of the Company's printer Cox (later Cox & Baylis) probably explains why. We can picture perhaps one or more compositors being loaned by Cox to assist Wilkins in setting Devanagari and then Bengali type, learning well under his stern eye and gradually relieving him of the burden more or less altogether. Thus it was that Cox & Baylis went on to print a whole series of Sanskrit and Bengali texts at their Great Queen Street premises. This impression is reinforced by the 'day book' which frequently records types being loaned to Cox from Wilkins' equipment – 19 October 1811 four cases of Roman and Italic letters on English body and a fifth on 22 October; 7 January 1813 a pair of cases of Sanskrit types with another pair the very next day; 24 January 1815 two cases each of Sanskrit and English; 29 December 1815 five cases of Bengali types and all spaces.

Until the rediscovery of this new material, it was totally unknown that Wilkins had ever experimented with the design and manufacture of a Modi fount. Without doubt he was prompted again by the need for text-books at Haileybury, in this instance for the teaching of Marathi to the Company's recruits destined for Bombay. Furthermore, the majority of Modi printing has always been undertaken by lithography, a technique ideally suited to reproduce its cursive character and introduced at Bombay for this purpose in the early 1820s. Wilkins employed for Modi the same typesetting technique as that used for Bengali – basic characters, floating vowel signs, and reduced forms – but the quality of the design is superior. The reason for this may be that the Modi script presents shapes to the designer which, although in some respects complex, are easier to translate into metal type than the idiosyncratic sorts of the Bengali fount. The shaping of the curves, which has been gracefully executed, would not have been unknown to a professional European punch-cutter. A number of the characters bear some affinity to the Devanagari script but Wilkins has treated these in quite a different manner to his Sanskrit fount, producing types which are more successful than the Modi founts prepared at the Courier Press, Bombay, in the late 1790s for printing the Company's regulations, and at the Serampore Mission Press, Bengal, by 1810 for printing the Marathi New Testament. The drawings in Wilkins' own hand testify that the obvious elegance of this fount is not solely due to the skills of the punch-cutter. The quality of the line, the treatment of tight internal counters so as to avoid fill-in, and the weight distribution have been handled with greater skill than his fourth Bengali fount. Inconsistencies in design are evident, but not obstrusive, and would perhaps have been remedied had the fount ever been put to practical use.

Unfortunately no works printed with Wilkins' Modi types can be traced and the matrices are in such pristine condition that it is possible that they were never used. This makes the dating of Wilkins' work on Modi very difficult but, given his preoccupation with other oriental typefaces upon his return to England, particularly his Devanagari, it is perhaps reasonable to suppose that he experimented with Modi only after about 1812 when the East India House Press was wound up. The Modi fount would thus be Wilkins' last and perhaps greatest achievement. Even by the time of his death it does not appear that his contemporaries knew of the fount's advanced state of preparedness and no one took up the task of completing it. Thus printing with Modi types never took root in England. When in 1839 J.R. Ballantyne (later to become another librarian at the India Office) published at Edinburgh *A grammar of the Mahratta language. For the use of the East India College at Haileybury*, the work was not typeset as the preface explained: 'With respect to the mechanical execution of the work, the lithographic press has been employed, because no fount of Mahratta types was to be found in London'. Ironic, but had he known of Wilkins' fount Ballantyne might not have had to complain about that 'pestilent compound of soap and lampblack', lithographic ink. The sample of Modi text shown in the specimen

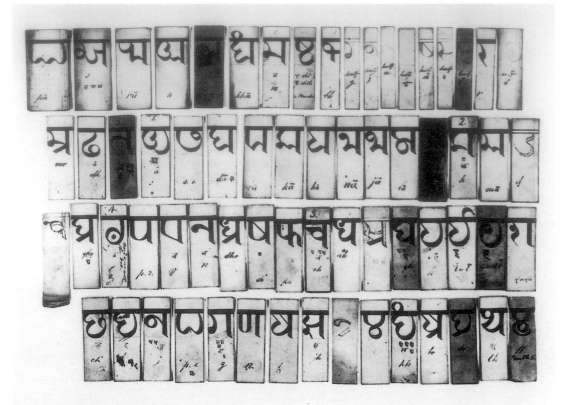

6. The complete set of Wilkins' Modi drawings.

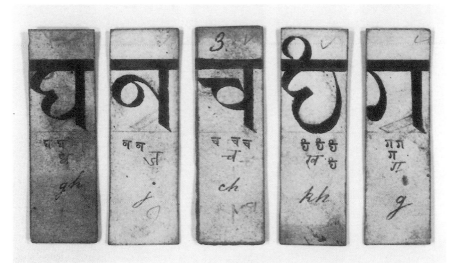

7. Close-up of Modi drawings.

(figure 1) was chosen from a Marathi grammar produced by lithography and which thus possesses no relationship to the fount. It no doubt contains orthographic errors, in part due to the incompleteness of Wilkins' fount and in part to the difficulty of translating cursive Modi chirography into type.

Finally, the presence in Wilkins' box of a few hand-cast types in the Gujarati script was equally unexpected. Although similar in style, they cannot be identified with any other known early Gujarati typeface and we can only assume that they were also the result of Wilkins' own experimenting. But in the absence of any supporting evidence – matrices, punches or drawings – this is impossible to substantiate. Perhaps that evidence was among the printing materials handed over to Cox after Wilkins' death. It remains to be ascertained whether any or all of those materials could possibly still be preserved in the archives of Cox & Wyman Ltd. today to shed more light on Wilkins' important role in the early development of Indian typography in England.

Fiona Ross specializes in non-Latin type design and typography. From 1978 to 1989 she worked for Linotype Limited, being responsible for the design of Linotype's non-Latin founts and typesetting schemes. Since 1989 she has worked as a consultant, author, and visiting lecturer. Ross holds a B.A. in German, a Postgraduate Diploma in Sanskrit and Pali, and a Ph. D. in Indian Palaeography from the School of Oriental and African Studies (London University), and she is a Fellow of the Royal Society of Arts.

Graham Shaw is Head of Asia, Pacific, and Africa Collections at the British Library in London. After graduating in Hindi and Sanskrit from the School of Oriental and African Studies, University of London, in 1969, he began his career in the School's Library before joining the British Library in 1974. He has published widely on printing and publishing in South Asia, including *Printing in Calcutta to 1800* (London, 1981) and *The South Asia and Burma Retrospective Bibliography. Vol. 1: 1556–1800* (London, 1987).

NOTE

In 1982 the India Office Library and Records became part of the British Library, and the Wilkins collection is now housed in the Library's Asia, Pacific and Africa Collections at 196 Euston Road, London NW1 2DB.

The authors would like to acknowledge the help of Mr James Mosley of the St Bride Printing Library in the preparation of this article. All photographs reproduced by courtesy of Mr Trilokesh Mukherjee.

ABCDEFGHIJ
KLMNOPQRS
TUVWXYZGE
EF

ılmnjnruhkꝼꞅ
vxyzwáéíóú
coꝺeꞇabdqp

1. Master drawings of the capitals and lower-case from Monotype archives. Reproduced by kind permission of the Monotype Corporation.

The Colum Cille Irish Type

BY DERMOT McGUINNE

The problem of making a useful and readable modern Irish type involves creating Latin letters that preserve the forms that became traditional in the medieval monasteries of Ireland and that still work in the modern world. In the 1930s Colm Ó Lochlainn sought the advice of Stanley Morison on his plan for a new typeface suitable for setting modern Irish prose, though in the end Ó Lochlainn described himself as 'one who tried and failed!' (Matrix 12, 1992)

In 1926 Colm Ó Lochlainn set up his own printing business in Dublin.[1] He recalled that: 'when I decided to set up my press in Fleet Street, it gave me great joy to find that a large sign board hung outside the premises. This I took down and painted with the sign of the Three Candles which has been much admired . . . "Three candles that light up every darkness: Truth, Nature and Knowledge" was very suitable as a legend for the sort of book we meant to issue, and so the name of the Candle Press was chosen.'[2] Ó Lochlainn was not an admirer of the popular Irish printing types available at the time and was particularly outspoken in his criticism of these design departures from the earlier round Petrie style which he so much appreciated. In addition he argued for the provision of a complete range of weights, and italics and small capitals for a Gaelic typeface, and expressed these sentiments so strongly in an article in the *Irish Book Lover*[3] that it prompted William Burch of the Monotype Corporation to take an interest in the project: 'In the past we have been only too desirous of co-operating with recognised authorities on Gaelic, in order that we could produce a face or faces which would be considered as something better than those which have already existed.' He pointed out the difficulties in producing an italic Gaelic and concluded: 'However this question is one in which we are very interested, more especially after reading your articles. I should appreciate very much the opportunity of discussing this matter with you personally if you could spare the time to come over [to London] for this purpose, and bring with you any specimens of ancient printing, or hand written specimens in Gaelic, in faces which you think are preferable to those which we have prepared.'[4]

Thus was sown the seed for what was to become the Colum Cille type. The graphic designer, Dara Ó Lochlainn, a son of Colm, points out that: 'The genesis of this type was a conversation between Stanley Morison and Colm Ó Lochlainn in April 1929.[5] Morison had been appointed as typographical adviser to Monotype in 1922 ('the Corporation didn't hire me, I hired them' was Morison's version), and in this capacity he was to play a major role in helping Ó Lochlainn realise his dream.

On 1 October 1929 Ó Lochlainn was appointed as part-time director of the department of printing in the Municipal Technical School, Bolton Street, Dublin, and to help formulate his plans he decided to visit schools offering similar courses on the continent. Morison, congratulating him on his appointment, offered to introduce him to his many 'friends in the German print centres.'[6] Ó Lochlainn wrote on 15 July 1930 asking Morison if August would be a good time to visit 'the people in Germany'. He reminded him of his offer 'to accompany me to Leipzig and I need not repeat that I would value highly the introductions you would give me to these Continental people . . . I expect to be free about the 10th August.'

In his article 'An Irish Typographical Link with Germany', Ó Lochlainn gives an account of his visit to Germany:[7] 'In the summer of 1927 [actually 1930] I left London, armed with letters of introduction from Stanley Morison to Julius Rodenberg of the Deutsche Bucherei in Leipzig, to Julius Rodenberg of the Deutsche Bucherei in Leipzig, to Rudolf Koch of Offenback, who was Klingspor's chief type designer and punchcutter, and to other lights of the book and type world in Germany. . . . On another day', he continues, 'we went to meet the artist Walter Tiemann (designer of Tiemann Antiqua), who presided over the Akademie für Kunst und Buchgenerbe, a comprehensive school embracing every kind of technical and process teaching and specialising in art training for book design. There a year later [1931] I brought my disciple Karl Uhlemann – half German already – and left him for a year under Dr Tiemann. The next summer I collected him from his father's people in Marburg on the Lahn; and he returned to work with me at the Three Candles.' The visit in 1930 to Germany was most eventful, Ó Lochlainn records: 'My voyage of exploration took me to Antwerp (Plantin Museum),

Cɼiɼc lim	Chɼiɼc wichin me
Cɼiɼc neum Cɼiɼc im ɒeꝼaiɒ	Chɼiɼc in my headway Chɼiɼc in my wake
... Cɼiɼc iɼɼum Cɼiɼc úaɼum	Chɼiɼc alow and Chɼiɼc aloꝼc
Cɼiɼc ɒeɼɼum Cɼiɼc cuacum	Chɼiɼc on my ɼighc hand Chɼiɼc on my leꝼc
Cɼiɼc illuɼ Cɼiɼc iɼiuɼ Cɼiɼc ineɼuɼ	Chɼiɼc wich me waking walking and ɼleeping
Cɼiɼc i cɼioiu cech ɒuini ɼoɒomɼcɼúcaɒaɼ	Chɼiɼc in each heaɼc chinkɼ on me
Cɼiɼc i nꝼin cech óin ɼoɒomlabɼacaɼ	Chɼiɼc on each congue ɼpeakɼ to me

2. Prayer from St Patrick's Breastplate, set in Colum Cille

Leipzig, Frankfurt, Offenback and Mainz . . . and so began my friendship with Rodenberg, Hartmann, Jost and Konrad Bauer and, most fruitful of all, with Rudolf Koch and his son Paul which lasted until they died.'[8]

In a letter to Ó Lochlainn dated 16 September 1930, Morison states: 'I am very glad that you have happy recollections of the day you spent in London. I am only too happy to have shared it with you.' And with a remark that would suggest that discussion had taken place regarding the production of a Gaelic type he states: 'As to the Gaelic business, I feel a little more disposed to occupy my mind with the question as a result of seeing the *An Fiolar*.' Ó Lochlainn had sent Morison a copy of *An Fiolar*, the Annual Journal of St Joseph's College, Roscrea, in which the Irish sections were printed using Monotype Series 24 Gaelic. In this journal extensive use was made of engraved blocks to print title headings and larger text, hand written in a round style of letter.

Ó Lochlainn had, at this time, the idea of the development of a Gaelic type progressing at two fronts, one with the Monotype Corporation and the other with the Klingspor type foundry in Offenback. In September 1930, seemingly as a result of queries he made during his visit to Germany, he received a letter from Klingspor stating that 'Dr Rodenberg from Leipzig tells us, that you are interested in our "Hupp Unziale" as well as in our "Hammer Unziale", specimen books of which types we are sending you today under separate cover.'[9]

In 1932 an article by Ó Lochlainn appeared in *Gutenberg Jahrbuch* entitled 'Irish Script and Type in the Modern World' in which he states: 'Already one German type designer Victor Hammer [see article on p. 29] has found in the Irish Uncial the inspiration for a very beautiful ornamental type "Hammerschrift" which has been cut by Gebr. Klingspor of Offenbach and I submit that in Irish handwriting from the year 800 to the present day there is an unlimited fount of inspiration for the design of types for Advertising Display, Ornamental bookwork and Poster work.'[10] Victor Hammer wrote to Ó Lochlainn on 15 July 1932 describing his own study of Irish manuscripts and the influence they had on his type, and again on 29 July 1932 Ó Lochlainn received another letter from Hammer acknowledging receipt of a copy of Ó Lochlainn's article and informing him that he would be in England during September and October. He enclosed a prospectus of his Samson Uncial type (an improved development of the Hammerschrift type), and went on to say: 'I would be delighted to cut, either myself or with my pupil Paul Koch – Rudolf Koch's son – an entire Irish typeface.'

At this time Ó Lochlainn sought to adapt Hammerschrift for use in Gaelic. Hammer had come to London in mid-October 1932 and in pursuit of this aim Ó Lochlainn visited him there, concerning which he recalled: 'Dr Klingspor . . . was much interested in my proposed extension of Hammerschrift to fit it for a ᴀ b ʙ c ᴄ ᴐ e f g ᴣ h i j ᴋ l m

n o p q ʀ s ᴄ ᴛ u v w x y z

á Á é í ó ú ḃ Ḃ ċ Ḋ ḋ ḟ ᵹ́ ġ ṁ ṗ ṡ ṫ

1 2 3 4 5 6 7 8 9 0

3. The 'Baoithín' type with redesigned A, B, D, G and T, and aspirated characters, adapted from Hammerschrift in 1932.

printing Modern Irish – especially display matter, certificates and diplomas, so I redesigned A, B, D, G and T in proper Irish scribal form, gave all five vowels an acute accent, and aspirated (dotted) B, C, D, F, G, M, P, S, T. I crossed to London and spent a night with Hammer at the Austrian Embassy, where we considered and approved my innovations. Rudolf Koch, or perhaps Paul, cut the punches, and I called the type Baoith'n: for Colm Cille's last written words were "Reliqua scribat Baitenus". Let Baoith'n (his disciple at Iona), write the rest, just as I had designed "the rest" for Victor Hammer'[11] (figure 3).

In a letter dated 31 October 1932, Morison expressed sorrow at having missed Ó Lochlainn while he was in London. Perhaps this was just as well for it is not clear to what extent Ó Lochlainn kept him informed with regard to his dealings with Hammer. Ó Lochlainn, it would appear, discussed the possibility of himself cutting the punches for a text size which Morison comments on in a letter dated 23 November 1932: 'Victor Hammer came to see me last week [after his meeting with Ó Lochlainn], and I was rather taken with his universal benevolence, but I did not care to argue with him on the first occasion of meeting. To my mind, the suggestion that you should cut the punches argues a misunderstanding of the position. Hammer appears to me to inhabit some mental monastery in which a worship of beauty and culture and the like is carried on in an atmosphere steaming with aesthetic complacency. I hope this does not sound uncharitable.' Indeed there may have been an element of playing one off against the other on Ó Lochlainn's part, for as early as April 1932, Morison had written to Ó Lochlainn urging him to work on a Gaelic alphabet: 'If you will design a humanistic Gaelic, I will get it cut. The new political line makes this a very opportune moment.' Later in a letter of 12 June, he asked again: 'Will you undertake to design a lower-case of Gaelic which shall go with the Gill Sans capitals used on the Customs declaration? If you will, I will get Gill to work over the designs and you will then have the first of all sensible alphabets for displayed Gaelic.'

Ó Lochlainn applied himself to these urgings for in a letter to Morison on 26 July 1932 he says: 'After much delay I am acknowledging your little book about the Hebrew Type [sent on 28 April 1932] and your recommendations. I have been trying to see what can be done to make Irish type follow these lines but so far have nothing to show except rough pencil sketches . . . I will be going to Germany the end of this week and will probably see Rodenberg and some of the others also but I am not going to work very hard while I am there.'

It was on his return from this visit to Germany that he brought Karl Uhlemann back to Dublin, having left him there the previous year studying with Dr Tiemann. Ó Lochlainn got Uhlemann to work on drawing up the alphabet. Uhlemann, who died in September 1992, still possessed his original drawing of the capital letters which is dated 21 December 1932 (figure 4). It is interesting to recall Morison's offer: 'I will get Gill to work over the designs', for the Monotype archives contain an undated set of drawings clearly based on Uhlemann's design and from which the first set of characters were cut (figure 1). It was not until September 1933 that evidence of this work emerged. Morison wrote to Ó Lochlainn: 'The alphabet looks good to me. I am not sufficiently up in the palaeography of the thing to be absolutely sure that your serif treatment is thoroughly unobjectionable.' After some comment on various individual characters he continued: 'However, it is such an enormous gain to get a set of Capitals I really ought not to do any more than congratulate you on the design.' Later in a letter of 18 September 1933, Morison again commented: 'The Sans Serif Gaelic appears to me to be very satisfactory. I should say myself that the lower-case n is too narrow. We are making a few sorts of the New Gaelic in 14-point. They will be ready, I hope, by the time you arrive', and later, on 30 September, Morison wrote: 'I think you should be very pleased with the trial characters of your Gaelic as shown on the accompanying proof. I should like the foot of the Capital **B** to be opened out a little more, but I have no other criticism to make. The trial characters seem to me to promise a really fine fount' (figure 5). Again on 30 October 1933, Morison added further approval: 'The accompanying new proof, I think, does go still further modernising the alphabet, and I cordially approve.'

There followed a number of letters from Morison urging some response from Ó Lochlainn: 'If there is any News about the Gaelic I should be interested. If it is abuse, rather than news, I shall still be interested.'[12] Ó Lochlainn was reluctant to rush into approving the sample prints. The cause for this delay was that he was having alterations made to many of the letters. He was clearly unhappy

4. Karl Uhlemann's first drawings of the capitals dated December 1932.

5. Trial A, dated 26 September 1933 (reduced).

Amⲓꝛꝛ ꟓamⲓꝛ ꝛam maꝛꝛ Baꟓ aꟓⲓm ⲓꝛ mam am
mammⲓꝛ Dⲓꝛꝛ ꟓⲓmmⲓꝛ mⲓmⲓꝛ Eⲓꟓꝛ ꟓⲓꝛꝛⲓm ꝛamꟓ
Ꝼammⲓꟓꝛ am ꝛⲓꝛam ⲓꝛꝛam Bamⲓꝛ ꟓⲓꝛꝛam ꟓⲓꝛꝛ
Amⲓꝛꝛ ꟓamⲓꝛ ꝛam maꝛꝛ Baꟓ aꟓⲓm ⲓꝛ mam am
mammⲓꝛ Dⲓꝛꝛ ꟓⲓmmⲓꝛ mⲓmⲓꝛ Eⲓꟓꝛ ꟓⲓꝛꝛⲓm ꝛamꟓ
Ꝼammⲓꟓꝛ am ꝛⲓꝛam ⲓꝛꝛam Bamⲓꝛ ꟓⲓꝛꝛam ꟓⲓꝛꝛ
Amⲓꝛꝛ ꟓamⲓꝛ ꝛam maꝛꝛ Baꟓ aꟓⲓm ⲓꝛ mam am
mammⲓꝛ Dⲓꝛꝛ ꟓⲓmmⲓꝛ mⲓmⲓꝛ Eⲓꟓꝛ ꟓⲓꝛꝛⲓm ꝛamꟓ
Ꝼammⲓꟓꝛ am ꝛⲓꝛam ⲓꝛꝛam Bamⲓꝛ ꟓⲓꝛꝛam ꟓⲓꝛꝛ
ABDEꝾ   aꟓⲓmꝛ

with their appearance, and on 30 July 1934 he wrote: 'At last I have the revised letters to send you' (figure 6). He enclosed new sketches for a, D, G, I, M, N, P, and R, and stated: 'The cap A which appears on this I do not think we need bother about. My draughtsman [Uhlemann] heard some people criticising our angular A but I think I should stand firm for it as it certainly gives us a definite distinction between caps, and lowercase, and this is what we want if ever small-caps are to be made.'

Ó Lochlainn continued to push for an extended range to the fount: 'My anxiety is that the font should be as perfect as possible so that yourselves will not suffer through adverse criticism. There is a general feeling that a variety of type would be desirable, and I am glad that my efforts coupled with yours, have brought the type to such an advanced stage that now only some minor changes are required. I wish that the type should be called Colum Cille as he is par excellence, the patron of Irish scribes.'[13] Following this instruction the Monotype records for series 121 show an entry dated 20 February 1935: 'To be known in future as Colum Cille.'

Shortly after this Morison became somewhat disenchanted with the project, for he frequently referred to the financial risk involved to Monotype, and on occasion, it took great persuasion on the part of Ó Lochlainn to effect changes called for. In his letter of 20 March 1935 he was quite forceful: 'The re-designed cap B seems quite satisfactory but the new D [d] is wrong entirely and I do not know where you got it as I referred you to the Rudolf Koch Memorial Inscription for my own D in order that you would see exactly how the thick stroke proceeds across the whole top of the letter. Whatever else is done or not done this D must be cut right before we proceed any further.'

Ó Lochlainn contributed an article to *Progress in Irish Printing* entitled 'Gaelic Script and Modern Type' in which he gave a brief account of the development of Irish type design and mentioned his Colum Cille was 'now nearing completion'. He went on: 'This is an attempt to combine the inspiration of scribal forms with the formal elements of printing type design. An entire elimination of non-essential scribal motifs has resulted in a severe yet attractive face which composes in a soldierly line, legible and clear and free from angularity, even in tone colour without the monotony of some modern sans-serifs. Through the kind offices of my friend Stanley Morison, I was given every opportunity of dropping and changing until at last my dream-type has become a reality. The elements used are simple. No serif is allowed except a small 'lead-in' from the left. Lower case l is the first element and from this and the second – the l.c. o – all such letters as a, b, d, p, g. etc. are formed. The o again gives, in combination with a horizontal line, the t and g, those two unruly letters which seem to resist all efforts at formulisation. The capitals have been brought all to line and definitely Roman forms have here and there been used, historically and scribally defendable, and exceedingly clear and useful, in view of the intention to develop small capitals and italics at a later stage. All the additional letters not needed for Irish are also included, as well as the normal forms of d, g, t, s, r, thus rendering the type usable for display work in any language.'[14]

Ó Lochlainn used the 14-point size from a supply of foundry type (he had not yet received any matrices), for the setting of invitations and various small jobs in Irish, but unfortunately this new type did not immediately find favour with printers in Ireland. Morison noted this in his letter to Ó Lochlainn on 7 December 1938: 'We are sorry to have to report that no enquiries for matrices of this design have followed its use in your publications, and we have not, therefore, found it necessary to put in hand any further sizes. Notwithstanding, we are prepared to cut a 12-point, a 10-point, or an 8-point if you will order any of these sizes; and we think we could promise you delivery within five or six weeks of the receipt of your order.'

Ó Lochlainn requested that he 'proceed at once with the cutting of the 10-point Colum Cille' to which Morison replied on 9 January 1939: 'We will proceed at once with the cutting of the 10-point Colum Cille if you will send an order for it. You are at present our only customer, and I cannot tell you how we prize you. If you send in the order at once the fount of 10-point shall be completed within six weeks at the most.' On the 23 January 1939 Ó Lochlainn wrote:

6. Revised drawings to trial no. 1, dated 30 July 1934.

'Herewith a definite order for the 10-point to be executed as soon as possible.' He attached a sheet containing a number of redesigns and alterations, and commented regarding a second enclosure: 'The other sheet contains the first italic alphabet ever planned for Irish (figure 7), at which let Nations tremble! . . . I would like you to study this *very carefully* and let me have your remarks. I myself am well satisfied with it – indeed I think it will look even nicer than Roman as it retains the inscriptional character and only follows scribal tradition in its slope.' He then reminded Morison that: 'Now the only thing that is wanting is an alphabet of small caps.'

On 25 January Morison wrote: 'As for the italic, I have first of all to acknowledge receipt of your drawings, and congratulate you on the effort. The only criticism I have to make concerns the lower-case g, the form of which appears to me to be a very difficult affair for a stone carver. On the whole, however, I think that the lower-case is satisfactory. You notice no doubt that the letters n, u and h are very narrow sorts compared with a, d and e. I fancy in 10-point they will look very narrow indeed. In fact you have altered the proportions from the roman very materially indeed.'[15] On 6 February Morison sent a photographic print of the italic drawings reduced to 10-point, from which the relative lightness and narrowness of some of the sorts is quite evident. Ó Lochlainn thanked Morison and asked: 'Do you think the general line of this too thin? and would it be strengthened in cutting? . . . Many thanks for the interest you are taking in this. You do not know what balm it is to the soul of the neglected Type designer whose obsession is Gaelic!'[16] On 26 April 1939, Ó Lochlainn asked for an early delivery of the necessary matrix case for the 10-point 'as I am closing in on the big MacNeill book.' In the same letter he further pushes to realise his initial goal of a complete range to this type: 'By the way some of those who are interested in the type have been asking me about a black to work with it. Will it be necessary for us to make new drawings or will your artist work out a heavy version of the alphabet.'

He was still pursuing this matter over three years later when he wrote in September 1942: 'I suppose this is a bad time to be talking about extending the range of Colum Cille, but we do need badly the 14-point which was never completed. If you think anything can be done I will mark on the 12-point sheet all the sorts which we require. If that were once finished we could proceed with an 8-point which could be set either solid or on 10-point.' Morison replied: 'This is a bad time to talk about extending the range of Colum Cille. Look into the characters that you really want and let me know. I do not make any promises but I will do what I can.'[17]

Ó Lochlainn put his new type to good use and with it produced a range of

A B C D E F Ᵹ
H I J K L M N
Q P R S T U V
W X Y Z A E G
A V I O

a b c o e ꜰ f Ᵹ
g h ı ȷ k l m n
o p q ꞃ r s т u
v w x y z t ꞃ d

books that were remarkable for their typographic excellence. Among the titles to first use the 10-point was an attractive small book *Cúpla Laoi as Edda* by Pádraig de Brún. On the reverse of its title page is printed the statement: 'Columcille is ainm dom chló so. An chuallacht Monotype a ghearr éó litreacha a tharraing Colm Ó Lochlainn.'[18] (The typeface is Colum Cille. It was cut by the Monotype Corporation from letters supplied by Colm Ó Lochlainn). Regretfully the Colum Cille type did not prove to be very popular, the Three Candles Press being the only printing house offering this face for some time.

The preference among printers for the more angular minuscule based alphabet which Ó Lochlainn so disliked, together with the ongoing lobbying for the use of the roman character for the printing of Irish, tended to polarise the situation, creating extremes: those supporting the roman character for printing Irish, and those supporting the more traditional Irish character, with little room for this Irish type with roman characteristics. This led Seán Jennett to comment: 'Because he is a printer, Mr Ó Lochlainn understands that a type is not a version of calligraphy, and he has produced an eminently printerly character, based on the Petrie designs. It has unfortunately not proved popular; perhaps because it has too many affiliations with roman – the capitals L, M, N for example. This is the only Irish type with the rest of the roman alphabet designed to match, and certainly the only one with an italic.'[19]

Jennett's article prompted Karl Uhlemann to seek clarification from Ó Lochlainn regarding the authorship of the designs. He states that he asked Ó Lochlainn to acknowledge his leading role in the design and to disassociate himself from the statement made by Jennett. Ó Lochlainn replied to this request in a letter to Uhlemann: 'That article in The British Printer was not inspired by me, although considerable use was made of things I had written elsewhere. All I did was to send, when requested by the Editor, a few samples of *Colum Cille*, and *Baoithín*. I have never met the strangely named Mr Jennett – I hope he is not an ass as his name would seem to indicate.'[20]

In a 1959 review of Sir Cyril Burt's *A Psychological Study of Typography*, Ó Lochlainn praises the introduction by Stanley Morison, and more generally his on-going work in typographic design, with a sad note regarding his own efforts: 'His [Morison's] success is apparent to all; and I salute him as the best living type designer. This from one who tried and failed!'[21]

Dermot McGuinne received his primary degree and early training as a typographer and graphic designer in the United States, where he later held the position of Art Director of the University of Iowa Press and Publications for a number of years before returning to Ireland. He was awarded his doctorate from Trinity College, Dublin, for research undertaken into the historic development of the Irish character in print. He is presently Senior Lecturer and Head of Department of Fine Art at the Dublin Institute of Technology. He is author of *Irish Type Design – A History of Printing Types in the Irish Character* (Irish Academic Press, Dublin, 1992), together with various articles on related aspects of this topic.

NOTES

1. Prior to locating the Three Candles Press in Fleet Street Ó Lochlainn worked from his family home in Rathgar. Shortly afterwards he moved to 39 Harcourt Street where he operated his press from a backroom of the Craftworkers Studio and from there he moved to 44 Dawson Street using the imprint of the Candles Press.

2. Colm Ó Lochlainn, 'A Printer's Device', *Irish Book Lover*, vol. XVI, (Jan.-Feb. 1928), p. 15.

3. Colm Ó Lochlainn, 'The Printer on Gaelic Printing', *Irish Book Lover*, vol. XVI, p. 63, p. 87.

4. W. I. Burch, 'Gaelic Printing', *Irish Book Lover*, vol. XVII, (March/April 1929), p. 38.

5. Dara Ó Lochlainn, 'Irish Scribal Work as an inspiration for new type Design', *The Black Art*, vol. 2, no. 4, (1963), p. 102.

6. I wish to thank Mr Dara Ó Lochlainn for giving me access to the unpublished correspondence which took place between his father, Colm, and Stanley Morison, and for permission to quote therefrom.

7. Colm Ó Lochlainn, 'An Irish Typographical Link with Germany', *Book Design and Production*, vol. VII, no. 1, ed. James Moran, (Spring 1964), p. 34. Written in 1964, it seems that Colm Ó Lochlainn had mistaken the timing of some of the events recorded in this article, by three years in certain instances, e.g. he gives 1927 as the date in which he went to Germany with letters of introduction from Stanley Morison, while their correspondence would indicate that this took place in 1930.

8. *Ibid.*, p. 37.

9. Klingspor Foundry, 'Letter to Ó Lochlainn', 26 Sept. 1930.

10. Colm Ó Lochlainn, 'Irish Script and Type in the Modern World', *Gutenberg Jahrbuch*, (1932), p. 12.

11. Ó Lochlainn, 'An Irish Typographical Link with Germany', p. 39. St Columcille (Columba) together with his fellow Irish monks established an abbey on the island of Iona, west of Scotland, in 563. It seems he was a most prolific scribe, with the earliest known surviving Irish manuscript book *The Cathach* (the battler) being attributed to him. He died in 597.

12. Letter from Morison to Ó Lochlainn, 24 Nov. 1933.

13. Letter from Ó Lochlainn to Morison, 19 Feb. 1935.

14. Colm Ó Lochlainn, 'Gaelic Script and Modern Type', *Progress in Irish Printing*, (1936), p. 85.

15. Letter from Morison to Ó Lochlainn, 25 Jan. 1939.

16. Letter from Ó Lochlainn to Morison, 16 Feb. 1939.

17. Letter from Morison to Ó Lochlainn, 6 Oct. 1942.

18. Pádraig de Brún, *Cúpla Laoi as Edda*, Dublin: Three Candles Press, 1940.

19. Seán Jennett, 'Irish Types: 1571–1958', *British Printer*, no. 71, (1958), p. 54.

20. Letter from Ó Lochlainn to Karl Uhlemann, 19 March 1958.

21. Colm Ó Lochlainn, 'Reviews', *The Irish Book*, vol. 1, (1959–62), p. 54.

Dr McGuinne's book *Irish Type Design* gives an historical account of the development of printing types prepared for use in the Irish language.

εἶπεν αὐτῷ, Ἀγαπήσεις Κύριον τὸν Θεόν σου, ἐν ὅλῃ τῇ καρδίᾳ σου, 22-23
καὶ ἐν ὅλῃ τῇ ψυχῇ σου, καὶ ἐν ὅλῃ τῇ διανοίᾳ σου. αὕτη ἐστὶν ἡ
μεγάλη καὶ πρώτη ἐντολή. δευτέρα δὲ ὁμοία αὐτῇ, Ἀγαπήσεις τὸν
πλησίον σου ὡς σεαυτόν. ἐν ταύταις ταῖς δυσὶν ἐντολαῖς ὅλος ὁ
νόμος κρέμαται καὶ οἱ προφῆται.

Συνηγμένων δὲ τῶν Φαρισαίων ἐπηρώτησεν αὐτοὺς ὁ Ἰησοῦς
λέγων, Τί ὑμῖν δοκεῖ περὶ τοῦ Χριστοῦ; τίνος υἱός ἐστι; λέγουσιν
αὐτῷ, Τοῦ Δαβίδ. λέγει αὐτοῖς, Πῶς οὖν Δαβὶδ ἐν Πνεύματι
κύριον αὐτὸν καλεῖ λέγων, Εἶπεν ὁ Κύριος τῷ κυρίῳ μου Κάθου ἐκ
δεξιῶν μου, ἕως ἂν θῶ τοὺς ἐχθρούς σου ὑποκάτω τῶν ποδῶν σου;
εἰ οὖν Δαβὶδ καλεῖ αὐτὸν κύριον, πῶς υἱὸς αὐτοῦ ἐστι; καὶ οὐδεὶς
ἐδύνατο αὐτῷ ἀποκριθῆναι λόγον· οὐδὲ ἐτόλμησέ τις ἀπ' ἐκείνης
τῆς ἡμέρας ἐπερωτῆσαι αὐτὸν οὐκέτι.

❡Τότε ὁ Ἰησοῦς ἐλάλησε τοῖς ὄχλοις καὶ τοῖς μαθηταῖς αὐτοῦ λέγων, 23
Ἐπὶ τῆς Μωσέως καθέδρας ἐκάθισαν οἱ γραμματεῖς καὶ οἱ Φαρισαῖοι·
πάντα οὖν ὅσα ἂν εἴπωσιν ὑμῖν, ποιήσατε καὶ τηρεῖτε· κατὰ δὲ τὰ
ἔργα αὐτῶν μὴ ποιεῖτε· λέγουσι γὰρ καὶ οὐ ποιοῦσι. δεσμεύουσι
δὲ φορτία βαρέα καὶ δυσβάστακτα, καὶ ἐπιτιθέασιν ἐπὶ τοὺς ὤμους
τῶν ἀνθρώπων· αὐτοὶ δὲ τῷ δακτύλῳ αὐτῶν οὐ θέλουσι κινῆσαι
αὐτά. πάντα δὲ τὰ ἔργα αὐτῶν ποιοῦσι πρὸς τὸ θεαθῆναι τοῖς
ἀνθρώποις· πλατύνουσι γὰρ τὰ φυλακτήρια αὐτῶν, καὶ μεγαλύ-
νουσι τὰ κράσπεδα, φιλοῦσι δὲ τὴν πρωτοκλισίαν ἐν τοῖς δείπνοις,
καὶ τὰς πρωτοκαθεδρίας ἐν ταῖς συναγωγαῖς, καὶ τοὺς ἀσπασμοὺς ἐν
ταῖς ἀγοραῖς, καὶ καλεῖσθαι ὑπὸ τῶν ἀνθρώπων ῥαββί. ὑμεῖς δὲ μὴ
κληθῆτε ῥαββί· εἷς γάρ ἐστιν ὑμῶν ὁ διδάσκαλος· πάντες δὲ ὑμεῖς
ἀδελφοί ἐστε. καὶ πατέρα μὴ καλέσητε ὑμῶν ἐπὶ τῆς γῆς· εἷς γάρ
ἐστιν ὁ πατὴρ ὑμῶν, ὁ οὐράνιος. μηδὲ κληθῆτε καθηγηταί· εἷς γὰρ
ὑμῶν ἐστιν ὁ καθηγητής, ὁ Χριστός. ὁ δὲ μείζων ὑμῶν ἔσται ὑμῶν
διάκονος. ὅστις δὲ ὑψώσει ἑαυτόν, ταπεινωθήσεται· καὶ ὅστις ταπει-
νώσει ἑαυτόν, ὑψωθήσεται.

Οὐαὶ δὲ ὑμῖν, γραμματεῖς καὶ Φαρισαῖοι, ὑποκριταί, ὅτι κλείετε τὴν
βασιλείαν τῶν οὐρανῶν ἔμπροσθεν τῶν ἀνθρώπων· ὑμεῖς γὰρ οὐκ
εἰσέρχεσθε, οὐδὲ τοὺς εἰσερχομένους ἀφίετε εἰσελθεῖν.

Οὐαὶ ὑμῖν, γραμματεῖς καὶ Φαρισαῖοι, ὑποκριταί, ὅτι περιάγετε τὴν
θάλασσαν καὶ τὴν ξηρὰν ποιῆσαι ἕνα προσήλυτον, καὶ ὅταν γένηται,
ποιεῖτε αὐτὸν υἱὸν γεέννης διπλότερον ὑμῶν.

Οὐαὶ ὑμῖν, ὁδηγοὶ τυφλοί, οἱ λέγοντες, Ὃς ἂν ὀμόσῃ ἐν τῷ ναῷ,
οὐδέν ἐστιν· ὃς δ' ἂν ὀμόσῃ ἐν τῷ χρυσῷ τοῦ ναοῦ, ὀφείλει. μωροὶ
καὶ τυφλοί· τίς γὰρ μείζων ἐστίν; ὁ χρυσός; ἢ ὁ ναὸς ὁ ἁγιάσας τὸν
χρυσόν; καί, Ὃς ἐὰν ὀμόσῃ ἐν τῷ θυσιαστηρίῳ, οὐδέν ἐστιν· ὃς δ'
ἂν ὀμόσῃ ἐν τῷ δώρῳ τῷ ἐπάνω αὐτοῦ, ὀφείλει. τυφλοί· τί γὰρ
μείζον; τὸ δῶρον; ἢ τὸ θυσιαστήριον τὸ ἁγιάζον τὸ δῶρον; ὁ οὖν
ὀμόσας ἐν τῷ θυσιαστηρίῳ ὀμνύει ἐν αὐτῷ καὶ ἐν πᾶσι τοῖς ἐπάνω

1. The specimen page for *The Four Gospels*, reduced from 17.5 × 12 inches (see page 202), margins not indicated.

The Oxford University Press and Robert Proctor's Greek Types

BY J. F. COAKLEY

Major university presses are precisely the patrons that have both the need and the funds to buy or commission new classical Greek typefaces for use in publishing the classics. J. F. Coakley's essay in Matrix 13 *(1993) not only traces the story of Robert Proctor's distinctive Greek type but gives an insight into the ins and outs of getting a typeface project through the maze of an academic institution.*

The distinctive Greek type known sometimes as the 'Otter' type, the intellectual offspring of Robert Proctor (1868–1903), is quite well known to, and appreciated by, printing historians.[1] The type, double pica in size and with separate kerned accents,[2] was made for hand setting, and this fact, together with the eccentric design of some of its sorts (especially the whole of the upper case, which Proctor made disproportionately tall) has rendered it in some respects a private press curiosity. It did, however, represent a pleasing and justified departure from the Porson types which were the nineteenth-century fashion in printed Greek; and its influence has been widely felt through Monotype series 192 New Hellenic Greek, whose designer Victor Scholderer was an admirer of Proctor's achievement.

The opening chapter of the history of the Proctor type, covering its design, production, and use for an edition of the *Oresteia* of Aeschylus, has been admirably set out by John Bowman in a 1989 article in the *Transactions of the Cambridge Bibliographical Society*.[3] The *Oresteia* was published by the Chiswick Press in 1904, the year following Proctor's mysterious (perhaps suicidal) death. The subsequent history of the type has to be pursued at the Oxford University Press, where the type reposed from 1905 until 1982. In what follows I recount the next two chapters, so to speak, of this history: the publication of the *Odyssey* in 1909 and *The Four Gospels in the Original Greek* in 1932. Two parties were involved: Proctor's trustees (in particular, Sydney Cockerell and Emery Walker) and the OUP (the printers Horace Hart and John Johnson and their colleagues on the publishing side) and there is a human as well as a typographical interest in their relations over three decades. Finally, at the end of this article the story of the type is brought down to date.

The Odyssey

Horace Hart, the Oxford University Press Controller, had an eye to acquiring the Proctor type even while it was still in use at the Chiswick Press for the *Oresteia*. 'If you think it is worth having', he wrote to Charles Cannan, the Secretary to the Delegates (11 January 1904), 'I believe I could get it for the Oxford Press, when the books for which it is being used are disposed of.'[4] Cannan was not interested and passed on to Hart the view of one of the Press delegates, the Regius Professor of Greek Ingram Bywater, who 'dislikes it beyond words, except as an archaic monument'. In October, however, Hart received a proposal from Emery Walker which made the type a matter of business.

Proctor had left no will, but he had written that his Greek type, matrices and punches should become the property of Walker, his partner Cockerell, and Proctor's colleague at the British Museum Alfred W. Pollard. The three men, all of whom had helped Proctor in various ways with the type, considered it their duty to carry out the publishing programme which he had laid down, namely the *Odyssey* and the poems of Theocritus. The Chiswick Press had already advertised for subscribers to these books, and Proctor was supposed to have prepared at least part of the texts for the press (though it seems these papers were never found); but the matter had got no further. Now, Walker evidently saw the possibility of appealing to Hart's empire-building inclinations to get Oxford to print the books. He wrote to Hart (22 October), 'If you were able to do this, we [Cockerell, Pollard and Walker] should be inclined to let the type remain with the University Press, to be used for printing such Greek texts as we might mutually approve, under Mr. Cockerell's and my typographical direction.' Hart went to call on Walker five days later, and they discussed the terms of business further. Henry Frowde the OUP's London publisher would take over the subscription list; if the subscriptions covered the printing costs, or, failing that, if the Delegates could be induced to subsidise the publications as 'learned' works, Hart would go ahead. Walker must have encouraged Hart to believe that Oxford might also acquire William Morris's types, of which Cockerell (though not Walker himself) was one of the trustees. 'I did not press the point of these types,' Hart recorded, 'because I thought that any arrangements for them will necessarily follow the arrangements for the Greek types.'[5]

To Walker, the chance to have the Proctor types (and a hope for the Morris ones) must have seemed a sufficient inducement to offer, and he chose to believe that Hart and Frowde would proceed with the two books. When nothing happened, he had to be reminded by Hart, who went to see him again in February 1905, that it was a simple matter of printing business and that the books would only be undertaken if the subscriptions covered his expenses. Yet Walker realised that printing the books and having the type would be matters of prestige, and that, whatever Hart said, he did wish to do the work. He intimated that if Oxford would not print the books, 'somebody else' – Cambridge was evidently understood between them – would.

Although Hart warned him that the Delegates would probably not be willing to take the books on as loss-makers, after the interview was over, Walker renewed the suggestion. This brought Cannan into the discussion. He and Hart exhanged memos both disclaiming any wish to proceed with the books, and Cannan was firm that the Delegates must be kept out of it. Yet Hart had already made arrangements for the Proctor type to be packed up at the Chiswick Press for delivery to Oxford, and for his part Cannan wrote to Frowde that 'it would be a pity if Pollard got into relations with the Cambridge Press. The Cambridge Press has I think sold the Bible that Cobden Sanderson printed, and they have got their 'Cambridge type'. If they have sold their Cambridge type books they will jump at this.'[6]

Negotiations started which went on until October. Cannan proposed terms which Frowde could put to Walker: Theocritus (a shorter book) to be printed first, if possible without promising the *Odyssey* ('Morris didn't *begin* with the Kelmscott Chaucer'), and the Delegates' imprint not to be used. The other side proved insistent, however, in particular that the *Odyssey* should come first. Cannan applied himself to composing an imprint which would avoid bringing in the delegates, two possibilities being: OXONII E TYPOGRAPHEO ACADEMICO TYPIS PROCTORIANIS and, ΕΞ ΕΡΓΑΣΤΗΡΙΟΥ ΤΥΠΟΓΡΑΦΙΚΟΥ ΑΚΑΔΗΜΙΑΣ ΤΗΣ ΕΝ ΟΞΟΝΙΑ. Hart estimated the cost of printing in the same format as the *Oresteia*, quarto on Batchelor's 15 x 20 ins Kelmscott hand-made paper, in black with red shoulder-references. For 350 copies, this came out at £450, so that at £3 per copy, 150 would need to be sold to break even. Although only forty-two subscribers had been enrolled and it seemed unlikely that this goal could be reached, the Trustees would not consider any economies, such as dispensing with the second colour. Instead, they applied to Mrs Proctor, who offered a guarantee against loss of £100 after two years. A smaller edition of 225 copies was eventually decided on, which Frowde thought a reasonable risk, and Cannan gave his blessing.

Typesetting therefore began in February 1906. The text of the *Odyssey* to be followed seemed to interest no one very much, and it was decided to reproduce a standard Oxford edition of 1896 by D. B. Monro. (Since the type existed in only one size there could of course be no notes or *apparatus criticus*.) Some questions were still undecided, such as the use of the alternative *nu* and *pi*, and it was one point among others on which Hart found the Trustees hard to deal with. 'They seem to be very touchy about the Proctor types,' he wrote after an interview with

2. The Proctor type
(part of Romans
8.28-9, set at the
Jericho Press

οἴδαμεν Δε ὅτι τοῖς ἀγαπῶσι τὸν θεὸν πάντα συνεργεῖ εἰς ἀγαθόν, τοῖς κατὰ πρόθεσιν κλητοῖς οὖσιν. ὅτι οὖς προ-έγνω, καὶ προώρισεν συμμόρφους τῆς εἰκόνος τοῦ υἱοῦ αὐτοῦ, εἰς τὸ εἶναι

Pollard in March. Proctor had used these alternative letters unsystematically (as it seems) in the *Oresteia*, and Pollard evidently thought they should be used in the same way again, but he was unwilling to specify where, or indeed to deal with the Greek copy at all. (In the event, the letters were not used anywhere in the *Odyssey*.) In the appearance of the type on the page, however, the Trustees and especially Walker took the closest interest, and asserted their right to the final say in every decision. The Printer's files contain pulls of the first few pages of the text marked up by Walker, directing for example that the title should be broken into three lines and not two. Hart wrote on the page, 'Alter it & begin working once more.' The most serious problem was encountered on p. 17 where there was a long line which ran up against the shoulder-note and would require to be turned. Astonishingly, Pollard insisted that rather than turn the line, the page-size for the whole book should be widened to accommodate it. Perhaps the final order for the paper had not been made, but two signatures worth of hand-made paper and typesetting would have to be written off. Nevertheless, it was decided to start over with another Kelmscott paper from Batchelors, 16½ x 22½ ins (with a flower watermark), and printing restarted in January 1907 when this arrived.

There were some further interventions from Walker and Cockerell (though not Pollard, who must have given up this duty) over the next two years. Even when the fifty-ninth and last signature, numbered λλλ, was reached in April 1909, Walker showed that he had not lost his interest in the details. In the colophon on the last page the words *Oresteia* and *Odyssey* were naturally set in italics, but Walker commented 'We [Walker and Cockerell] neither of us like to use italic when not absolutely necessary.' Again – *Hart's Rules* notwithstanding – Walker had his way and the titles were printed in roman.

If it seems now remarkable that Walker was allowed to dictate to the printers as he did while the Press bore most of the financial risk, it is anyhow clear that his instincts were good. Walker wrote to Hart on 22 April 1909; 'I think we may all of us now meet Proctor's ghost without compunction.' Hart may or may not have shared this feeling of *pietas* toward Proctor, but he and his men had at least

to their credit an undeniably fine (if somewhat forbidding) book, and possession of 1689 lbs. of the Proctor type.

The Four Gospels

The story of Proctor's type reads quietly until 1926. In 1912, Hart got permission
from Walker and Cockerell to use the type to print an address for the University
of Liverpool to send to the University of Athens.[7] In 1913 Walker asked the Press
to send some of the type on loan to the Central College of Arts and Crafts in London where there was a plan to print an edition of Hesiod with English translation. Some 120 lbs. of type were sent, in a pair of cases and seventeen pages of
diss, but the project was overtaken by the war and was evidently never proceeded with.[8] In 1920, on the other hand, Walker refused a request from the Medici
Society for enough type to set up a sentence in Greek for an Eton College war
memorial volume.

Under Fred Hall, Hart's successor 1915–25, the OUP did little or no luxury
printing, and certainly none in Greek. It was at Hall's funeral, however, that
Walker mentioned in conversation with someone from the Press the idea, which
he attributed to J. W. Mackail, that 'the Press might like to print a New Testament' in the Proctor type. John Johnson, the new Printer, was himself a classical
scholar, and Walker no doubt hoped he would be naturally sympathetic to such
an idea, the more so since Johnson had let it be known that he had plans for rais-
ing the standards of work done at the Press. Even so, when he wrote to Johnson
with the formal proposal (5 March 1926), Walker thought fit to mention that the
type was only 'lent' to Oxford, and that:

> Cockerell being now a Cambridge man has suggested that we should house the
> type at the Cambridge University Press, with a view ultimately, perhaps after my
> death, or perhaps before that event, that we should give it to that Press. When I
> mentioned the matter that I had a tentative suggestion for its use in printing the
> New Testament Cockerell at once agreed that if you had any thought of going on
> with the scheme it should be done while the type is still in your hands.

This was certainly an ungenerous statement if it were to be taken to mean that
the type would be lost to Oxford whether or not any further printing was done
with it. Johnson must have thought so too, and replied to Walker (9 March) in
characteristic style:

> My dear Walker,
>
> We are now old friends and therefore I think you will not mind me saying
> frankly how great a blow your letter is to me coming as it does at the start of my
> new career.

We have housed the type for so many years and we have borne so great a part of the burden (an increasing burden, increasing naturally as the study of Greek has declined) of the printing of Greek in this country during recent generations that the action which you contemplate hits us (and especially me) hard.

As you know I am myself hardly in harness, but for the last month I have been digging into the question of our Greek founts and preparing to disinter the Baskerville and other founts. It would have been a noble range unequalled, I believe, in Europe.

Of course I know that the Proctor type is not our own and that we have never touched it without your permission. But we have been good fathers to it all these years and good fathers to Greek.

Knowing me I know you will forgive my cry of distress.

Meanwhile I am laying your proposal for the New Testament before the Secretary.

The Secretary, R. W. Chapman, was as unenthusiastic about the look of the type as his predecessor Cannan had been. Sales of the *Odyssey* had also been less than encouraging: Mrs Proctor's £100 had been asked for and received in 1912, in exchange for which the Trustees had been given thirty-nine of the unsold copies in 1920 when it was reckoned that the book had just about repaid its costs. There were still nineteen copies in stock at the current price of £6. 6s. 0d. (of which the last seven were remaindered in April 1940). Even so, like Johnson, Chapman did not wish to lose the type, especially to Cambridge. In the course of a meeting in London, Johnson and Chapman looked at a copy of the *Odyssey*. Chapman wrote:

When we met at Amen House the other day I was compelled to admit that the Odyssey is a much more attractive book than my recollection of it. I think really the book I was familiar with was not the Odyssey but the Oresteia, in which the huge red capitals make I think an affected and ugly book. But though I don't like the type in all its particulars, the Odyssey is no doubt quite an event in the history of Greek printing. I don't think we should find it nearly so difficult today to sell something as Mr Frowde did many years ago; and if it would secure us from total loss of the type I think it would be quite worth while to do *something*, though I shrink from the New Testament. Why not Theocritus, which would come very appropriately from the present Printer to the University of Oxford?

Theocritus was Chapman's nominee, not from any memory that it had been the next book on Proctor's agenda, but from an idea that Johnson might use the opportunity to publish the text on which he was himself working.[9] The suggestion went no further, Johnson's edition being not yet ready for print; but it was at least a signal of willingness on the OUP's publishing side to undertake the risk of something.

In exchange for this willingness Johnson hoped to get some concession about the type from Walker and Cockerell. In April he had separate meetings with both of them. That with Cockerell was evidently less than completely amicable, though Johnson commented to Chapman that 'He is a good-hearted chap behind the Cockerell manner.'[10] To judge from the absence of mention of the type, Cockerell must have been adamant that Cambridge should have it. Walker paid a visit to the Press on 16 April which was friendlier, but during which Johnson had still to defend himself. He recorded:

> I spent almost the whole day yesterday with dear old Emery Walker. I never met a man who made himself more at home in a printery. As he moved round with me he adapted himself exactly to the department and was able to give them some anecdote or other benefit of his experience. I suggested to him, and he is going to propose, to Cockerell that the matrixes of the type shall be deposited in Oxford and only the type in Cambridge. . . . I told him that he might account that the penalty for our failure (if there has been a failure which I do not necessarily admit) to use the type during the last twenty years, that we should have to pay for the casting if ever we needed it. We should still have to obtain permission before we used it.

Whether even this concession was acceptable to Cockerell is not clear, but no promises were put on paper.

The Delegates no longer included Professor Bywater (†1914), and Chapman was able to get his recommendation accepted: not the whole New Testament to be published, but some shorter text. Chapman wrote to Walker on 15 June putting another suggestion, Marcus Aurelius, instead. No reply came; Johnson and Chapman inferred that Cockerell was going to insist on the New Testament. Chapman wrote on 12 November: 'I fear the dice are loaded against us; and if the New Testament, the whole New Testament and nothing but the New Testament is made a sine qua non I am afraid we must abandon the unequal contest.' It turned out however that Cockerell had gone back to an idea earlier thought of, that the edition should be of just the Four Gospels, but that somehow he and Walker had forgotten to pass this on to Johnson. Once received, however, the proposal was quickly agreed, and plans for the edition could proceed.

These plans occupied most of a year and it was not until the autumn of 1927 that production actually started. The delay was not due, as one might have expected with a text like the New Testament, to any decision-making about the text to be followed. Again, no one was interested in this, and in the event the edition of A. Souter (OUP 1910) was chosen and followed exactly.[11] There was, on the other hand, a good deal of trouble over typography, mostly from Cockerell, who seems to have taken over the role played by Walker with the *Odyssey*. Johnson at first produced a specimen of a page (Matthew 22.37–23.20) in folio (figure 1). In this size (the pull is on a page 17½ x 12 ins) the type appears to splendid advantage, and the headlines in red in the over-large capitals do not overpower the solid mass of lower case in the lines below. It would have made a magnificent edition – but, as Johnson told Chapman (22 January 1927), Cockerell wanted the *Odyssey* quarto format. 'Cockerell's contention is that he and others will read the Gospels in this form and that the folio would be ornamental and not practical.' This was not a forceful argument: 'ornamental' was precisely what the book aimed to be. But Cockerell's peremptory manner made it impossible to argue this or any other point. On the next revised specimen, in quarto, the printers set the headline Κατὰ Ματθαῖον in caps and lower case, since as Johnson put it the caps 'simply crushed everything else on the page'. After consultation, however, Cockerell and Walker insisted on all caps, and requested that the sorts should be trimmed to achieve closer letter-spacing. This kind of nicety made for expense, as did the other specifications of the book if it was to follow the format of the *Odyssey*. The same paper was still available to order from Batchelors at a cost for thirty-six reams of £151. But, Johnson wrote, 'we can hardly afford to argue with two such obstinate men as Walker and Cockerell about this paper or a hand-made paper slightly less expensive.'

In fact, Johnson had come to consider Cockerell a friend – one who, moreover, had brought work to the Press in the shape of two lucrative books from the Roxburghe Club – and he now wished to carry through the book in the best style rather as a favour, or as Chapman called it, a 'liturgy'. Even when the book was published and Cockerell asked for a royalty – to Chapman's incredulity – Johnson found words to excuse him. 'It is his not altogether unattractive cross-grainedness, coming out in a slightly perverse form of pleasantry. In his perverse ways he has stood a very good friend to me.'

The Four Gospels in the Original Greek was four further years in the press – a leisurely progress, it would seem, although printing had to be interrupted once in 1930 for the type-foundry to order matrices and cast new type for certain accented sorts which had been exhausted. The book was published in the spring of 1932 in an edition of 350 copies. The title-page, itself an impeccable composition in Caslon capitals in red and black with an engraved Oxford device, this time carried the formula 'the Clarendon Press' in recognition of the Delegates' responsibility for it. At 309 pages, the book is a more comfortable size than the *Odyssey*, and the presswork is even better than in the earlier book (in the copies I have examined anyway). Walker wrote to Chapman (4 June), 'The book is certainly one of the finest specimens of modern typography extant and I cannot help thinking that it would be difficult to find any book printed in Greek letters to equal it.' Even while regretting that the book was not a folio, I think these comments need not be much discounted.

The fate of the type

Johnson still affected to understand that the type was to go to Cambridge after the Gospels were finished. It is, however, to be suspected that he hoped his friend Cockerell would not after all insist on removing it from Oxford. Some such hopes would explain the unusually fulsome language in his letter to Cockerell of 19 May 1932 promising a royalty on the unlikely event of there being any profit in the Four Gospels.

> I think you know the task was undertaken as a gesture of affection for you and Emery Walker and in commemoration of the domicile which this University had offered to the type for a good many years. Even in the more prosperous days when the work was planned, the thought of any ultimate profit was held to be out of the question and actual loss was envisaged. Without this it would not indeed have been the gesture which it was designed to be.

If Johnson calculated that one gesture would elicit another, he was right, although the response was not one of complete magnanimity. Cockerell conferred with Walker, who had likewise just received three copies of the new book with the printer's compliments, and wrote to Johnson (5 June 1932) offering the type, punches and matrices – for sale. Johnson declared himself to be honoured, and offered £50. Eventually this became £100 (£50 to each man) in two instalments.

So the Press became the legal owner of the Proctor materials. The punches and matrices had lain at the Miller and Richard foundry in Edinburgh since their first and only use in 1903. Johnson was dismayed to be told in answer to his first enquiry that they could no longer be found; but they were soon turned up, and ninety-seven punches and 102 matrices were duly accessioned in the OUP foundry on 5 September 1932.

Johnson immediately made use of his new purchase to print a Greek book independently of the Trustees. A Greek millionaire Pan. Aristophron had been excavating the ancient Academy of Athens at his own expense since 1929, and he wished to publish a tract entitled Πλάτωνος Ἀκαδήμεια: ἢ περὶ γενέσεως τῆς πρὸς ἀνεύρεσιν αὐτῆς ἰδέας (*Plato's Academy: the birth of the idea of its rediscovery*) in a lavish format. Johnson offered him the Proctor type, and the work, a large quarto of forty-nine pages, appeared in 1933. There were 333 copies: three on vellum, thirty-one on Japanese vellum, and 299 on specially-made handmade paper with a watermark of Plato's head and the words ΠΛΑΤΩΝΟΣ ΑΚΑΔΗΜΕΙΑ. A shorter second part, subtitled Ὁμολογία (*Confession of Faith*) in the same format followed in 1937.[12] Much space might be taken up in describing these luxurious volumes. Among their interesting typographical features is the use of 18-point Gill Sans to match Proctor for a few necessary words in Latin script; but everything possible in the books was in Greek, including the imprint and Johnson's name (Ἰωάννης Τζῶνσον Τυπογράφος). They are inflated works, however, with lines too heavily leaded (the type had always before been set solid) and margins too wide, and with the general aspect of vanity books. (They did, indeed, cost the author £467 and £172 respectively.)[13]

A couple of ceremonial ephemera were printed in the Proctor type in 1937 and 1938 and a title-page in 1940,[14] but then it fell into disuse, as far as I can tell, until 1964 when it appears in some of the headings in *The Greek New Testament* edited by R. V. G. Tasker.[15] The text of this edition was printed in New Hellenic, and it is the only time in which the Proctor and New Hellenic types, so well matched, have ever appeared on the page together. The reason is no doubt that the Proctor types were trade height, and therefore not easily combinable with any other types in use at Oxford. In 1965 it was decided to recast the type to Oxford height, presumably to facilitate its occasional use in the future. The old type (which was 'wide 2-nick') was melted[16] and the new (1-nick) was put into the cases.

In 1982 as a result of my much-daring request to buy some of the Proctor type, the contents of the cases were divided. Half the type went to the St Bride Library and the other half to my press, then in Lancaster. Its condition suggested it had never been used since its casting in 1965. Waiting for a worthy text to come along, I used the type in some jobbing work and two type-specimens. Then my friend David Scott proposed an edition, with his translation, of the daily Greek prayers, known as the *Preces Privatae*, of Lancelot Andrewes (1555–1626). (To be exact, it was just the introduction to each day's prayers, a text of suitably short length.) This we published in 1993. It was the first time that the Proctor type had been used in a bilingual volume, and although it is unlikely to take anything away from the glory of the *Odyssey* and the *Four Gospels*, I hope it will stand in this good company.

J. F. Coakley taught in the Religious Studies department at Lancaster University from 1976 to 1993. His private press and typographical research were extracurricular activities. The Greek type treated in his article was one among a number of exotic types that he collected from printers in Britain who were then getting out of letterpress. (Another language, Syriac, was the subject of an earlier *Matrix* article, "Some Syriac types in Oxford and Cambridge," *Matrix 10*, 1990.) In 1993 he moved to Harvard University in the United States, his native country. There he teaches in the Department of Near Eastern Languages and Civilizations and is also on the staff of the Houghton Library. Exotic-language printing is still one of his interests. His own printing is done at the Jericho Press, which is a garden shed belonging to a house in Oxford where the family spends part of each summer.

NOTES

1. E.g. V. Scholderer, *Greek Printing Printing Types* 1465–1927 (London 1927), 15; D. B. Updike, *Printing Types: Their History, Forms and Use* (Cambridge, Mass. 1962), ii. 215–16; and J. H. Bowman, *Greek Printing Types in Britain in the Nineteenth Century: A Catalogue* (Oxford 1992), 70–71.

2. A kerned Greek accent is illustrated in P. Gaskell, *A New Introduction to Bibliography* (Oxford 1972), 32.

3. 9 (1989), 381–98.

4. Documents quoted in this article are found in the archives of the Oxford University Press, which I consulted by kind permission of the Secretary to the Delegates. The main sources for the years down to 1932 are 'Oxford Packet 199.5' and the Printer's file on Proctor Greek. I should like to thank Peter Foden for turning these up for me and for much other friendly help.

5. The Kelmscott types are never again adverted to in any of the papers I have seen of Hart or of John Johnson. It is hard to say whether Johnson may have still hoped to get them in the 1930s. The types were bought from Cockerell by the Cambridge University Press in 1940.

6. He need not have worried: the 'Cambridge type' books were a failure. See M. Black, *Cambridge University Press 1584–1984* (Cambridge 1984), 209–10.

7. There seem to be no copies of this document preserved in Oxford or Liverpool.

8. In a letter of 27 December 1921 Walker speaks of needing to remind the School to either go on with the book or return the type. There is nothing to show that they did either. What became of the type is unknown to me.

9. Johnson had discovered a manuscript in Egypt in 1913–14. He eventually handed over the work to A. S. Hunt and it was published under their joint names (*Two Theocritus Papyri*, OUP 1930).

10. On the 'Cockerellianism' (i.e., tactlessness) of Cockerell, see W. Blunt, *Cockerell* (London 1964), xvii–xviii, 260–74.

11. So we have for example Souter's square brackets around John 7.53–8.11; but the significant blank line in Souter separating Mark 16.9–20 off from the authentic part of the gospel has been thoughtlessly suppressed.

12. On Aristophron and his excavations see further P. Aristophron, 'Plato's Academy', The Nineteenth Century and After 122 (1937), 676–84; and J. Travlos, Pictorial Dictionary of Ancient Athens (London 1971), 42-3. Aristophron's work, broken off in 1934, was resumed by others in 1955.

13. Aristophron had two other editions of his book printed at the OUP: in 1934 a small and attractive Greek-English edition using new Hellenic; and in 1938 a very lavish English translation of both parts, large quarto on hand-made paper with illustrations in black and green, mainly rather obscure pictures of swans, by E. Fraser. The bill for the latter book was £792.

14. In the John Johnson Collection in the Bodleian Library are two broadside addresses: (1) to Athens University from the Universities of Birmingham, Bristol, Durham et al, dated 24 March 1937; and (2) to the Archaeological Association in Athens, from St. Andrews University, dated 8 September 1938. The title-page of 1940 is noted by Bowman, art. cit. (n. 3 above), 396.

15. Perhaps because of its limited purpose (to give the text underlying the New English Bible New Testament of 1961) this is an undeservedly forgotten book. I should like to call it the edition of choice for typographically sensitive readers of the Greek New Testament.

16. One packet of the old type does survive at the St Bride Printing Library.

THE FOUNT

ABCDEFGHIJKLMNOPQRSTUVWXYZ&

abcdefghijklmnopqrstuvwxyzfiflffffiffl

1234567890   ft❨§‡y.,:;!?''""=~()[]—

ABCDEFGHIJKLMNOPQRSTUVWXYZ&

abcdefghijklmnopqrstuvwxyzflffffiffl

1234567890   ftggy§‡❨=~[]()''.;~!?

Treyford type

John Johnson and the Treyford Type

BY PETER FODEN

Graily Hewitt's calligraphic Treyford type, commissioned in the late 1920s by John Johnson, the Printer to the University of Oxford, flew in the face of the typographic orthodoxy of the time. In Matrix 13 *(1993), the same issue that contained the previous essay on Proctor's Greek types, Peter Foden traces another tale of how a new typeface can gain and lose its credibility.*

Treyford is an oddity. Although launched in 1928, at the time of the Morisonian typographical renaissance and of the New Typography of the Bauhaus school, it conforms to the ideals of neither. In contrast with other Monotype faces cut during the late twenties, Treyford is calligraphic rather than typographic, an Arts and Crafts script transposed into lead type.[1]

Odder still is the fact that Treyford was commissioned by John Johnson, Printer to the University of Oxford, shrine of typographical tradition. For two years the new type enjoyed the active patronage of the University Press, until in 1930 the young Stanley Morison published a hostile review in *The Fleuron.*[2] Oxford however continued to display the fount in its type specimens until 1966, and advertised its availability until at least 1976.[3]

The rise and fall of the Treyford type is well documented in the archives of the University Press. It is a human story, and much of it is told in the inimitable flowing prose of Johnson himself.[4] The following is his own summary of the history of the fount, told in a typical letter to Geoffrey Cumberlege:

> I am sending you out the only existing specimen of the Treyford type, which at the moment is as rigidly proprietary as Fell!!
>
> The origin of it lay not only in artistry, but also in diplomacy. Graily Hewitt, the greatest scribe of our time who has also paid much attention to typography in its origin and development, was staying with me and showed me some drafts which embodied his own life's study and which out of timidity (he is one of those curious creatures – recluse and genius) he had never shown to anyone.
>
> This was very early in my career as Printer when I was faced with problems as multifarious as you have to face in the USA. Undoubtedly Oxford printing had fallen to a very low level (how low perhaps only a very few know) and I thought it might be diplomatic for Oxford to put out, for the first time for more than 100 years, a wholly new type which could not fail to be provocative. This I thought

would itself call incidental attention to what I hope would prove a general renaissance of Oxford printing. It was the only money I have put down and written off as sheer advertising since I have been in office.[5]

William Graily Hewitt (1864–1952) had indeed a proven record, almost as calligrapher to the nation. A pupil – like Gill – of Edward Johnston, he had taught the Art of Writing at the London County Council Central School of Arts and Crafts since 1902. At the end of the Great War, it was Hewitt who inscribed the memorial records of many public schools, colleges, Inns of Court, regiments, and the House of Lords.[6] John Johnson entertained great respect for Hewitt, fellow member of the Double Crown Club and his senior by nearly twenty years, and the tone of his letters between 1926 and 1930 implies a growing friendship. Johnson's first approach recorded in his letterbooks was a relatively formal letter ('Dear Mr Hewitt') dated 13 November 1926, inviting Hewitt to lecture on handwriting to all the printing apprentices of the Oxford district. Graily Hewitt was to deliver his lectures on Friday 7 and Friday 21 January 1927. On both occasions he was invited to spend the weekend at Johnson's home in Oxford. Nearly two years later, Johnson looked back to the conception of the Treyford fount on Hewitt's first weekend visit:

> It is beginning to be a very long time since you were sitting in front of my fire in Linton Road and rather timidly disclosed the original photograph of your ideas.[7]

Johnson was an instant convert. When Hewitt came to Oxford to deliver his second lecture on Friday 21 January 1927, he was charged to bring with him 'the specimens of the type which you have been designing' because 'they would be of the greatest possible interest to Mr Shand and myself.' James Shand, then just twenty-one years old, was Johnson's right-hand-man. Shand had been taken on as assistant printer by Johnson's predecessor Frederick Hall directly from the London School of Printing. His combined ability and charm quickly won Johnson's respect, confidence, and even dependence. Johnson's background was in archaeology, not typography. He was not a printer by training and consequently appears to have given his technically qualified young assistant responsibility far beyond his years. The decision to commission this unusual new typeface seems to have been taken jointly by Johnson and Shad, and with only one deviation the design process was handled entirely by Shand.

Printer and Assistant Printer alike were convinced that Hewitt's proposals had merit:

> Personally I think that the Oxford University Press is on to one of the biggest and most interesting experiments in modern typography.[8]

Johnson saw the 'experiment' as something of an advertisement. Publication of the new type was to draw attention to his renaissance of the Oxford Press, part of his mission 'to rebuild this ancient Press, to give it new buildings, to re-equip it, to give it even a new spiritual background.'[9] He did not think, however, that Treyford would be the new Fell. He did not envisage any commercial success, but saw himself (or rather the University Press) as an art patron:

> I am afraid we have the majority of modern typographers agin us, but I have always justified it on the ground that even if the world outvotes you, you have every right to be heard and it is only a University Press which could afford to give you the hearing.[10]

Graily Hewitt's proposed 'type' was nothing more nor less than his own calligraphic script mechanised for mass-production. 'It is based on the authority of script, but with the individuality, the idiosyncrasy of the scribe removed, and the modifying, generalising influence of the machine admitted.' Hewitt's calligraphy was inspired by his study of both mediaeval and renaissance manuscripts, from which he had developed a series of canons of excellence, expressed in his vindication, *The Pen and Type Design* (London, The First Edition Club, 1928). Above all, he wished his type to be 'uniform or regular in . . . height, breadth, method of construction, direction, alignment'; he wished for a pen-like rhythm of thicks and thins; and he demanded consistency of treatment throughout. As with the more conventional renaissance roman and italic types under scrutiny during the typographical revival, the ultimate sources of letter forms were eighth-century Carolingian minuscules (the ancestor of the lower case), and Roman inscriptional capitals (the ancestors of the upper case). Hewitt chose to disregard all historical developments which had involved cutting letters in stone or metal, and to regard descent through the nib as the only legitimate line. In doing so, he was courting disaster, since emergent typographical orthodoxy was firmly anchored in the traditions of punchcutting and letter carving.

The process of converting Graily Hewitt's designs into type was delegated to James Shand from the outset. During the weekend of 22 and 23 January 1927 in Oxford, Hewitt identified his preferred handwritten letters. Armed with this specimen, Shand went directly on Monday 24 January to Fetter Lane to meet W. J. Burch, the managing director of Lanston Monotype. So began an eight-month triangular correspondence, with Shand acting as intermediary between artist and manufacturer. He spent a number of weekends at Hewitt's home, Phillis Mead, Treyford, near Midhurst in Sussex, learning to play golf between the discussions about typography and calligraphy, and on one occasion taking an amazed Hewitt to visit the Monotype factory at Salfords. To apply the name Treyford to the fount must have seemed very appropriate to Shand under these circumstances, and Johnson agreed to it on 25 April 1927.

Most modifications of Hewitt's original designs were in fact made at the suggestion of Burch, and out of technical necessity. Hewitt's serifs for example Burch thought likely to 'overhand and foul the next letter', and so were curtailed.[11] Hewitt's upper-case J similarly required too much kern, and so was shortened at Burch's request.[12] Treyford's size was also decided by Burch. When he first saw the designs, he wrote that they would be unsuitable for a body of 12-point or less. Shand felt that the height and depth of Hewitt's ascenders and descenders would require a 16-point body. Burch on the contrary stated 14-point to be most versatile, and so Treyford was cut to this size. In practice, however, it was always leaded.[13]

Johnson intervened in the design and manufacture process only once – over the controversial perpendicular descender of the y. As early as 24 January, Burch had objected to this as resembling an inverted h. The calligrapher was however adamant that consistency dictated this form. Shand accepted Hewitt's arguments and repeated them to Burch, who was equally convinced that it spoiled the fount. By 7 February, after a weekend in the country, Shand had persuaded Hewitt to prepare alternative designs for v, x, and y, but a week later Hewitt's artistic temperament rebelled and Shand backed down – 'the force of your remarks were so clearly evident that we agreed to cancel any attempt at an alternative form.'[14] Johnson was however still unhappy, and as he witnessed the reactions of his friends to the new type became more and more concerned that this one idiosyncracy would blight the whole fount. On 22 August he made an eloquent attempt to persuade the artist:

> By the bye I have often and often wondered about the vertical Y of your fount. My own taste, as you know, is as receptive as can be and I quickly accustom myself to the unusual and like it very well. On the other hand I have been watching the effect of it on all my friends, typographical friends and artistic friends. Of course one discounts a good deal of criticism forthwith. One knows exactly those of one's friends who resent anything even slightly new. Only one man has actually liked it. . . . My worst shock came from my best friend, Bernard Ashmole the present Director of the British School at Rome. He is one of the best scholars on Greek and Roman Sculpture now living and has the keenest sense of form of any man I know. He liked the fount enormously, but said that the Y gave him a curious back-handed sense for the whole fount. He pointed out that this was because Y is so frequently in English a terminal letter and that the Y therefore thrusts itself at you on the page. He even advocated having two classes of Y, one for the terminal poition and the other (which might be straight) for the medial position.
>
> I give you this for what it is worth, but I do believe that we gain enormously by getting the point of view of the artist of the sense of form who is able to see the wood clearly without being embarrassed by the trees.[15]

Hewitt gave way and sent an alternative design directly, but was later to regret his compromise:

> Of course I lament throughout the change in the **y**. And if you will set such a sentence as 'Is it nothing to you, all ye that pass by' as now set and as set before with the straight **y**, I am hoping and thinking you will personally agree with me, that the alteration is but a sort of pretty sop thrown to convention to propitiate a prejudice. I made the curl only to please Mr. Johnson. I don't believe in it, but believe rather that in spite of his fears the uncompromising straightness, perpendicularness would have been quite soon accepted and appreciated and have given the work a better chance than this weakened substitute of the Army Club cigarette alphabet. However that's me, and I did my very best to please others than myself. Not the safest thing to do after all.[16]

Punches for all the lower-case roman sorts and some of the upper-case were cut by Monotype during March and April 1927, and matrices were sent to Oxford on 21 April.[17] Shand was impatient to give Treyford a trial, and by 25 April type had been cast at Oxford and two variant specimens printed on different papers using the lower-case roman and only **B, E, G, H, N**, and **O** of the upper-case. On 10 May, Shand reported to Hewitt 'I have two or three interesting little jobs which I would like to try it on.' His patience was rewarded on 27 May: 'The balance of the "Treyford" matrices have arrived and I am very busy (and a little excited) setting up the first page.' This 'first page' was probably Hewitt's 'Defence' of his type, printed as a single page specimen. Shand worked quickly, and specimens of the complete roman fount were despatched to the designer on 27 May 1927.

Hewitt and Shand had perhaps learned by their mistakes with the roman sorts, and faster progress was attained in the drawing and cutting of the Treyford italics. Tracings of Hewitt's designs for the lower-case were sent to Monotype on 11 June, and proofs and matrices were returned to Oxford on 27 June. A specimen of the whole alphabet was completed by 4 July, and Hewitt was delighted with it.[18] The only remaining sorts were the italic figures, which Shand thought unnecessary but Hewitt demanded, and which were cut during July 1927. The fount (including the hardwon alternative **y**) was finally complete by 24 September 1927, when rejected sorts were weeded out, and the only later changes were adjustments in alignment of individual sorts.

Treyford got a mixed reception. First impressions were on the whole good, and there was little indication that it would retreat so swiftly into obscurity.

Until June 1927, no one but Johnson, Shand, Hewitt, and a small circle of Monotype personnel was aware of the new fount. Once specimens of the roman sorts were available however, Johnson began to canvas the opinions of his friends:

> Foss was with me yesterday (I think you have met him from time to time at the Double Crown) and was let into the secret. He said he liked the type very much and said, what most of us have said, that it grew on him while he was looking at it.[19]

Johnson respected the views of Hubert Foss, who was himself a very accomplished book designer (as well as publisher, printer, and musician). Johnson also asked his friend Strickland Gibson, Keeper of the University Archives, what he thought, and Gibson, well aware of Treyford's palaeographical inspiration, was effusive. On receipt of the complete specimen on 2 July 1927, Gibson wrote:

> The folio sheet is truly a fine sight; the italic ranges excellently with the roman. I think the G. H. type must be a great success, and I hope that you will receive adequate reward for your enterprise. Now I want to see a whole book of it.

Gibson was as good as his word, and commissioned the first book to have been set in Treyford.[20] Oliver Simon was also sent a copy of the completed specimen. His judgement has not survived in full, but he apparently thought it 'arty'.[21]

Some professional typographers saw artistic merit in Treyford before Morison made this view untenable. W. J. Burch was forced by Shand to give his opinion of Hewitt's designs, and he wrote to Johnson on 24 January 1927 that 'Generally speaking, the face looks very well', and that he found the 'general appearance of the face . . . very agreeable'. Whatever less favourable comments had been received, Shand was nothing but encouraging towards Hewitt: 'Your type goes a wide round of approval with, of course one or two vehemently adverse criticisms. But the more noise the merrier!'[22]

Having seen specimens of the Treyford romans, Johnson began in June 1927 to consider what should be the first publication using Oxford's new proprietary type. His earliest intention was to publish first a setting of Hewitt's own vindication of Treyford, but when he was invited to enter Pierpont Morgan's competition to design the Revised *Prayer Book of the American Episcopal Church*, he could not resist the temptation to set one of Oxford's two entries in Treyford (the other, safely and predictably, to be set in Fell): 'we propose to have a fling with your type and shall expect you to draw for us some magnificent rubrication. It will be the greatest fun, although I do not expect anything will come of it.'[23] Johnson was right: the competition was won by Updike.[24] Whether Oxford's failure was a result of poor typography must be discussed by professional typographers. It has to be admitted that Johnson was preoccupied with many other projects at the time, including the *Revised Book of Common Prayer*, and clearly did not expect to win. Both Fell and Treyford specimens were put together hastily, the Treyford even before the alignment of some sorts had been finalised, and the Fell specimen looks odd because it uses

Hewitt's initials which had been designed to accompany Treyford.

During the next two years, Johnson and Shand appear to have seized every opportunity to publicise Treyford and encourage its use. In November 1927, W.G. Constable of the National Gallery wanted printing his *Catalogue of Paintings by Italian Masters in the possession of W. H. Woodward,* and Shand designed and printed specimen pages in Poliphilus, Caslon, and Treyford.[25] Publication of Hewitt's 'Vindication' was delayed since Johnson's intention was to have it published by the First Edition Club whose account with the Press was outstanding – Johnson had refused to commence setting the Treyford book until A.J.A. Symons paid his bill.[26] The debt was paid in February 1928, and Shand began to design Hewitt's apologia. Specimens and proof slips were sent to Symons on 20 April. At the same time, Hewitt was sent specimens of all setting in Treyford then under way at Oxford: a type specimen for an exhibition at Cologne; *Horne's Orion* for the Scholartis Press; G. W. Wheeler, *Bodley's Early Catalogues;* and specimens and proofs of his own book.[27] *Bodley's Early Catalogues* and *Orion* were both published by 4 June, and Johnson commented to Hewitt on 16 June that 'The type is creating all the interest it deserves.' On 29 June, Shand tried to peddle his wares to Monotype, offering to produce a number of the *Monotype Recorder* in Treyford, an offer which does not appear to have been taken up.[28] *The Pen and Type Design* (a rather snappy title from the author after printers and publisher had toyed with several more cumbersome versions) was finally published around the end of October 1928, proofs having earlier been sent to B. H. Newdigate and Stanley Morison for review in the *London Mercury* and *Fleuron* respectively. Newdigate's review was published in the *London Mercury* in December 1928, and was favourable towards Hewitt's 'very beautiful' fount. Johnson and Shand continued to persuade publishers to consider setting prestige works in Treyford. In October 1928, Denis Cohen of the Cresset Press proposed having *Gulliver's Travels* printed at OUP. Johnson's reply is suggestive: 'There is nothing that Shand or I would like better than to do more work for you', but he must know the name of the proposed artist before committing himself, in order to satisfy 'the sanctity of my imprint'. As a postscript he adds 'This book could hardly be more suitable for one of our proprietary founts.'[29] The proprietary fount which Johnson and Cohen had in mind at this point was Treyford. Specimens of *Gulliver* set in Treyford and in Baskerville were despatched to Cohen with estimates in January 1929,[30] and a specimen of Catullus set in Treyford.[31] During February 1929, Shand was designing a book set in Treyford for the Arts Workers' Guild (Miller, *Ruskin Reconsidered*), a body who would clearly have appreciated Hewitt's calligraphy.

Stanley Morison's long awaited review of *The Pen and Type Design* was published in the final issue of *The Fleuron* in 1930. Graily Hewitt had dreaded being 'dealt with' by Morison for some time, and with some justification, since *The Pen and Type Design* was very antagonistic towards Morison's views, particularly in its championship of the pen versus the chisel. Shand asked Morison on 22 February 1929 'to assure him yourself that you have no malevolent intentions'. Morison in turn admitted to Johnson 'My only feeling about Mr Hewitt is that I am afraid of him'.[32] The last significant item set in Treyford for a number of years was *Two Letters of Petrarch to Boccaccio Printed as a Specimen of the Treyford Type Designed by Graily Hewitt for the University Press, Oxford* 1929, published as an insert in *The Fleuron*. Two letters containing allusions to calligraphy and fine books were selected and introduced by Morison, illustrated with two collotype facsimiles, the whole designed by James Shand and set in Treyford (figure 2). Morison himself thought it 'a fair shewing of the fount'.[33] In his review, Morison took his cue from Hewitt's own apologia, and was merciless: 'Mr Hewitt is not, in our opinion, welcome to dismiss the printer as a mere corrupt imitator of the more highly endowed scribe.' As far as Morison was concerned, the design of type should be determined by the historical processes of carving letters in stone and punchcutting. Hewitt's crime (and incidentally John Johnson's as sponsor) was to deny the centrality of this dogma.

What is most significant about Morison's review of Treyford however is its effect. Hewitt was later to upbraid Johnson with his 'lack of championship . . . in or about 1930, over the Treyford Type,[34] a charge which Johnson was unable to deny. Some brave publisher had defiantly considered using Treyford in the wake of Morison's demolition: 'The first result of your article on the Treyford Type in the *Fleuron* is that I am to set in it a work of some magnificence.'[35] But no record survives to say who this was or what the magnificent work was to have been. Johnson does not appear to have encouraged his customers to use Treyford, partly perhaps because the enthusiast Shand had left the Press for the commercial world in 1929. It is a sign of Morison's growing dominance of typography that none of the typographers, publishers and printers who had warmed to Hewitt's work during the period 1927–9 dared to use Treyford after 1930. Its use during the thirties seems to have been limited to jobbing printing for Hewitt's own Manuscript Club, and its one revival for bookwork seems to have been for Viscount Carlow's Corvinus Press in 1936.[36] At the height of the OUP's enthusiasm for Graily Hewitt, around 1927, it appears that he was encouraged to write a book on handwriting by Humphrey Milford, Publisher to the University, but when his manuscript was finally delivered in 1937, it was rejected.[37] A full bibliography of the Treyford type remains to be compiled: after a clutch of minor titles published during 1927 and 1928, the list would be a short one.

It seemed when writing this article that Treyford would never again be used for letterpress composition. All type was melted down in 1966, and the fount

2. One of the *Two Letters of Petrarch to Boccaccio* which were set in Treyford to illustrate Stanley Morison's review of the type in *The Fleuron* (1929). The letters dealt with handwriting, fine books, and master-and-student relationship reminiscent of that which existed between John Johnson and James Shand until 1930. The extracts were in fact chosen by Morison, and the designer was Shand himself. Now printed from a new casting of the type for the use of the Whittington Press.

THIS YOUNG MAN'S character has won my affection to such an extent that he is as dear to me as a son of my own would be, and perhaps dearer, because a son, as is the way of our young men, would wish to rule, whilst he is studious to obey; he consults my desires rather than his own pleasure, and that without any wish or hope for reward, but out of pure affection and perhaps the expectation of self improvement by converse with me. He came to me two years ago, and I wish that he had come earlier, though much earlier it could not have been because of his age. Four of my friends had promised me their help in making a fair copy of the confused mass of my prose letters, I myself being distracted by many affairs. Would that the quality of the letters were equal to the quantity! All four abandoned the attempt halfway, but this young man has completed the task alone, and copied, not all the letters, but enough to make one not too enormous volume; their number, if I include this letter, will amount to three hundred and fifty. *You shall see them, please God, written in his hand, not in the rambling and ornate letters affected by our calligraphers, or painters perhaps we should call them, which delight the eye at a distance, but are fatiguing on closer application. As though letters were invented for some purpose other than that of reading, and as if the very word did not mean, as the prince of grammarians[1] says 'a path to reading'[2] My pupil's letters are disciplined, clear, and helpful to the eye, and no liberties are taken with orthography or grammar.*

[1] Priscian   [2] *legitera*

withdrawn. The matrices of all OUP's withdrawn Monotype founts were lost during the nineteen eighties. However, the recently re-established Merrion Monotype Company discovered they still had the Treyford punches, and a fresh set of matrices was struck for the Whittington Press, from which the type was cast that has been used to set the specimens that illustrate this article.

Stanley Morison's condemnation of this typographical experiment had depended upon the insoluble link between metal technology – punchcutting – and typography, which has also now been swept away. Perhaps it is therefore time for some bright young typographer, another James Shand, to reconsider Graily Hewitt's calligraphy as 'type'.

Peter Foden has worked in local, institutional, and business archives in Britain over the past dozen or so years. About half that time was spent at the Oxford University Press, discovering a world strangely suspended between academia and commerce. He began the job of organising OUP's heritage, presenting the results of his research through lectures, publishing, and museum displays. The collections span more than three hundred years of the history of book design and manufacture, from the seventeenth century when John Fell endowed the University with the means of printing books well, to the twentieth in which a colourful procession of academics-turned-craftspeople (notably John Johnson) pushed the bounds of book production into fine art.

NOTES

1. A similar roman fount was however cut by Louis Hoell for the Bremer Presse in Munich and used for their 1923 English-language prospectus of the Iliad and Odyssey set in Hoell's Greek type.

2. *The Fleuron*, volume 7 (Cambridge and New York, 1930), p. 180.

3. Oxford University Press Monotype Type Specimens, 1962, 1969, 1976. The only matrix cases were in store at the University Press until at least 1976, but are now lost.

4. The Printer's Letterbooks contain a copy of every letter sent out from the Printer's Office during John Johnson's period in office (1925–46). There are four series: Delegates' letters, Amen House letters, General letters, and Private letters. The Private letterbooks include correspondence concerning the development of what is now the John Johnson collection in the Bodleian Library, but also much business correspondence, particularly with Johnson's close friends in the private presses. All letters quoted in this article written by Johnson or James Shand are preserved as copies in either the General or Private series. Carbons of some also survive in two files on Treyford: the file of correspondence with Monotype, 1927–56, and Johnson's own file of correspondence with Graily Hewitt (containing type specimens), 1927–43. Extracts from the archives of the University Press are published by kind permission of the Secretary to the Delegates of the Press.

5. John Johnson to Geoffrey Cumberlege, Vice-President and Manager, Oxford University Press, New York, 4 September 1928.

6. Article on William Graily Hewitt in *Who was Who*, 1951–1960, p. 516.

7. John Johnson to Graily Hewitt, 29 September 1928.

8. James Shand to W. J. Burch, 25 January 1927.

9. John Johnson to Graily Hewitt, 10 August 1943.

10. John Johnson to Graily Hewitt, 10 February 1928.

11. W. J. Burch to James Shand, 1 February 1927.

12. W. J. Burch to James Shand, 8 February 1927.

13. G. W. Wheeler, *The Earliest Catalogue of the Bodleian Library*, printed in 1927 for Strickland Gibson, for example, was set in 14/15-point Treyford (OUP Rough Estimate Book 26, p. 375).

14. James Shand to Graily Hewitt, 14 February 1927.

15. John Johnson to Graily Hewitt, 22 August 1927.

16. Graily Hewitt to James Shand, 9 October 1927, concerning the Oxford entry for the new American Prayer Book competition.

17. Very full records survive of the design process, in original correspondence preserved in the OUP archive, and in the Monotype index cards and working drawings. I am grateful to David Saunders, Typographic Consultant to Monotype Ltd., for photocopies of the Treyford index cards and for copies of some of the drawings.

18. I have seen only one surviving copy of the folio specimen (Bodleian Library 25839.a.3). It is a handsome document printed in black on hand-made paper with two red initials (the six-line I and

T designed for the American Prayer Book). Two columns of text – Hewitt's 'Defence' – give the appearance of a medieval manuscript. This was perhaps the most effective layout for Treyford. The alphabet at the bottom of the specimen lacks the curled y and the italic figures, so dating it to July 1927.

19. John Johnson to Graily Hewitt, 11 June 1927. Hubert Foss was Oxford's first Music Publisher, and typographical adviser to Henderson and Spalding.

20. G. W. Wheeler, *The Earliest Catalogue of the Bodleian Library*. The Press estimate is dated 30 September 1927.

21. James Shand to Oliver Simon, 26 July 1927.

22. James Shand to Graily Hewitt, 26 July 1927.

23. John Johnson to Graily Hewitt, 24 June 1927. I am grateful to Dr John Bidwell for our discussions about the American Prayer Book competition.

24. James Shand to Graily Hewitt, 20 April 1928.

25. 30 copies printed at the University Press in 1928 (40 pp., royal quarto). Unfortunately the archives do not indicate the type of the finished book, and there is no copy at the Press or in the Bodleian Library.

26. John Johnson to Graily Hewitt, 7 February 1928.

27. James Shand to Graily Hewitt, 20 April 1928. See *Matrix 11*, pp. 179–83.

28. James Shand to W. J. Burch, 29 June 1928.

29. John Johnson to Denis Cohen, 22 October 1928.

30. Oxford University Press Rough Estimate Book 28, p. 155. Specimen pages set in Baskerville and Treyford have been pasted in. An estimate and specimen set in Fell Great Primer were made on 19 February 1929 (Rough Estimate Book 28, p. 205. See also *Matrix 11*, pp. 88–89).

31. James Shand to Denis Cohen, 18 January 1929.

32. Stanley Morison to John Johnson, 23 June 1930.

33. *ibid.*

34. Graily Hewitt to John Johnson, 9 August 1943.

35. John Johnson to Stanley Morison, 27 November 1930.

36. Louis Golding, *Pale Blue Nightgown* (see A. J. Flavell and Paul W. Nash, 'A Nice Young Man', Viscount Carlow and the Corvinus Press, *Matrix 12*, p. 70).

37. Memo from Sir Humphrey Milford to John Johnson, 31 March 1937: 'Graily Hewitt, dear man, by the way, is ten years late with the delivery of the MS.' Hewitt's book, *Handwriting – Everyman's Craft*, was proposed to the Delegates of the Press for publication on 5 February 1937 but was 'ploughed' by them on 30 April 1937. *Handwriting* was published in 1938 by Kegan Paul, Trench, Trubner and Co.

ABCD
EFGHIK
LMNOPR
STUVW
XYZ
JQ

1. Wood-engraved initials made by Eric Gill for the Golden Cockerel Press

Letters are Things:
The Wood-engraved Initials of Eric Gill

BY SEBASTIAN CARTER

Eric Gill not only carved letters in stone and turned his designs into type, he also produced a large number of engraved titles, initials, and alphabets for book publishers. In Matrix 15 (1995), Sebastian Carter describes how some of these engravings, as well as the original Golden Cockerel type, were rescued from the scrap heap and ended up in his possession.

Most readers of *Matrix* will be familiar with the magnificent engravings Eric Gill made for the Golden Cockerel Press edition of *The Four Gospels* of 1931. In them he emulated the historiated initials found in medieval illuminated manuscripts, in which pictures illustrating the text which follows are intertwined with the opening letter. Sometimes, too, smaller subsidiary initials later in the same text also pick up themes in a less exuberant way. Gill took this idea and gave it a twentieth-century look – both in the figures, which are unmistakeably his, and also in the relative thriftiness of means, plain black on white.

The actual design of the letters, of course, is outstanding. Gill's practice, as described by John Dreyfus,[1] was to engrave a fluid white outline which was then cleared by an assistant, usually R. J. Beedham; after that, any large areas of white were cleared with a power router. The example of a chapter opening from *The Four Gospels*, which Dreyfus illustrates with proofs of both Gill's outline engraving and the final block, makes it clear that Beedham sometimes showed considerable interpretative skill in deciding what Gill meant in certain figurative details, such as people's hands. Nevertheless, this system involved a rather un-Ruskinian subdivision of labour, and a first glance at Gill's often-stated principles might lead one to think it was against them too; but it was made necessary by the great output of the workshop. In particular the long sequence of marginal decorations for the Golden Cockerel *Canterbury Tales* would have been inconceivable done in any other way.

For another well-known category of work, the small book-labels, this practice was not necessary. The lettering was almost always engraved in white line on black, and needed no laborious clearing. Although Gill's labels are less accomplished than those of his one-time pupil Reynolds Stone, many have a rough elegance and the best, such as the early one for John Rothenstein (Physick.175) or the late one for Thereze Mary Hope (P. 883), are splendid examples of their kind. Often the lettering seems to improve when combined with an illustration, as in the charming bookplate for Miriam Rothschild (P. 834) with its leaping deer, or the device for the British Medical Association (P. 913), from which I recently printed a small edition before the block was put for safety in a bank vault.

Far less well known is Gill's work in engraving plain unadorned lettering, in positive black on white, either as lettering pieces or as alphabets. Often this can be mistaken for type, and indeed Fiona MacCarthy in her biography[2] illustrated a cover for the Golden Cockerel Press 1930 Spring List (P. 625), which is entirely engraved, as an example of the type which Gill designed for the Press, to which it is similar. Throughout his career, he produced a long series of titles and alphabets for Count Harry Kessler, first when Kessler was working at the Insel Verlag, and later for his private press, the Cranach Press. Most of these represent Gill in his most all-in-a-day's-work manner, and often look like line-blocks of lettering by someone else. Quite a lot of them are not in the Victoria and Albert Museum collection, which comprises the artist's own set of proofs given to the Museum by his widow in 1952, and so do not appear in John Physick's catalogue, which is based on that collection.[3] (This is not in itself a mark of uncharacteristic or second-rate work: the catalogue begins in 1908, and so omits the beautiful and astonishingly mature titling-piece engraved for the magazine *The New Age* in 1907.) They are illustrated in the appendix to Christopher Skelton's edition of the complete engravings,[4] which also shows a pair of remarkable two-colour initials engraved for Kessler by Gill jointly with the French sculptor Aristide Maillol: Gill cut the letters and Maillol the second-colour block showing the figure and flower which are interwoven with them. These blocks (G. 11, 12) are dated 1910, and so were cut about the same time as the bizarre episode when Kessler tried to persuade Gill to go and work with Maillol: Gill got as far as Maillol's studio at Marly-le-Roi outside Paris, and then turned back, deciding that such a venture was not for him. Despite this, he continued working in a collaborative way with Maillol, who of course illustrated some of the most beautiful Cranach Press books. They combined in 1925 to make a Cranach press-mark with Gill's lettering and Maillol's figure (P. 313), and Gill cut some sets of white initials set in black rectangles for Maillol himself to engrave with ornaments (P. 314, 500), as well as designing some ornamented initials himself, such as those for the 1931

Cranach edition of Rilke's *Duinese Elegien*, which was set in Edward Johnston's strange chancery italic.[5]

Of the alphabets of what might be described as one-off wood type, the first
example was cut for the St Dominic's Press at Ditchling in 1918 (P. 146). It is a
nine-line-pica version of Caslon, and is not readily indentifiable as Gill's work. It
was for Robert Gibbings at the Golden Cockerel Press, a decade later, that his
more characteristic titling alphabets were done. All these sets of blocks were
described by Physick as 'woodcuts', and Skelton followed him in this; but whereas the Ditchling set looks as if it probably was, the Golden Cockerel ones are all
engravings on end-grain boxwood. There were two main sets, P. 552–3, both
made in 1928. P. 552, the smaller, is cut on a four-and-a-half-pica body, except for
the J and Q, which are larger to accommodate the tails. The bigger, lighter alphabet is six-line-pica, again with the J and Q larger.

After Robert Gibbings sold the Golden Cockerel Press to Christopher Sandford in 1933, the printing shop at Waltham St Lawrence was closed down and
the type and other material were transferred to the Chiswick Press, where Sandford was a director. There it was used for Golden Cockerel publications until the
closure of the Press and the selling of the name to the New York publisher
Thomas Yoseloff. With the name, Yoseloff bought the type, and as he did not
need it, he put it into storage in Bentall's furniture warehouse in Kingston-on-
Thames – where coincidentally Gill had carved the name on the main shop
front.[6] There it languished, virtually forgotten, until the Rampant Lions Press
took an interest in the type in 1971. We were planning an edition of the *Greek
Anthology* for a customer who had made some translations, and were going to
set the Greek in 18-point New Hellenic. My father Will thought that the 18-point
Golden Cockerel Roman, designed by Gill in 1929 for *The Four Gospels*, would
go very well with the Greek, and wrote to Christopher Sandford to find out what
had become of it. Sandford explained the position with Yoseloff, and put us in
touch with his London agent in the Charing Cross Road. Here our customer got
a firm brush-off from an assistant, and as the *Anthology* project languished, we
did not pursue the matter. However, I had noticed that one of the directors of
Yoseloff's English company was a friend of mine, Peter Cowie, who ran a small
film publishing imprint called Tantivy Press which had come under the Yoseloff
umbrella. Three years later, I was discussing an edition of Gill's *Essay on typography* with Deighton Bell, the Cambridge bookseller, and we thought that the
14-point size of Golden Cockerel would suit the book if we could use it; so I
wrote to Peter to see if he could use his influence to get permission. This new
move was successful, Yoseloff gave us permission to borrow the type, and I went

down to Bentalls in June 1974 to inspect it. The warehouse was one of those vast places with a lift big enough to take a removal lorry up to the top floor. In one of the bays I found the Golden Cockerel material, which consisted of quite a few cases of the 18-point Gill type in almost pristine condition, together with tin boxes of individual sorts, and standing pages of the 14-point size, much more worn. There were also the 24-point and 36-point titlings, and several other miscellaneous cases.

It was immediately obvious that the 18-point and the titlings were the only usable parts of the collection, so I took away some of the cases and left the rest behind. After more discussions with Deighton Bell we decided that to set the *Essay on typography* in a big 18-point would be pretentious, and agreed to print the *Psalms of David* instead. The daunting job of hand-setting this book was eased by the assistance of two American students who came to the workshop during this period, Kate Emlen and Anne Geer, but even so it took slightly over a year to complete the printing.

By around 1980, we had become so used to having the Golden Cockerel type in the workshop that we enquired of Thomas Yoseloff if he would be prepared to sell it. As the storage and insurance charges at Bentalls were becoming a burden, he generously agreed. The worn pages of type were scrapped, but we invited the St Bride Printing Library to take sample founts of the 14-point, which we have not got, and the 18-point, which we have. The matrices, which Christopher Sandford had kept back, were deposited by him in the Cambridge University Press collection of private press typographical material, and are now in the University Library. Other than this, the Rampant Lions Press has all the Golden Cockerel type in existence. The 18-point roman has a rugged power which makes it suitable for the classics – I can imagine doing a Shakespeare in it some day. The 36-point titling is in my opinion Gill's most beautiful typeface, far superior to the Perpetua titling which Stanley Morison praised so extravagantly.

Before the scrap people collected the residue of the material, I went down to Bentalls to check that nothing important had been left behind. This was fortunate, since one of the cases turned out to contain quite a few of the engraved wooden letters Gill had done for Golden Cockerel. (It is a testimony of the mess everything was in that even after this, when James Mosley of St Bride went down to collect his founts, he found some more.)

The most interesting pieces were some of the smaller initials from *The Four Gospels*. The bigger historiated ones Gill used to fill with gesso, mount on little pedestals and sell as miniature sculptures; but several of the small ones survived in printable form. There is a T with a flamboyantly devilish serpent squiggling down the margin introducing the temptation of Jesus in the wilderness in Matthew, and later in the same gospel an **A** interlaced with a whip introduces the scourging of Jesus. There is a foliated **B** which begins the parable of the fig tree in Luke. And there are two words, WHEN and JESUS. The second appears at the end of the first chapter of Matthew,'. . . and they called his name Jesus'. It then reappears over the page with the other one at the beginning of the chapter, 'Now when Jesus was born. . . .' (The big picture **N** must have had the gesso treatment, and the **OW** was among the blocks which went to St Bride.) Both words are re-used later: WHEN to open the Palm Sunday account in Matthew, and the JESUS in Luke.

These engravings are shown as illustrations together with a few other initials from Golden Cockerel books. The Rampant Lions collection also has a number of unadorned assorted initials ranging from the quite large to the very small. The core of the collection, however, is the two alphabets mentioned above, P. 552 3. P. 552 is complete, and I have printed it that way, but P. 553 is short of D, G, N and T, and so I have printed a selection from this (figure 2). The purpose of these alphabets may seem a bit puzzling: when initials are needed for a particular text, it is usual to make only the letters required, and that is what Gill usually did. A single alphabet is virtually useless for setting words, where duplication is inevitable in all but the rarest cases. (Unusually, *King Lear*, *Hamlet* and *Macbeth* are each possible – but not *Othello*.) The Cockerel procedure seems to have been to make electros where required, several of which came with the collection, but the wood letters seem to have been used chiefly as initials, since many of the blocks such as the **T** and **L** with vacant space in them have been rather crudely stepped off with a saw to take inset lines of type.

A case where they were used for whole words was in the one book produced during the Sandford years which approaches *The Four Gospels* in grandeur, the *Paradise Lost* of 1937. This was the first time the 18-point Golden Cockerel roman had been used for poetry, and one of the few times Sandford used the type at all, in either size, which accounts for its good condition. Sandford, writing in *Pertelote* (1943), challenged any pernickety printer to find fault with the presswork, which is not at all bad; but the book is let down by the feeble wood-engravings, by Mary Groom. The 36-point titling appears throughout for two-line initials, but a few of the openings of the books into which the poem is divided use the wood alphabets for words. At the beginning, SING is set in P. 552, while Books 8 and 10 open with words set in P. 553. Electros must have been used: there is a repeated **O** in Book 8 (in the words NO MORE), and a nicked **H** in Book 10, whereas the wood master is undamaged.

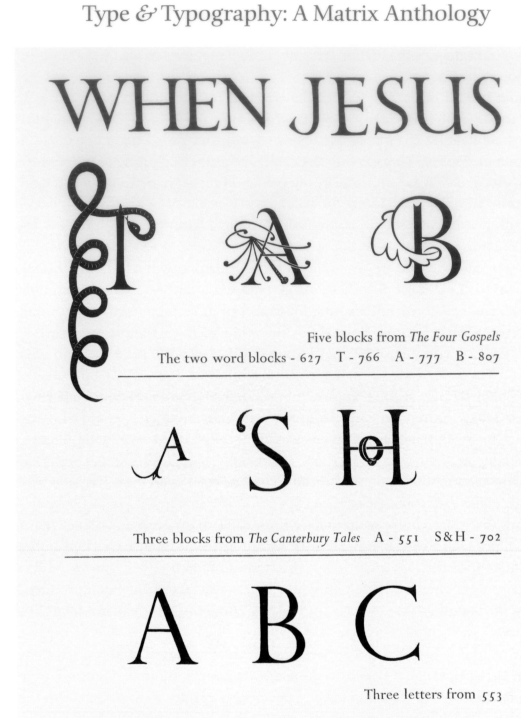

Five blocks from *The Four Gospels*
The two word blocks - 627   T - 766   A - 777   B - 807

Three blocks from *The Canterbury Tales*   A - 551   S & H - 702

Three letters from 553

2. Designed for *Matrix* by Sebastian Carter at the Rampant Lions Press, Over, Cambridge. The blocks were originally printed from the wood and are given their numbers from J. F. Physick's catalogue.

One final category of block was included with the Gill engravings we inherited (several of which have his monogram scratched in the side): these are blocks designed by Gill but entirely engraved by Beedham, not just finished by him. They are reproduced by Skelton in his appendix on Beedham. There is a set of foliated capitals (G/B.1) and some big letters with swashes including a J which was used in *The Four Gospels* (Mark, Chapter 1). About half of the blocks which the Whittington Press borrowed for their *Miscellany of Types* on pp. 83–5 were from this group.

When *The Four Gospels* was published in 1931, my father Will, then aged nineteen, bicycled over to Waltham St Lawrence with some money saved up to buy a copy. When Gibbings found that he was a printer, he allowed him a trade discount off the sale price of eight guineas. The book, a treasured possession ever since, is now joined by the type in which it was printed, together with several of the engravings and many other beautifully engraved letters by this twentieth-century master.

Sebastian Carter was born in 1941, and studied English literature and the history of art at King's College, Cambridge. After university he worked for a number of publishers and designers in London and Paris before joining his father Will Carter at the Rampant Lions Press in Cambridge, which he now runs from his house outside the town. Here he has produced a long series of fine editions, often in rare typefaces such as Eric Gill's Golden Cockerel Roman and Hermann Zapf's Hunt Roman. Highlights have included Milton's *Areopagitica*, Samuel Beckett's *As the story was told*, and T. S. Eliot's *Four Quartets*, as well as a number of typographical display pieces such as *A printer's dozen* and most recently *In praise of letterpress*. He writes extensively on printing and typography, reviewing regularly for the *Times Literary Supplement* and the British Printing Historical Society's *Bulletin* and *Journal*. He guest-edited the 1990 Eric Gill number of the *Monotype Recorder*, and wrote the section on 'The Morison years' in the centenary number in 1997. His *Twentieth century type designers* (1987; new edition 1995; now out in paperback) has become a standard work. With only two exceptions, he has contributed to every number of *Matrix*.

NOTES

1. *A Typographical Masterpiece, An account by John Dreyfus of Eric Gill's collaboration with Robert Gibbings in producing the Golden Cockerel Press edition of 'The Four Gospels' in 1931*, The Book Club of California, 1990.

2. *Eric Gill*, Fiona MacCarthy, London, Faber and Faber, 1989.

3. *The Engraved Work of Eric Gill*, J. F. Physick, London, HMSO, 1963.

4. *The engravings of Eric Gill*, Christopher Skelton, Wellingborough, 1983.

5. *Italic Quartet, A record of the collaboration between Harry Kessler, Edward Johnston, Emery Walker and Edward Prince in making the Cranach Press italic*, John Dreyfus, Cambridge University Press, 1966.

6. Catalogue No. 633 in *The Inscriptional Work of Eric Gill*, Evan Gill, London, Cassell, 1964, and in David Peace's expanded version, *Eric Gill, the Inscriptions*, London, Herbert Press, 1994.

1. A proof of a W, one of the early copperplate initials belonging to the Oxford University Press museum. The original pulls used in *Matrix 17* were taken on Rives Heavyweight paper using a rolling press, by Jim Nottingham of the Department of Fine Art, University of Reading, who has described the process in *Bulletin 41 of the Printing Historical Society* (Summer 1996).

Bishop Fell's Overlooked Bequest in the OUP Museum

BY PETER FODEN

Rummaging through the collection of the Oxford University Press can turn up unexpected treasures. Alongside the well-known and highly influential Fell types, bequeathed to Oxford by Bishop Fell in the late 17th century, are more than fifty copper engravings of decorated initial letters. In Matrix 17 (1997), *Peter Foden sorts them out and traces their origins.*

The Fell Types belonging to the Oxford University Press include not only text founts (ranging from 'English' black letter to Coptic, Samaritan and Syriac), but also typographic flowers and wood-engraved decorated initial letters. Stanley Morison identified six distinct series (if not alphabets) of the latter.[1] He hypothesised the copper-engraver Michael Burghers as the cutter of the 'untypographical' series of 14-line pica decorated initial letters, upon the twin arguments that the designs are Dutch in style and the technique that of metal engraving.

The inventory of Fell's printing equipment annexed to the earliest printed specimens of the Fell Types (dated 1693) refers to '26 copper letters'. There survive in the OUP Museum collection no fewer than fifty-seven small copper plates engraved with decorated initial letters: could some of these plates possibly have been commissioned by Fell himself? The answer is probably 'Yes'. A number of other copper-engravings (by Michael Burghers and others) survive which were commissioned to illustrate books issued by Fell's Press between 1672 and 1686, most remarkably the plate for the half-title of Fell's first schoolbook, an edition of Aesop's Fables, of which this plate is the only relic.[2]

This is no new discovery, despite its omission by Morison. The original line-and-wash drawings for some of the initials (and also for headpieces and tailpieces of which plates also survive) were discovered and acquired for the Delegates of the Oxford University Press in about 1923.[3] Reproductions of some of the drawings were reproduced by the Cresset Press in 1931,[4] although the commentator A. F. Johnson oddly refers to the survival of 'blocks' rather than plates, implying that he thought them to be cut in wood rather than copper. Had they indeed been cut in wood, then doubtless the earliest of them would have been studied in Morison and Carter's great work on the Fell Types. For it was of course axiomatic to their generation of typographers that 'type' could only mean a raised printing surface, and these intaglio letter forms were therefore categorically not typographic.

These fifty-seven copper plates may or may not conform to the reader's definition of 'type', but some of them may nevertheless have belonged to Fell's Press at Oxford in the late seventeenth century, and may even have been commissioned by him for use alongside Walpergen's romans or italics. It is therefore worth asking the question whether these letters were indeed Fell's. There is nothing particularly unique about the designs. The concept of illuminated initials alive with birds and beasts, thronged with mythological, legendary, or scriptural characters, is of course older than printing. What may however be unique is the survival in one place of designs and plates, as well as the survival in libraries of books in which they were used.

Let us then take a closer look at the surviving plates and designs, with a view to establishing which of them might have been commissioned by Fell during the period 1672–86. We may immediately discount the initial T illustrated with a view of the Clarendon Building (built 1712–13). It has been concluded by Helen Mary Petter, who is the best authority upon this period of Oxford engraving, that the line-and-wash drawings now in the OUP Museum were made by Henry Aldrich in about 1700 expressly for the embellishment of the first folio Clarendon (published 1702–1703).[5] The subjects of these illuminations are diverse: mostly classical, there are nevertheless some Biblical scenes (A for Adam and Eve is for example a common theme from the sixteenth century onwards), and some allegorical symbols (such as A for the Arts, in which a seated and luminous angelic figure is surrounded by harp, globe, books, palette, armour and anchor, and holds a laurel wreath for the victor in these pursuits). For some designs there is no corresponding plate in the OUP Museum collection, and I suspect (but cannot prove without an exhaustive examination of all Oxford books of the period) that some of these have never been engraved.

Of the remainder of the collection of plates, there is one series which can be easily set apart. Seventeen smaller plates, each one measuring approximately 48 mm. square, share an identical border design stringed with pearls, and are illustrated with scenes from classical mythology.[6]

A ACTAEON, hunting in a forest, has glimpsed the nakedness of Diana bathing. As a punishment, Diana has turned him into a stag, and his own hounds are about to devour him.

B BELLEROPHON resists the advances of the wife of his host, King Proteus. She subsequently accuses him falsely, and his punishment is the task of slaying the Chimaera.

C CERBERUS, the three-headed guardian of Hades, is captured by Hercules – his Twelfth Labour.

D DEIANEIRA, the lover of Hercules, is abducted by the Centaur Nessus as he ferries her across a river; Hercules (left) retaliates by shooting Nessus with his bow.

E EVANDER (THE ARCADIAN PAN) – he is playing a pipe under a tree and an ox lies down to sleep.

F FORTUNA, her sail billowing, rides her dolphin across the sea.

G GANYMEDE is flown to Olympus by an eagle; the eagle is actually Jupiter who has fallen in love with Ganymede. This plate is not extant, but appears twice in Wood's History.

H HELLE and her brother Phrixus flee from their father Athamus and step-mother Ino on the back of a golden ram, but Helle falls through the clouds into the sea where she forms the Hellespont.

I ICARUS also falls from the sky as the hot sun melts the wax of his wings.

L LICHAS is thrown by Hercules into the sea (Deianeira had sent him as a messenger to Hercules when she heard of his infidelity, but the love-potion which she sent was, unbeknown to her, poisoned by Nessus – hence Hercules' harsh treatment of the messenger).

M MARSYAS about to be flayed alive by Apollo after their musical contest. Apollo's lyre (here something like a violin) lies at his feet.

N NEPTUNE, his trident raised, rides his chariot across the waves, drawn by Hippocampi.

O ORPHEUS plays his lyre [this plate was later altered to Q, thus making a nonsense of the mythological theme].

P PAN, unmistakeable here with his single eye and pan pipes, makes his music.

Q QUINTUS CURTIUS, a knight in armour, spurs his horse over the mountains and through the middle of the letter Q.[7]

R ROMULUS & REMUS suckle their wolf foster-mother.

T TRIPTOLEMUS, by whom man learned to grow cereals, was almost murdered in his bed by Lyncus, but Demeter saved him by turning Lyncus into a lynx.

V VULCAN at work in his forge.

The forms of the letters are sculptural, but tend to be very broad and crudely proportioned, with a minimum of shading, always to the left of verticals and beneath horizontals. The letter-forms are not dissimilar from the woodblock capitals printed in the early Fell type specimen books, but the P and R are open. The engraving is not of the purest technique, but the composition of most of the initials is very strong, particularly where there is action such as Neptune rising from the sea and throwing his trident.

The concept of such a mythological alphabet was not new in the seventeenth century. Gabriele Giolito has used such an alphabet of woodcut initials in books printed in Venice from 1539 onwards.[8] Some subjects in the Oxford mythological series are identical with those for the corresponding letters in Giolito's alphabet, but the composition and execution are, for the most part, dissimilar. These initials therefore belong to a very old European corpus of emblems.

Three initials belonging to this series were used in the printing of Anthony À Wood, *Historia et Antiquitates Universitatis Oxoniensis* (1674), together with an engraved title-page by Robert White for which the plate also survives (very worn) in the OUP Museum collection, and other engraved initials and ornaments. These three initials G, H and T are used with no particular relevance to Wood's subject matter (the histories of Magdalen College G, Brasenose G, Jesus College H, and St John the Baptist College T), and so I would conclude that this alphabet had been designed in or before 1674 for another publication. The alternative conclusion would be that the design and creation of such a 'display fount' was simply part and parcel of equipping a new Press, but against this I would point to the essential unitics of style and subject within this series. As well as copper initials, the compositor has used some of the fantastic wood-engraved initials attributed by Stanley Morison to Michael Burghers (viz: A, H, M, P, R, & S): did he do so because the appropriate copper-engraved initials were not available at the time? The family likeness in this series of copper initials is so strong that I do not believe this to have been the case – all must have been cut at about the same time and with a common purpose in view. I suggest that the wood-engraved 'Dutch Bloomers' were used in order to expedite production (copper gives way to wood in the histories of Academic Halls from p. 340 onwards) by reducing the number of printings of these sheets from two (on different presses with the consequent problems of accurate registration) to just one on a hand-press. Moreover, the Halls (unlike the Colleges) did not justify so expensive a process as engraving.[9]

Ten other copper-engraved initials of which the plates survive were also used in Wood's *Historia et Antiquitates*, and so may be proved to have belonged to

Fell's Press. Similar hatching techniques suggest that some may share the same engraver, but themes and typology are various. O is the ring of the Zodiac held by a bearded classical figure floating in space between the sun, moon, and earth, and was used as the initial for the Address to Charles II with which the *Historia* is prefaced, and again at the beginning of Wood's history of Christ Church (p. 246). *Liber primus* opens with what may have been a specially-commissioned capital H – Athene holding spear and gorgon shield against the background which is recognisable as the Oxford skyline (Oxford being identified as a latter-day Athens); at her feet stands her owl symbolic of wisdom, and the foliate border bears the arms of the four nations of Britain at its corners. King David, playing his harp, was used to introduce the second book of Wood's history, and the histories of University, Wadham, and Pembroke Colleges: this capital D is bordered with only a double fine line. The initial T opening the history of Balliol College and repeated at the beginning of Wood's *Fasti Oxonienses* (p. 386) is decorated with an ancient battle scene whose lines are rather firmer and stronger than the others used in Wood. Another extant plate for an initial C is illustrated with a bishop kneeling beneath a sunburst, and this precedes the history of Merton. Exeter College's initial S shows a man wrestling with a lion – perhaps Samson. A group of these plates is Biblical or mystical in inspiration, and the histories of Oriel and Corpus Christi Colleges commence with an initial R illustrated with the instruments of the Passion. The initial C employed in the histories of Queen's College and Trinity College is apparently by the same hand as these Biblical designs, but shows an eagle sitting on a branch beneath a smiling sun (if this is also intended to be Biblical, then it may represent John the Evangelist). I am at a loss to explain the illustration behind the initial P in the histories of New College and All Souls: it appears to represent a horseman in sixteenth-century doublet and hose who has been felled from his mount by an explosion or flash of light, and a soldier who holds up his round shield against the same peril. Could this perhaps (as it is by the 'Biblical' hand) be Saint Paul on the road to Damascus? An initial A is revealed by the open curtains of a royal tent, decorated with fleur de lys and Tudor rose; this does not belong to the 'Biblical' group of initials, but is used at the beginning of the history of Lincoln College.

Here, then, are twenty-seven extant copper plates for initial letters, and one design for which no plate survives, which may be proved to have been used by Fell's Press as early as 1674. Most of the remainder of the fifty-seven surviving plates are accounted for by designs taken from Aldrich's drawings of *c.* 1700. The 'odd men out' it will be impossible to classify or date without further research

EXAMPLES OF THE OXFORD DECORATED COPPER INITIALS

The surviving copper plate engravings may be divided into two groups chronologically: the first (see examples 2, 3, and 4) were acquired or commissioned by Bishop Fell in or before 1674; the second group were engraved c. 1700 from designs by Henry Aldrich, Dean of Christ Church and Editor of Clarendon's History (see examples 5 to 8).

2. Athene, clearly identified with her gorgon-headed shield and owl, guards the spires of Oxford, the Athens of Britain (note the arms of the four nations at the corners of the border). See page 231.

3. Another capital H, upon whose crossbar sits an angel carrying a shield (this is not the arms of any Oxford college).

4. Neptune: an example of the mythological alphabet described on p. 228.

5. The liberal arts: one of the initials designed by Aldrich (but the border has been added by the engraver, who may be Michael Burghers although he has not signed the plate).

6. A terrifying figure of death stalks beneath a tropical palm tree. Note the monogram MB (Michael Burghers). This is the only in-line initial in the Oxford collection.

7. Two classical females converse against a background of pyramids. Another Aldrich-Burghers production.

8. A victorious king in his chariot leads his captives. The composition is Aldrich's, but the strong – some would say crude – line engraving and hatching are typical of Burghers' work.

among the output of the Oxford Press during the late seventeenth and early eighteenth centuries, but I suspect them to be post-1686 on stylistic grounds. What, however, is the origin of the mythological alphabet which I hypothesise may correspond with the 'twenty-six copper letters' of the Fell inventory? They were not created for Wood's History (in which only three were used apparently at random and for which they have no relevance). Nearly all the myths to which they refer are to be found in one source – Ovid's *Metamorphoses*. And we know that Fell and his Partners intended to publish an annotated edition of Ovid, since the right to do so was expressly reserved in their 1675 agreement with Stationers' Company.[10] I should like to propose, as a working hypothesis for future research into illustration of Fell's books, that at least these seventeen extant plates (but perhaps an entire alphabet of twenty-six letters) were commissioned by Fell for just such a thoroughgoing edition. It would not have upstaged Sandys' English translation printed by John Lichfield of Oxford in 1632 (illustrated by Francis Clein), but it might have been more than a match for the school editions purveyed as a monopoly of the Stationers' Company.

And what of the half-dozen initials of Biblical or Mystical theme which were also used in Wood's History? Do we here catch a glimpse perhaps of Fell's aspirations for Oxford's Bible and liturgical publishing? His first Bible and Prayerbook (1675) were small quartos and used four-line pica wood-engraved initials, but these larger copper-engraved initials (King David, Samson, St Paul) would have been fitting ornaments to a very grand folio edition of either Bible or Prayerbook. As early as 1671, Fell had written 'I have a great mind, if it be possible, that we may be benefactors to the Nation in the matter of bibles', and he had appointed Richard Allestree, Regius Professor of Divinity, editor-in-chief of a new annotated Bible, but the project came to nothing.[11] Such initials as these would have been eminently suitable for such a project. Oxford, however, had to wait for its folio Bible until John Baskett produced the very grand but very flawed Vinegar Bible in 1717.

Peter Foden has worked in local, institutional, and business archives in Britain over the past dozen or so years. About half that time was spent at the Oxford University Press, discovering a world strangely suspended between academia and commerce. He began the job of organising OUP's heritage, presenting the results of his research through lectures, publishing, and museum displays. The collections span more than three hundred years of the history of book design and manufacture, from the seventeenth century when John Fell endowed the University with the means of printing books well, to the twentieth in which a colourful procession of academics-turned-craftspeople (notably John Johnson) pushed the bounds of book production into fine art.

NOTES

1. Stanley Morison, *John Fell, the University Press, and the 'Fell' Types* (Oxford, at the Clarendon Press, 1967), chapter XI, pp. 188–194.

2. Anne Becher, in *PHS Journal* 1997.

3. A. F. Johnson attributed the acquisition to John Johnson as Printer (who displayed them alongside the copper plates in his 'Record Room of the Press'), but the drawings were already in the possession of the Delegates by December 1923, when one of them was reproduced on the cover of the OUP advertising journal *The Periodical* (Vol. IX, No. CXXII, 15 December 1923) and was stated to have been 'lately, with many others, . . . purchased by the Delegates'.

4. A. F. Johnson, *Decorative Initial Letters* (London, The Cresset Press, 1931), pp. 174–179.

5. Harry Carter, *A History of the Oxford University Press, Volume I to 1780* (Oxford, at the Clarendon Press, 1974), introduction.

6. I am very grateful to my colleague Jenny McMorris for her help in identifying the mythological subjects of these initials. Most are to be found in James Hall, *Dictionary of Subjects and Symbols in Art* (London, John Murray, 1974).

7. A difficult and uncertain identification, but I follow A. F. Johnson, *op. cit.* p. 102.

8. A. F. Johnson, *op. cit.* pp. 102–103.

9. It is ironic, therefore, that the copy of Wood which I am studying now (bequeathed to the Press Typographic Library by Sidney Squires, typefounder) has been carefully marked to show the 'Dutch Bloomers' but the copper engraved initials were clearly of less interest to him.

10. Agreement between Sir Joseph Williamson, Sir Leoline Jenkins, Thomas Yate, John Fell, and the Stationers' Company, 9 March 1674 [new style 1675], printed in John Johnson & Strickland Gibson, *Print and Privilege at Oxford to the year 1700* (London, Oxford University Press, 1946), pp. 165–167.

11. Harry Carter, *A History of the Oxford University Press* (Oxford, at the Clarendon Press, 1974), pp. 59–60.

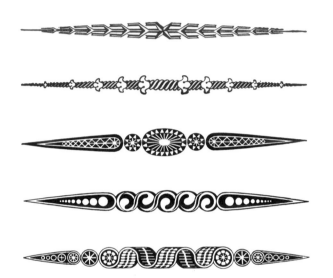

Swelled rules designed by Edward Bawden.

Borders and Swelled Rules Designed by Edward Bawden for the Oxford University Press

BY MICHAEL JOHNSON

The decorative elements of letterpress printing begin with borders and rules. Those created after the Second World War by Edward Bawden gave a bold new look to books and printed ephemera. Michael Johnson's essay in Matrix *16 (1996) celebrates Bawden's work as it is converted into digital form and given a new lease of life.*

In 1948–9 Edward Bawden designed a series of border units and swelled rules for the exclusive use of the Oxford University Press. Vivian Ridler, then Assistant Printer at the Press, commissioned the work from this well-known painter and designer, and asked the Monotype Corporation to manufacture the border units for use on OUP's Monotype casters. This article draws on correspondence and drawings surviving in the OUP and Monotype archives, as well as an interview with Vivian Ridler. Finally, samples of a newly digitised version of the borders are shown.

Edward Bawden (1903–89) often drew border motifs in his graphic design work, and this reflects a widespread interest during the inter-war years. Douglas Bliss, a fellow student at the Royal College of Art in London in the 1920s, noted Bawden's early interest. 'He was a student much impressed with an article by Francis Meynell on Printer's Flowers which appeared in *The Fleuron*.'[1] Examples of Bawden's work which used drawn borders include a poster series for the London Underground (1927–8)[2] and the title-page of Ambrose Heath's *Good Soups*, published in 1935 (figure 1). The latter is of interest here, as it has certain similarities to some of the OUP border designs (numbers B1203–5). Bawden also had his borders made into metal type early on in his career. The Curwen Press, for whom Bawden did much work, produced both a delicate arabesque ornament which appears in their 1928 type specimen book,[3] and a series of solid geometric designs[4] (figure 2). Bliss also noted that 'The Curwen Press was justly proud of the borders and typographic ornaments he [Bawden] provided for their title-pages, some of which had international acclaim.'⁵

Probably in late 1948, Ridler commissioned Bawden to design some contemporary versions of swelled rules and printer's border units. Ridler had a high regard for Bawden's work and had first met him in 1947 at the Royal College of Art in London, where they were both part-time teachers. Over lunch in Oxford, Ridler showed him some 'ornamental dashes' from a Caslon specimen book of 1844, and asked him to take on the work.

In a letter dated 3 January 1949, Bawden commented in relation to the 'lovely examples of Victorian swelled rules' that Ridler had sent him, that he had not attempted 'a similar elaboration of detail & richness of colour', but instead felt that 'plainse [*sic*] effects might be more serviceable'. Bawden mentions that he had designed corner pieces as well as units for setting in a line and that the design ideas could be further extended: 'it requires no more than a crossword intelligence & unlimited time for doing so.' He then promised to draw enlarged versions of any preferred design.

Of the border units, three styles were apparently designed. Ridler decided against producing the first design. The second design was produced in three variants (later numbered B1203–5 by Monotype) at 24- and 36-point. Finally, the third design was produced in four variants (B1206–9) at 18- and 24-point. Shown below are the final forms of the second and third designs (at 24-point) that Monotype manufactured for the OUP.

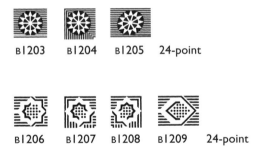

Figure 3 shows Bawden's rough sketches for three designs, which survive in the OUP archive. The first design was drawn at a height of ⁵/₁₆ in. (about 22-point) and the second and third designs at ³/₈ in. (about 30-point). The enlarged versions, at a height of 2 ins, only exist for the rejected first design (figure 4). The enlarged drawings of the other designs have not been found in the OUP or Monotype archives, but this probably reflects the fact that they were 'working' drawings. The first design appears to show that Bawden refined the rough sketches when he came to produce the enlarged 2 in. versions.

2. Letterpress border units designed by Bawden during the inter-war years for use at the Curwen Press.

1. Title page designed by Bawden for Ambrose Heath's *Good Soups* (image reduced from original page size of 188 x 124 mm).

On 23 February 1949 Ridler acknowledged receiving the border designs. A fee of ten guineas per border was agreed by the Printer (Charles Batey); Ridler commented that Monotype 'will probably take several months to do their part'.

A month later, Bawden sent working drawings for the 'three other type unit borders' and commented on the hours he had spent making them 'geometrically true and regular' while not producing something that differed too greatly from the accepted design. He suggested that photostat enlargements be made to test the designs before punchcutting began. Ridler replied the same day, saying that this was unnecessary as Monotype would carefully check the designs. Bawden also wrote that he hoped to draw the swelled rules within two or three weeks, for line block reproduction and suggested a fee of five guineas for each.

When OUP received Bawden's artwork for the swelled rules it was sent out to be photographed and two zinc masters produced. From these zincos, electroplated copies were made at the OUP and used to print from. A specimen book entitled *List of Ornaments, Borders & Swelled Rules in use at the University Press, Oxford* (October 1954) refers to 'Edward Bawden Rules' and states that 'Four electros. were made of each from two zincos. supplied in June 1949.' The swelled rules appear in two different sizes (with widths of 3 ins and 4 ins); the photographic nature of the process meant that an enlarged or reduced version of the artwork was easy to produce. Shown opposite the start of this article (p.236) are the swelled rules at the smaller of the two manufactured sizes. Bawden's artwork

3. Bawden's rough sketches for border units supplied to the Oxford University Press in about January 1949. The rejected first design is shown above, followed by the second and third designs which have an O.K. beside them. The second design contains the circle and oval motif (actual size, but rearranged).

for the third and fifth rule is known to survive in a private collection; both of these rules were drawn with a width of 8 ins.

About this time, Monotype also began manufacturing the border designs. As the first step in Monotype's production process, ten-inch pencil outlines were drawn of each border design (figure 5). These were drawn in mirror-image due to the subsequent manufacturing process. It is probable that Bawden's artwork would have been enlarged onto a glass screen and traced around in pencil. In addition to refining the design detail, the functional aspects concerning the alignment of one border piece to another were considered. Square border units having an equal point size and set width are the easiest for composition as they can be combined even when rotated ninety degrees to one another. However, two of the seven borders (B1205 and B1209) have a width of 1¼ ems and this was the subject of some discussion at the time. Bawden refers to the 1¼ em width units as 'lozenges'.

The ten-inch drawings survive in the Monotype archive and carry some additional information, which is unusual. On the B1203 border unit, the draftswoman has signed and dated her work, M. Bishop 13.1.49. This date must be erroneous going by the correspondence between Bawden and Ridler. At the top of the ten-inch drawing is the line 'M92535 of 1.3.49 for O.U.P. FROM CUSTOMERS ORIGINAL DRGS.' which also supports this view. 'M92535' is Monotype's matrix order number. The M indicates an order placed in the United Kingdom, as compared to Continental orders (CM), Overseas orders (OM), and American orders (A). It notes the drawing scales used (300 and 450) that correspond to the two point sizes (24- and 36-point) that were manufactured. There is also a slight variation in the centre line on the drawing which corresponds to the 24- and 36-point versions. The words 'Black' and 'White' have been added as clarification during the subsequent cutting of the wax pattern.

The outline on the ten-inch drawing was followed using a pantograph so as to cut a wax pattern at a smaller size. This pattern was then made into metal. This provided a guide for the engraving (again pantographically) of a steel punch with the design. The punch was initially 'cut fine' which means that the image area was made thinner than on the ten-inch drawing. Beneath the top of the punch, the metal was bevelled so that it became progressively thicker. Slivers of metal were removed from the top of the punch (known as 'facing down') until the thickness of the image matched the ten-inch drawing. The border units B1203–5 would have been particularly tricky as the black and white lines have an equal thickness which makes any variation noticeable. The ten-inch drawing of B1203 shows that the horizontal lines slightly overlap the em width assigned to the character. This overlap was removed by grinding during the manufacture of the punch. It was done at this stage to ensure that the type that was subsequently cast, would have a perfect join between units. The next stage was for a matrix to be struck from the punch, and type cast from this matrix. This was proofed and the whole process repeated until a satisfactory border unit was achieved.

Bawden was given an opportunity to comment on Monotype's work. In a letter dated 26 July 1949 from Banff School of Fine Arts, Alberta, Canada (where he was briefly teaching), Bawden says that he had received the photostat enlargements of separate units and would consider the modifications suggested by Monotype. From subsequent letters it appears that Monotype submitted their own design for one of the corner pieces, the one later adopted as B1204. Bawden comments that Monotype appear to have provided 'an ingenious solution to an awkward problem.' Later the letter shows two delightful drawings of

4. One of the enlarged drawings by Bawden for the rejected first border design.

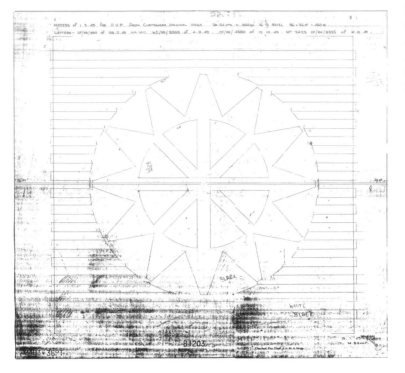

5. Monotype's drawing of 1949, for the border unit B1203. (Image reduced from original size of 13x14 inches).

6. Part of a letter dated 26 July 1949 from Bawden to Ridler referring to the second border design.

the border design which is something like this :- seems to be quite satisfactory & it could be proceeded with if the ~~Montype~~ Monotype people agree.

With best wishes

Yrs sincerely

Edward Bawden

First design

1 2 3 4 5 6 7 8 9 24 pt.

Second design

B1203 B1204 B1205 24 point

Third design

B1206 B1207 B1208 B1209 24 point

7. Newly digitized version of the three border designs.

B1203 and B1205 (figure 6), but leaves open the question of the B1204 unit.

On 5 October Bawden writes that he returns the type border designs and that the Monotype version of the problem corner piece (B1204) is certainly better than his own. Bawden notes that he 'cannot work out a compromise between the cornerpiece & the long & short border units which would be perfect: possibly a perfect solution does not exist within the limitations imposed by the border units themselves.' Further 'the irregularity of the corner-piece must be accepted, I believe, & I don't believe the Monotype version will look bad provided it is *not* joined to a square unit (as on the sample) but is followed instead by a lozenge: in fact, I would suggest that my own square unit for the border is put aside & not used, instead lozenge units in succession ought to be used or perhaps lozenge & cornerpiece units alternating. I wonder whether this rigmarole is clear to you?'

Bawden appears to be saying that B1203 should be abandoned, and only B1204 and B1205 should be used, (see below, left side). On the right hand side is the combination of border units that Bawden apparently wanted to avoid (which uses B1204 and B1203).

uses B1204 (corner piece) and B1205   uses B1204 (corner piece) and B1203

This was perhaps because the apparent misalignment and size variation of the corner piece (B1204) compared to the connecting units is more noticeable in the right hand example than the left.

In a letter dated 20 October, Monotype appears to be writing in response to an instruction from Ridler not to manufacture B1203. Monotype pointed out that if only B1204 and B1205 were made it would be difficult to compose the border to an even number of ems as the lozenge (B1205) equals 1¼ ems of body in length. He also commented that the revised corner piece they had produced needed to be a square unit of one em. On 21 October, Ridler conceded that the square unit was probably necessary, and asked for that and the rectangular one to be included when cutting the design.

When Bawden had initially submitted his rough sketches on 3 January 1949 he commented 'The borders probably are more successful than the rules'. Almost fifty years later, Vivian Ridler confirms that the borders did prove to be of more use at the Press. Bawden's designs were used at the OUP on such items as a Bible supplement for the *Printing Review* magazine[6] and a four page quarto booklet that was part of the OUP's contribution to the Festival of Britain in 1951.

A newly digitised version of the border units

The author has recently digitised the border designs using the FontStudio program on an Apple Macintosh computer; figure 7 shows various samples of these. From this a PostScript format fount was generated for use on Macintosh or IBM-PC computers. Monotype's ten-inch drawings were used as the principal reference source for the second and third designs (B1203–9); occasionally minor modifications were necessary to ensure that neighbouring borders aligned exactly. The relatively regular and symmetrical nature of the designs meant that the most efficient method was to plot points at exact co-ordinates, whereas it is

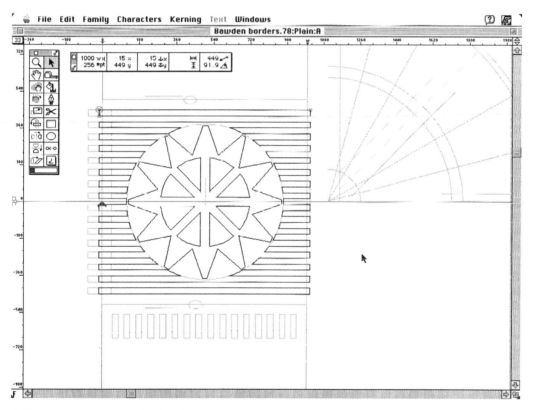

8. The editing window of the FontStudio program showing the digitized outline of border unit B1203. Note the greyed lines which are in the background layer and were used in constructing the border unit. The tool box at the top left of the screen, enables enlarged and reduced views, and manipulation of the outline such as rotation, enlargement and skewing. Individual points on the outline can be moved using the cursor (their exact co-ordinate position is shown in the readout box at the top of the screen).

Figure 9. Sample of the newly digitized second border design in use for a piece of ephemera.

usually easiest to scan the images and manually trace over them to create a digital outline. Figure 8 shows the finished B1203 border unit in the editing window of the FontStudio program. The greyed lines show some of the construction lines that were also used to create the geometrical shapes. One quarter of the circular elements were created and then electronically duplicated three times to make a complete circle. It is interesting to compare how Bawden's original sketch, Monotype's letterpress version and this newly digitised version differ.

Vivian Ridler recently saw the rough sketches for the rejected first design again, and commented with renewed interest on their potential. Bawden's sketches and the enlarged drawings have been used to produce a digitised version. This required some interpretation of the design. For example, the cross within a circle on the rough sketches (figure 3), becomes a cross within an oval in the enlarged version (figure 4). In order to reproduce Bawden's sketches in digital form, nine border units have been produced. Finally, figure 9 shows a recent piece of work using the digital version of the second border design.

NOTES

1. Douglas Percy Bliss, *Edward Bawden*, The Pendomer Press, Surrey, 1979, p. 45.

2. One of these posters is shown in Herbert Simon, *Song and Words, A History of the Curwen Press*, 1973, p. 179.

3. *A specimen book of types & ornaments in use at the Curwen Press*, The Fleuron Ltd, printed at the Curwen Press, 1928. The borders are also illustrated in *Matrix 5*, eight page insert preceding page 33.

4. Illustrated on p. 27 in 'The printed work of Edward Bawden', Hamish Miles, *Signature*, number 3, July 1936, p. 23–39. Also illustrated in *Matrix, op. cit.* 3.

5. Bliss, *op. cit.* 1. Similar praise is given in Robert Harling, *Edward Bawden*, Art and Technics, London, 1950, p. 40.

6. *Printing Review*, volume 18, number 62, Coronation 1953 issue.

After studying at the Department of Typography and Graphic Communication, University of Reading, United Kingdom, in the mid-1980s, **Michael Johnson** worked for Monotype Typography in their Type Drawing Office. This included various type design projects, as well as early development work on Monotype's TrueType fonts. In 1990 Monotype released his bitmap-style typeface Zeitgeist as part of their Classics library. After a couple of years working and travelling in the Far East and Australia he joined Oxford University Press, where he works on the text design of reference books, including many of its dictionaries. In 1999 he and Philip Atkins wrote, illustrated, and published their own guidebook to Oxford, called *The Heart of Oxford* (reviewed in *Matrix 19*). The book is set in Darjeeling, a typeface designed by Johnson, and based on his handwriting.

1. Many historic type decorations were re-cut in the 1920s and 30s, encouraging new contemporary work. This specimen of type decorations comprises 822 separate pieces, and was composed and printed in England by the Workshop Press, Hanna's. Thaxted.

A Collection of Printers' Flowers

BY MARK ARMAN

The background for Bawden's borders, in the previous essay, is the history of printers' flowers, from the 15th-century arabesques based on Islamic rugs and architecture to the floral exuberance of Victorian ornament. Mark Arman, in Matrix 9 (1989), surveys their revival in the 20th century, leading to the creation of new type ornaments by modern designers like David Bethel.

A few presses continue to use metal types, but yearly their numbers diminish as letterpress printing gives way to modern technology. In the last ten years the process has gathered speed and such august establishments as the Cambridge and Oxford University Presses have switched over to new methods; printing houses like the John Roberts Press and the Curwen Press have ceased trading altogether. Included with other material that went for scrap were printers' flowers which a few years ago decorated and enlivened the page. Generations of these embellishments have disappeared, even as in the late 1940s and 50s lithographic stones were discarded in favour of metal plates. I can remember lithographic printers in the Midlands and in the City who had stones stored in racks extending from floor to ceiling: like standing type they awaited repeat orders and like metal type their bulk, weight and the need for special storage contributed to their demise.

The use of printers' flowers always has depended on fashion, and the debate on how and when they should be used continues: the same considerations have occupied the minds of printers in every century since printing began. There have been periods when decorations fell from favour and were not used at all; but from the sixteenth century to the present day, fine examples can be found where judicious use of ornament is fully justified and delights the eye of the beholder.

Because so much has been destroyed and because replacements are no longer available, an interest in what is scarce is stimulated. The collector is attracted to those things that are difficult to find: the magpie delights in accumulating treasures; what is known to be rare is prized. Thus the typographer who begins with an interest in type is in danger of becoming a collector, and his discoveries may lead him to collecting printers' flowers. This is precisely what happened to me, as my collection began modestly in 1949 and now has developed beyond the confines of reason. A sortie in the summer of 1988 proves the point, for it yielded about 6cwt of nineteenth-century type decorations; although this is the largest, over the years there have been a number of smaller acquisitions and many of these finds date from the 1880s and before.

Soames Forsyte, the man of property, had great possessions – more than he could use: his pleasure was restricted to looking at his pictures and assessing their worth. Fortunately few people have a passion for old types and fewer still for printers' flowers. Since their cash value is largely irrelevant, to enjoy these possessions the collector must try to use them; if he is able to add intellectual enjoyment by discovering their history, so much the better.

The article 'Printers' Flowers and Arabesques' by Francis Meynell and Stanley Morison which appeared in the first issue of *The Fleuron* in 1923, traces the use of arabesques back to the fifteenth century when Aldus Manutius used them as binders' stamps. The designs were earlier and hailed from the Middle East, reflecting the Islamic architecture of that region. *Flowers and Flourishes* (1976) by John Ryder goes further and covers a wider range of flowers and their history: it includes a facsimile reproduction of *A Suite of Fleurons*, the preliminary enquiry which Ryder printed on his own Miniature Press in 1956. Vincent Steer in his *Printing Design and Layout* (1937) illustrates a wide range of basic designs and classifies them according to their origins and periods. These three sources of information are essential reading for anyone wishing to pursue the subject.

Eventually my collection of printers' flowers grew to the point where I could no longer remember what I had and some system of reference and recording became essential. A specimen print of each design was made and these were pasted six to a page on A4 sheets in a loose-leaf binder. Spaces between designs were reserved for notes, and these included whatever information became available – Monotype reference numbers, foundry particulars, historical notes, so that for example the name of the printer who first used the design and the places where it was subsequently used would be recorded. Broad classifications such as Renaissance, Rococo or Classical were shown. Much information was gleaned from facsimile illustrations in D. B. Updike's *Printing Types*, and in Joseph Blumenthal's *Art of the Printed Book 1455–1955* and his *Printed Book in America*. Many designs were traced in Stephenson Blake and William Caslon specimens issued between 1885 and 1924, in the Vincent Figgins specimen of 1815 and the Edmund Fry specimen of 1828. The 1785 William Caslon specimen which was reproduced in the *Journal of the Printing Historical Society* No. 16 (1981–82) also proved invaluable. Monotype identification was achieved using their 'Specimen of rules, borders and figures' which is currently obtainable.

Typefounders' specimens rarely give any indication of the age of a design, whether it be type or decoration: often the specimen is undated, though the contents of the page may give an indication by referring to known events. Sometimes it is possible to establish when first a design was introduced by tracing it back to the founder's earlier specimens: for example the Garland ornament which was based on an eighteenth-century Robert Adam design, first appeared in Stephenson Blake's 1914 specimen and disappeared after 1924. Similarly the Floral ornament can be found in their 1885 specimen and continues into the 1920s. Thus we are able to establish that the Garland may have lasted a little over ten years, the Floral for perhaps forty. This is a fairly rough and ready method but more exact information is difficult to find; sadly it tells us nothing of the designers who created them.

In the typographical revival of the 1920s and 30s, printers' flowers, particularly those of the sixteenth, seventeenth and eighteenth centuries, were brought into use again. Francis Meynell at the Pelican Press, and later with his Nonesuch Press, and in the earlier part of his career Stanley Morison at the Cloister Press, played important roles in promoting their use. The Monotype Corporation responded to a growing interest and re-cut many of the early arabesques and a number of the designs of Luce and Fournier. It was a time of re-assessment, revival and excitement, and much of this is reflected in the Monotype publications then issued to the trade.

Originally *Monotype Recorders* were sent free to every printing office equipped with their machines, and offered for general sale at 2s–6d: today they appear in antiquarian booksellers' catalogues and vary in price from £5 to £10. In addition to this publication, because so much that was new was being produced for an expanding market, a series of well designed, sometimes lavish, *Newsletters* were issued under the inspired direction of Beatrice Warde. As so often happens give-aways are treated as throw-aways, and now after fifty years these information sheets are difficult to find. These *Recorders* and *Newsletters* have provided me with much information on the borders which were then being issued, and have provided valuable material for my Fleuron Index. Often experimental arrangements involving intricate and subtle combinations were included when new designs were made or old ones re-issued; references to the designer and his work also appeared.

The Spring 1960 issue of the *Monotype Recorder* is devoted entirely to printers' flowers and is described as 'A Grammar of Ornament'. In it designs are classified, their use analysed and a multitude of arrangements are displayed: fortunately copies can still be found and it is well worth getting a copy if at all possible – I think my copy cost £5. The most useful of the *Newsletters* in my possession is No. 119 which was printed by Benteli SA of Switzerland. It is presented in French, the designs are in black, red and green on a high quality antique stock, and all periods from the sixteenth century to the present day are fully represented. In addition to this visual feast there is a folded sheet giving reference numbers of all the 155 designs displayed, showing them in groups of origin. I have found all the *Newsletters* I have acquired useful but particularly those which unfold to provide broadsheets measuring 22½ x 17½ ins. I have five in this series all issued between 1957 and 1959 and they show Arabesques, Fournier, Classical, nineteenth-century Gothic and finally twentieth-century designs.

Once my *Fleuron* Index was established I was able to decide what gaps in the collection needed to be filled. Most of the designs which were missing were available at one time from the suppliers of Monotype sorts, but in recent years the number of these founders has declined, and even more disastrous, those that remain have reduced the range of what they have available. So it was necessary to shop around finding a border here, a corner-piece there, a design in 12-point at one establishment, 18- or 24-point at another. Apart from Mouldtype and Horsfalls there are some small suppliers who have accumulated matrices, and in building a collection or filling up spaces all these sources of supply must be tried. Apart from Monotype material many valuable additions came from Stephenson Blake whose restricted range is still available.

Making the collection and researching the history of individual pieces occupied about seven years; it then became apparent that use of all this mass of material could best be achieved by creating displays in some kind of publication. An attempt to do this in a small way was made in my first little book *Flowers & Fancies for a Workshop* published in 1981 and then in *Patterns in Print* in 1984 [see "Patterns in Print" in *Matrix 7*, pp. 115–120]; but the collection was growing so rapidly that more was needed. In 1988 *Fleurons, their Place in History and in Print* was produced showing 130 different designs on 26 pages of decorative arrangements. It was felt however that to use to the full the material collected for the Index the historical notes should be used. In doing this the main classifications for printers' flowers became apparent.

There was excitement in tracing designs back to their origins, in discovering that the first known use was in Verona in 1478; and in tracing them to the printing centres of Europe. Famous names were associated with these decorations; in Lyons, Henri Estienne was the first printer to use them and of course in that city Garamond, Guillaume Le Bé, Jacques Sabon and Robert Granjon all produced

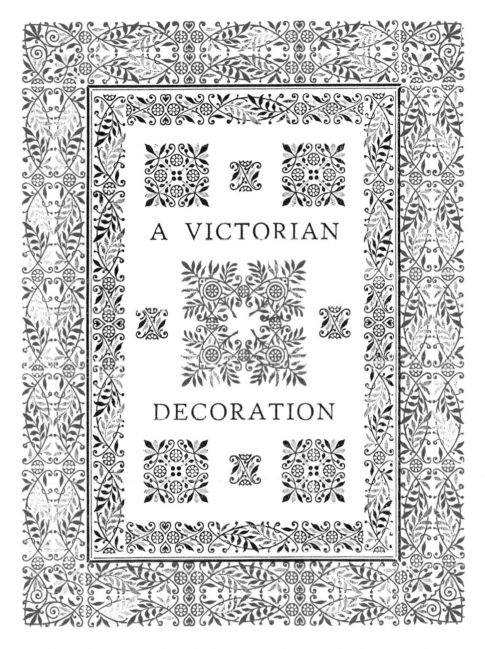

2. Fleurons printed at the Workshop Press. Printing in two colours is achieved as follows. The chase is locked into the bed of the press and then the quoins holding the forme are loosened. The types to be printed in a second colour are carefully removed and 3-point leads, cut to size, are inserted in their places: the types are then replaced and the forme is locked up again with these types standing 3 points proud of their fellows. Since the Farley 24 provides for the height of the inking rollers to be set automatically with the impression cylinder, and both are adjustable by calibrated drum, the height is then adjusted so that the second colour is printed. At the end of the run the types used are removed and replaced with quads and spaces, the height of the cylinder and inking rollers is returned to normal and printing the main colour can proceed. This method is particularly suitable for printing complex fleuron combinations in two colours, but it is only possible using a proofing press with micro-adjustment and automatic inking. This example, c. 1885 was issued by Stevenson Blake and is presented here as seven different units of the same design.

type decorations. It is their developments of the arabesque that figured so prominently in the revivals which took place between 1920 and 1960.

The influence of Louis Luce and Pierre Simon Fournier in the first half of the eighteenth century continues with us today. The Rococo style which they created forms our second group of decorations and many of the Monotype re-cuttings of these designs are available today: the Fournier Star and the Pineapple Flower were specially re-cut for John Ryder for his *Flowers & Flourishes*. Generally the designs appear to be very small and simple, but when cast at an angle of 45 degrees they allow great variety of arrangement.

The latter half of the eighteenth century saw the arrival of neo-classicism with type ornaments which harmonised perfectly with the Modern types of Didot and Bodoni. Borders became heavier and the trend was carried through into the nineteenth century by Fry, Figgins and Henry Caslon, in whose specimens they were displayed. This was the period of the Grape & Vine-leaf border and of the entwining leaves of the English Rose design, both of which are still available from Stephenson Blake. It was the time when Fat Face types became fashionable and these were matched by solid geometric borders which added further weight to the page.

The fourth group of ornaments appeared after the Great Exhibition of 1851 when designs became finer in line, fussier and more likely to be used to create intricate and complex Gothic patterns. They were used also to create background tones, combining large numbers of 12-point types (or their equivalent in size) to simulate architectural features such as church windows and buildings. By 1885 borders tended to become larger and unit pieces equivalent to 24 x 48 points appeared in combination designs such as Stephenson Blake's Floral Ornament or their Marigold series of decorations.

The final group contains flowers of the twentieth century which are representative of our times. They are the work of a number of outstanding designers who, unlike their predecessors, need not be anonymous. Percy Smith and Edward Bawden produced designs for the Curwen Press, at least one of which was taken up by Monotype and is still obtainable. Berthold Wolpe's ornaments for the Fanfare Press were shown off in *A Book of Fanfare Ornaments*, published by Fanfare in 1938. David Bethel, whose two Glint units were issued in 1957, was responsible for a number of other designs. John Peters, Elisabeth Friedlander and Will Carter all contributed to the type decorations of the 1950s and 60s.

There has always been enjoyment in collecting things, be they coins, first-day covers, matchboxes or vintage cars. Collecting types and later type-ornaments has given me the same satisfaction but has extended far beyond the mere accumulation of materials: it has opened up new avenues of experiment, given new opportunities for pattern making, and through research a knowledge of the past. It is this that I wish to convey in writing of an absorption which has taken up so much of my time.

3. Pierre Simon Fournier was born in 1712. He produced a wide range of type decorations in the 18th Century Rococo style which for many years replaced the Arabesque.

In 1980, **Mark Arman**'s interest in typography grew to such an extent that he decided to set up the Workshop Press. He began with an Adana HQ Flatbed press, which enabled him to print larger sizes than the 6 x 4 inches that he already owned. He found that by removing the rollers, he could print a small book two pages at a time, he produced his first book, *Flowers and Fancies*, for a workshop. A small Albion, a Fairly 11, a Farley 24, a Model 4, and an 18-inch guillotine followed, and as this equipment was acquired over several years, so were the typefaces that he collected from many sources. Apart from a new fount of Caslon Old Face, Arman accumulated a very large collection of types which were no longer available. These included arabesque and rococo decorations, which were to become an obsession and lead to a number of books and publications. In fifteen years the Press printed thirteen letterpress books in editions limited to fewer than 180 copies, all of which were bound in the workshop. Most of them had two-colour illustrations of type designs and decorations.

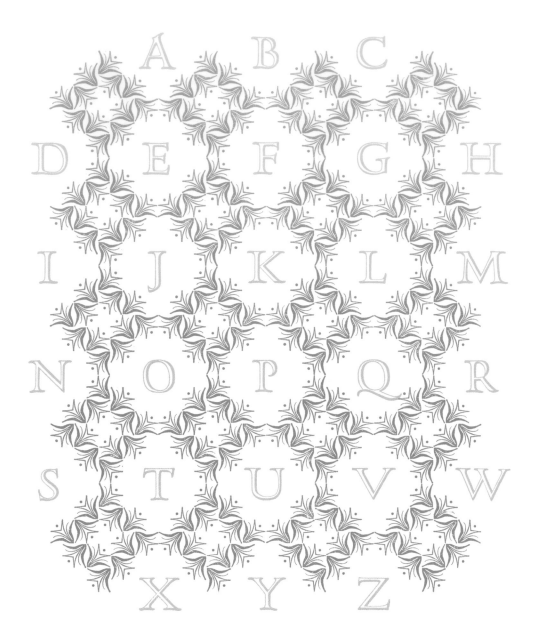

Glint borders (released in 1956) with Hadriano Open capitals. (Printed by Michael Tarachow at Pentagram Press for *Matrix 13*).

Creating Printer's Flowers

BY DAVID BETHEL

In Matrix 13 *(1993), David Bethel gives his first-hand account of creating stylish, complex printers' flowers and ornaments like Glint for the 1950s Festival of Britain exhibition – a project in which he was encouraged by Monotype's dramatic publicity director Beatrice Warde.*

The idea of designing new printer's flowers today when, except for a few enthusiasts, the practice and the traditions of printing from metal have been virtually superseded by electronic and photo-mechanical processes, would seem eccentric. Indeed, it is difficult to imagine how the copyright of such designs could be protected, hence their commercial value would be questionable.

In the decade after the Second World War, the problem was quite different. The struggle to re-establish trade and commerce in the United Kingdom and in continental Europe caused a resurgence in printing generally and this continued the pre-war processes and attitudes. In addition to the needs of advertising and publicity, a gradual release of controls on paper saw the book trade flourish and with it a nostalgic return to the traditions of the fine book valued by many of those who purchased them. The Leipzig Book Fair, among others, became an annual show-piece for well-designed books, and decoration featured in many books exhibited.

Despite the influence of the pre-war Bauhaus on post-war typography in England, Germany, the Netherlands and Switzerland, decoration was not eschewed by all those who set standards in typographic design. In the immediate post-war grey decade, helped perhaps by the seminal influence of the 1951 Festival of Britain exhibition, there was a need for embellishment, for decoration on artefacts, in architecture, in interior decoration and in print in the UK and elsewhere. Austerity had produced limits of tolerance in the public and it was against this background that I began to design a range of printer's flowers for the Monotype Corporation.

In the 1930s, Monotype had led the way in reviving printer's flowers and other typographic decoration under the guidance of Stanley Morison who had edited *The Fleuron,* launched in 1922 and published both in London and New York.

Through this medium he brought to the interested public a number of essays on the subject, including 'Printer's Flowers and Arabesques'. In his time at Monotype after his appointment as consultant in 1922, he authorised the re-cutting of a large range of printer's flowers from the sixteenth, seventeenth, eighteenth and nineteenth centuries.

Typefounders in the UK and in Europe issued revivals and survivals from their own stocks of historic units. The number of historic flowers well outweighed contemporary designs. In England, the Curwen Press had commissioned some new designs in the early 1930s from Edward Bawden, Paul Nash, Harry Carter and Percy Smith, but these were for their exclusive use. Their 1928 Specimen Book contained the legend, '*In the use of ornament, the Curwen Press endeavours to use contemporary work or none at all.*' Berthold Wolpe designed a set of units for the Fanfare Press *c.* 1937 and in the USA, Bruce Rogers, Thomas Maitland Cleland and Walter Dorwin Teague, among others, designed printer's flowers for American Type Founders, but these were conservative in style: a salute to the past. One casualty of the war was new design and I *think* that the Glint border and corner units which I designed and Monotype produced were the first post-war original designs for printer's flowers.

The Glint border unit started not as a design for a printer's flower, but as a bookbinder's brass. As a post-graduate student I had to choose to study and practise two crafts and bookbinding was one which I chose. The decorative bookbinding material then available to students at least was very limited and did not have the scale or weight for any of the books I wished to bind, so I decided to produce my own by the traditional method of engraving and filing the end of a square brass shaft mounted into a wooden handle. In the course of engraving, it occurred to me that the process had some affinity with the production of the steel punches from which type matrices are formed. Some two years after graduation I experimented with a calligraphic motif that I had sketched originally for translation into a binder's brass: the outcome was the border unit of Glint.

Having decided on the final form of the border unit, a corner unit was needed. Corner units can be designed by holding a mirror at 45 degrees across the border unit and using the resulting image – half the border unit and its mirror reflection – as a corner unit. This will link up two lines of the displayed border at 90 degrees to each other around the sides of a square or rectangle. However, in the case of Glint, this method did not produce a satisfactory result and the corner was designed as a separate unit in its own right but, by using elements similar to those used in the border unit, it was satisfactory as a corner pair to the border.

I now had two decorative units which were related in form and style and which could be used together or separately. Apart from style and form, they shared another factor: each was mathematically proportioned. This was the most important factor in their ability to be combined in seemingly an endless number of different permutations. The two units, along with a design for a continuous border, were submitted to Monotype in April 1956. I knew the method employed by Monotype in producing typographic material for hot-metal printing. Each punch was cut from a master drawing of a prescribed size using a pantograph-linked router. This set certain limitations to any design for there had to be an allowance for the shoulder of the matrix from which the unit of type was to be cast.

Morison himself approved the continuous border and Glint and I was made an offer for the purchase of the designs. The first proofs of the border and corner unit, with reference numbers B.1309/10, were sent to me on 29 August 1956. C. W. Geoffrey Paulson, the Monotype Sales Director, wrote, 'I thought you would like to see the proofs of these immediately and to know that we regard the Border and Corner Unit as a very nice design indeed. Certain complications were experienced in cutting these designs but the result has come up to our expectations and we are confident that it will prove a success.'

Beatrice Warde, the Monotype Corporation's publicity manager, who as a young American post-graduate student writing under a nom-de-plume as 'Paul Beaujon' (equal opportunities were far from certain then), had found fame for the results of her research into the designer of what is now known as Garamond's roman, christened the corner and border units as Glint. She wrote to me on 21 September 1956, 'Do let me congratulate you on your new border designs B.1309/10. The moment I saw the work's proof, I rushed out a leaflet for our next News-letter (figure 1). It's the 20th century rival of the famous "Antwerp" arabesques – and has limitless combinations.'

In 1928, Frederic Warde, Beatrice's husband the typographer, had produced a book *Printers Ornaments, Applied to the Composition of Decorative Borders, Panels and Patterns* for the then Lanston Monotype Corporation which, in Beatrice's words in a letter to me was, 'to illustrate the uses of its decorative material'. This material was, of course, the re-cutting of the historic units selected by Stanley Morison in the 1930s. The Antwerp arabesques, i.e. those by Christophe Plantin (1514–89), were shown in a range of combinations not hitherto brought together in one collection, with others devised by Frederic Warde. No doubt Beatrice Warde had this essay on the inventive use of printer's flowers in mind when she generously referred to my Glint units as 'the 20th century rival of the famous "Antwerp" arabesques'. Not a claim that I would have made.

Mrs Warde wrote to me again on 23 October 1956 in her own handwriting which was based on the style of the late fifteenth-century Italian humanistic cursive hand (on which, incidentally, Bembo type was based), and said, 'Working out combinations of your border is becoming a mania with me. Every time I try to stop, something brand-new emerges, generally by accident. I impose a stamp wrong-way round on the paper and behold another possibility. I'm longing to know how many of them you have worked out yourself. Sarah Clutton [her personal assistant] and I, between us, have evolved 75 and are only beginning to explore the 2-colour possibilities.'

Monotype, in producing the 18-point version of the Glint units, had indicated that any smaller size would not be useful. I disagreed and thought that a 12-point version would be particularly useful for multiple combinations to make all-over patterns etc. In November 1956, I asked Mrs Warde whether any further thought had been given to produce a 12-point size set of units and whether there had been any trials on a 9-point version, suggesting that a print of the 18-point could be photographically reduced to the two sizes for a visual assessment of its viability. She must have taken up what I had said for I received a letter from Geoffrey Paulson written on 11 January 1957 to say that they had worked on a 12-point version and enclosed a proof for my inspection. He wrote, 'This size appears to have worked out successfully without any modifications to the drawings. We have had made a photographic print of the 18-point trial proof reduced to 9-point and send you a copy herewith. I think you will agree that the character of the original design is lost in the smaller size and this feature, together with any technical difficulties which might be experienced in cutting, means that we shall not go below 12-point. I think you might also like to see proofs of the 18D and 24-point and 24D which we have recently made.' It was not until April 1957 that I was sent proofs of the 12D, 14-point and 14D sizes.

Much later I learned that it was Beatrice Warde who had championed the production of a 12-point version, believing that it would be a best seller of interest to book designers as well as to jobbing printers: and she was right.

No one was more surprised than me when Glint had an immediate success. A *Monotype Newsletter* was devoted to Glint and went as a mail-shot to all the Corporation's clientele in the UK and overseas. The units were even popular in India with its own different traditions of decoration, often full of symbolism. Whether they found any symbolism in Glint I never discovered. There they were marketed as Butterfly Flowers.

Beatrice Warde encouraged others to experiment and invent new combinations. She invented the Glint Game and explained how this could be played. 'It is played with a stamping pad and two metal stamps of type, those two units

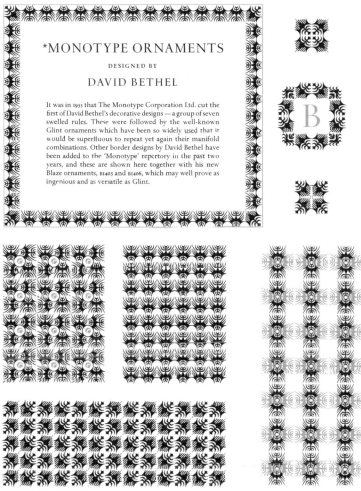

1. First page of leaflet from the *Monotype Recorder* (reduced).

*REGISTERED TRADE MARK

designed by David Bethel which, in combination with each other or themselves make up the almost incredibly varied range of "different" borders, all-over patterns, tail-pieces, factotum initials etc. which is only briefly indicated by the few combinations shown in the following pages. Working on graph paper, one puts down a print of (say) a corner and then, after tossing the stamp in the air, one puts the second print up against it, not knowing which of the four sides of the square will be uppermost. Wherever way it falls, the two prints will combine; thereafter with the help of a pocket mirror, one follows up that hint, with due reference to the rhythms and counterpoints which are basic to the fascinating "grammar of ornament". One can play this game indefinitely, because the little units are mathematically proportioned. It is not by accident that they coalesce under your eyes into much larger and more spectacular ornaments. That, I think, is the essentially "twentieth century" thing about them. This is the age of the mathematician: even those of us who are still defeated by arithmetic can sense the absolute dependence of our modern civilisation on mathematical thinking. David Bethel's feat of design (which incidentally involved a technical feat of punch-cutting) has that steely-feathery look which puts it in the advance current of modern decorative design: but it took more than off-hand sketching to evolve anything as protean as these units.'

In Antwerp, the home of Christophe Plantin, a Glint Club was formed to play the Glint Game. I heard of no other clubs that were formed but I did receive many results from people playing the game. At that time, very few people in the UK had a television set and I suspect that today, the Glint Game could not have competed with it. In October 1969, Beatrice Warde presented me with her graph-paper book in which she had made the Glint trials, or at least some of them, for there were not seventy-five versions in it.

Looking back, it is difficult to identify why Glint had such an immediate appeal. There were a plethora of typographical ornaments, flowers, arabesques etc. available but these were re-cuttings of historical material from the past 450 years and had been used over and over again in various combinations. Those from years before the nineteenth century had almost all been designed to embellish books, whereas the need in the late 1950s for type decoration was much wider. Many of the early-twentieth century designs in the Art Nouveau and Art Deco styles had been designed for promotional material, but in the 1950s these did not seem to fit the taste of the time although they were to enjoy a revival in the 1970s and 1980s. Book designers, advertising and publicity designers were looking for something new (as they always are). With its combinability and lack of historical derivation, Glint apparently met the current needs of those in advertising, publicity and promotion.

There may have been other reasons. In the scientific and technological research world, among the factors used to evaluate research projects submitted for grant support, 'timeliness' is a highly rated criterion. There is little point in funding research which is unlikely to meet needs as perceived at the time of evaluation. So it is with design of all kinds, to be successful commercially, a design must be timely in its appeal. Beatrice Warde thought that Glint's appeal was essentially in its mathematical proportioning and thereby appealing to a technological society. Whatever their attraction, Glint combinations could produce so many weights that they could be used to embellish books, advertising material and publicity matter. And, their launch was timely.

Encouraged by the success of Glint, I began to design a series of type ornaments of Monotype. My taste is for typographic ornaments which have the characteristics of type, that is, that they have been conceived as engraved units for

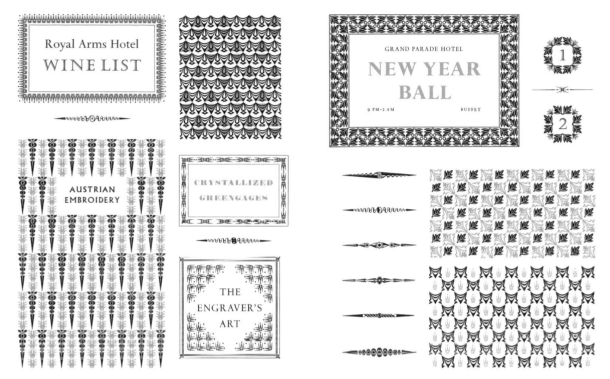

2. Interior pages of pages from the *Monotype Recorder* (reduced).

punch-cutting and have not been produced from drawn masters with pen or brush characteristics and then reduced on a machine-controlled pantograph. In other words, if one had the technical skill, such designs should be produced in the traditional way that type was produced before the twentieth century.

Not all designers would agree with this contention for there is a reasoned view that successful typographical decoration should contrast in form and feeling with the text type. Further, that it was only the lack of modern technology that forced the type designers of the past to produce their work the way they did, with an engraved look to it. In this century, the use of pantograph engraving machines in matrix production meant that original designs could be produced in any drawn medium and reproduced, given certain technical limitations. The Deberny et Peignot Art Nouveau borders numbers 2750 6, issued around 1910, retain their drawn look. The Pan ornaments by Professor Walter Brudi for D. Stempel AG in 1958 have a brush-drawn look. Imre Reiner's Primula ornaments for the Amsterdam Typefoundry *c.* 1950 are essentially calligraphic pen forms and Crous-Vidal's Fugue d'Arabesques for the Fonderie Typographique Française, also *c.* 1950, set out to be in complete contrast to any typeface with which they may be used.

On the other hand, E. R. Weiss's ornaments designed for the Bauer Foundry,

3. Final page of the
Monotype Recorder
insert (reduced).

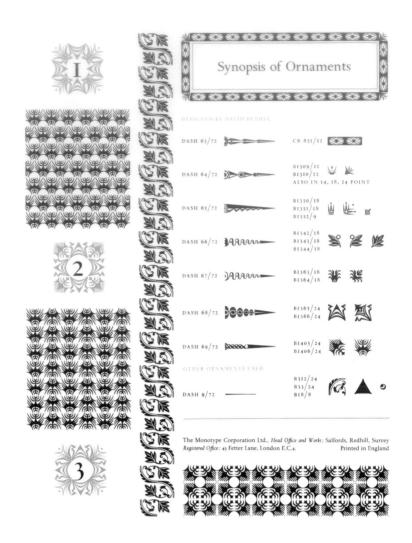

Frankfurt-am-Main in 1911–13, and Elizabeth Friedlander's set of ten units designed in 1958 for the Monotype Corporation (ref. B.1332–41), have the characteristics of type, of being engraved. I warm to this approach and devised a simple engraving method for producing designs for printer's flowers.

The method is to cut an inch-square piece of linoleum (of the kind that is used for making linocuts), and engrave the design on it, mounting the engraved pieces on a wooden one-inch square shaft. Using a stamping-pad and graph paper, trials then can be made of borders and combinations of the unit. When necessary, the piece can be altered, rejected or re-engraved very quickly. When the border unit seems satisfactory, a corner unit can be produced in the same way using a mirror set at 45 degrees to the border for the first approach. Fair impressions of the result can then be enlarged to the size prescribed by the typefounder, in my case, Monotype.

By 22 December 1956, two new sets were designed and despatched to Monotype: these were the Leaf and the Coronet designs.

The first typographic decorative motif used by early printers was the vine leaf. As I have shown elsewhere, the vine leaf as a motif in printing was adapted from the Roman custom of using it, a symbol of the wood of life, on altars and inscribed memorial tablets as a word-spacer and as border decoration. It is not always appreciated that, in the Renaissance, with which the birth of printing in Europe coincided, despite the great step forward taken in the spread of learning and literacy which the partnership of Renaissance thinking and printing produced, symbolism, a form of non-literate visual communication, was still important. Indeed, even printers, themselves purveyors of the written word, used symbols as the devices by which they became known. These printer's devices, incidentally, became increasingly complicated in their symbolism in the first 200 years of printing, a paradox, for the spread of the word through the printed book should have reduced the need for visual symbolism.

The leaf motif used as a printer's flower has had many forms during the whole lifetime of printing. The design has changed to meet changing taste with the greatest changes in the nineteenth and early twentieth centuries. The private press movement revived the vine leaf symbolism. William Morris at the Kelmscott Press, Emery Walker at the Doves, C. H. St John Hornby at the Ashendene, Lucien Pissarro at the Eragny and Charles Ricketts at the Vale presses, all had specially designed vine leaves in their typographic repertoire.

Alongside the private presses, the typefounders in England and in the USA who supplied the jobbing printers also produced leaf designs. These were largely a revival of another, more recent tradition, the so-called 'Old fashioned Christmas', with which holly leaves were associated. ATF and DeLittle did produce some vine leaf motifs for both book and poster work. My Leaf designs were meant to revive the vine leaf tradition yet also be seen as useful for the seasonal trade. There were three units, a border mirror pair and a corner which could be used as a border alone or with the border pair. The border unit designs included a symbolic berry which, when the units were combined, made a visually geometrical foil to the leaf shape. The original designs were engraved, and enlarged as drawings to meet the Monotype specifications. These were accepted by Monotype on 11 January 1957 and put into production. As with most of my designs of printer's flowers, a number of combinations can be made with the Leaf units.

I have not found a crown or coronet motif as a printer's flower anywhere before 1685 and that was in a book, *Epistolarum* printed by M. Flesher, London. The crown and coronet are symbols of authority and, in seventeenth-century

Britain, symbols had a special significance. Emblem books were popular, giving explanations of the symbolism used. The English Civil Wars, which ended in 1649 with the beheading of King Charles I, had not only riven the country into two main factions – the parliamentarians and the cavaliers – but saw the formation of a large number of religious and political groups at a time when it was not always safe to proclaim one's allegiances without fear of reprisal. In this situation, the idea of proclaiming one's beliefs and antipathies by symbols was attractive.

The crown was clearly a symbol understood by all and, after 1660 when Charles II was restored to the throne, it was used on proclamations, official documents of all kinds and books printed with authority. Typographic crowns and coronets can be found in typefounder's catalogues from former Imperial Austria, nineteenth-century Hungary and Italy, and eighteen-century pre-revolution France. For example, Fournier cut some excellent crowns and used them in his *Modèles*, published in 1742.

My Coronet border unit was not meant to look royal or official but to have a modern, charming appeal, a kind of Cinderella's Prince Charming look. It was accepted by Monotype at the same time that my Leaf units were accepted, but with a caveat. Geoffrey Paulson wrote on behalf of Monotype on 31 January 1957, 'It is, of course, sometimes necessary – if a design is difficult to adapt to suit our manufacture – to ask the designer to modify it; we may also require you to help in relation to a corner piece to ensure that our views coincide with yours but such requests will be definitely limited.'

My help was asked for and I was requested to design a corner piece to accompany the Coronet border unit, I think by John Dreyfus, Monotype's consultant (although I cannot find the letter). After a number of trials, my response was to send off two corner piece designs. One was from a 45 degree mirror version of the border unit, the other a much smaller unit which echoed the base of the border unit. In each case I wanted to retain either the dots or the parallel lines which featured in the border unit. The corner piece designs were readily accepted and the Coronet suite was put into production almost straight away and issued as B.1350, 51, 52.

By April 1957, I had designed further units and had submitted them to Monotype. They were accepted on 10 May although they were not produced and issued until the following year. For some reason, these border and corner units did not get a name. Perhaps the motif was too abstract and its geometrical elements, a triangle and curves slightly reminiscent of Art Nouveau forms but unmistakably of the mid-twentieth century, did not (and do not) lend themselves to baptism.

I still regard them as worth using. I would like to see them used in large bookwork with Plantin Old Face, perhaps on a title-page and as tail-pieces for a Shakespeare edition. Not that it is likely that anyone now can think in the lavish terms that were available not so long ago to designers such as Bruce Rogers. They were allocated order numbers B.1365/66.

On 10 June 1957, I sent two more border and corner units off to Monotype. One, for obvious reasons, I labelled Scorpio. It has movement, its 'legs' crawl across the page, yet at times it looks derived from plant form. On 20 June, Doris Weller of Monotype, secretary to the Typographic Committee, replied: 'These have been studied and we are seriously interested in no.2 [Scorpio] but must make careful tests before reaching a decision . . . it will probably be a couple of months before we can let you know the result'.

I did not have to wait long, for Doris Weller wrote again on 25 July to say, 'Further to our letter of 21 June, we have now completed our tests on the above [Scorpio] design and enclose for your examination two prints (in duplicate) showing various combinations of the borders reduced to 18-point. You will note we have purposely arranged a slight space between each unit as this will be essential for manufacturing purposes . . . we shall be interested to know if you are satisfied with our proposed rendering of it.' I was satisfied and the units were put into production and issued in 1958 in one size only, 18-point as B.1363/64.

The last border and corner units that I designed for Monotype, named Blaze, were accepted in October 1957 and issued in 1958 with the order numbers B.1405/06. They were named by Beatrice Warde who liked the units comprising Blaze, 'because it can be shooting in all directions over the page.' Like Scorpio, the border unit could face left or right and, in combinations, made something like a 'Tudor rose. In other combinations, there is a hint of the Imperial Russian eagle. In the main, its use is in all-over patterns and some very handsome examples have been made by graphic designers.

My designs were followed by those of Elizabeth Friedlander, John Peters, Peter Burnhill and Keith Chapman, all for Monotype, a spring flowering which dried up after a relatively short blossoming.

David Bethel graduated from the West of England College of Art and the University of Bristol, England, in 1951, having majored in Graphic Design, and he was immediately appointed Lecturer in Graphic Design at the Stafford College of Art; in 1953 he became its Head of Department. He moved to the Coventry College of Art & Design as Vice-Principal in 1956, in charge of the Design & Printing Departments. There he developed courses in book and technical illustration and typographic design and practised as a graphic and typographic designer. In 1969 he moved to the newly-formed Leicester Polytechnic as Deputy Director; he was appointed Director in 1973, developing it to become the De Montfort University in 1992. While practising as a designer and Polytechnic Director, he represented the United Kingdom on the OECD and EEC committees for higher education, served on the Hong Kong University & Polytechnics Grants Committee, and was the founder-chairman of the Council for Academic Accreditation, among many other assignments in South Africa, Colombia, etc., bringing whenever possible recognition of the value of design. His degrees include four Doctorates, in Law, Letters, Education, and Design, and he was awarded an O.B.E. in 1983.

Music fount completed in 1988 by the author.

Cutting a New Music Type

BY STAN NELSON

Typesetting music is a special and highly technical aspect of typography, especially in metal. Stan Nelson, in an essay in Matrix 8 *(1988) that nicely complements the following essay on setting plainchant, describes the enormously complex process of cutting the punches for a font of plainchant.*

Certain old books hold a special fascination for me. There may be something about the look of the type or the feel of the paper that is exciting (though I prefer not to think about the smell). Among the various old books that I have admired through the years was a volume of red and black plainchant music, a Gradual. It was very attractive with its deep red lines and the scattering of square, black notes that were clustered across the page.

I didn't consider printing such material since, after all, where would one find old music types? A modern Monotype fount of plainchant just doesn't have the character of the older founts.

24-point Monotype plainchant, cast by Paul H. Duensing, Kalamazoo, Michigan.

Then, during one of my many forays into *Fournier on Typefounding*, translated by the late Harry Carter [see *Matrix 7*, pp. 150–155], (my Bible on the subject of hand-typefounding), my eye was caught by the title of Chapter VII, 'Cutting Red and Black Plainchant'. The instructions were very clear and seemed quite easy. I was particularly attracted to a line stating that 'The old red and black plainchant is made from fifteen punches'.[1] I had just been cutting a fount of letters and by comparison this seemed too simple to be true. With fifteen punches, over thirty matrices could be struck (two per punch) and the entire fount of music cast. It was an irresistible prospect! With such a fount I could print a Mass, or perhaps there was a mediaeval music group dying for period scores. However, I didn't really need an excuse since for me exploring the process has always been an end in itself.

Of course, before getting too involved in this project, it occurred to me that I ought to find out a little more about plainchant and its use. Several helpful sources turned up. *Four Hundred Years of Music Printing*, by A. Hyatt King, published by the British Library, London, 1964, was very informative, as was *Grove's Dictionary of Music*. . . . A quick look in these references gave me some basic information about plainchant.

Plainchant (which is synonymous with plainsong or Gregorian Chant) is a very old form of music used since mediaeval times in Christian liturgies. It consists only of melody (the tune) and does not use harmony (chords) as we know it. Ironically, even as I began to cut a new plainchant music it had already become pretty much obsolete, and with the exception of some religious orders, it is not used very much now in Catholic worship. This is largely due to the fact that it worked better with the older Latin Mass and pre-Vatican II worship practices than with the current liturgy. Vestiges of plainchant are still sometimes used in Church of England services. [See 'The Setting of Plainchant' by Sister Valerie Cryer which follows.]

Plainchant has a very different appearance from modern, polyphonic music. It uses a form of mediaeval notation with a four-line stave, in contrast with modern music having a stave with five lines. The notes have completely different shapes from modern music. There have been two basic styles of plainchant and for a while both were used concurrently. One early form, known as the 'Gothic' style, had diamond shaped note heads and thick tails that sort of resembled horseshoe nails (figure 1). The other form of plainchant was known as 'Roman' and it was the more common form that Fournier discussed and which I have been cutting. It had square note heads and the tails of the notes were very thin (figure 2).

Plainchant was 'not based on modern "major" and "minor" tonalities or keys, but on the eight "church modes" or scales, each of which was thought to embody different kinds of emotional appeal.'[2] In plainchant the clef was movable, as opposed to the modern 'treble' or 'base' clefs which do not usually change position. The position of the clef indicated the particular mode or key that was to be sung.

Though plainchant notation had ways to indicate longer and shorter notes, rhythm was also dependent upon the text being sung. Notes could be held for varying periods of time where the text required it. 'It was completely divorced from post-renaissance metric rhythms, with regularly recurring "strong" and "weak" beats, in order to let the syllables being sung receive appropriate emphasis, wherever they fell.'[3] Some notes were connected together, usually on one long syllable.

Early printers certainly had their hands full when printing music. Music types

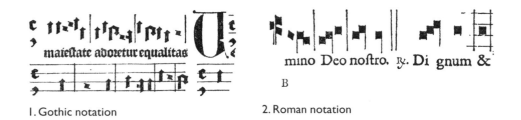

1. Gothic notation   2. Roman notation

required a greater level of precision in their manufacture and use than the letters needed for printing ordinary text. The notes had to be spaced accurately both horizontally and vertically if the correct note values were to be represented. In the earliest music the staves could not be printed with the notes, so that accurate types, imposition and presswork were necessary if the notes were to fall exactly on or between the lines as required.

For some printers the solution was to avoid altogether the difficulty of printing music, printing only the stave lines and leaving the notes out entirely, to be filled in later by hand. This can be seen as early as 1457 in Fust and Schoeffer's famous Psalter with the red and blue initials. But many others successfully met the challenge of music printing. The earliest example of printed music is thought to have been produced in Southern Germany, possibly near Constance, around 1473 and is of the Gothic style. The earliest dated piece is by Ulrich Han, of Rome, and was printed in 1476.[4] It almost seems redundant to say that this music was in the Roman style. The success of early printers in dealing with the problems of music printing is demonstrated by the surprising amount of music printed in the incunabula period. 'Before 1501, nearly 270 liturgies with music appeared, and about a score of books containing musical examples' were produced.[5]

By 1525 printers were beginning to use more economical, single impression founts of plainchant because they required half as much presswork as the older, two colour music. Yet, red and black plainchant continued to be cast and used for centuries because it really looked better than the single impression founts. Single impression music types showed many more breaks in the stave lines and if the types weren't very well made, the results could be pretty rough. In comparison, the stave lines of red and black chant are much wider and, because they are not separated between every note, there are far fewer visible joints. Despite the greater cost of two impressions, the red and black music is colourful and quite pretty. Red and black founts were cast

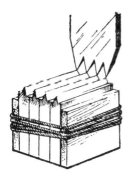

3. 12-point centre-face rule, used as a pattern for the stave lines.

through the eighteenth century so that examples can be seen in the specimens of the typefounders Fournier and de la Cologne of France, and Rosart of Belgium.

Having made up my mind to proceed with this music, I read Fournier's instructions through very carefully and began the project by tying four pieces of 12-point centreface rule together with a piece of string (figure 3). This formed a pattern for the exact spacing of the lines of the staves. Because at that point I had not decided whether I would actually cast my stave lines (one *can* use printers' rule instead of cast units) I proceeded to cut a brass 'face' gauge having notches cut to the dimensions of the various notes. These notches were 12 points wide, for the square heads of the notes; 36 points for the tails of the notes and 48 points for the overall body of the notes.

As I mentioned before, fifteen punches are needed. These consist of the following characters:

There are a few shortcuts that I could have taken with this music. By using modern printers' rule and by altering some of the notes it is possible to reduce the number of characters required to print this music from fifteen to ten punches. As I have said, rule can be used to print the stave lines. The vertical lines that separate the measures can also be cut from printers' rule. The notes falling third and fourth from the right in the above illustration are called catch notes. They come at the end of a line and indicate the first note to be sung in the following line. These catch notes can be made from similar but wider notes. But, attractive as these economies might seem, I decided to go for it and to make all of the characters as they would originally have been required. There seemed no point in being remotely practical while making such an anachronistic music! Anyway, rules would have looked too mechanical and I wanted to have the exact feeling of the old founts.

I prepared suitable lengths of water-hardening tool steel (I use a steel purchased from Colt's Industries, crucible steel division) and using my face gauge, I laid out the first note. The gauge indicated the height and width of the note and these were marked on the polished face of the steel with a scribe. A small tri-square was used to draw the parallel sides of the note with accuracy.

This simple square note was easy to cut; but, of course I had to complicate the matter by adding little serifs that I had seen and admired in Rosart's specimen of this music. The first punch was followed by one for the 'clef' that is used to indicate the mode (or key) being sung. I used a counter-punch to form the inside of this note, since the serifs made it an enclosed space. (The counter-punch is a separate, small punch that is cut in the shape of the interior of the character. After being hardened it is hammered into the face of the punch being cut.) Next came the two notes that resemble 'quarter' notes and come in a right and left hand version. The tails of these notes indicate the movement of the voice to the next note and give the visual effect of the note having been joined to the one following it. After these punches were finished, I cut the diamond and rhomboid notes followed by the sharp, flat and natural. That left the stave, which was, because of its size, a difficult punch to cut.

The punch for the stave is very large in four-line plainchant. It has four lines, spaced exactly 12 points apart and it has to be at least four lines of pica, or 48 points wide. (Ideally, the notes will be 12-points wide and when four are combined will match the width of the stave unit). By making the stave units as much as five or six times the width of the notes the number of joins or breaks in the stave will be reduced, thereby improving the look of the music; but, in four-line-pica (48 points) it is very difficult to make such wide types.

A special scribing tool was needed in order to mark the face of the punch for the stave. While referring frequently to the pattern of tied 12-point rules, a steel scribe was filed so that its four teeth matched the pattern rules exactly. When the points were perfectly spaced and of exactly the same width the scribe was hardened. This scribe was drawn across the face of the polished steel punch, leaving marks that showed just where the lines were to be cut. The punch for the stave was cut for the most part with files but the final shaping and adjustment of the lines was done with gravers. These small sculpting tools, made of very hard steel, come in a variety of shapes and are ideal for carving designs into the face of the steel punch. By very slow and careful work the four lines of the staff were made to appear straight and even.

Once this large punch was finished I hardened it in the usual manner (by heating it red hot, quenching it in water and then reheating it to a straw colour) and then prepared to strike a matrix. This was the largest matrix that I had ever struck and frankly it was a problem. Because of its size this large punch would require enormous force to enter the copper matrix blank and a great deal of distortion was certain to take place as so much copper was displaced by the punch. I chose a generous piece of copper so that there would be plenty of metal to work with and I annealed it by heating it until it was almost glowing red, then quenching it in water. (Surprisingly, although this process hardens steel, it softens copper). I struck the punch into the copper using a heavy hammer while holding the punch with my fingers. I have heard of mind-numbing boredom but this was finger-numbing and *not* boring in the least. I had to anneal the copper three times while I was striking the matrix. This music has a deep depth of drive and of course the copper strike curled as the punch was sunk into its surface. Fitting this matrix required a lot of filing and caused grey hair. Matrix justification is never easy in the best of situations and in this case I hated to think about having to re-strike this monster, so I had to be sure that I didn't file too much metal away. Much careful filing on the face, sides and head (or end) of the matrix eventually resulted in a justified mat. When cast, the stave units needed to be exactly 48 points wide and line exactly at each side. I was pretty successful in this regard.

I had some problems striking the notes with the long tails. The punches didn't want to sink straight in, as the tail tended to go in deeper than the note head and one unlucky character was broken and re-cut on two separate occasions. That really made my day. When the strike was not level (which often happens) the face of the matrix had to be filed and adjusted until the cavity was level with the surface of the matrix, or else the face of the cast type would not be level. Of all the problems encountered in fitting a matrix, this is the one that gave me the most grief. Other concerns were to get the character vertical on the body and to fit the character close or tight so that the face of the type and the side of the type are at an angle of almost ninety degrees. This permits the compositor to combine various notes so that they almost appear joined.

Of course in discussing the fitting of the matrices I have neglected to mention that this step of the process is impossible without a type mould, and for this project I didn't have a 48-point mould to work with. In addition, a mould required for casting plainchant must have an adjustable stool-abutment to position the matrix under the mould. Such a stool is almost unique to a mould for music because it must move over a much greater distance than the kind of stool used in casting letters. If the previous sentences didn't make much sense, remember that movable types were always cast in adjustable type moulds that were adapted to cast each character by sliding their two halves closer together or farther apart. The face of the type is formed in a matrix which is fixed below the mould, closing the cavity which forms the body or 'shank' of the type. The matrix is accurately held in place by the stool-abutment and the registers (figure 5).

An old form of screw adjustable stool is described by Fournier as follows. '[Alignment] is usually regulated by means of a device called the stool-abutment, which fits on the bottom-plate of the bottom half of the mould. The stool itself is inside this contrivance and is made to move in and out by means of a screw so that the staff-lines of any matrix may be adjusted to their proper position in

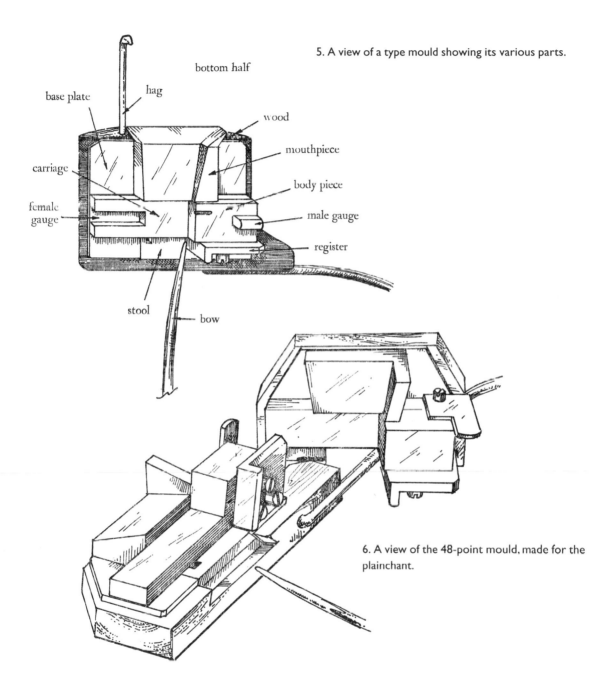

base plate

hag

bottom half

5. A view of a type mould showing its various parts.

wood

mouthpiece

carriage

body piece

female
gauge

male gauge

register

stool

bow

6. A view of the 48-point mould, made for the
plainchant.

relation to the mould. The apparatus is a hindrance to the caster because it projects considerably form the mould, and the accurate adjustment of the matrix for alignment is a delicate operation.'[6]

Fournier's solution to this awkward arrangement was to fit a metal dovetail to the bottom half of the mould that contained two separate pieces of steel that had been dressed to exactly 12-point thickness. By removing the first of these two pieces the matrix would be moved 12 points closer to the base plate of the bottom half of the mould. Removing the second piece moved the matrix 12 points further. The effect of this movement was to cast three different notes from one matrix. The same character was cast in three different positions on the body of the type, thus representing three different tones. If some of the notes were turned upside down, a total of five or even six notes could be cast from a single matrix! The advantage of Fournier's stool-abutment lay in its accuracy and the ability to make rapid changes of alignment. Each time the older screw abutment was changed it had to be carefully fiddled with to get it back into alignment, so that the notes would be in exactly the right place. I chose to make a mould with Fournier's improved stool.

Each time that I make a type mould I usually try something different. No two are made quite alike. In this case I made the 48-point mould in the late-nineteenth-century manner (even though it had Fournier's stool-abutment) because I felt it would be a bit faster and easier to complete. The fit of the mouthpiece on this mould came out particularly well compared to some of my previous efforts which had been a bit less precise. Refer to my sketch of this mould (figure 6) for some idea of its appearance.

After completing a usable 48-point mould, I fitted the matrices for this music and then discovered that it was a beast to cast. I am constantly impressed with how miserably difficult it is to cast type by hand, particularly in very small or very large sizes. After much experimentation I determined that I had to use a softer alloy than is required for smaller types and that many characters would have to be poured twice. The first ladle of metal was given a hard shake to drive the alloy into the matrix in order to get a good face. Then a second pour would fill the body of the type. Sometimes (read that as often) the face would not be complete, or I would have to cut a hole in the foot of the type in order to get the second ladle of metal into the hollow middle of the type. Of course the problems in casting were worse with the staves, which are wide. Simple, narrow notes are not so hard to cast. Still, details in the face frequently gave trouble. Coating the mould and the matrix with soot helped some. Soot seems to insulate the hot metal from the cold surfaces of the mould long enough to improve the cast.

After being cast the sorts were dressed to smooth and finish them and to rub away any overhanging parts near the face that would get in the way of a close fit. This rubbing was performed on a smooth piece of sandstone that had been made perfectly flat. The feet of the types were trimmed in a dressing bench, which is simply a large wooden (in my case) vice that holds the types face down while a knife cuts away the rough nubs left on the feet after the 'jet' or sprue is broken off. Again, it was important that the various notes fit closely in order to create certain patterns of notes. Some combinations were next to impossible to set with separate characters and required special punches if they were to be used.

Now that all of this work is finished the types are ready for use in printing liturgical music. The specimen illustrated on page 268 is the first complete example of this music fount and, though it was begun in 1978, this project lay dormant for a long time. Resurrected this last year, the final work was completed and this specimen printed in 1988. That's just ten years for a supposedly 'simple' project requiring 'only' fifteen punches!

'A life of letters.' It's a phrase that fits **Stan Nelson** well. The son of a minister turned English professor, he grew up with a love of learning and books. He began to play at printing while a young boy, when he was given a toy printing outfit. His early efforts at calligraphy and block carving led eventually to efforts to cast his own printing type, a goal that was finally realized with the cutting of his Robin type, and the establishment of his own personal type foundry. Along the way, Nelson graduated from Morningside College in 1970, spent two years teaching high school art, and then began working at the Smithsonian Institution, with the National Museum's Graphic Arts Collection, where he has been toiling away for the past 28 years. He is noted for his expertise in typefounding, as well as his knowledge of printing technology, and has traveled internationally to deliver lectures and demonstrations on these subjects.

NOTES

1. Harry Carter, *Fournier on Typefounding* (the text of Pierre Simon Fournier's *Manuel Typographique*), Burt Franklin, New York, 1973, p. 57.

2. John Fesperman, (memo) *re Plainsong*, 29 December 1987.

3. Ibid.

4. A. Hyatt King, *Four Hundred Years of Music Printing*, The British Library, London, 1979, p. 16.

5. Ibid, p. 8.

6. Harry Carter, *Fournier*, pp. 153, 159.

SURE-ly * he hath borne our griefs, and car-ri-ed our sor-rows. ℣. Yet we did es-teem him stric-ken, smit-ten of God, e-ven af-flic-ted. ℣. But he was woun-ded for our trans-gres-sions, he was brui-sed for our i-ni-qui-ties. ℣. The chas-tise-ment of our peace was up-on him: and with his stripes we are hea-led.

The Setting of Plainchant

BY SISTER VALERIE CRYER

Sister Valerie Cryer of St Mary's Press has experience in hand-setting plainchant, the notes used to represent Gregorian chant on paper. Her essay in Matrix 4 (1984) *ties her own contemporary practice into a tradition that stretches far back before the advent of printing.*

I have been asked to write a description of the setting of plainchant at St Mary's Press, the private press of the Community of St Mary the Virgin. As this is a form of music which may be unfamiliar to many, it might be appropriate to begin with a short history of the chant itself.

Plainsong is, as its name suggests, 'even, level plain song'. It is a very ancient form of liturgical music thought to have evolved with the growth of the early church and originating in the musical traditions of Palestine, Syria, Armenia, Asia Minor and Greece. Little is known of this period as the earliest extant manuscripts date from the 9th century A.D. Documents from the Middle Ages ascribe to Gregory the Great the enormous task of revising the liturgy of the church. He was Pope from 592–604, and his revision formed the basis of worship for succeeding generations, thus plainsong came to be known as Gregorian chant. Nevertheless, the chant was inevitably exposed to later influences and in some cases the early principles were lost. These corruptions culminated in another great reform, this time led by Pope Pius X, who published an encyclical on church music in 1903.

By this time, St Mary's Press had become actively involved in the preservation of the chant, and indeed there are records of a letter from Pius X to Sister Emma asking to see examples of her printing. The Community was founded in 1848 and one Sister Eliza laid the foundation of the present press as far back as 1854, when the first 'Rules and Regulations' were printed. The vigour and enthusiasm of this woman, who taught at the school then dashed home up the hill to run off tracts for the vicar on a small hand press, led to the establishment of the printing room. Our archives are frustratingly unconcerned with the machinery and equipment used in those days, but a turning point in the history of the press was reached in 1890 when Dr George Herbert Palmer first visited it. In collaboration with Mother Lucy and Sister Emma, he set up for the Community the use and printing of plainchant – including the major undertaking of translating the texts from Latin to the vernacular.

A diary kept by Sister Emma records the phenomenal amount of work they got through, though again there is a paucity of material regarding equipment. An entry for Monday, 26 July 1897 reads: 'Music type came from Paris' and again on Saturday, 27 November 1897: 'Music type came from Paris.' On Wednesday, 1 December 1897: 'Sent Deberny's bill to the bank to be paid' – this is the first reference to the name on the type chart. Whether or not our existing type actually dates from this period I am not able to discover. There is also no mention of precisely how much the type cost, though a later reference states that the princely sum of £3 1s. 10d. was paid for two cases of music. A final, rather quaint, entry reads: 'Maude went in laundry cart to station to collect the two cases of modern music and one of Gregorian from Mr Woodward.' This is dated 4 September 1903 and there are no further entries about the acquisition of type or the skill to use it.

I find it difficult to describe on paper the method of setting plainchant, although some years ago Sister Dorothy Clare achieved the remarkable feat of teaching the enclosed nuns of Stanbrook Abbey by post! The layout of the two type cases required accompanies this article. The lower diagram represents the basic music case, the upper that of the 'peculiars' (the origin of this term I have not discovered, but it is very apt!).

Plainchant has a four-line stave, and in the type these lines are provided singly or in pairs and in various lengths, incrementing in halves. The compositor must work from three cases, two of music and one of the type face chosen for the text (see figure 1). The skills of setting Gregorian chant have been handed down in our Press through an oral tradition and there are few basic rules. These are mainly related to spacing: a line length equivalent to G or F on the basic chart (i.e. 1½ must be allowed after each clef and also before) and after full, half and quarter bars. This may be reduced to 1 (see D and E on the chart) if necessary, always retaining the same spacing each side of the bar line. A hair space (see A and A bis) is inserted between any flat and the note it relates to. Flats are shown in the top row of the peculiars case, nos. 4–8. A final rule concerns the guide notes which occur at the end of the line to indicate to the singers the pitch of the first note of the next line. No space is ever allowed after a guide, and the space between it and the final note on the line may never exceed 2, or the equivalent of H or I on the basic chart.

This allows limited flexibility for the compositor who wishes to lengthen or

CASSE DE PLAIN-CHANT

DEBERNY & PEIGNOT, PARIS

1. Layout of the plainchant case, published in Paris by Deberny & Peignot

shorten a line, because it must also be remembered that in plainchant the sylla-ble is positioned exactly beneath the note or group of notes it belongs to (there are no harmonies). Thus a relatively short syllable such as '-ya' of 'alleluya' may have a very extended neum which makes positioning the line break almost impossible. Alternatively, a single syllable such as 'Christ', spread because of its capital letter, may be attached to a single punctum (the basic note of plain-chant). Thus it behooves one to set words and music concurrently, so that the approach of bar lines or the end of the stick can be anticipated and successfully negotiated with due regard to spacing.

A further difficulty that besets the compositor is that the plainchant type does not appear to correspond to any exact point size that I can discover (ours is only labelled small, medium and large – the example reproduced on page 278 was set in the large type). Peculiars may be the depth of two or more lines, therefore the lines have to be brought to the same length when they are used. However, the process is somewhat simplified when one remembers that the lines increment in halves, thus making it a matter of simple arithmetic.

Let us imagine we are commencing to set a line of music, having already determined the length of stick required. One begins with a quad as always, fol-lowed immediately by the clef (see nos. 1, 2 and 3 on basic chart). The hypothet-ical copy shows that no note appears on the top two lines for a considerable space, so a long, double line is inserted after the clef (see O on basic chart). If the first note should occur on the bottom line, then the third line must extend over it in order to keep it in position. It must also be long enough to allow for the spacing required after the clef and the length of the clef itself, thus a single line of 2½ or 3 length (see L and N) is next inserted. The bottom line contains the first note. A space of 1½ must be allowed after the clef, plus ½ for the clef itself so a single line of 2 is placed, with the note fitting snugly in position against it (see 1 and no. 17 on basic chart respectively). Further lines are then inserted until the estimated position of the next note (or group of notes) is reached, the text being set as one proceeds.

This continues until the end of the stick is reached, when one probably encounters difficulty in tightening the line! This often involves spreading the music or shortening the spaces between groups of notes – rarely can it be achieved by the simple insertion of a hair space (see A and A bis on basic chart) at the end of the line. This kind of juggling requires a cool head and much patience as notes will easily slip into the wrong position when lines are removed. A further hurdle is that one always sets music with nicks to the back – confusing when setting text simultaneously with nicks to the front.

It is hard indeed to convey on paper the deep satisfaction that setting the chant affords, but perhaps the orderly beauty of the finished product speaks for itself. The rich monastic tradition that lies behind it and the painstaking skill of those who reproduced it by hand all contribute to making the setting and printing of plainchant a rewarding and enjoyable task.

Sister Valerie Cryer learned to print at the private press of the Community of St. Mary the Virgin, Wantage (United Kingdom).

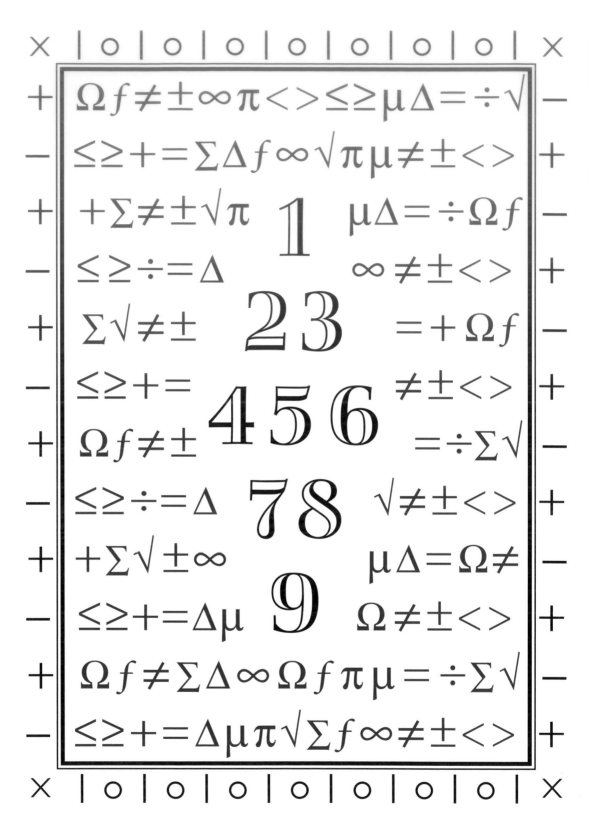

Smaragd figures with Symbol Greek

The Printing of Mathematics

BY DAVID WISHART

If typesetting music is a specialist art, the setting of mathematics is even more complex – a challenge that has bedeviled printers since the earliest days of printing books. David Wishart, in Matrix 8 *(1988), shows the changing standards since the 15th century for representing mathematics on the page, and the intricacies of reproducing it in metal type.*

> Philosophy is written in this grand book, the universe, which stands continually open to our gaze. But the book cannot be understood unless one firsts learns to comprehend the language and read the letters in which it is composed. It is written in the language of mathematics.
>
> Galileo Galilei:[1] The Assayer (1623)

Galileo wrote these words almost 150 years after the publication of the first printed arithmetic book (the *Treviso Arithmetic*, 1478). Several such arithmetics appeared across Europe, written in the vernacular, containing instruction in 'the mercantile art' (i.e. book keeping) and were widely available for the expanding class of traders and merchants at the beginning of the Renaissance. Prior to the invention of printing, this instruction was transmitted by professional 'reckon-masters' and through the apprentice system. With the slight loosening of the control of the guilds and companies, these books enabled the rising, independent entrepreneur to educate himself in the methods of business without a master.

Algebra may be thought of as the first extension of arithmetic. Thus, we know that the number 4, added to 3, gives 7, but it would be tedious to write out every case of this calculation. Rather, we wish to ask the general question: if a, b and x are numbers, what is the value of x so that $x + a = b$? Problems involving areas give rise to ideas of multiplication: for example, can we construct a square field whose area is 2? We would write this, today, in the form:

find the number x such that $x^2 = 2$.

However, these relations were not written in this way in the early printed books which, as in other spheres of activity, followed the manuscript traditions of the preceding generation. The relations were expressed in words, the unknown and required number being referred to as *cosa* [= the thing, in Italian]. The second of the above relations would have been expressed as

cos. quad. aeq. num. 2.

i.e. the thing squared [*quadrata*]^2 equals the number 2.

The first printed algebra appeared in Italy in Italian in 1494.[3] It was set in a black letter, as was the *Whetstone of Wit* (1557), the first algebra book in English. The latter's author, Robert Recorde,[4] referred in his sub-title to algebra as 'the Cossike practice' so wide-spread was the use of *cosa* (and its German version, *Coss*) in this sense. Recorde's principal claim to fame is his introduction of =, the sign for equality, 'bicause noe 2 thynges can be moare equalle'.

Some other symbols had been introduced during the first half of the sixteenth century and the corresponding sorts made available to printers. About 1500 in Germany,[5] the signs for the operations of addition (+) and subtraction (–) were introduced and the sign √ for the square root appeared at the same time (although this had to compete with [Latin: *radix*, a root] for several decades).

A major advance was made towards the end of the sixteenth century by François Viète[6] who started to use upper-case letters in place of *cosa*, although he did not complete the transition to a symbolic language which would be recognisable today. Thus, the expression which in today's notation we would write

$$A^2 + 2AB + B^2 = (A + B)^2$$

appeared in a mixed form as

A quadratum + A in B bis + B quadrato. Quae ideo aequabantur
A + B quadrato.

The remaining steps to transform mathematical notations from a mediaeval into an understandably modern form were taken during the first half of the seventeenth century. Thomas Harriot[7] made several important innovations in his posthumously published book on the practice of algebra (1631): he used lower-case letters in place of Viète's upper-case; he introduced *ab* to represent the multiplication[8] of *a* and *b* (instead of A in B, as above), and used *aa*, *aaa*, for A quadratum, A cubus etc.; and he also started the practice, to which we still adhere, of printing all mathematics in italic (whether in the text or displayed). Finally for this very brief survey of the mathematical background, René Descartes[9] (1637)

introduced an important notation writing, for example, a^2 for aa, a^3 for aaa, etc.
(In fact, for many years aa continued to be printed for a^2 on the grounds that it
was easier to set – the compositor did not have to go to a sorts box for the superior 2 – and it took up the same space on the line.) He also simplified Harriot's
brackets (which indicated that all the terms under, or over, the bracket are to be
included in the square root operation) to a straight line.

These algebraic notations (and the sorts), combined with the decimal representation of numbers, were now ready for the next generation, the generation of
Newton, to carry out the programme enunciated by Galileo at the head of this
essay – to describe the physical world in terms of mathematics.

Not every new idea in mathematics generates a new symbol but many do.
Printers and type-founders have, from the beginning, responded (with praise-
worthy flexibility) to the demands of authors in the creation of new sorts,
although authors have often shown little understanding of the problems of
composition.[10] (In Monotype's 4-line system, discussed below, Monotype
claimed that 8000 characters and symbols were available in 1967.) Sometimes,
however, rather than going to the expense of cutting new punches, an ingenious
printer would create a compound character by some judicious filing. Thus
Thomas Simpson[11] required an unusual set of characters

$$\text{℥, ℥', ℥'' &c.}$$

for use in a text-book published in 1750. These were clearly constructed by filing
the top of Caslon's ℥ and juxtaposing the standard sorts for minutes and sec-
onds of arc.

It will be apparent from the above summary that mathematical notations
have grown somewhat haphazardly, with the result that printers were having to
stock increasingly large quantities of sorts. From time to time, editors have
issued guidelines on notation. This would be partly to control the symbolism
used in the journal so that authors and readers communicated through a common language and partly to control the proliferation of sorts. The earliest of
these known to me dates from 1708. It appeared in a journal called *Acta Erudi-
torum* in which many of the important mathematical developments of the period were reported: the editor was G. W. Leibniz,[12] one of the great polymaths of
his time. His instructions to authors ran thus:[13]

> We hereby issue the reminder that in future we shall use in these *Acta* the Leib-
> nizian signs, where, when algebraic matters concern us, we do not choose the
> typographically troublesome and unnecessarily repugnant. Hence we shall pre-
> fer the parenthesis to the characters consisting of lines drawn above . . . ; for

example, in place of $\sqrt{aa + bb}$ we write $\sqrt{(aa + bb)}$. . . . As regards powers, $\overline{aa + bb}^{\,m}$ we designate them by $(aa + bb)^m$; etc.

The expression $\sqrt{(aa + bb)}$ is certainly typographically less troublesome than its alternative for which a length of 1-point rule (known as the *vinculum*) has to be cut to size and justified (usually in a line by itself). Leibniz's influence in this country was not great and appears to have been totally ignored by English mathematicians, as in this example from Simpson.

$$\overline{rr - 2brx + xx}\Big)^{\frac{1}{2}} \times \overline{rr - 2crx + xx}\Big)^{\frac{1}{2}} \times \overline{rr - 2arx + xx}\Big)^{\frac{1}{2}}$$

It is clear from reading Legros and Grant[14] that Leibniz's recommendations on the use of brackets had been largely adopted by 1916; but other notations had been invented which involved the cutting and justification of rule and they still felt it necessary to inveigh against these.

> Typography may be defined as the craft of rightly disposing printing material in accordance with specific purpose; of so arranging the letters, distributing the space and controlling the type as to aid to the maximum the reader's comprehension of the text.[15]

A definition of mathematical typography would not differ from this. It differs from the typography of prose only in the complication of that which is to be comprehended and in the corresponding variety of types to be controlled. Because a mathematical text will require type in several point sizes and varieties of sorts in each of these sizes, hand-composition is slow.

The early handbooks had very little to say of Algebra. In his inventory 'Of Letter', Moxon wrote: 'Besides *Letters* he [the Printer] Provides Characters of Astronomical Signs, *Planets, Aspects, Algebraical* Characters, Physical and Chimical Characters, &c. And these of several of the most used bodies'.[16] He did not give a list of 'Algebraical Characters' nor did he make any mention of mathematical composition. John Smith (1755) appears to have been the first to have given a list of signs and a little homily (but no instruction):

> These and several other Signs and Symbols we meet with in Mathematical and Algebraical works; tho' authors do not confine themselves to them, but express their knowledge in different ways; yet so as to be understood by those skilled in the science. In Algebraical work, therefore, in particular, gentlemen should be very exact in their copy, and Compositors as careful in following it, that no alterations may ensue after it is composed; since changing and altering work of this nature is more troublesome to a Compositor than can be imagined by one that has not a tolerable knowledge of printing. Hence it is that very few Compositors are fond of Algebra . . .[17]

This passage remained the only statement on mathematical composition for a long time (it was copied *verbatim* by several authors during the eighteenth and early nineteenth centuries).[18]

The most substantial writing on the hand-composition of mathematics is found in Lefevre[19] who devoted ten pages to the subject. 'The composition of algebra' he asserts 'is one of the most difficult to perform. It consists particularly in the building up of formulae which requires great attention'. Most of his advice still stands as current practice: that signs (e.g. $+, -, =, \times$) have the status of words and should be word-spaced within a formula; that mathematical prose needs to be punctuated like any other prose; that the disposition of type to aid the reader's understanding should have some symmetries (e.g. two similar expressions to be set above the other should be aligned vertically); he gives two examples to illustrate his practice, thus[20]

$$8x \; + \; 9y + \; 8z \; = 2700$$
$$12x \; + 12y + 10z \; = 3600$$

$$ax \; + by \; + \; cz \; = d$$
$$a'x \; + b'y \; + \; c'z \; = d'$$
$$a''x + b''y + \; c''z \; = d''$$

Finally he considered, in detail, the setting of a substantial formula. Rather than follow Lefevre's formula, I will discuss an expression exhibiting some more recent trends in mathematical notation.

Setting by hand will be discussed first. We must suppose that the compositor works at a double frame since he will need to have two double cases (roman and italic) of the text type, a case of mathematical sorts (containing signs, super and sub-scripts and etc.) and a case of (unaccented) Greek on the frame and, depending on the work, he may also need to have a case of bold near to hand (although bold was not often used until this century). The text will be set in roman with italic used sparingly for emphasis. As noted above, it is a long-standing convention to set the mathematics in italic (with the occasional help of some Greek).

Let me therefore follow Lefevre's description of setting by hand, using the equation in the copy below. Superscripts and subscripts form an important part of modern mathematical notations and (as here) there are occasions when it is necessary to use what are called second-order super- and sub-scripts (i.e. superscripts on superscripts, subscripts on superscripts, etc.). The building up of formulae requires even greater attention today than it did in Lefevre's time.

A compositor in a house accustomed to setting mathematics will set 'displayed' expressions of this kind automatically in italic. From each section of such a formula, we take first the widest parts and set these (properly spaced), centred within the measure of the page (using 24-point spacing), so that the composing stick will contain

$$P_{N_1+m} = N_1 + m\ \binom{N_2-N_1}{} \alpha^m \beta^{(N_2-N_1)-m}$$

Take out the terms to the right of the = sign and put them in a safe place, then insert 6½ points above and below the first terms. Bring back the term $N_1 + m$ (note the convention that all numbers are set in roman): cut a piece of 2-point rule of its exact length and centre the C above it: replace the 2-point space and the first 24-point parenthesis so that the composing-stick now contains

$$P_{N_1+m} = \frac{C}{N_1+m}\ \Big($$

take now the $N_2 - N_1$; put a 2-point lead below and centre the m: and penulti-mately, insert the second 24-point parenthesis followed by another 2-point space:

$$P_{N_1+m} = \frac{C}{N_1+m}\binom{N_2-N_1}{m}$$

finally, complete the setting of the expression by placing 6½ points above and below the remaining terms.

$$P_{N_1+m} = \frac{C}{N_1+m}\binom{N_2-N_1}{m} \alpha^m \beta^{(N_2-N_1)-m}$$

The development of Monotype technology brought many benefits to mathe-matical type-setting but there was still quite a lot to be done by hand.[21] The fol-lowing piece of copy contains the above expression.[22]

```
        The usual technique for solution in series leads to a pair of

        solutions only one of which is relevant here, and this gives
```

$$(63)\qquad P_{N_1+m} = \frac{C}{N_1+m}\binom{N_2-N_1}{m}\alpha^m\beta^{(N_2-N_1)-m}$$

```
    where the constant C is to be adjusted to make  ∑_{N1}^{N2} P_n = 1.
```

Before anything else is done, it will be marked up for the keyboard operator who will insert the necessary extra characters into the matrix-case. He will set the displayed material in italic unless told not to do so: it is important that any symbols in the body of the text be marked on the typed copy and the Greek letters should be marked the first time they appear. The 11-point Modern No.7 will emerge from the Monotype caster in the form

$$P_N i_{+m} = N_1 + mx\ N_2 - N_1 x \alpha^m \beta^{(Ni - Ni) - m}\ C\ m$$

The galleys from the caster would then go to the 'maker-up' who would turn it into

$$P_{N_1 + m} = \frac{C}{N_1 + m} \binom{N_2 - N_1}{m} \alpha^m \beta^{(N_2 - N_1) - m}$$

In August 1958, all those who attended the International Congress of Mathematicians in Edinburgh received a copy of *The Monotype Recorder*[23] devoted to the typographical problems of setting mathematics. Towards the end of the issue there is a brief description of a new system for the setting of mathematical texts which had been designed to do away with many of the time-wasting activities of the 'maker-up'.

Within the procedure used before 1958, the 'maker-up' had to add most of the first and second order characters as well as the large sorts, to create many of the two-line formulae from components cast on one line and to insert horizontal rules and leads as required. These were his principal time-wasting activities. The ingenuity of the 4-line system lies in the way the text is separated for setting so that almost the only things left for the 'maker-up' are the insertion and justification of the rule for a fraction and the insertion of the large sorts.

The 4-line system takes the two lines of a deep formula separately and treats each of these as two 6-point lines so that (with the insertion of 2-point rule or lead, as appropriate) the total depth is 26 points. The type-face used for the principal characters is 10-point Times (series 569, especially designed for this type of work) and it is obvious that, for example, the bowl of the *P*, in (63), cast on a 6-point body will seriously overhang. To support this overhang, the keyboard operator inserts a shoulder-high space of the correct unit width and in the correct place on the top line. The top line will therefore look like this:

$$\theta \qquad \theta\ \theta\ \theta\theta\ \ \theta\ \ \theta\theta \qquad \theta m \theta_{(N_2 - N_1) - m}$$

where the θ represent the supporting shoulder-spaces for the characters of the second line which will now look like this:

$$P_{N_1 + m} = N_1 + m\ \ N_2 - N_1\ \ \alpha\ \beta$$

The third line is then

$$\theta \qquad \theta$$

and the fourth

$$C \qquad m$$

The 'maker-up' cuts a 1 on 2-point rule for the fraction (and inverts it) and a 2-point lead to separate the two lines within the parentheses. The other terms are centred with 7 points above and below (7-point leads would have been available). Spaces of the unit-width of the large parentheses have been cast in the correct places in all four lines so that the 'maker-up' has now only to remove these spaces and insert the 26-point sorts which (along with the other large 'fences') were already cast and available in case. Other expressions which had been noted as occuring frequently in the text being set would also have been pre-cast to be inserted by the compositor at the make-up stage (these would have included, for example, the = cast on a 26-point body). Note also, that the procedure recommended by Lefevre, of setting first the wider half of a fraction, is again used here so that the width of the fraction bar is determined without a trial setting.

The 4-line system is designed for the setting of displayed formulae: mathematics in the text is usually dealt with by the insertion of the necessary characters into the matrix-case used for text-setting (10-point Times, Series 327). The normal 15 x 17 matrix-case arrangement (MCA) allows for 251 characters and 4 spaces. The MCA for 4-line mathematics has available 341 characters plus spaces.[24] The basic arrangement has 200 characters and 51 blanks. Of the characters, 153 are 10-point (a complete fount of upper and lower-case italic and all the non-roman characters of a Greek fount; lower-case roman and figures but no upper-case roman, since one would only have conjunctions in the middle of a display – one would never start a sentence there; and some signs) and the remaining 47 for characters required in superior and inferior positions (the same matrix will cast in either position): of the 51 blanks, 43 can be used for first- and second-order characters and the remaining 8 for additional 10-point characters. Thus, 341 = 153 + (2 x 47) + (2 x 43) + 8, in addition to the high and low spaces.

A special Button-bank was designed to go with this arrangement. Since, as we have seen, the spacing of mathematics is complicated, every character key has engraved on it the unit value of the character and the blank keys carry their matrix-case positions.

During recent years, commercial type-setting has been taken over by computers: printers have melted down their lead, sold their matrix-cases and invested large sums of money in a rapidly changing technology. This development has taken place in mathematics as in other disciplines. After a period of fairly ghastly typography (the late seventies and early eighties), several wordprocessing packages have been written to handle mathematics, one of the most interesting of which is TEX, devised by Donald Knuth, a computer-scientist at Stanford University. In his first paper,[25] Knuth surveyed the typography of *The Transactions of the American Mathematical Society* from its inception in 1900 and described the decline in the 1970s as a result of which he 'regretfully stopped submitting to the American Mathematical Society, since the finished product was just too painful for me to look at'. He therefore turned his thoughts to the design of a flexible system which would handle both ordinary prose and mathematics of any complexity. Since Knuth writes well, the interested reader should consult his work directly and I will not attempt to describe TEX here. Suffice it to remark that, as Monotype 4-line succeeded by dividing a mathematical expression into ½-lines which were cast separately and then put together, so TEX succeeds by dividing the text into units which are key-boarded (these he calls 'boxes') and then 'glued' together. His notion of 'glue' is essentially a procedure for justification (horizontal and vertical) of almost infinite flexibility. Similar procedures were developed into the layout programs now included in the so-called 'desk-top publishing' packages.

The 500th anniversary of the publication of Pacioli's *Summa* was celebrated in 1994. During 400 of these years, mathematical notations developed slowly; since 1900, the number of mathematicians and the quantity of mathematical notation has increased enormously. Using Knuth's METAFONT program, it is now possible for an author to design any desired character or, indeed, the very face in which the work is to be printed. Its unbridled use could lead to anarchy; let us hope that the mathematical community can exercise restraint.

David Wishart retired from the University of Birmingham (England) in 1988 after teaching mathematics there for thirty years. During that period he also acted as copy-editor and editor for the *Journal of the Royal Statistical Society*, B. This article was written to record, before it was forgotten, a technology which had died. Long before he retired, Wishart had started the Hayloft Press. In 1983 his first booklet was published (*The Last Crisis* by Tom Paine, commemorating its first publication in 1783). Commemorative publications have played an important rôle in the Press's output since: e.g. the bi-centenary of Shelley's birth in *I am Ozymandias* (1992) & the centenary of Jacob Burckhardt's death in *London Observed* (1997). (The latter was computer-generated.) Ever since the beginnings of the Press, the collection of interesting types has been an important activity: there is a Corrector's case-rack for 4-line mathematics; some unusual roman, italic, & blackletter; and several non-Latin type faces – Greek, Hebrew, Russian, Old Church Slavonic, Egyptian hieroglyphs. The Egyptian types have been described in several articles in *Matrix*, and a survey of the non-Latin types at Oxford may be found in *Matrix 21*.

NOTES

1. Galileo Galilei (1564–1642): an intellectual giant of his time. He was a natural philosopher who saw clearly the relationship between Physics and Mathematics. He was a pioneer in his approach to Physics; his mathematics was essentially old-fashioned.

2. Whence the printers' term *quad*.

3. Luca Pacioli (1445?–1515?): *Summa de Arithmetica, Geometria, Proportioni et Proportionalita*, 1494.

4. Robert Recorde (1510–1558): he qualified as a doctor and wrote also (in English) a popular medical text (1547), *The Urinal of Physic*.

5. Michael Stifel (1486?–1567).

6. François Viète (1540–1603): a politician, he did his major mathematical work during 1585–1590, while out of office. His printer did not always distinguish between + and †, although he was consistent within a single line.

7. Thomas Harriot (1560–1621): in addition to his mathematical innovations, he developed a telescope and was observing sunspots at the same time as Galileo.

8. This is the algebraic form of multiplication which complements the arithmetic form, $a \ x \ b$, introduced in the same year by William Oughtred (1574–1660).

9. René Descartes (1596–1650): Philosopher and Mathematician. These notational innovations may be found in his *Geometry*. It is interesting to note that his printer did not have an en rule for the minus sign but used instead two hyphens.

10. J. E. Poole (1967), 'The non-mathematician sometimes wonders if in fact this vast range [of characters] is really required. When an author insists that a new character or symbol has to be coined because nothing in existence has, for him, just the right usage or nuance of expression, does this stem from ego or necessity?' The author was typographic technical adviser to Monotype.

11. Thomas Simpson (1710–1761): *The Doctrine and Application of Fluxions*, London, 1750.

12. G. W. Leibniz (1646–1716): mathematician, diplomat, philosopher, philologist.

13. F. Cajori, *A History of Mathematical Notation*. University of California, 1928.

14. L. A. Legros and J. C. Grant, *Typographical Printing Surfaces*. Longman, Green and Co., 1916.

15. S. Morison, *First Principles of Typography*. Cambridge University Press, 1936.

16. J. Moxon, *Mechanick Excercises in the whole Art of Printing*. London, 1683, (reprinted, OUP, 1962).

17. J. Smith, *The Printer's Grammer*, 1755.

18. P. Luckombe, *The History and Art of Printing*, 1771; C. Stower, *The Printer's Grammer*, 1808.

19. Théotiste Lefevre, *Guide Pratique pour le Compositeur*, Paris: Didot, 1873. Of the principal symbols listed in the text, only = still has the status of a word; his practice of setting upper case mathematics in roman is now only followed by some of the more traditional French printers.

20. J. Southward, *Practical Printing*, 1882. Southward misunderstood Lefevre and printed the two examples as one, at the same time aligning the xs, ys and zs (as is my practice today).

21. T. W. Chaundy, P. R. Barrett and C. Batey, *The Printing of Mathematics*. Oxford University Press, 1954.

22. D. G. Kendall, Stochastic Models in Population Growth. *J. Roy. Statist. Soc.*, B, 1949.

23. Arthur Philips, Setting Mathematics. *The Monotype Recorder*, v. 40, no. 4, 1958.

24. Monotype Information Sheet No. 156, March 1959.

25. D. E. Knuth, Mathematical Typography. *Bull. Amer. Math. Soc.,* 1979. His writings on typography are collected in *TEX and METAFONT: new directions in typesetting,* published by The American Mathematical Society, 1979.

I am indebted to Mr Julian Roberts and to the staff of the Bodleian Library for their assistance in the preparation of the historical material in this article; to Mr Nigel Roche of St Bride Printing Library for directing my attention to the printers' handbooks; and to Mr Duncan Avery of the Monotype Corporation and Mr Derek Copp of Mouldtype Foundry Ltd. for information on the 4-line system.

1

FIRST VOICE

— We were not told they had been wrecked, only we heard their voices
in dry wells of villages behind grey churches
in the cry of rust-splashed birds — wood water-ripe
blacker than rotting fruit, bulks hugged by tangled weeds
where time flows like the shadow of a fish,
cold poise of throats snatches of limbs
stone shimmering through corpse-green slime
eyes water-worn, the lips salt-gnarled —
painted ships.

          We searched the sea-caves,
only the breath of ancient love stretched in their dampness
green pools of silence like a mermaid's eyes.
Memory seeps away in that long sleep of slime
where no arms reach to stroke the wounded stone.
Shreds only of green bronze cling to their rust shapes —
a boy watching a pecking bird? a man? the apple rolled out of his hand?
"Why," you had said, "must the hands of robbers
be the last flesh to touch them?"

          Remember those gestures of limbs
when midday was swelling, lechery of light.
The hunt was over,
he lay there killed by the accurate wounds of Acteon's hounds.
Death swings an artist hand, life snapped

[1]

Reproduced from *The Elegies of a Glass Adonis* by C. A. Trypanis, published by Chilmark Press. Designed and printed by Will and Sebastian Carter in 1967, using Arrighi italic designed by Frederic Warde in 1925.

Some Notes on the Design of Poetry

BY SEBASTIAN CARTER

Poetry requires no special characters, like mathematics or music, but arranging lines of verse on the page of a book requires careful thought and sensitivity to the text. In Matrix 4 *(1984), Sebastian Carter invents an imaginary client to describe the real problems of printing poetry. His essay is in part a response to the one following.*

In the early 1980s two eloquent manifestos for the printing of poetry by hand caught my attention: Clifford Burke's *Printing poetry* was published by the Scarab Press of San Francisco in 1980, and Glen Storhaug's article 'On printing poetry aloud'. Both writers (and it should be said that both are first-rate practitioners of what they preach) argue that the physical form poetry appears in makes a positive contribution to its message. Storhaug says that careful design and crisp impression on good paper seize the reader's interest, and are the visible equivalent of the Anglo-Saxon minstrel's call for attention, 'HWÆT!' Burke makes the complementary point, that the excellence or poverty of the typographic form, and the choice of materials, declare an attitude towards the text's status: 'the printer is the text's first critic'.

Storhaug's article, which follows this one, is too short to go into particulars, and although Burke's book is one of the best accounts of both the philosophical and practical aspects of small letterpress printing I have come across, I feel it needs some comment on the business of designing poetry. I apologise in advance that though I respect the seriousness of both writers, my attitude may seem at first a degree less reverential than theirs.

The teachers of English literature used to make, I remember, extremely heavy weather of the difference between poetry and prose, and we had to write laborious essays on the subject, leaning heavily on Coleridge's *Biographia literaria*. It is a great relief to me now, as a working printer, simply to accept that there is a clear division between prose writers, who do not complain when the typographer cuts their lines to fit his page, and poets, who think they know best about the way their writings are laid out.

Nine-tenths of the time this does not matter: the typographer can cope. Most poets keep within a metrical foot either way of the pentameter, and this is about right for a comfortable page. Milton, Dryden, Pope and Wordsworth wrote pages of blank verse or heroic couplets which you would be hard put to set badly. The proportion of the sonnet sequence, arranged two to a page, is virtually idiot-proof. But sometimes poets get it into their heads that their phrases need more space, or less, and group them in very long, or very short lines, recklessly unmindful of the extra work they are making for the printer, and even sometimes plaintive that the results look less than wonderful.

An extreme case is that of Browning's 'A toccata of Galuppi's'. It is a marvellous poem, but its effect on the page is inevitably marred by its very long fifteen-syllable line, which has to be turned over – at any rate in any edition which also includes 'A woman's last word', which alternates six- and three-syllable lines. (In the Penguin Browning, dated 1954 and therefore presumably with Hans Schmoller's approval, 'A toccata' is further distorted by justifying the broken long lines on the measure, the turn-overs being mostly of one to three words. Indeed, an instructive chamber of typographical horrors might be assembled of ways in which short turn-overs are accommodated.) A solution to the problem, if Browning had recognised it *as* a problem, would have been to break the lines halfway along at the rhythmical pause, and print the stanza as a six-line one, with only the second, fourth and sixth lines rhyming:

> As for Venice and her people,
>   Merely born to bloom and drop,
> Here on earth they bore their fruitage,
>   Mirth and folly were the crop:
> What of soul was left, I wonder,
>   When the kissing had to stop?

But many poets seem to think that a variety of line lengths is a virtue, and a snappy new stanza form shows invention. Such a one was John Donne: in the fifty-five *Songs and sonets* there are over fifty different stanza forms, over forty of which were apparently devised by Donne. But at least he spares us excessively long lines.

Of course, the humble printer is there only to serve the poetry and do his best, but I sometimes wish that poets had better typographical eyes, or had been better advised. Clifford Burke recommends reasoning with the author in awkward cases, but Donne and Browning are unfortunately beyond the reach of reason.

When a manuscript arrives in front of a would-be poetry printer, and he has been inspired by Storhaug and invigorated by Burke, how should he proceed? Burke writes well on the choice of tools and materials, and wonderfully well on workshop practice and the physical delights of hand-setting and printing; the few pages on 'The two-page spread' in his chapter 'The poem on the page' are excellent, but I would like him to have written more. During the conference of small press printers in San Francisco in 1979 I went to a class he gave on just this subject, and I wish I could convey how invigorating his teaching style is. What follows is a fictionalised account of our working methods at the Rampant Lions Press, which are close to his on most but not all points, with some reflections.

Matthew Prenderghast, a retired merchant banker, has since his undergraduate days been a clandestine poet. His collection of sonnets *Love's offering* appeared in 1934, just before his first marriage, in a privately printed edition of 125 copies, produced at the Fanfare Press vaguely under the control of Stanley Morison, and set in Frederic Warde's Arrighi-Vicenza type. At various times since then works have been sparingly added to the canon: some sprung-rhythm musings in the manner of Hopkins written during a brief religious phase, an Horatian ode to Anthony Eden during the Suez crisis, and some celebrations of family life and the joys of grandchildren, written in a comparatively free style, some of them with very long lines.

At the suggestion of his friend Angus Wildsmith, Mr Prenderghast has approached us with the poems; an added spur is the fact that we now have the Warde Arrighi types in our collection, since he very much wants the new book to look as much like the 1934 *Love's offering* as possible. Independently, Angus tells us that the poems are not bad, and that Prenderghast is well heeled. We write to Prenderghast explaining that we cannot publish the book, but would be happy to print it for private distribution; he replies that this is just what he had in mind, and how much will it cost?

To make an estimate requires an outline design. What format should the book be? What should be the area of the type page? How many pages will it make? Is it possible to maintain the style of the 1934 book? Warde's Arrighi is a very, some might say exaggeratedly narrow italic: sometimes the kerns sit on the shoulders of *two* adjoining letters. In the 1934 book Morison, true to form, did not lead it, and the page area, with one sonnet to a page, was very small, 21 ems deep on a 14 em measure. With a narrow type there is the advantage that the disparity between long and short lines is less than with a wider one, which, aside from their attractiveness and informality, is why we often favour italic type for poetry, as Francis Meynell did for other reasons; but we decide that the delicacy of the Warde type is unsuitable for the free-verse domestic poems, let alone the Horatian ode, and moreover it has to be hand-set, which would be too time-consuming. We opt for a type which can be machine-set, finally choosing 12-point Ehrhardt italic on a 14-point body, which has almost exactly the same x-height as the 18-point Arrighi, but is slightly wider.

We have now to decide on the measure. We first do a character count of the longest lines. The longest is a freak line, in a poem on the birth of a first grandson, which has 82 characters; the next longest has a more manageable 68 characters which, in the type we have chosen, will squeeze into a measure of 26 ems. We feel it would be better to turn the one freak line over rather than distort the whole book for its sake. Burke advises us to consult the author about this, and in due course we do, but only after we have made all our other decisions: in our view anyone who writes such a line *must* expect it to turn over. Even our 26 em measure means a lot of quadding out in most of the other poems – the sonnets average around 43 characters a line, visually about 17 ems, and the ode is narrower still – and if we were setting by hand we would set the narrower poems on shorter measures; but as they are being set by machine it is more economical to stick to the one measure.

We have next to consider the page depth. The measure we have had to adopt because of the longer line lengths and wider type makes it impossible to keep to the small format of *Love's offering*, but we think it likely that we shall decide to begin each poem on a new page. To determine where best to break the longer poems, our practice is to draw a chart of the poem lengths, with gaps for the stanza breaks, which Burke recommends as well.

From the diagram opposite we can see that a fairly clear break could be made after line 15, which would comply with Mr Prenderghast's request for a book with one sonnet to a page as in 1934. The fifth and ninth domestic poems are awkward, in that they would end the page with either a single line from the stanza over the page, or a two-line white space which might suggest that the poem had ended.

My preference in these cases would be for the less attractive but also less ambiguous first option: designers tend to be too pre-occupied with the look of a spread, and consequently to rate the hiatus of turning the page more highly than does the reader, who treats a book more as a continuous flow. Readers are

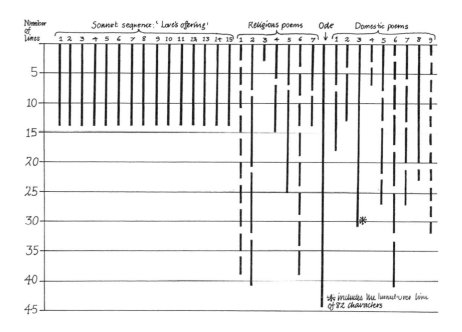

more likely to object to a confusing ambiguity, such as you might get from a turn-over which looks like a new poem: as Burke writes: 'If, for example, a long poem leaves a three-line widow and the book also contains untitled haiku, then the widow will look more like an untitled haiku than the end of a long poem.' In our book, just such a confusion may arise, since the three-line turn-over in the first of the domestic poems would look like the third of the religious poems, which is a short three-liner; but fortunately the latter is titled, so the confusion would be only momentary. I have often felt that the use of an arrow or printer's fist set discreetly at the end of a page where a poem is to continue over would prevent this kind of ambiguity.

In any case, reflection shows us that a fifteen-line page is far too short, and would make a book of a landscape format. (Although one should not completely rule out such a format for poetry if a particular stanza form suggested it, in the case of a collection of poems it would be highly arbitrary.) There is another clear break at line 32, which would allow two sonnets to be set to a page; in the sixth religious poem this will mean a break in the middle of a quatrain, which is acceptable. The proportions of the page will now be quite pleasing.

As I have said above, as an indication that the poem is to carry on over the page, a mid-stanza break is preferable to one which falls neatly at the foot of the page. But there is a further factor to consider, which is how to affirm in the case of a poem with irregular stanzas that there is a stanza break when it falls exactly at the page foot with no room for a line space, as happens here in the second religious poem and the sixth domestic one. One's typographical training revolts at the idea of dropping the head of the next page by a line. Since the action of turning the page is enough to create the momentary pause that the poet intended, it does not greatly matter unless the book is likely to serve as the copy text for another edition, when the next designer will need to know where the breaks occur. One might add a hollow square to the arrow or fist mentioned above; or adopt the solution of the new Finneran edition of Yeats of printing an appendix listing the cases where stanza breaks and page endings coincide.

With the poems arranged in this way, some of the pages will be full, and others, especially the third religious poem, empty. What to do about this, if anything, is a matter of personal preference. Some might prefer to insert this three-line poem at the foot of the previous page. To me, this is a compromise, and looks like one. Others will drop the tops of the shorter poems and arrange them around some notional optical middle line, a solution which Burke rightly condemns as the 'pogo-stick effect'. Provided that the outer margins of the page are reasonably wide, a short poem should look at home on its own at the head of a page.

At this stage we can make our quotation: we know the extent of the book (with half-titles before each section, prelims and blanks at the beginning and end it makes 48 pages); we can decide our paper format (Imperial Octavo), choose our paper and estimate printing time. We put our proposals to Mr Prenderghast; he accepts the logic of our decisions and our price and gives us the go-ahead. We get the book set, paged up, proofed and corrected, and we are ready to go to press. By now we should have confronted the question of how to position the poems on the page, by making either an exact paste-up or some form of universal page layout. What rules should we follow?

The conventional wisdom, as set out by Burke, is that the poetry 'should be visually centred [laterally] within the area normally allotted to a prose type block' (opposite, A). Burke acknowledges the drawbacks of this method: an isolated long line in an otherwise narrow poem will drive it to the left or straggle into the margin, and similar distortions will happen in most highly irregular verse forms. Burke also objects to the effect of a very short page which is kept aligned at the head (opposite, B). Allied to this is what might be called the 'anthology problem': how are you to arrange poems of different widths on the same page? Figure C shows the conventional solution on the left-hand page,

A   B   C

which to me looks a mess: I greatly prefer the look of the same poems arranged as on the right-hand page. Nevertheless, Burke suggests modifications to the method rather than scrapping it altogether, except for the convenience of having a fixed left-hand margin when designing a trade poetry edition for someone else to print.

We at the Rampant Lions Press used to follow this visual centering method, and to make the kind of adaptations in the awkward cases that Burke suggests; but I have revised my views for two reasons. One is simple irritation at the effect of a jumping left-hand margin which you get when you leaf through a book planned in this way if the poems vary in width to any great degree. Book typography is a three-dimensional affair, the third dimension being the sequence of the pages viewed in time. The continuity of the sequence is just as important as the look of a single spread, and if anything the former should condition the latter.

Secondly, I think the idea of placing poems as though on a notional prose spread is basically misguided. You are using as a frame a set of four invisible margins of which only one, the head, is ever stated. Poems make dynamic shapes which need more secure fixing than this. At the same time, one of the things that distinguish them from prose is precisely their awkward, irregular shape, which prevents their ever being balanced like blocks of text. We should forget completely about those ghostly rectangles and carefully calculated proportions which define the prose spread, and deal simply with what we have, difficult but lively shapes. It does not matter that every page is different: that is the way poems are. It may seem paradoxical to be recommending at the same time that the leading edges, the top and left-hand margins, should be constant throughout the book; but with continuity on these two vital sides, the eye will relish variety on the other two. It is enough to anchor the prow; we can let the stern swing free.

At all events, we are happy with the book, and so is Mr Prenderghast.

Sebastian Carter was born in 1941, and studied English literature and the history of art at King's College, Cambridge. After university he worked for a number of publishers and designers in London and Paris before joining his father Will Carter at the Rampant Lions Press in Cambridge, which he now runs from his house outside the town. Here he has produced a long series of fine editions, often in rare typefaces such as Eric Gill's Golden Cockerel Roman and Hermann Zapf's Hunt Roman. Highlights have included Milton's *Areopagitica*, Samuel Beckett's *As the story was told*, and T. S. Eliot's *Four Quartets*, as well as a number of typographical display pieces such as *A printer's dozen* and most recently *In praise of letterpress*. He writes extensively on printing and typography, reviewing regularly for the *Times Literary Supplement* and the British Printing Historical Society's *Bulletin* and *Journal*. He guest-edited the 1990 Eric Gill number of the *Monotype Recorder*, and wrote the section on 'The Morison years' in the centenary number in 1997. His *Twentieth century type designers* (1987; new edition 1995; now out in paperback) has become a standard work. With only two exceptions, he has contributed to every number of *Matrix*.

On Printing Poetry Aloud

BY GLENN STORHAUG

In the second issue of Matrix *(1982), Glenn Storhaug arguing from his own experience as a letterpress printer, insists that it is possible, with sufficient care and attention, to make a poem spring alive from the printed page.*

When a poet comes to the front of the platform to commence a reading he or she may – if the reading is a proper occasion – have to work hard to win the audience's full attention: drink may be flowing, friends may be chatting, the air may still be ringing from a musical interval just ended. But even if the reading is a more sober affair the audience may not be prepared for the transition from everyday to heightened language. So the poet takes a deep breath (inspiration) and then, in a measured breathing out of the poem's words, puts a spell on the audience (*spell* derives from the Gothic *spill* meaning *recital*).

In eighth century Britain the same preoccupied audience was alerted to a recital by a loud 'HWÆT!' from the minstrel. 'HWÆT!' meant 'listen!' (rather than the literal modern English translation 'what!') and survives as the first word on manuscript transcriptions of many Old English oral poems. Thus *Beowulf* opens with

> HWÆT, We gar-dena   in geardagum,
> Þeodcyninga   Þrym gefrunon,
> hu ða æÞelingas   ellen fremedon!

which translates as '*Listen!* (or, *Here we go! Prepare for a long journey!*) We spear-Danes heard of the glory of the people's kings in former days, how the princes performed deeds of valour!' 'HWÆT!' could have cut like a knife through the smoke-filled air of the mead-hall.

This formulaic shout, like the performance of the contemporary reciter, is needed to prepare the audience, tune the senses. It is the aim of this essay to consider how the poem *on the page* can alert the reader in a similar manner, can shout 'HWÆT!' to ensure that the poem is read as a poem and not as prose cut into differing line-lengths.

Many contemporary poets feel that printed poetry fails because a book simply cannot shout 'HWÆT!'. Basil Bunting maintains that 'poetry lies dead on the page, until some voice brings it to life, just as music on the stave is no more than instructions to the player'. As a printer and publisher of poetry I must face this challenge, just as I must face the less specific challenge of such commentators as Marshall McLuhan who believe that print has reduced human sensibility and imagination. McLuhan's book *The Gutenberg Galaxy* makes interesting reading for anyone who has just been holding a composing stick with reverence. 'Alphabetic man', he writes, 'was disposed to desacralise his mode of being.' And he summarises thus: 'As the Gutenberg typography filled the world the human voice closed down.'

The assertion, then, is that poetry is essentially performed, shared by an audience for whom traditionally its sounds had magical powers, and so is drastically reduced when read silently by one person sitting in a corner with a book. Firstly, the poem is not a communal event when on the page, and secondly it has no vocal energy since the modern reader does not, like the medieval manuscript reader, mouth the words aloud. (McLuhan describes how the scribe's close-fitting words, with almost no punctuation, forced the reader to vocalise in order to make sense of them, while a printer supplies sufficient punctuation for the reader to follow a complicated sentence with eyes only. Speed-reading techniques take us even further from the sound and feel of the words.)

I hope to show that committed small press poetry publishing (where the publisher is also letterpress printer and sometimes poet – and it's bound to be committed as there's no money in it) can meet the challenge represented by silent, passive, solitary reading. A new book from a lively poetry press is an event, a performance in which poet, printer, publisher and reader all participate and, if successful, it is a book that will be *heard*.

The poem is said to lie dead on the page, but what kind of page is assumed? Those who argue exclusively for the oral tradition do not distinguish between the standard mechanical page and the page produced with typographic skill by a lively imagination in sympathy with the sound of the poem. Many a poetry book from the big publishing houses, produced economically and quickly, has a look of sluggish uniformity about it: a standard layout grid has been applied throughout and minimal point size, leading and margins combine to give a feeling of tightness which makes a cage of the paper and ink, a cage in which to trap the poem. The reader doubles up to enter the cage for a text that may prove so self-effacing that he or she gives up and turns on the television – even though the poem may have held that reader spell-bound when recited at a local festival. The successful page, on the other hand, releases the text to meet the reader. Generous margins (with no unnecessary folios or other clutter) and ample leading create space and light against which the words stand like branches against the sky or images in stained glass: light shines *through* rather than *on to* the poem so each word is given a three-dimensional presence. Sharp printing (ideally letterpress) of a carefully chosen face at least 12 points in size – with careful word spacing acting as punctuation where the poem demands it – is of course essential for the achievement of this effect. Silence and speech, as light and shade, work in measure on the page, the poem breathes, the poet sings in the reader's head.

Handbooks of typography are quick to recommend this face or that, this spacing or that for the setting of poetry, all with the good intention of slowing down the reading pace while keeping things tight enough to prevent the breaking of long lines. And some poets have been quite specific about the correct face for their work or for poetry in general. My intention is not to add to or disagree with these rules and regulations, rather it is to distinguish between poetry printed according to the handbook or house style and poetry printed according to its own particular shape, sound and sense.

Happily a good deal of poetry resists any layout grid imposed upon it and forces the designer-compositor to listen with care and set as appropriate. A poem that breathes with long and short lines, long and short sections, forces the compositor to set and space accordingly. In this regard the hand-setting of poetry for letter-press printing will always be more of an event, more of a collaboration between poet and printer, than will any cold-type system used for photo-lithography. The letterpress hand compositor not only feels the weight of each word – and the weight of the surrounding space   in his stick, he also has to wrestle with all the different margins as he locks up his four or eight pages in the chase. We have already seen the importance of these margins and spaces, the light essential to the black of the text, and only in letterpress do these spaces have such a presence during composition. In a page containing a poem set to a wide measure but with many short lines, the spaces will demand more attention, and weigh more, than the type. And I do not think it fanciful to suggest that the reader of the finished book can sense this long and laborious involvement of the compositor: it is an important part of the event. In his poem *Ode to Typography* Pablo Neruda described this aspect of the printing-a-poem-event. The extract shown on page 308 celebrates a linotype event but it is still worth quoting. It also serves to illustrate the way words work in ample space.

There are notable exceptions to the letterpress-only rule. A sense of immediacy attends many of the duplicated poetry publications – among the best are those from *Writers Forum* and *Galloping Dog* – a sense that there is no time for

But,
when
writing
unfolds
its roses,
and the letter
its essential
gardening,
when you read
the old and the new
words, the truths
and the explorations,
I beg
a thought
for the one who orders
and raises them,
for the one who sets
type,
for the linotypist
and his lamp
like a pilot
over
the waves of language
ordering
winds and foam,
shadow and stars
in the book:
man
and steel
once more united
against the nocturnal wing
of mystery,
sailing,
perforating,
composing.

the lengthy business of conventional printing and publishing, a feeling that the poem must be typed, duplicated and distributed *now* if it is not to lose its voice in the process. And photo-lithography gives great scope for inspired jumbled-together paste-ups of text and illustration simulating the act of creation itself: a remarkable example is the *Big Huge* issue of *New Departures*, which is in every way an event.

So the book need not be an expensive letterpress edition in order to keep the poems within it alive; this would hardly meet the challenge that poetry has a traditional function within the community. But letterpress – which is the ideal medium for so many reasons – need not be exclusively expensive. Small presses have always managed to price at least some of their letterpress books very modestly: sometimes only pamphlets but often paper or board bound books too, usually subsidised by the collector's items. These presses invariably go bust, but new ones appear to take their place. The letterpress books produced in London during the late 1960s from such poetry presses as Trigram, Cape Goliard and Fulcrum were astoundingly cheap. Michael McClure's *Hymns to St Geryon/Dark Brown* from Cape Goliard and Lorine Niedecker's *North Central* from Fulcrum (printed by Asa Benveniste of Trigram) are among scores of books that launch their poems into the air, each page forever alive with the effort and imagination and pleasure that led the poem through the stick and onto the Wharfedale.

There is a great difference between reading such a book and reading a standardised volume in a standardised series from one of the big houses. Only the former is designed for language that is working full out, playing on all its sounds and senses and so demanding an audience especially attentive with eye and with ear. No distractions, no crampings, only leaping words against enough white to cut out everything else in the world. The first sound such books make as we turn over the blank pages from end-paper to title-page, blank pages blanking out all our daily preoccupations, is a sharp and beautifully printed 'HWÆT!'

As writer, editor, and teacher, **Glenn Storhaug** has always been fascinated by the way typographical design affects the reader's response to text – particularly poetry. He established Five Seasons Press in 1977, only a few miles from Capel-y-ffin (on the border between England and Wales), where Eric Gill designed some of his finest typefaces. The Press produced hand-set and hand-printed books, broadsides and pamphlets up until 1996, favouring Ehrhardt and Sabon as house faces. The attempt to steer a middle course between private press publishing (which tends not to focus on new or 'difficult' writing) and more commercial literary publishing (which tends not to prioritise the book as an object) led to some confusion in the respective marketplaces. Five Seasons is still busy, on behalf of other publishers, with typography and book design, but now – sadly – this is of a more electronic nature.

Left: From Ode to Typography by Pablo Neruda. Translation by Carlos Lozano © Chicago Review by whom it was first published (Vol. 17, no. 1, 1964).

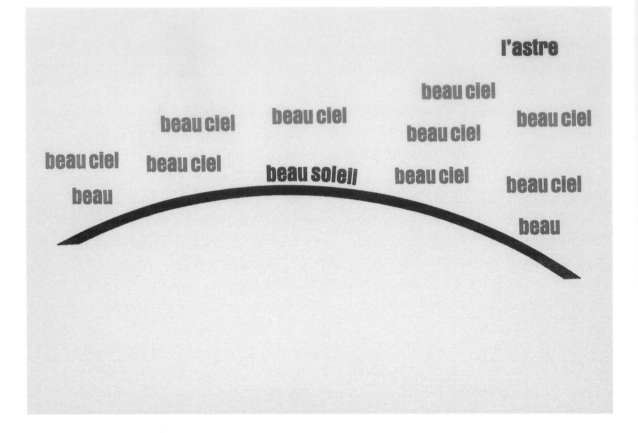

1. 'l'astre'

How Far the Abracadabra

BY PHILIP GALLO

The setting of concrete poetry, where the physical form of the poem is a part of the poem itself, is always a collaboration between the poet and the printer. In Matrix 8 (1988), Philip Gallo both tells and shows his own experience in working with the material, in every sense of the word.

Whatever led me to Concrete Poetry began at the Typographic Laboratory in Iowa City – at that time (1965) still under the direction of Harry Duncan – and it began almost immediately, with my second project there, an essay attributed to Jonathan Swift, and which I entitled 'Bric-A-Brac'. The essay satirised people who bought books by the foot to adorn their already-magnificent bookcases, and among other uses for books was the suggestion they be turned into kites. So I made an ornamental page in the shape of a kite and, ever the modernist, inserted in the manner of William Burroughs' cut-ups the paragraph from *Gulliver's Travels* in which he satirised The Order of the Garter – and included in the typographic topiary on which the the two birds stand the motto of The Order, 'Honi Soit Qui Mal Y Pense'.

Following that I set in 24- or 30-point Hadriano Stone Cut an Abracadabra. I never even proofed it, held prisoner as I was (it was magical, after all) by the triangular arrangement of letters, imagining what it would look like printed – a vision which seldom holds true as the proof is quick to show. And even now uninked type has great appeal to me, the letters sinuous, and in the right light, almost alive, in the rectilinearity of the locked-up forme. It was also in Iowa City that I named the press The Hermetic Press, after a Troyer Ornament that looks like a scarab.

2. "Bric-A-Brac"

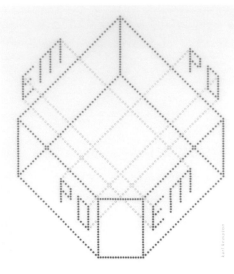

3. The Kempton poem

The usual delay ensued, and it wasn't until 1968 I set my first concrete poem (and very self-consciously called it *Concrete Poem Number One*); and then suffered another hiatus so that it was not until 1970 I printed it, in Texas, where at that time I was teaching. The poem itself was a field of ampersands reversed out in Royal Blue from 12-point Caslon and Caslon small caps, with one in 24-point replacing the A in a 12-point setting of the word 'AND'. Others were upside down, and one step-leaded; and all of which were driven by who-knows-what typographic muse. A friend I sent one to said he saw love and sex and death in it (among other things) – remember, this was the psychedelic seventies – and I wrote back, Yes, but did you see the ampersands? Which brings up type and the typographic in concrete poetry, and what prompts these notes on the production of *Five Visual Poems*.[1]

First of all, I called the portfolio 'visual' poems rather than 'concrete', as that term – tending as it does toward the semantic, the politicised, and the artifact or 'word as object' – is so narrow. And of the poems, only the Kempton and Helmes is most properly concrete. My own is almost calligramme-like, and Ian Finlay does refer to his as a visual poem; and as the Williams poem is a rendering of a literary text, i.e., poem, as the word is most generally understood – the decision seemed obvious, even though, and without hesitation, I would describe myself as a concretist.

Now, all that notwithstanding, to the practical matter at hand. From the standpoint of the typographer the Kempton poem (figure 3) was the easiest; from that of the printer, most difficult. If I divide typographer from printer, I should explain that I earn my living as an advertising typographer for a photocomposition shop, and that I have learned to deal with art directors – which is to say that in the Kempton piece the typography was already there, composed on an IBM Selectric and camera-ready for either offset or xerographic reproduction. My decision to reset was based on the challenge the hand-setting presented and also the fact that I thought I would get a better result from type than a plate. I have also seen some new work by Kempton that was done on a Smith-Corona 7000 with variable pitch, and if I can find a willing typecaster I hope to print one of these.

So it follows then that it was only necessary to reconstruct the diagram, a simple enough procedure complicated by aberrant incremental error introduced into the forme. Over 51 picas I was beginning to wonder whether all those 6-point ems were square, even after having made sure the nicks were always up. And further complicated by the introduction of 1-point brass spaces between ornaments to balance the 1-point leading between lines. It would have made quite a pie, set solid. And of course, I did the dumbest thing. After having worked out a grid pattern and numbering the squares, I forgot to flop the thing and work off a light-table; so everything turned out backwards. But by then I was quite expert at handling these lines, and the correction only took the better part of a day. Then there was the inevitable lock-up problem and here I did suffer some skewing and made hair-paper corrections as best as possible. Mr Kempton wrote back that he liked the way the poem turned out and was very pleased that I had not corrected the missing solid circle of the letter P, which in the manner of the Hopi he had omitted that the evil spirit which might inhabit the forme could escape.

The pale blue Magnani seemed to suggest itself, as the poem has a blueprint-like quality to it – and also the cool surface lending itself to the rigidity of line. The choice of mauve for printing the name was one of those fey, art director choices, and letterspaced to go with the openness of the poem. Also use of lower-case was prescribed by the fact that Kempton eschews capitals in his orthography, an orthography that uses k for the hard c and z for the plural s. One disturbing fact, however, and one that should always be kept in mind in non-traditional typography, is the very strength of that long history of 'orthodox' typography. Many people flop the poem to get the name on the horizontal, something I had not anticipated, as I thought the poem read quite clearly right to left, left to right, top to bottom, and mirror-imaged, Karl Kempton being dyslexic and working these inversions as part of his art. In point of fact, the vertical axis was chosen to divorce the name from the poem itself and I handled the name in the Williams poem in the same manner, like a photo credit line.

I chose Times Semi Bold to most approximate the face on the rubber-stamped poem of Scott Helmes (figure 4). The Times seemed closest to what could also have been Century or Bookman; now please do not go running to your typebooks to check this out. I once heard that Ed Benguiat, when questioned what prompted ITC Benguiat, said 'I was shooting for Times Roman'. So you see how far afield one might ramble.

In the setting I rigidly maintained the correct spacing of letters and missing letters down the length of the forme, varying considerably from the uneven spacing of the original. I did not think it in the nature of type to randomly attempt a disorder, which in fact was the natural result of the hand-stamping. That is not to say I dislike fields. In fact I print on a Poco proof press (inking by hand) and there is no throw-off on the return. So I always use a sheet of newsprint on the return to prevent offset. Oftentimes in the printing of second colours, initials or ornaments, I have ended up with some rather attractive fields, some of which I have saved; though as a printer I subscribe to the theory that an efficient army buries its dead, and no bad sheet should remain to be seen.

As for paper and choice of colour, I used Okawara with a very light grey ink to disappear the letters into the paper, which seemed appropriate to a poem that is primarily de-constructive. And depending on how light strikes the sheet, the grey is quite fugitive and hints at the tonality of the original. I printed damp (as I did the other four poems) so the ink got into the paper better. Of course, the larger size – 42-point, and boldface at that – solved many of the problems associated with printing on Japanese papers, and there was not much of a slurring problem, nor significant lack of coverage.

The poem by Ian Hamilton Finlay (figure 5) was worked out closely in correspondence with him, the final design is actually by a friend of mine, who thought mine too modern. I had justified to the measure the five cap text lines, and she redid the layout with 'RUMBLINGS . . .'' letterspaced to the measure, and the others letterspaced to match, and centred – which is what you see. As for typeface I suggested Caslon or Baskerville, and Finlay chose Caslon. The ornament is from a Caslon specimen sheet (1798) and is reproduced from D. B. Updike's *Printing Types*. Finlay wrote back that he thought it added 'just the right neo-Gothic note'.

Also choice of paper was governed by his desire for a sort of handbill feel, and we settled on De Wint. The smaller size Caslon gets a little lost in the heavily textured De Wint, something I had not anticipated; but an art director might counter by saying that there are areas of black and there are areas of grey, and certainly footnotes would fall into the latter. Also to be taken into consideration is that the text is printed in sepia, and some contrast is lost by way of that.

Of the poems, it is the most conservative in treatment, governed primarily by the fact that it is quite

4. Poem: Scott Helmes

intentionally period-allusive. Finlay seemed pleased with the result, and subsequently I printed a tiny poem for him using Times Roman, a face he would appear to favour. An attempt to woo him with a showing of Felix Titling and Calligraphia – both of which I thought amenable to his work – proved unsuccessful.

Perhaps an aside is in order. For me, Times Roman seemed an unusual choice, and I did have to special order it. I would say that in the United States, Times Roman is primarily an ad face, which would suggest it does not have the anonymity – if anything, it would be considered sturdy – that I would assume it to have in England or Scotland, as a serviceable and unprepossessing face, much as the ubiquitous Helvetica has become in the United States. So allusiveness is rather a chancy thing, as evidenced by the use of Legend to suggest things Oriental.

As was the Finlay poem, the other two poems were rendered from literary texts. The Jonathan Williams poem (figure 6) was part of a manuscript, *Aposiopeses*, which I have since printed, but the text of this seven-line poem presented itself almost immediately as a visual poem. To my mind it was so obviously a tent card on the piano, that my use of the prism was to suggest the tent card, and further accentuated by bleeding the rules off the sheet.

The poem was printed entirely from plates. The type is Univers Condensed, obliqued 27° on an Alphatype CRS 9943. The short horizontal rule that adjoins each long rule is actually a 34-point Univers lowercase l backslanted and the rule keyboarded to crash into it. Each rule and accompanying type element were film output off the machine. The prism could have been keyboarded, but the operator was becoming recalcitrant, so that was done with a ruling pen. In the printing everything is interdependent, and I consider myself quite fortunate that the indigo line ('play it') intersects the upper-righthand corner of the prism. At least, it is supposed to. I hope the one you see does.

I used Arches Buff for three reasons. I use it a lot. Damp, it is dimensionally stable over a long time (ten runs taking ten days). And the buff colour enhanced the lighter shades in the prism,

Strawberry Hill[1]

"PRECIPICES,
MOUNTAINS,
TORRENTS,
WOLVES,
RUMBLINGS..."[2]

...*Wildcats,
Corsairs...*[3]

❁

[1]"I am going to build a little Gothic Castle at Strawberry Hill. If you can pick me up any fragments of old painted glass, or arms or anything, I shall be excessively obliged." – HORACE WALPOLE (1717-1797). [2]"WALPOLE TO RICHARD WEST,"From a Hamlet among the Mountains of Savoy," 1739. [3]Carrier-borne aircraft of World War Two.

IAN HAMILTON FINLAY

5. Poem: Ian Hamilton Finlay

which might otherwise have been lost on the white.

The 'lipstick' poem (figure 7) is an actual snippet of conversation, that is to say, a found poem – one of a series called Over-Heards. It is composed from University of California Old Style and rules. No plates were used. The type is step-leaded, and the curlicue of cigarette smoke was locked into a balsawood s-shaped forme.

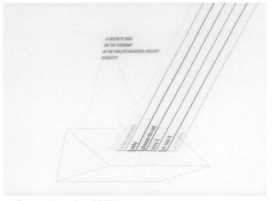

6. Poem: Jonathan Williams

The step-leading was accomplished by setting each letter horizontally, nick turned to the right, instead of up, in a 12-pica line of its own, and letters in the upper lip being a separate setting from the lower lip. Then these lines were gathered and justified to a 40-pica measure, and the two formes put together. For one who is not a type-

7. The 'lipstick' poem

caster, it was a fascinating lesson in widths, to see which and how many of the characters were on 14-point bodies, others 16 and so on; I believe the smallest body was 8-point. This method of setting made it very easy to move the characters up and down to get the correct curve, and as each letter was independently justified on a line of its own, horizontal moves could be made by the insertion of paper or 1-point leads.

I hope there's not too much colour (red, blue, gold, green and two shades of grey – there are times I think it disintegrates) and I am curious what it would look like all in black. In part, the colours resulted from the difficulty of lock-up and maintaining consistent colour through successive runs. And the choice of paper, Rives Heavy, was made on the basis that I am quite familiar with how it prints, though in my estimation, not as well as the Arches, which is a most forgiving paper.

The greys are not very legible, but legibility is not a primary concern, as this poem is meant to be looked at, not read, and eventually the viewer will find his way to the faint tendril of smoke, which is both title and documentation. If at this point I veer toward the pictographic, the primary impetus remains typographic, and it is at this point as a concretist I would have my work both end and begin.

The story of my finding a paper for the folder is a case of serendipity. The paper is a very nice Japanese Tarei – there are some folders on Inomachi – with four deckles and a matt finish; and I subsequently did some folders on an Inomachi with a satin finish.

I was going to screenprint the folders with a high coverage vinyl or lacquer, but kept delaying that as the odours are so long to clear from the paper, especially with the vinyls. Then one day the obvious presented itself. The folders could be made to fit the press if cut to size and folded, rather than the 25 x 19 in. sheet unfolded. By reducing the packing on the cylinder of the press I was able to insert a few sheets of mylar between layers of the folder and eliminate most of the blind embossing effect of the impression. So then I was able to change typefaces from Eurostile to 24-point Castellar 600 with 8-point (Didot) Inserat Grotesk – the Inserat homage to the abandoned Eurostile.

I suppose it is only right that the conclusion of one project lead to another, and I was fortunate that way too. After having found the paper in a small gallery in one of the richest and most insular suburbs of Minneapolis, my friend and I repaired to a Polynesian restaurant, where we successfully idled away the afternoon in such fashion as to warrant the waiter a really big tip – postscript to which, I was able to write a longish and splendidly (to my mind) cynical poem called 'Afternoon at the Paper Merchant's'.

Since its inception over thirty-five years ago, **Philip Gallo** has operated the Hermetic Press continuously as a medium for typographic art and concrete poetry. Its primary purpose at the beginning was the production of small works in the manner of the Fluxus movement. From there the press moved into the area of concrete and visual poetry, celebrating its 25th anniversary in 1991 with a broadside suite featuring among others work by Ian Hamilton Finlay and Jonathan Williams. In the '90s the press was closely associated with Granary Books of New York City, in the production of full-scale artists' books, including collaborations with John Cage, Carolee Schneemann, Timothy Ely, Buzz Spector, and Robert Creeley. These books have been acquired by museums and collectors around the world. In the last several years, Gallo has been working in the digital area, combining letterpress printing with inkjet and laser printing. These new books would qualify as artists' books, but the thrust is the highly decorative, much in the manner of what was formerly the exclusive domain of the illustrated book. Concomitant with this new work are typographic works meant to be viewed entirely on the electronic platform, either as PDF files or as QuickTime files generated in Flash.

ABCDEFGHIJKL

abcdefghijk

TUVXYZ

ABC
DEFG
HIKL
MNO
PQR
STUV
XYZ

Eric Gill's Gill Sans typeface, the digitized version from Monotype

Sans Serif

BY RICHARD KENNEDY

Richard Kennedy's light-hearted meditation on sans serif type, in Matrix 3 *(1983), touches on the 20th century's vehement arguments about the appropriate kind of typeface for the modern world.*

When Eric Gill produced his Gill Sans at the end of the twenties, it seemed to appear everywhere. I looked about for guidance. Leonard Woolf had taught me to worship Caslon Old Face like he did himself, with an almost religious fervour. Gill Sans seemed almost heretical. However I do not know what his reaction was to the new type, because I had already left the Press when it appeared. It seemed to symbolise the new life style of the thirties and I connected it with functional furnishing and abstract art. Sans serif was taken up by the London Underground. Herbert Read's *Art Now* was printed in Gill Sans and Wyndham Lewis' *Blast* had already appeared in a sans serif typeface. Serifs were thought of as decorative excrescences out of keeping with the functionalist age. Teachers proclaimed that children found sans serif type easier to read, a fact which Sir Cyril Burt discredits in his *Psychological Study of Typography*. In fact they find Old Style the easiest of all the type founts.

My own reaction to Gill Sans was to consult Uncle George, as I always did when in doubt. He however proved to be prejudiced on the subject owing to the fact that he was having a violent dispute with a woman sculptor, whom he had commissioned to do a piece of sculpture for the Royal Geographical Hall, of which he was the architect. The work she produced was a statue of a naked boy, in what was then described as the modernistic style, from which she had omitted the genital organs. She was unable to persuade Uncle George that the male genital organs were a decorative excrescence and could be compared to serifs. He vehemently protested that type was one thing and the human body quite another. But it is surprising how very close the relationship is between the two, as the following story indicates.

Al Ghazzali, a famous Sufi philosopher, tells how, on his travels he came upon a woman having difficulty in giving birth to a child. Her helpers, who evidently knew a thing or two of which modern gynaecologists are ignorant, resorted to typography. They printed out a placard on which they drew the

Roman numerals one to nine and alongside these they drew the same numerals in Arabic script. After reading the placard the woman was at once able to give birth to her baby. The contrast between the formal Roman numerals and the flowing Arabic script evidently sorted out the muscular tangle in which she had got herself and enabled her to relax.

Sir Cyril Burt does not take his study of typography to this depth. He is concerned with visibility and believes that serifs help the eye to travel along a line of type by making bridges between the letters.

However, Professor Robert Ornstein has opened a new dimension on the subject by popularising the knowledge relating to our right and left brains or cerebral hemispheres, and their relation to each other. It seems the left brain is more concerned with logic and formality whereas the right brain is spiral and holistic, rather than linear like its neighbour, and is concerned with the organism itself and natural movements across the body from right to left, the opposite way to which we read a line of type. It is probable that serifs mitigate the difficulty the right brain finds in travelling along the line from left to right, the way we read it in the West.

This would explain why children and women who are apparently more under the domination of their right hemisphere find Old Style more acceptable than sans serif type and why adult male intellectuals might appreciate abstract art and cubism, where straight lines predominate and organic forms and decoration are banished. The serif is like a pinch of sugar which induces the right brain to move along a line in a direction contrary to its inclination.

In the case of posters where there is no lateral movement ('Help the Aged' for example), serifs are generally omitted. Advertisements in women's magazines and children's books make a generous use of them.

The craftsman using a tool works away from his body, left to right, hence the direction of the letters engraved on the Trajan Column. Some other races however form their alphabet from the movements of the hand holding a quill or a brush or crayon, which travels naturally from right to left like that of the artist drawing the curves of the human body. Maillol, the French sculptor, is a case of an artist overcoming the disadvantage of using a tool to express the organic world, and when it comes to an etching needle or a pen this disadvantage is fairly minimal.

In Michelangelo's decorations on the walls of the Sistine Chapel, one of the sinners being cast out of Paradise has his hand over his left eye, which suggests that Michelangelo had some knowledge of the function of the right and left brain. Is the man blinded by the more formal classical nature of Paradise or by the void into which he is falling? We can only guess. Our eyes are connected contra-laterally to the respective hemispheres of our brain. Although they both see the same image the left eye would emphasise its organic nature, the right its more formal aspect.

I must say I have considerable sympathy for this unfortunate sinner. I am a very right-brained person and consequently have considerable difficulty in filling out my cheque stubs. This is increased because the numbers on the cheques are printed in computer type, which includes numerous dashes and dots and squiggles attached to figures made out of straight lines. It is designed to satisfy the computer brain which is creating a void into which I am falling. So far the girl behind the counter has saved me. Economic measures I feel sure will bring about a world of tapes printed in computer code and from which books will be banished. Caslon Old Face will be a far off dream.

Richard Kennedy was superannuated from Marlborough College when he was sixteen, and went to work for Leonard and Virginia Woolf at their Hogarth Press in 1927. Here he made the tea, printed book jackets on the treadle press, and helped Virginia to set type, as he described in *Matrix 1* and in *A Boy at the Hogarth Press* (Whittington Press, 1972). His second volume of autobiography, *A Parcel of Time* (Whittington Press, 1977), describes his childhood and early struggles with reading, and he went on to become one of England's best-known illustrators of children's books. He illustrated *The Song of Songs* (1976) and many other titles for the Whittington Press, and contributed several witty and eclectic articles to *Matrix* up till his death in 1989.

Drawing by the author.

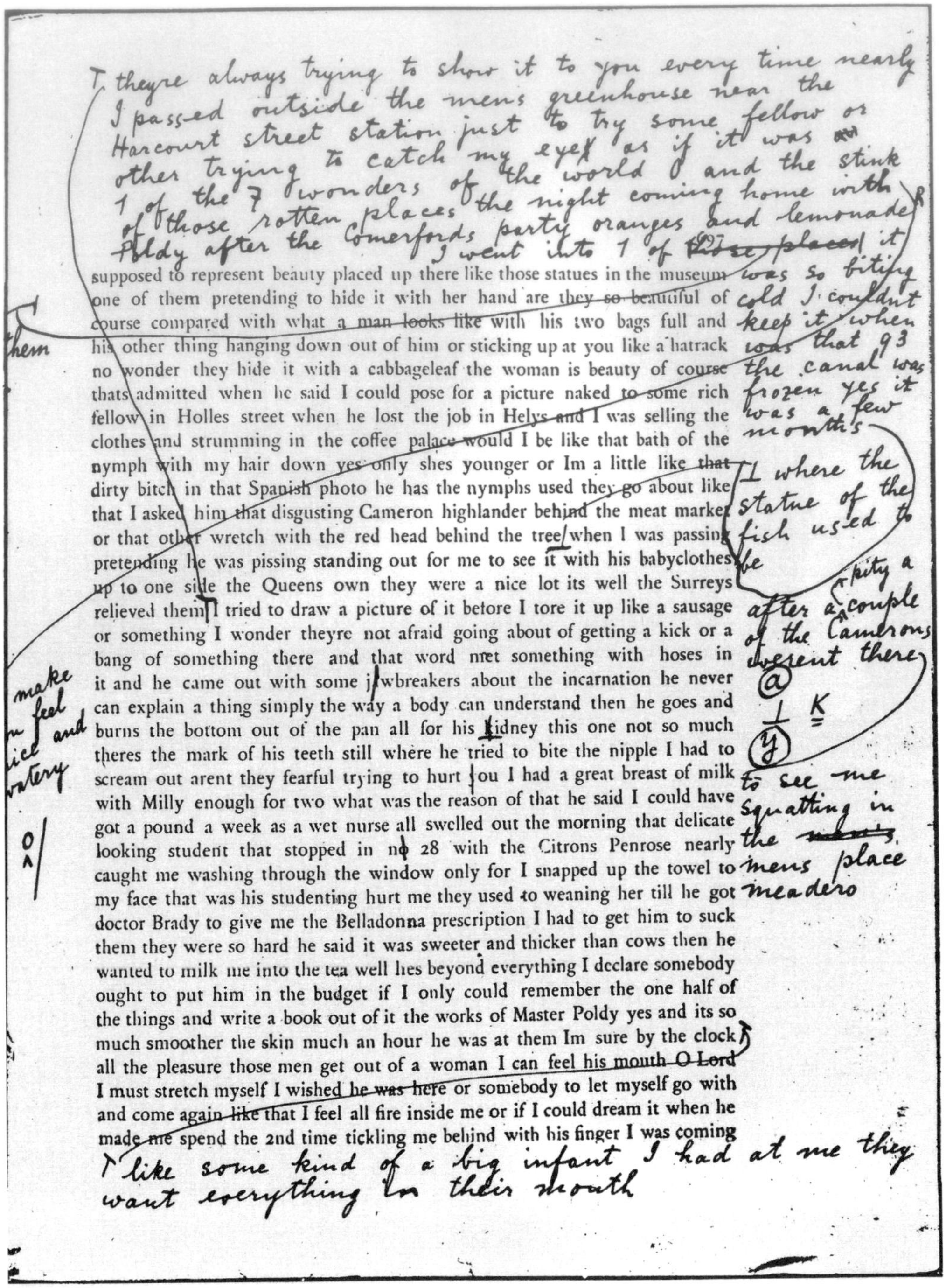

Handwritten at top:

theyre always trying to show it to you every time nearly I passed outside the mens greenhouse near the Harcourt street station just to try some fellow or other trying to catch my eyes as if it was one of the 7 wonders of the world O and the stink of those rotten places the night coming home with Poldy after the Comerfords party oranges and lemonade I went into 1 of those places it

supposed to represent beauty placed up there like those statues in the museum
one of them pretending to hide it with her hand are they so beautiful of
course compared with what a man looks like with his two bags full and
his other thing hanging down out of him or sticking up at you like a hatrack
no wonder they hide it with a cabbageleaf the woman is beauty of course
thats admitted when he said I could pose for a picture naked to some rich
fellow in Holles street when he lost the job in Helys and I was selling the
clothes and strumming in the coffee palace would I be like that bath of the
nymph with my hair down yes only shes younger or Im a little like that
dirty bitch in that Spanish photo he has the nymphs used they go about like
that I asked him that disgusting Cameron highlander behind the meat market
or that other wretch with the red head behind the tree when I was passing
pretending he was pissing standing out for me to see it with his babyclothes
up to one side the Queens own they were a nice lot its well the Surreys
relieved them I tried to draw a picture of it before I tore it up like a sausage
or something I wonder theyre not afraid going about of getting a kick or a
bang of something there and that word met something with hoses in
it and he came out with some jawbreakers about the incarnation he never
can explain a thing simply the way a body can understand then he goes and
burns the bottom out of the pan all for his kidney this one not so much
theres the mark of his teeth still where he tried to bite the nipple I had to
scream out arent they fearful trying to hurt you I had a great breast of milk
with Milly enough for two what was the reason of that he said I could have
got a pound a week as a wet nurse all swelled out the morning that delicate
looking student that stopped in no 28 with the Citrons Penrose nearly
caught me washing through the window only for I snapped up the towel to
my face that was his studenting hurt me they used to weaning her till he got
doctor Brady to give me the Belladonna prescription I had to get him to suck
them they were so hard he said it was sweeter and thicker than cows then he
wanted to milk me into the tea well hes beyond everything I declare somebody
ought to put him in the budget if I only could remember the one half of
the things and write a book out of it the works of Master Poldy yes and its so
much smoother the skin much an hour he was at them Im sure by the clock
all the pleasure those men get out of a woman I can feel his mouth O Lord
I must stretch myself I wished he was here or somebody to let myself go with
and come again like that I feel all fire inside me or if I could dream it when he
made me spend the 2nd time tickling me behind with his finger I was coming

Handwritten at bottom:

like some kind of a big infant I had at me they want everything in their mouth

Left margin handwritten:

them

make u feel nice and watery

O/∧

Right margin handwritten:

was so biting cold I couldnt keep it when was that 93 the canal was frozen yes it was a few months

I where the statue of the fish used to be pity a after a couple of the Camerons present there

⊥ K = (y) to see me squatting in the mens place meadero

'Seems to See with his Fingers': the Printing of Joyce's *Ulysses*

BY GLENN STORHAUG

How did the French typesetters who actually set James Joyce's masterpiece deal with transmitting genius into print? Glenn Storhaug's researches into the pragmatic problems of printing a work that defies convention, published in Matrix 6 *(1986), bridge the gap, in a very real sense, between theory and practice.*

Special delivery services, despatch riders and express postal systems might well depend on business from the printing trade for their survival; the manufacturers of those labels loudly announcing 'Press matter: Urgent!' should have a secure future. The writer of this piece lives with his family, nine bean-rows and two cylinder presses in the apparently peaceful depths of the Herefordshire countryside, but spends much of his time pulling proofs and pasting mock-ups in a frenzy of missed deadlines, dashing to railway station or post office with ink and glue still wet.

Once the typesetter has the copy for a book it's downhill all the way in a headlong rush of proof-readers, printers, binders and publishers all with their eyes fixed on the delivery date circled in red on the calendar. Obstacles are not welcome in this race, least of all the boulders strewn on the track by that monstrous impeder of progress called AUTHOR'S ALTERATIONS. The author may think that changing the word 'rock' to 'molehill' creates no more obstacle than a molehill on the ground; to the harrassed compositor it will feel, if it occurs in the middle of a tightly spaced narrow-measure paragraph, much more like a mountain. (At least this *was* the problem when founts of founder's type adorned the Garden of Eden – before computer screens seduced all but the readers of *Matrix*.)

To stand calmly in the midst of this rush-to-turn-galleys-into-books-for-sale, carefully resetting type again and again, gently sliding those galleys in and out of the rack day after day, altering a comma here and a paragraph there, all this calls for much patience and level-headedness. In the history of western book printing these qualities have never been more thoroughly tested than in a small printing shop at 13 Rue Paul Cabet in Dijon, where for the best part of ten months from spring 1921 to February 1922, early in the morning until late every night, twenty-six compositors set and reset by hand a 732-page novel written by a strange Irishman living in Paris. His publisher, an American who had never published so much as a pamphlet before, had given permission for as many stages of proofing, altering, re-proofing and re-altering as the author required. The patience shown by the Maître Imprimeur Maurice Darantière, his compositors and their foreman Maurice Hirchwald, and the generosity shown by Sylvia Beach the publisher (who used as imprint the name of her bookshop, Shakespeare and Company) enabled James Joyce, the author, to compose about one third of his novel *Ulysses* actually in the margins of the proof sheets. Some pages of his book went through as many as nine different proofs, firstly in *placard* form (eight approximate pages of type not properly imposed but printed broadside on a large sheet) then as page-proofs proper.

Sylvia Beach's biographer, Noel Riley Fitch, has found the following account of the composition of *Ulysses* in an early draft of the publisher's memoirs: 'I let [Joyce] have as many proofs as he wanted and [he] crowded them with as many additions as he could get onto the page. The final proofs contained more handwriting than print. . . . After the *bon à tirer* had been returned with Joyce's and my signature, and the printing had begun on our beautiful hand-made paper, the printers would receive a telegram with several extra lines to insert – but they were so obliging. . . .'

Whatever frustration she must have felt is here forgotten, just as Joyce's own exasperation with the inevitable typesetting errors ('I am extremely irritated by all those printer's errors' he wrote in November 1921) was quite forgotten in his own account of the printing in a letter written ten years later to Bennett Cerf of Random House (who had to wait until the obscenity ban in America was lifted in 1933 before he could go ahead with his edition of *Ulysses*). 'This brave woman [Sylvia Beach] risked what professional publishers did not wish to, she took the manuscript and handed it to the printers. These were very scrupulous and understanding French printers. . . . It came about that thanks to the extra work and kindness of Mr Darantière . . . *Ulysses* came out a very short time after the manuscript had been delivered [!] and the first printed copy was sent to me for my 40th birthday on the 2nd of February 1922.' Joyce omits to say here that only two days before the first copies were despatched on the 7 a.m. express from Dijon to Paris, he had returned a final set of corrected proofs to Darantière with approximately 150 words added in the margin of one page of Molly Bloom's monologue (figure 1).

Darantière is described as forever throwing up his hands in despair as more alterations arrived in the post, but he and his assistants *did* see it through to that vital publication date. (Without which Joyce may well have continued revising almost *ad infinitum*, creating an open-field novel constantly transformed by an ever-developing experiment with language; as with the painting of the Forth Bridge, the beginning of the novel could appear decidedly flaky by the time the later revolutionary episodes like Oxen In The Sun, Ithaca and Penelope were composed.)

Of course the typesetters, who spoke no ordinary English and certainly no Joyce-English, struggled to understand and implement the author's alterations added in his impossible hand-writing. Joyce complained to Robert McAlmon that the printers were 'boggled by all the **w**'s and **k**'s in our tongue and can do only about 100 pages at a time until they print off.' *100 pages!* In more forgiving moments Joyce recognised how valiantly the compositors were working, as in this letter to Harriet Shaw Weaver written in October 1921 – with an optimistic publication date: '*Ulysses* will be finished in about three weeks, thank God, and (if the French printers don't all leap into the Rhône in despair at the mosaics I send them back) ought to be published early in November.'

Since the first publication of *Ulysses* (only three months later than Joyce's prediction) the Darantière printers and their working methods have received no complimentary mention, let alone detailed study, in any of the hundreds of books and theses about *Ulysses* that relentlessly issue forth from the academic Joyce industry (Joyce knew he would 'keep the professors busy') even though more and more of this research has a 'textual' discipline. Those twenty-six compositors *have* been in the news, but only because we now have a clearer idea of the number of errors in the printed text that they were (most excusably) responsible for.

To discover all these errors, a computer has hummed away in the University of Tübingen in Germany for some seven years, using a programme called TUSTEP that had taken another ten years to develop. An international team of scholars, led by Hans Walter Gabler, has collaborated on a remarkable quest for the *true text* of *Ulysses*, not to be found in a complete authorial manuscript (no such thing exists) but instead in a massive disarray of 'documents of composition and pre-publication transmission: the holograph drafts, fair copies and typescripts as well as the proofs for the first edition with

Joyce's numerous autograph corrections, additions and revisions' to use Gabler's own description. At last, as Joyce scholars around the word held their breath, the computer produced an electronically typeset correct text which was published, complete with a 'synoptic analysis' of the route the questing computer took through all the textual overlays and revisions, by Garland Publishing Inc. in New York in 1984 – in three impressive volumes embellished with the Homeric bow designed by Eric Gill for the first Bodley Head edition in 1936.

This publication, properly known as *Ulysses A Critical and Synoptic Edition*, is a quite remarkable achievement, of enormous value to Joycean scholarship and also of importance to the general reader who until now has been puzzled by many a Joycean wordplay that turns out to be a mere misprint.

Some 5000 errors in all are corrected, so it is not surprising that the enthusiastic reviews of the Garland edition usually contain some condescending remarks about the foolish French typesetters who did not appreciate the significance of the text they were marring. The present writer set out to restore the balance a little by researching into the Dijon printing firm as it operated in the 1920s. The intention was to publish a piece in *Matrix* combining an appraisal of the just-published Garland edition with some new insights into the daily routine of Darantière and his staff during 1921 and 1922. The search for new material on Darantière proved so slow and frustrating (for example the University of New York at Buffalo would not release its collection of correspondence between Sylvia Beach and Darantière) that this article now appears long after the Garland edition has become an established classic and has indeed been reissued as a three-volume paperback set – with 'some thirty corrections in the reading text made since the hardcover edition was published', so nobody's perfect, not even the TUSTEP computer programme. What's more, 16 June 1986 saw the publication of the first British trade editions to use the new computer-set type: two Penguin editions, one with line numbers for students, and the new Bodley Head edition (also line-numbered) which looks most elegant notwithstanding Bodley's Design Director feeling more than a little reluctant to exchange the bold-looking narrow-measure Plantin setting of the 1960 Bodley Head edition for the wide-measure grey offset-printed Garamond decreed by the computer. The point of the wide measure is to avoid the word-breaks that Joyce abhorred (though there are still at least two hyphenations in very long portmanteau words in the Circe episode) and the point of using the Garland computer tapes (produced at Tübingen) is to avoid any errors of transmission creeping in. But it seems they do creep in: the Garland text correctly has no punctuation at all in the final Penelope episode until after the last 'Yes.' while in both the Penguin and Bodley Head texts a full point has crept in at the end of an earlier paragraph: 'they might as well throw you out in the bottom of the ashpit.'. The 1960 Bodley Head text has 'ash pit' as two words – incorrect, we are now told – but at least no full point after.

I wish I had contacted Bodley's Design Director, John Ryder, a good deal earlier as he could have saved me all those weeks I spent writing to the firm of Darantière in Dijon and receiving no reply. The trade department at the French embassy had supplied their new address and in no time I expected reminiscences from the 1920s and archival material to arrive by registered post. It was John Ryder who explained why this never in fact did happen: even though a modern printing firm in Dijon may be using the name, the old firm of Darantière had long ago moved and had indeed been taken over by Alberto Tallone. I then wrote to the Italian Master Printer's widow, Signora Bianca

2. The 'Succes' cylinder press on which all eleven impressions of the Shakespeare and Company Ulysses were printed (1922–1930).

Tallone, and learned from her that Alberto Tallone had started as an apprentice at Darantière's in 1931, after Darantière had moved from Dijon to Chatenay-Malabry near Paris (taking all his equipment with him). In 1936 when Tallone bought the Imprimerie with Count Govone he moved it to the Hôtel de Sagonne in Paris and worked there virtually uninterrupted until he returned home to Alpignano near Turin in 1958. Returning with him to Alpignano was the flatbed cylinder press that Darantière had used to print the first edition of *Ulysses* nine years before Tallone joined him as apprentice. The machine was built for Darantière in Dijon in 1920, only months before Sylvia Beach first approached him about *Ulysses*. It was built under the 'Succes' trademark by Franco Pozzoli and was used at Dijon, then at Chatenay-Malabry then at the Hôtel de Sagonne and then at Alpignano right up until 1983. Now Signora Tallone has donated it to the Museum of Printing at Lingotto-Turin. She has kindly supplied the photograph of the machine reproduced on page 327. Signora Tallone also wrote on my behalf to M. Roger Lautrey who had worked in Paris as Tallone's assistant and earlier had been Darantière's pressman in Dijon. Sadly this gentleman, who probably ran the first sheets of *Ulysses* through the press in 1921 and '22, is not well enough to reply to Signora Tallone's request for reminiscences.

So I have failed to balance the resounding praise for the new computer-text with an original portrait of the Imprimerie Darantière battling away with Joyce's 'mosaic' of proof-alterations. But I hope enough of the picture has been painted to indicate the dimensions of their task and the remarkable patience with which they saw it through to the final machining. The noted textual scholar Hugh Kenner would no doubt dismiss me as an irrelevant romantic for taking issue with his remarks published in the *New York Times Book Review* in 1980, written at a time when he was eagerly watching the development of the new 'critical text' in Germany: 'The book of the century, beyond doubt James Joyce's *Ulysses*, was set in type the Gutenberg way, by hand. There had been typesetting machines for thirty-odd years, but *Ulysses* was surely the biggest book of any importance to be set by hand since William Morris handset the Kelmscott Chaucer in 1893–96. Of course Morris intended a gesture. Whether Sylvia Beach, Joyce's publisher, intended anything special when she signed up a firm that specialised in hand composition is something I'd like to know. I'd guess she was innocent.' Darantière certainly was special: he was recommended to Sylvia Beach by Adrienne Monnier whose Cahiers editions he had printed. Besides producing the letterpress work for such fine editions as Apollinaire's *Calligrammes* with lithographs by De Chirico, published by Gallimard, he was to work for such diverse publishers as Gertrude Stein and Trianon. Kenner maintains that hand composition in a foreign language invites errors that keyboard setting might avoid (since the text has to be 'memorised' as the compositor moves from copy to typecase) but I feel quite sure (though I have no proof) that there was no Monotype installation around Paris that would have produced a better text. Sympathy and patience were surely as important for this venture as mechanical accuracy. And after all, Joyce himself sometimes mis-corrected the proofs as Gabler has now proved, substituting one error for another while his concentration was on a later part of the novel he was still preparing as original manuscript. By no means was Darantière's team responsible for all 5000 errors corrected in the Garland edition. Many errors were made by the motley crew of typists (hired to prepare copy for the printers) and then missed by Joyce, quite understandably considering the strain he and his eyes were under. Then of course there have been errors of transmission ever since: corrections in all subsequent editions have led to further errors. A particularly inaccurate text was the first American printing by Random House, which inadvertently used as copy an error-ridden pirated edition (produced by Samuel Roth to look like the ninth impression of the Shakespeare and Company edition). On the first page of the Random House first edition we find that Buck Mulligan (who in other editions 'went over to the parapet' on the top of the Martello tower) here 'pointed his finger in friendly jest and went over the parapet . . .'.

Ulysses looks best when printed in a workmanlike way, respectful of the text. The Shakespeare and Company editions take one directly to Joyce's demanding novel with no distractions. The next main edition, printed in Leipzig for the Odyssey Press in 1932, comes in two paperback volumes very well produced but obviously lacking the 'presence' of Darantière's productions. The superb first British publication produced by Western Printing Services in Bristol for John Lane, The Bodley Head, in 1936 was printed in its large format only in the edition of 1000 numbered copies. It was then reprinted by offset litho rather unsuccessfully (with a photographically reduced page size) and issued as the standard trade edition until John Ryder produced an excellent new design for the 1960 re-setting of the text. But all down the line to the first Penguin edition in 1968 old errors were perpetuated and new errors introduced into the text. There is only one edition of *Ulysses*, however, that is a real disaster, and it also happens to be the most lavish. In 1935 The

Limited Editions Club in New York published an enormous edition of *Ulysses* with etchings by Matisse. The artist supplied twenty preliminary drawings and six etchings whose large size (11½ x 9 ins) was no doubt the argument for using double-column setting for the text. The result is almost unreadable, littered with word-breaks and distracting fiddly display-setting quite out of keeping with the strong clear lines of Matisse. Joyce stopped signing copies of this book when he realised that Matisse had absentmindedly illustrated Homer's *Odyssey* instead of Joyce's *Ulysses*.

After all the misadventures of Joyce's text, with odd bits appearing and disappearing in unreliable typescripts, then the magazine serialisations that were later completely rewritten, then the long lineage of errors in edition after edition, it is quite proper for the scholars – and the general reader – to be delighted by the arrival of 'The Corrected Text' as proclaimed on the covers of the new Bodley Head and Penguin editions. The Garland three-volume edition is testimony to the skill and patience of Gabler's team of textual scholars, and to the new technology they employed. But we should not forget that pioneering dedication to the text, to the text as it was still growing, that was shown by Darantière and his compositors. With today's pressures on an increasingly capital-intensive printing industry it is highly unlikely that such a long and profound – if at times reluctant – collaboration between an experimental writer and his printer and publisher could happen.

Of course Joyce wanted above all to see *Ulysses* printed 'as written' (though as Gabler's team found, it is not so easy to discover where it *is* written). But Joyce had all the time in the world for people and no time at all for machines. I do not think it trite to suggest that he would have felt as uneasy in the computer room in Tübingen as he would have felt easy and comradely in the composing room at 13 Rue Paul Cabet in Dijon. This is not simply because he was 'of his time' – for he was more than that anyway. The first edition of *Ulysses* carries the following notice above Sylvia Beach's initials but apparently composed by Joyce himself: 'The publisher asks the reader's indulgence for typographical errors unavoidable in the exceptional circumstances.' He knew better than anyone what the printers had to contend with, and he understood and valued the typographical arts. In the novel he takes Bloom to the pressroom of the *Freeman's Journal* in Dublin. 'He stayed in his walk to watch a typesetter neatly distributing type. Reads it backwards first. Quickly he does it. Must require some practice that. mangiD kcirtaP.' We could playfully suggest that it is significant that Joyce is describing not setting but distribution, the relaxation after the concentration of setting and printing and meeting the deadline. After all, Joyce chided the printers while they set, but praised them later in his letter to Cerf written around the time they might have been distributing the first setting of *Ulysses*. Bloom returns to consider the typesetter after the 'reading backwards' has led his thoughts elsewhere. 'How quickly he does that job. Practice makes perfect. Seems to see with his fingers.'

As writer, editor, and teacher, **Glenn Storhaug** has always been fascinated by the way typographical design affects the reader's response to text – particularly poetry. He established Five Seasons Press in 1977, only a few miles from Capel-y-ffin (on the border between England and Wales), where Eric Gill designed some of his finest typefaces. The Press produced hand-set and hand-printed books, broadsides and pamphlets up until 1996, favouring Ehrhardt and Sabon as house faces. The attempt to steer a middle course between private press publishing (which tends not to focus on new or 'difficult' writing) and more commercial literary publishing (which tends not to prioritise the book as an object) led to some confusion in the respective marketplaces. Five Seasons is still busy, on behalf of other publishers, with typography and book design, but now – sadly – this is of a more electronic nature.

DIE KUNSTISMEN

1924
1923
1922
1921
1920
1919
1918
1917

HERAUSGEGEBEN VON EL LISSITZKY

1916
1915

UND HANS ARP

1914

LES ISMES DE L'ART

1924
1923
1922
1921
1920
1919
1918
1917

PUBLIÉS PAR EL LISSITZKY

1916
1915

ET HANS ARP

1914

THE ISMS OF ART

1924
1923
1922
1921
1920
1919
1918
1917

PUBLISHED BY EL LISSITZKY

1916
1915

AND HANS ARP

1914

EUGEN RENTSCH VERLAG
ERLENBACH-ZÜRICH, MÜNCHEN UND LEIPZIG

1925

Title-page page from *Die Kunstismen*.

El Lissitzky 1914–1924:
'Prouns' to 'Die Kunstismen'

BY ADELA SPINDLER ROATCAP

Lissitzky's books, produced in the creative ferment of Russia before and after 1917, were revolutionary both politically and artistically. Adela Spindler Roatcap shows, in Matrix 17 (1977), *how they were a supreme expression of the hope and creative freedom that attended the early days of the Bolshevik revolution.*

For those of us whose parents or grandparents suffered disenfranchisement and exile or incarceration and death as a result of political changes following the 1917 Russian Revolution, there may be little consolation in the fact that the Soviet flag, red with a yellow hammer and sickle, was designed by a young Russian-Jewish architect who enthusiastically embraced the freedoms that the new political regime conferred upon him.

Lazar Markovich Elizer Lissitzky was born on 10 November 1890 (old style), in Polshino, a small town in the province of Smolensk, but like fellow artists Marc Chagall and Ossip Zadkine, he grew up in Vitebsk, in the Pale of Settlement where Jews were allowed to live during the Czarist regime. Lissitzky was a precocious child who, by 1905, was already 'book-building' – as he called writing and illustrating books. In 1909 his family sent him to study engineering and architecture at the Technische Hochschule at Darmstadt, where he managed to defray his expenses by completing architectural drawings for his fellow students, thus becoming unusually proficient at this task. In Darmstadt he adopted the aesthetic principle which he upheld for the rest of his life: 'Architecture – that is art in its highest sense, mathematical order.'[1]

Lissitzky spent his school holidays travelling. He went to France and Belgium and made a walking tour of Lombardy and Tuscany to see the masterpieces of the art of the past. In 1911 he visited his friend the sculptor Ossip Zadkine in Paris and was thrilled by the daring modern construction of the Eiffel Tower. In Brussels he visited the Art Nouveau architect Henry van de Velde, who had designed the house in Moscow in which Henri Matisse painted the famous murals *The Dance*. In Italy he made contact with Futurist artists – who had already 'exploded' old-fashioned notions of the printed

Two text pages from *Die Kunstismen*.

book, replacing typesetting with manuscript, printing with lithographic processes on wallpaper or cheap coarse stock and adopting the use of collage.

He continued 'book building': in 1913 he drew the cover for Konstantin Bolshakov, *Solntse na Izlete: Vtoraia Kniga Stikhov: 1913–1916*, (*The Spent Sun: Second Book of Poems: 1913–1916*) published in Moscow in 1916. His graphic style resembled the Futurist Rayonist art of Russian artists Michael Larionov and Natalia Gonchrova. When in 1924 Lissitzky was preparing the text for *The Isms of Art*, or *Die Kunstismen*, he included Italian Futurist Umberto Boccioni's definition:

> Futurists have abolished quietness and statism and have demonstrated movement, dynamism. They have documented the new conception of space by confrontation of interior and exterior. For us gesture will not anymore be a fixed moment of universal dynamism: it will decidedly be the dynamic sensation eternalised as such.

Lissitzky was forced to flee from Germany at the outset of the First World War. At the age of twenty-four he enrolled in Moscow's Riga Technological University, where in 1916 he obtained the diploma in engineering and architecture which enabled him to enter the practice of architecture in Russia. During this period he illustrated a series of Yiddish-language picture-books for children, such as Moshe Broderson's *An Unholy Story, or The Legend of Prague.* Each page of Broderson's text is a block of Hebrew lettering (written by a synagogue scribe), enclosed in Lissitzky's water-coloured border in an Art Nouveau style similar to Marc Chagall's early graphic work and to *Lubki,* the traditional Russian broadside. Twenty of the 110 copies of *The Legend of Prague* were issued in a scroll format, hand-coloured by Lissitzky and enclosed in a wooden casket shaped like a Torah.

As the October Revolution of 1917 erased the stigma of his Jewishness, bestowing upon him equal rights with all workers, Lissitzky hastened to present himself to the Committee for Art set up by the Soldier Deputies and eagerly accepted the chance of undertaking propaganda work on behalf of the revolutionaries. His first assignment was to design the flag which the leaders of the Central Committee of the Communist Party of the Soviet Union carried across newly renamed Red Square on 1 May 1918.

In 1919 he was invited by Marc Chagall to head the applied arts department and teach graphic art and architecture at the State Free Art Workshops at Vitebsk. Another new faculty member at Vitebsk was Kasimir Malevich, whose theories of 'Suprematism' rejected any imitation of natural shapes in favour of distinct geometric forms painted in pure colours against white backgrounds, such as his influential *Black Square,* or *Red Square.* Malevich managed to turn one of the crucial corners of art history – that of channelling current Futurist, Modernist and Abstract tendencies into 'Spirituality through Art'. 'The New Realism,' Malevich claimed, 'is . . . the Supremacy of pure emotion.' Lissitzky fell under Malevich's spell and in 1924, in *Die Kunstismen,* incorporated his poetic definition of Suprematism:

> Midnight of art is ringing. Fine art is banished. The artist-idol is a prejudice of the past. Suprematism presses the entire painture [*sic*] into a black square on a white canvas. I did not invent anything. It's only the night I felt in me, and it is there I perceived the new, which I called suprematism. It has expressed itself by the black plain that formed a square.

El Lissitzky decided to become a Suprematist artist. Henceforth, in his drawings, paintings and graphic designs, he portrayed three-dimensional abstract compositions   geometrical shapes based on the architectural drawings he had made at Darmstadt but altered to suggest that they might leave the two dimensional canvas or paper and float free in space. He named these compositions 'Prouns' meaning 'Projects for affirmation of the new', or 'the interchange station between painting and architecture', or even 'a . . . stage in the making of a new world out of the corpse of traditional painting.'[2] He adapted his 'Prouns' to many uses – architectural shapes and settings, mechanical structures, interior spaces and even furniture.

While he was director of the school, Marc Chagall had named the workshops in which teachers and students collaborated 'Unovis' or 'Affirmation of what is new in Art.' But soon Malevich managed to take Chagall's job and taught systems of 'non objective representation'. Everyone was urged to redesign all everyday items of utilitarian use in Vitebsk – fabrics, furniture, magazines and books. For *Unovis* El Lissitzky wrote:

> Building a book like a book moving in space and time, like a dynamic relief in which every page is a surface carrying shapes, and every turn of a page a new crossing to a new stage of a single structure . . . Gutenberg's Bible was printed with letters only; but the Bible of our time cannot just be presented in letters alone. The book finds its channel to the brain through the eye, not through the ear; in this channel the waves rush through with much greater speed and pressure than in the acoustic channel. One can speak out only through the mouth but the book's facilities for expression take many more forms.[3]

The symbol of *Unovis* was a red square within a black circle. Five copies of *Unovis* were printed using typewriter, lithography, etching and linocuts. During the winter 1919–1920, Lissitzky designed a Suprematist book for children, *Of Two Squares* (*Pro Dva Kvadrata*). The idea for this book may derive from the construction of a podium for public speakers, something like the famous *Lenin Podium* depicted on page 42 of *Die Kunstismen*. *Of Two Squares* is an amusing political fable, in which Lissitzky describes the confrontation between two squares: the red square symbolising life and the good revolutionary Communist order with its limitless possibilities, while the black square represented the bad old ways – chaos, egotism, death, and of course, the Czarist regime. Patricia Railing, in *More About Two Squares*, says that:

> This little book is also the moment when Lissitzky refined the use of his letter forms as pictorial images. He used letter, word and typography with his painterly images, page by page to create a dynamic and unified vision: picture + letter. . . .[4]

Since there was no suitable press at the school in Vitebsk, *Of Two Squares* was not printed until early 1922 in Berlin. In his *Typographical Facts*, Lissitzky explained his aims:

> In this tale of two squares I have set out to formulate an elementary idea, using elementary means, so that children may find it a stimulus to active play and grown-ups enjoy it as something to look at. The action unrolls like a film . . .

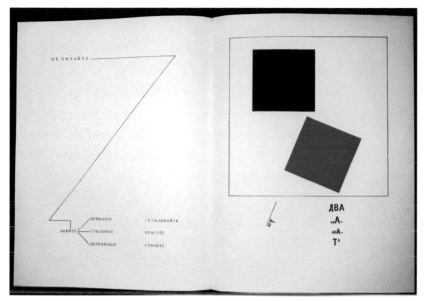

Merz

For the Voice

In 1921 El Lissitzky left Vitebsk to take over the faculty of architecture at the Free State Artists Workshop at Moscow, or 'Vkhutemas' which meant a 'higher artists and technical workshop'. It was there that Lissitzky came into contact with Professor Vladimir Tatlin, who in 1919 had begun designing a structure, vaguely reminiscent of the Eiffel Tower, which would serve as a news-gathering and broad-casting facility – the never realised 'Tower of the Third International'. 'Vkhutemas' was a stronghold of Constructivism. Susan Compton, in her *Russian Avant-Garde Books; 1917–1934* (British Library, 1994), suggests that at least in the field of book-design, Constructivism was not so much an 'art style' as a principle for shaping the new society. As the name suggests, Constructivism is about building. New metals, new forms of construction, new designs were fundamental to Constructivism art and thought. Constructivism was not about spiritual states but about doing things, creating environments in which the new order might be realised. Constructivism suited El Lissitzky's multi-faceted approach to art – he did not like to be idle, nor did he limit himself to a meagre output.

Soon Lissitzky was on the move again. At the very end of 1921, his head full of new ideas and a firm conviction in his heart, he travelled to Berlin, then a city overflowing with Russian emigres. His new task was to establish contact between German artists and the new generation of Soviet artists. Not so simple, post-war Berlin was a veritable witch's cauldron of avant-garde art movements. In Berlin, El Lissitzky met the satirical German artist George Grosz, who informed him that no less than seventy-seven artistic 'isms' were currently in use to portray the real soul of art in Germany. It may be here that the need for a book such as *Die Kunstismen* was established.

In 1922 Lissitzky's *Of Two Squares* was published by Skythen Verlag in Berlin. It had been printed in Leipzig by E. Haberland in an edition of ten unnumbered folios, fifty numbered and signed books and an unspecified amount of unsigned and unnumbered copies. Lissitzky made contact with the Bauhaus artists at Weimar. He met Theo van Doesburg in Amsterdam, where Lissitzky had gone to present a lecture. Full of enthusiasm for its design innovations, van Doesburg introduced *Of Two Squares* to his students and, as *The Suprematist Tale of Two Squares* had it reprinted in the Dutch art periodical *De Stijl*.

Late in 1922, Vladimir Mayakovsky, proclaiming himself a thoroughly modern man, flew to Berlin where the Soviet State Publishing House, Gosizdat, had a quite active branch and had promised to publish his latest book of poems. Lilly Brik was to be the editor and El Lissitzky was to design, illustrate and turn Vladimir Mayakovsky's poems into a Constructivist book. It was a small book, printed by Lutze & Vogt on cheap paper, meant to be carried in a coat-pocket or purse and brought out wherever a few people had congregated who might listen to new Communist fables. Many copies of *Dlya golosa*, (*For the Voice*, or *For Reading Aloud*) were worn to shreds or simply abandoned among the soiled dishes in countless cafes or cabarets. Lissitzky explained his design philosophy:

> . . . my pages stand in much the same relationship to the poems as an accompanying piano to a violin. Just as the poet unites concept and sound, I have tried to create an equivalent unity using the poem and typography.[5]

The excitement of the poems was certainly matched by the lucid typographical illustrations in red and black printed solely with the resources of the compositor's type case. Every possible two-colour printing technique, such as overlays and crosshatching, had been used. Each poem was given typographical identity and these symbolic images were used again on the thumb index. The brilliant orange cover depicts title and author in carefully balanced black letters which frame a red circle edged in black representing the open mouth of the reader. Some years later El Lissitzky recalled:

> We selected thirteen poems. The book was intended for reading aloud. To enable the reader to locate the individual poems quickly, I hit on the idea of using a thumb index (that is, alphabetical order). Vladimir Vladimirovich [Mayakovsky] agreed. Editions of our books were usually produced by large printing works, but the production manager at the Berlin office, Skaponi, found us a small firm because, he said, 'As this is a risky thing, it is better to work with a small printer – they will pay more attention to you there.' The compositor was a German. He set type absolutely mechanically. I made him a sketch-layout for every page. He thought we were crazy . . . [but] the printers became fascinated; they realised that a work which was so original in its form must also be remarkable in its content. They asked me to explain the meaning, and I translated the verses for them.[6]

The poems in *For the Voice* were not actually meant to be read as much as they were meant to be translated into sound by the human voice. Writer, artist and actor merged in the emotional message. During the decade immediately following the First World War avant-garde Russian artists had been influenced by the confluence of film, theatre, painting, graphic and book arts. They saw the theatrical stage as a large page by which theatrical designers or scenic artists and actors may reach the widest possible audience.

Vladimir Mayakovsky acquired the notion of the theatre as a series of integrated arts in 1911 when, as an eighteen-year-old art-student, he was taken to see Shakespeare's *Hamlet* directed by Edward Gordon Craig and presented by Konstantin Stanislavky at the Moscow Art Theatre. Marussia Burussia Burliuk, wife of the Russian Futurist artist David Burliuk, described Mayakovsky's reaction:

> . . . when Mayakovsky saw 'Hamlet' with us, even the plan of his own work began to grow in his mind. . . . Instead of decorations, movable screens of various sizes and cubes were used to portray the beauty and richness of the palace. Craig had some of the cubes covered with gold paper. In other scenes they appeared only gray. On the stage there were no doors, no windows, or furniture. Everything depended on the imagination of an onlooker.[7]

Not all of Lissitzky's projects were published. A book based on Aleksei Eliseevich Kruchenykh's Futuristic opera, *Sieg Uber Die Sonne*, or *Victory over the Sun*,[8] survives only as the manifesto: *The Painter on the Stage Progresses towards Architecture*.[9] A 'puppet portfolio' created for Kruchenykh's 'electro-mechanical peepshow', for which Lissitzky created a series of watercolour drawings, three of which were exhibited in Berlin in 1922, was partly printed by lithography in Hanover in 1923. El Lissitzky designed a handsome Suprematism cover and the photographic frontispiece of the author for Alexander Tairoff, *Das Entfesselte Theater* (*The Theatre Unchained*) published in Potsdam by Gustav Kiepenheuer Verlag in 1923. To his usual red and black, Lissitszky added a vermilion circle and rectangle and vermilion endpapers. He produced many magazine illustrations, book covers and posters. All of the many art journals which appeared in such profusion between 1922 and 1935 in Eastern Europe, Paris, England, Germany, Russia and the USA showed, in one way or other, a debt to Lissitzky's innovation in graphic design.

It may have been his editorial work on the avant-garde magazine *Merz* which inspired El Lissitzky to design the last books he would 'build' outside of Russia. *Die Kunstismen; Les Ismes de L'Art; The Isms of Art* was published in 1925 by Eugen Rentsch Verlag, of 'Erlenbach-Zurich, Munchen und Leipzig.'

Among Lissitzky's activities in connection with the Bauhaus in Weimar was a meeting held in the autumn of 1922 in which the European avant-garde artists participated, gathering almost in full strength at Weimar and travelling together to a great conference at Dusseldorf. They broke their journey at Hanover, where Lissitzky met the *enfant terrible* of German Dada, Kurt Schwitters and, through Schwitters, his future wife Sophie Kuppers, an enthusiast of the new art and a gallery director.[10] Soon Mrs Kuppers had purchased one of Lissitzky's best 'Prouns', was arranging exhibitions of his works in various German cities, and had invited the artist to give a lecture on the 'New Russian Art'.

Meanwhile, Lissitzky's constitution, which had always been frail, began to fail. In August 1923 he was diagnosed with pulmonary tuberculosis and the next February he travelled to Zurich to enter a sanatorium and was met at the station by another Dada artist, Hans Arp and his artist-wife Sophie Täuber-Arp. Arrangements had already been made for Lissitzky to edit an issue of Kurt Schwitters' Dada journal *Merz*. Lissitzky invited Arp to participate in the creation of issue 8/9 of *Merz*, which they nicknamed *Nasci*. With the help of Mrs Kuppers, Lissitzky was able to continue his graphic designs and theoretical writings as well as his experiments in photomontage while convalescing at the sanatorium at Orselino, near Locarno, in Switzerland. His page designs for *Merz* 8/9 (April/July 1924) were revolutionary indeed. Using a clear, deep blue and a vermilion red for the lettering printed on white stock he structured the entire issue around the exposition of the natural forms as they mutate into art styles. Lissitzky wrote the Introduction, which begins – 'We have had ENOUGH . . .', and several articles. As a distillation of all he had learned, Lissitzky published the following 'credo' in *Merz* 8/9:

Topography of Typography

1. The words on the printed sheet are learnt by sight, not by hearing.

2. Ideas are communicated through conventional words, the idea should be given form through the letters.

3. Economy of expression – optics instead of phonetics.

4. The design of book-space through the material of the type, according to the laws of typographical mechanics, must correspond to the strains and stresses of the content.

5. The design of the book-space through the material of the illustrative process blocks, which gives reality to the new optics.

The supernaturalistic reality of the perfected eye.

6. The continuous page-sequence – the bioscopic book.

7. The new book demands the new writer. Ink-stand and goose-quill are dead.

8. The printed sheet transcends space and time. The printed sheet, the infinity of the book, must be transcended.

The Electro-library.[11]

By the end of March, 1924, Lissitzky had finished editing, writing and illustrating *Merz* 8/9. Ideas for future work, as always, were plentiful. He wrote to Sophie Kuppers in Hanover: 'Have an idea for the final *Merz* issue of 1924: *"Last Parade of all the Isms from 1914–1924."* '

Impatient for the publication of *Merz* 8/9, he continued to visualise a book on the 'Isms of Art.' On 24 May, he wrote to Sophie '. . . Have various ideas on typography if I write the book,' and on 31 May he asked Sophie: 'Please bring me all *my negatives*, which are at the photographer's (be sure to have your Proun photographed). So that I can make prints, if it should be necessary . . . perhaps your large camera as well. . . .'

During the summer of 1924 'El' moved out of the sanatorium and with Sophie he rented a house in the village of Ambri-Sotto. Uppermost in his mind was finishing his current project. The idea had not appealed to Kurt Schwitters, but Hans Arp and Sophie Täuber-Arp were enthusiastic and they were invited to Ambri-Sotto. Lissitzky took several photographs of Arp: a *profil-en-face* portrait and a photomontage of Arp with his 'Dada Keyboard', which he finally used in 1928 for the cover of llya Selvinsky's *Zapiski Poet*, (*Notes of a Poet*), published in Moscow and Leningrad.

For *Die Kunstismen*, however, Lissitszy had in mind the visual effects of multiple copies in a display window and as he 'built' the book he used the most deceptively simple but direct visual and and textual approach. It was Hans Arp who edited the short paragraphs explaining in German, French and English, the sixteen art movements named on the cover:

> Film, Constructivism, Ver [secession], Proun, Compression, Merz, Neo-platicism, Pure art, Dada, Simultaneism, Suprematicism, Meta-physical art, Abstraction, Cubism, Futurism, Expressionism.

It was Hans Arp who found a publisher for *Die Kunstismen*: the firm of Eugen Rentsch Verlag. By the autumn of 1924 Lissitzky was ready to see his new book in print, but Hans Arp demurred. Early in November, Lissitzky, in desperation, wrote to Sophie:

> Thanks for the photo of Dix. It is not what I wanted (too ordinary). But Rentsch is in a hurry and he's right. As for Arp, it's like this: I sent him the finished foreword two weeks ago, and up to now no answer . . . I can't wait any longer because of Rentsch . . . you know how pleased we all were (Arp included) with the portrait of him which I did. I was proud to put my sign (eL) on the print I gave to Arp, to get a block made (you know I do that very rarely). The block proofs have arrived: and on this particular proof there is no trace of eL, and on the photograph itself the eL has been neatly scratched out . . . he has not handed over the Picabia photographs . . . the *Unovis* photos to Rensch . . . behind my back he has written to Segal, Hoch, Kassak. . . . It grieves me.[12]

Lissitzky's book covers conveyed a dynamism and directness equal to any of his posters. The cover of *Kunstismen* is dominated by a massive black 'K' and the dates 1924–1914 in red and black. The elongated red 'ISM' contrasts with the tiny 'us' of *KunstISM-us*, which is repeated sixteen times, to balance the sixteen 'isms' explained in this book. The title-page (see page 332) offers its message in three languages, announces that the book was published by El Lissitzky and Hans Arp, and repeats the ciphers of the years 1924–1914 to form a solid column on the right side of the page. The effect is one of absolute balance, of control of the uncontrollable 'isms'. The opening pages begin with a statement meant to comment on the meaning of 'Art' by Lissitzky's Suprematist master – Kazimir Malevich:

> The actual time is the epoca of analyses, the result of all systems that ever were established. Centuries brought the signs to our line of demarcation, in them we shall recognize the imperfections that led to division and contradiction. Perhaps we hereof shall only take the contradictory to construct the system of unity.
>
> Malewitsch [*sic*]

The typography of *Die Kunstismen* – squarish page, with solid pica rules separating the three columns of heavy sans serif type – make it one of the strongest and most exciting statements of twentieth-century book design.

The influence of Lissitzky's work on *Merz*, his attention to film and to the aesthetics developed at the Bauhaus were the aesthetic ideal for designing the page layout. In an introductory chapter, the sixteen 'Isms' are defined by Lissitzky and leading avantgarde artists and, preceded by Malevich's statement, printed in columns in German, French and English. Lissitzky's use of text and photomontage is kept to a minimum: a few dates and names identify the subject matter of the photographic items grouped on each page. For example on pages 41 and 42 Lissitzky introduces his own work under the heading of 'Prouns'. On page 41 he includes his *Proun 23, No. 6*, painted in 1919, accompanied by a small photograph of himself – crouching. On page 42 the famous sketch for the Lenin Podium, the inspiration for *Of Two Squares*, containing only one word: 'Proletarians'.

As *Die Kunstismen* went to press, El Lissitzky decided to return to the Soviet Union. While it was true that anti-Semitism was an ever growing force in the German art world and that his enthusiasm for art's great new mission in the socialist state had never diminished, his decision seems to have been a personal one: his beloved sister had committed suicide in Russia, he wished to console his grieving parents and unfortunately, his health was continuing to deteriorate. The happy Utopian goals of the 'new society' were becoming bogged down in civil war, famine and material want. Many splendid architectural plans were postponed or forgotten. Nevertheless El Lissitzky was still enthusiastic about his motherland. On 20 June 1925, he wrote to Sophie from Moscow, in his first letter from the USSR, of Kazimir Malevich, the Suprematist master of 'the Spiritual in Art', whose confrontation with the Constructivists led by Vladimir Tatlin was to result in Malevich being branded 'a non-person' (literally 'a mad monk'). Lissitzky wrote:

> Arrived late at night. . . . Next morning found Malevich. Tender embraces and great joy. . . . What he has written on architecture is completely opposed to my views, and in my opinion harmful. I told him that, and we agreed to appear in a public debate sometime. He was very pleased about the Isms book. . . .[13]

Lazar El Lissitzky continued his work for the Soviets – teaching architecture, designing books and posters and exhibiting his drawings and paintings. He died in December 1941, on the day that Sophie's German-born eldest son joined the Red Army to defend Lissitzky's motherland.

How the world turns – Lazar El Lissitzky's little books have become twentieth-century classics, not because of their propaganda content, but because of the inventiveness demonstrated by their designer. Lissitzky, who deliberately espoused poverty, created costly items avidly sought by capitalist book collectors and richly endowed libraries. The days of hammer and sickle are over and a new flag, one not designed by an artist, now flies over the Kremlin.

Adela Spindler Roatcap received her PhD in the History of Art from Stanford University in 1974, with a dissertation in Russian Medieval Art. She is currently a professor at the University of San Francisco – and an avid writer. Her interest in type and typography derives from her activities as a collector, lecturer, and writer about fine press books. In addition to articles in *Matrix*, Roatcap has contributed many articles relating to type, typography, and fine-press printing to *Fine Print*, *Letter Arts Review*, *Parenthesis*, and to *The Book Club of California Quarterly News-Letter*. This article was the result of a conversation with John Randle during a visit to the Whittington Press. When she asked John Randle which book designer he most admired, he enthusiastically brought out a facsimile page of *Die Kunstismen*, and during afternoon tea at Miriam Macgregor's, he vehemently explained why, to him, El Lissitzky's pages will always be the greatest achievements of Constructivist graphic design.

NOTES

1. Sophie Lissitzky-Kuppers, Herbert Read, Introduction, *El Lissitzky; Life – Letters – Texts*, London: Thames and Hudson, 1980, p. 19.

2. Lissitzky-Kuppers, *op. cit.*, pp. 21 and 35.

3. El Lissitzky, *Unovis*, No. 1, 1920, quoted in Patricia Railing, *More About Two Squares*, Cambridge, Massachusetts, MIT Press Edition, 1991, p. 37 and Lissitzky-Kuppers, *op. cit.*, p. 362.

4. Patricia Railing, *More About Two Squares*, Cambridge, Massachusetts: MIT Press, 1991, p. 5

5. Carol Hogben & Rowan Watson, *From Manet to Hockney; Modern Artists' Illustrated Books*. London: Victoria & Albert Museum, 1985, p. 190.

6. Lissitzky-Kuppers, *op. cit.* p. 25.

7. Susan O. Compton, *The World Backwards; Russian Futurist Books 1912–1916*, London: The British Library, 1978, p. 51.

8. *Victory over the Sun* was premiered in Moscow in 1913 with scenery and costumes by Kasimir Malevich.

9. Henning Rischbieter and Wolfgang Storch, *Art and the Stage in the 20th Century; Painters and Sculptors Work for the Theatre*, Greenwich, Connecticut: New York Graphic Society Ltd., 1969, pp. 128–139.

10. Sophie Kuppers and Lazar El Lissitzky were married in Moscow on 27 January 1927.

11. Lissitzky-Kuppers, *op. cit.*, p. 359.

12. Lissitzky-Kuppers, *op. cit.*, p. 54.

13. Lissitzky-Kuppers, *op. cit.*, p. 63.

JOHN- STON'S SANS LETTERS

LT

Johnston's Sans cut in wood-letter.

Edward Johnston and Letter Spacing

BY COLIN BANKS

The utilitarian nature of the lettering that Edward Johnston supplied to London Underground in 1916 belies its classical roots. Colin Banks, who with John Miles revised Johnston's work in the 1980s to give it new life in London Transport, wrote in Matrix 15 *(1995) about how Johnston saw the visual function of his letters.*

Frank Pick, the then Commercial Manager of London Underground Railway, commissioned a 'block letter' alphabet from Edward Johnston in 1916. It is thought of as the first modern sans serif type face, preceding that of Jacob Erbar (1922), and Paul Renner's 'Futura', Rudolph Koch's 'Kabel' of 1927 and Eric Gill's Sans of 1928. The lettering continued in vigorous use by London Transport for half a century. Then followed a decade in which it was increasingly put to one side until its revival in modified form for digital reproduction in the 1980s.

The wood and metal type for Johnston's sans became broken up and lost when licensed print suppliers to London Transport ceased trading in the early 1990s. The author was alerted to one such collection shortly before the closure of Ernest Jones, the Bermondsey printers who had in the past acquired a lot of print material from Waterlows. This led to a hasty rescue and the cataloguing of the wood-letter (there was no metal type) by Tim Demuth, Ian Mortimer and myself; and eventually the preparation of a folio volume of specimen pages printed letterpress from the original founts by the Libanus Press, together with an analysis of the development of the twentieth-century sans printed offset by the Senecio Press. This short account of Edward Johnston's theories (accompanied by some of the wood-letter printed by Libanus) develops some of the points made in the book.

I formed a partnership with John Miles in 1958 and one of our earliest clients was London Transport, so forging another link in the chain of design consultants employed by LT that has proved to be as enduring, if less distinguished, as that of Johnston himself. My principal teacher of typography had been Charles Pickering, who in turn had attended Johnston's calligraphy lectures in the late

1920s at the Central School of Arts and Crafts. Pickering had gone on to draw the final versions of 'London Underground Railway Block Letter Bold' in the 1930s. In 1981 London Transport asked me to prepare a 'visual audit' and report of all their graphic manifestations. One conclusion was that while individual promotional items of print looked decent enough, overall control of the identity had been lost.

LT's advertising agencies used different typefaces for different campaigns, driven more by the imperatives of short term effect than long term goodwill. More rational problems were the cost and length of time involved in hand-setting and a falling away in standards of spacing; then there was an extremely limited range of weights, styles and sizes.

My report emphasised to LT the significance of their typographic inheritance saying 'the lettering could act like a ribbon to tie in the disparate parts of the LT business into one well organised parcel'. This started a twelve year programme at Banks & Miles of drawing the sans letters in ways more fitting to modern usages and to computer origination.

The biggest problem we had was with Johnston himself and the way in which he had hung social theory (he set himself against industrial processes) and dogma about proportion on to lettering, and the way it was turned into type and then used at third hand far removed from the begetter. Much of that is discussed in the book *London's Handwriting*. I will confine myself here to writing about details of design and spacing.

When setting out letters, the sound principles advocated by Johnston can be summarised as follows:

> If the space inside a lower case o is equal to twice the width of the stroke that forms the o, then the apparent space between the o and next letter should also be twice the thickness of that stroke; and so on through the word. In this way when the spaces between letters are equally balanced by the spaces within letters an even flow will emerge in the pattern of the whole word, undisturbed by patches where letters are crowded together or pushed too far apart.

This is clearly much easier to achieve in arrangements of hand drawn lettering than in type where the possibility of a huge number of unpredictable letter conjunctions occurs. But the accumulated experience of five hundred years of type design has long since resolved the problem; the most common system used by type manufacturers is set out in Walter Tracy's *Letters of Credit* (Gordon Fraser, 1986) in chapter 10.

Wood-letter types, though, by tradition do not have predetermined spacing fixed by the 'shoulders' of each letter as cast metal type does; the correct amount of space needed between the letters is judged by eye and added by hand. London Transport's special sans lettering was initially and predominantly used in wood. Johnston applied himself to this problem with the doggedness characteristic of him and produced the table of spaces for LT's printers to follow that is printed here on page 352.

On the face of it his system seems logical and in the 1980s LT's Information Technology Department embarked on a similar but much more extended computer program to speed up the generation of computer typesetting and save 'memory'. It failed for the same reason that Johnston's system must, for both depended on the *conjunction of shapes* of the neighbouring letters, but neither allows for the *inherent spaces within each letter* (balancing the space inside of an o with the spaces each side of it).

When I showed Johnston's tables to Walter Tracy he commented, 'Why ever didn't the man go to a decent typographer for advice!'

Johnston was curiously unaware or wilfully indifferent to those five hundred years of typographical experience. The main principle of his block letter was that the thickness of strokes in the letterforms should be absolutely consistent throughout each fount and that is the way he drew them. The same year (1916) that he received this commission from Frank Pick saw the publication of what must still be the definitive work on its subject, *Typographical Printing Surfaces* by Legros and Grant. This was largely a reprinting of the longest proceedings ever published by the Institution of Mechanical Engineers, by Lucien Alphonse Legros in 1908.

One chapter in this very big book sets out in detail optical adjustments that have to be made in typeface design in order to achieve visually balanced characters. From this we can see that pointed shapes like that in the V need to be extended below the base line as do curved shapes shapes like the o, which also exceeds the x-height. We are shown how a lower case t often needs to lean backwards, and the dot over the i to offset to the left; how ink traps are opened up and potentially blobby terminals are guarded against.

Johnston used none of this expertise and was determined on his dogma of keeping all stroke thicknesses *precisely* the same, irrespective of whether they were horizontal, vertical or changing from one to the other, or of how dense or constricted were the shapes that these strokes encompassed. Horizontal lines do look thicker than vertical lines and by ruling out modelling of the thickness of a curved stroke, all sorts of problems occur which inhibit the development of the design into small sizes and into heavier weights.

This produced some very uncomfortable letters in Johnston's 'Underground

ABCDEFGH

PQRSTU

abcdefghij

tuvwxyzl2

A complete synopsis of Johnston's Block Letter fount, reproduced in the smallest size of the wood-letter, 5-line pica.

IJKLMNO

VWXYZ

klmnopqrs

34567890

Railway Block-Letter' notably O S and o s, but also to my eye give the alphabet a quirky individuality, something we were anxious to retain in the redrawing. In Johnston's defence (if Johnston's army of other admirers do not think *any* justification an impertinence) I would say that the realisation that his block letter was to be turned into type might have come to Johnston much later on, perhaps after the event; at first it only existed as litho tracing sheets for the use of a poster draftsman to copy onto a litho stone.

When the alphabets were first made into metal type in the 1920s, probably by the Shanks foundry, it looks as though the punch-cutters exercised much more interpretive freedom than was allowed the wood-letter craftsmen and a different but more conventional typeface resulted.

None of this is to deny 'Underground Railway Block-Letter' its place as the most revolutionary and inspirational of twentieth century letterforms.

NOTES ON SPACING THE BLOCK LETTERS, BY EDWARD JOHNSTON

1. A minimum of regularity is requisite, but it is not desirable to get perfectly regular spacing in straightforward work [i.e. the straightforward setting out of letters is better than the elaborate fitting and planning necessary to perfect regularity].

2. This is particularly so in printing, where it should be possible in nearly every case to get sufficient regularity by the ordinary setting of types together without 'leads' [i.e. letter spacing].

3. But to obtain a minimum of regularity without undue fitting, the Block letter type (for normal use) should be provided with their own margins (by a projection of the 'body' beyond the 'face'). The margins must vary – thus:

> a) The greatest for vertical strokes I

> For practical purposes the right sides of BCEGJX (narrow X) and both sides of S and U might be regarded as 'verticals' – (FKPR and Z and X (wide) would rank better with curves). Actually in each case they would be better for less margin (than verticals and curves).

> b) Less margins for curved strokes.

> c) The least (or none) for oblique strokes /.

4. By these varied margins sufficient optically regular spacing can be obtained in normal cases, thus:

> a) II Farthest apart.

> b) I Nearer together and)(still nearer.

> c) M Nearest (or even touching).

5. The chief difficulty is caused by the last (c) class of letters in conjunction with the two other classes (a and b).

The last class (c) consists of the obliques AWVY with which we may include L and frequently T.

If verticals be provided with margins wide enough to separate them from one another perfectly III this wide margin will be found too wide in conjunction with an oblique stroke IIV or VII.

6. This difficulty may be met in three ways (or by a combination of them).

1st, By a compromise in the margins (i.e. by making the margins of the verticals barely sufficient for inter-vertical spaces III which will give only a little too much space with obliques IIV, or:

2nd By giving verticals full spaces and making special combinations for all the oblique strokes AIIA etc., or:

3rd By making the space artificially by 'leads'.

7. The first (as used in ordinary printing) is probably the best way because it is straight-forward. The second would be almost too elaborate, as it would require about 100 combinations in addition to the ordinary alphabet of separate types. (A few combinations for extreme cases, however, such as LA AA VY WY TY would be advantageous).

The third would give the most even effect but would require 'leads' between all the letters and would require the use of 4 or 5 different 'leads' for the different combinations of vertical, curved, and ablique letters, thus:

for AA etc.

for OO etc.

for DI etc.

for ID etc.

In practice I should not expect this to work so well. It would tend to unnecessary spreading out and would probably lead to confusion (particularly in cases where there was a variety from the normal spacing).

If, however, it is your printer's regular practice to set Block letters with 'leads' between nearly all of them he might do best systematizing his 'leads' as indicated above.

8. But, if he does not practice such inter-letter 'leading' I should, on general practices, recommend the compromise (Note 6, 1st) and give approximately the following margins:

For vertical I a margin of say 2/5ths the stem width.

For curves) & (a margin of say 1/10th the stem width.

For obliques \ and / the least possible (or no) margin.

For L and T a very small margin.

By making these margins in fractions of the stem width they would be in right proportions whatever the size of the type.

I offer the above under the difficulty of not knowing how the BL Types are used. The only information I have is that they were 'cut in wood'. Doubtless you will be able to apply the above theoretical considerations to the practical conditions of your typography.

Colin Banks died on 9 March 2002 at the age of 70. After training at Medway and Maidstone Colleges of Art, Banks's first job was with London Typographical Designers, but a greater influence was his next employer, Ernst Hoch. In 1958 he set up on his own, but soon realised that he needed a partner; he was joined by John Miles in August of that year, to form Banks & Miles. The partnership's clientele included, among others, the Post Office, British Telecom, the European Parliament, the British Council, the Consumers' Association, and London Transport. In the 1970s, London Transport's advertising agency were finding the original Johnston alphabet too limited in range, and wanted to abandon it for Helvetica; but Banks & Miles suggested that a better course would be to increase the range of Johnston, while keeping its original character, and adapt it to modern production methods. This project occupied Colin Banks for a number of years, and it was one of which he was particularly proud.

ABCDEFG

abcdefghiklmnopqrstvxyz

HIJKLMN

abcdefghiklmnopqrstvxyz

OPQRST

abcdefghiklmnopqrstvxyz

UVWXYZ

Hermann Zapf's Optima type, the digitized version from Linotype

The Dust-jacket Designs of Hermann Zapf

BY JERRY KELLY

Hermann Zapf is best known, especially in the English-speaking world, for his typeface designs. Jerry Kelly's survey, from Matrix 17 (1997), *shows Zapf's mastery of design with type, most particularly in the composition of typographic book-jacket designs.*

The diversity and level of skills displayed by Hermann Zapf in the book arts is extraordinary. During the past half-century Zapf has been a recognised leader in the fields of type design, calligraphy, book design, and typography. Comparison could be made with Jan van Krimpen, Rudolf Koch, Eric Gill, Jan Tschichold and others in this century, each of whom made significant contributions to all these fields, but none can be said to have exerted such a strong and far-reaching influence on all the book arts as Hermann Zapf. Van Krimpen's type designs, while greatly admired by a select group, deserved more general acceptance, and his calligraphy is barely known among today's lettering artists. Gill's types and calligraphy are better known (and to this can be added his exceptional wood-engravings), but again his influence is generally limited. Koch had a tremendous impact in his day, indeed even on the young Hermann Zapf, who began his calligraphic exercises after viewing a memorial exhibition of Koch's work in 1935. Koch's influence was by far the greatest in his native Germany, despite the fact that several leaders in the graphics communities abroad, such as Stanley Morison and Francis Meynell in England and Melbert Cary in the United States, championed his work. Most of Koch's types were variants of black-letter scarcely used today. Of his roman founts only two – Koch Antiqua (otherwise known as 'Eve' or 'Locarno'), and Kabel – are seen at all today, and those only in limited applications. Tschichold designed only one type of note, Sabon (1966), and that fount does enjoy wide application today. His calligraphic work, like Van Krimpen's, is only known among a small group, despite its high quality. Similarly, his book design and typography is greatly, if not widely, admired by a small group.

Zapf's work, on the other hand, has achieved a level of acceptance – both by the graphic design community in general and those considering themselves 'fine printers' – greater than his predecessors or contemporaries. About a half-dozen of his nearly 200 alphabet designs are among the most used today, and several of his types are among the favourites of fine presses and distinguished graphic designers of our time. His calligraphy has been widely published and admired, and he is a much sought after author and lecturer in the calligraphic community. His type designs and calligraphy, as well as his meticulously produced publications, are popular not only in his native Germany but throughout the world, including England and the United States, where perhaps his popularity is greatest.

This is certainly not to say that popularity alone is indication of the quality of one's work. Surely much great work has gone un- or under-appreciated, and one can only wonder at the popularity of some things (certainly this is true for typefaces). However, in Zapf's case there is an appreciation by many of today's finest practitioners of calligraphy, type design, and typography, together with a popular acceptance, that make his situation extraordinary and perhaps unique. For such high-calibre work to be so admired by his peers and also so widely used must surely be a positive influence on the world of graphic design.

Zapf is best known for his type designs, which is understandable since his work in that field reaches the widest audience. With the advent of personal computers, with great masses of people using type in their day-to-day lives (for better or for worse), there is a proliferation of type founts. Most people use Zapf-designed founts without knowing it, to say nothing of the millions who read his types daily in magazines, newspapers, books and brochures totally unaware of their distinguishing characteristics and the effort and talent which went into their creation.

Next on a scale of popularity would be Zapf's hand-lettering. The calligraphic community is minuscule by comparison with the typographic one, but knowledgeable. Among practitioners Zapf's work (and name) is familiar as a high point to be admired and studied.

Zapf's typography, and in particular his book design, is less well known. Most of his book designs were done for German trade publishers such as S. Fischer, Büchergilde Gutenberg, Suhrkamp, and others. English-speaking afficionados of fine printing are remarkably provincial when it comes to the appreciation of books in foreign languages. I wonder what percentage of books on the shelves of today's bibliophiles who read *Matrix* are in a foreign language – I suspect it is small. Add to that the fact that by far the most of Zapf's book designs fall into the category of trade books, not fine editions, and one can see why his work in this area is so little known. What familiarity there may be would come mostly from Zapf's 1963 publication (reprinted in reduced format by offset in 1976) *Typographic Variations*, showing seventy-eight book and title-page designs by Zapf. While this beautiful book is an excellent selection of Zapf's work in this field, it necessarily shows only a small portion of each book; usually the titlepage, though in several instances text pages are also shown. Neglected are other aspects of a book's design such as binding and dust-jacket.

Of all the applications of Zapf's talents in the letter arts, book design in general and jacket design specifically are the ones where all of his talents – type design, calligraphy, and typography – can be seen together. In dust-jackets Zapf has had the opportunity to employ his types, lettering, and occasionally an image in a single design; the fields of type design and calligraphy are much more circumscribed applications.

Zapf's jacket designs fall into three categories: (1) typographic: employing only type (most often his own designs but in several instances other founts) in creative arrangements to attract the viewer; (2) calligraphic: employing mainly or entirely Zapf's hand-lettering for the wording on the jacket front and spine; and (3) those jackets with decorative elements: using an illustration or occasionally type ornaments for decorative effect. A few jackets overlap categories, using type and calligraphy, or calligraphy and illustration.

Zapf's first jacket design was for his own first publication as an author: *William Morris: Seine Werk und Leben*, published by Heinz & Blanckartz in 1948. An assortment of the elements mentioned above is combined in this jacket design: typography using Warren Chappell's Trajanus fount; calligraphy in a very finished uncial hand; and a rendering of Morris by Zapf, meticulously cut in metal by Zapf's friend August Rosenberger, the punch-cutter at the Stempel Foundry where Zapf's types were manufactured. Even a small ornamental fleuron makes an appearance on this jacket, though Zapf's jacket designs, like much of his typography and lettering, generally eschew ornament. Instead it is the careful placement of beautiful letterforms – either calligraphic or typographic – printed in tasteful colours on appropriate papers, that achieves the desired effect.

A couple of examples from among the totally typographic jacket designs are Bertrand Russell's *Philosophie* (Holle) employing meticulously spaced capitals of his own Michelangelo Titling design with the publisher's logo designed by Zapf; and *Amerikanisches Theater* (Büchergilde Gutenberg, 1958), entirely set in Garamond type. This straight-forward design is essentially a list

1. André Gide, *Die Pastoral Symphonie, enge Pforte, Eine Erzählung* (Büchergilde Gutenberg).

2. Vergil, *Bucolica* (Suhrkamp Verlag).

of the four plays included in the volume, but in Zapf's hands a cohesive and appealing arrangement is realised through the careful arrangement of the wording. Another example of a design incorporating the book's contents is the striking calligraphic jacket for Giradoux's plays. Other purely calligraphic designs we can cite are André Gide's *Die Pastoral Symphonie, Die enge Pforte, Eine Erzählung* (Büchergilde Gutenberg) (figure 1) in a flowing cursive style, and Carl Zuchemeyer's *Gedichte* (Suhrkamp) in formal capitals, among numerous others. The Gide lettering is based on Zapf's own elegant hand-writing. This jacket is printed in only two colours, a pale yellow and rich grey, yet one is not left wishing for more. Of the more ornamental jackets there are the Büchergilde Gutenberg's edition of Hoffmansthal's selected works in two volumes, employing Zapf's own Primavera ornaments blind debossed in combination with Walbaum type, or Zapf's edition of Homer's *Odyssey* for the same publisher (1966) which has Zapf's Attika borders blind debossed with Janson type on coated paper. Other jacket designs make use of pictorial elements, such as the frieze on the German edition of Joseph Campbell's *Hero of One Thousand Faces*, or the beautiful edition of Virgil's *Bucolica* (Suhrkamp Verlag) (figure 2) with a large reproduction of a Maillol

3. *Amorbach* (Hermann Emig).

4. Sigrid Wechssler, *Heidelberg, das Neckartal und der Kraichgau* (Hermann Emig).

woodcut from the Cranach Presse edition printed in red on the front. This jacket is printed in two colours on an elegant tan laid stock. The design, as well as the woodcut, is classical and elegant – totally appropriate for Virgil's work. Both of the aforementioned jackets have the images combined with Zapf's drawn open capitals, with their vigorous brush-drawn line. Further use of pictorial elements can be seen in the charming series of books on German localities produced by Zapf for the Oldenwald publisher Hermann Emig. The jacket designs for these books incorporate full-colour reproductions of earlier paintings with the title usually hand-lettered in a variety of styles, but occasionally set in an appropriate typeface.

By far the greatest number of Zapf's jacket designs employ his elegant calligraphy. His calligraphic work shows a thorough and wide-spread mastery of various calligraphic styles. Some of the earlier jackets have lettering in a black letter style, such as Willy Bremi's *Der Weg des Protestantischen Menschen* (Artemis Verlag) or *Amorbach* (Hermann Emig) (figure 3), but this was later generally abandoned in favour of the more modern looking roman and italic styles. In the Bremi jacket Zapf effectively combines classic roman capitals for the author, sub-title, and publisher with the title in textura. The title stands

5. Jean Giraudoux, *Dramen* [volume 2] (S. Fischer
Verlag).

6. Walter Benjamin, *Schriften* [volume 1]
(Suhrkamp Verlag).

out, but cohesion is achieved through the use of heavy, condensed roman capitals with the black-letter lower-case. An exception would be several of the
jackets for the Hermann Emig publications on German localities (an example
of which is mentioned above), where the occasional Fraktur or Textura design
fittingly connotes a German town. Another illustration shows, not one of the
black-letter Emig jackets, but rather Zapf's graceful italic lettering used on the
jacket for the volume on Heidelberg and its environs (figure 4).

Just as Zapf's type designs began with a black-letter fount (the Fraktur
design Gilgengart) but proceeded to almost entirely being variations on
roman and italic letterforms, so too in his jacket designs black-letter styles are
rarely seen after the first few years. Instead, myriad variations on roman
majuscules, minuscules, and italic or cursive styles dominate. For example,
formal roman capitals are seen in the Suhrkamp Verlag edition of Virgil's
Bucolica already mentioned, and also in the bilingual edition of René Char's
poems for the same publisher, but in the latter instance in a much more formal and modern variation. The roman minuscule in a simple yet strikingly
attractive arrangement is used for the two volume edition of Jean Giraudoux's
plays published by S. Fischer Verlag in 1960 (figure 5). The second volume of

7. Marcel Proust, *Auf der Suche* (Suhrkamp Verlag).

8. Hugo von Hofmannsthal, *Ausgewählte Werke* (Büchergilde Gutenberg).

the Giraudoux set is reproduced in our illustration. The roman lettering, while being classic, maintains a life and vigour, partly due to the lively rough edges and the restrained freedom of the letterforms. A more formal neo-classically influenced roman minuscule is used in Walter Benjamin's *Schriften* for Suhrkamp (figure 6). The Benjamin jacket reproduced (also the second volume of a two-volume set) is a more formal roman, based on a neo-classical style. It was rendered with a brush, while the Giraudoux lettering was done with a broad-edge pen.

Zapf has employed an assortment of cursive hands, ranging from the formal, restrained italic in Shaw's *Klassische Stücke*, to a brush written script based on Marcel Proust's handwriting for the multi-volume edition of his works published by Suhrkamp Verlag (figure 7). A few of the more unusual styles also make an appearance, such as uncial letterforms for the William Morris publication already mentioned and *Zucht in Schöne Sitte* (Reichert, 1977), or rustic letterforms as seen in Virgil's *Aeneid* (Suhrkamp Verlag).

While the greatest number of Zapf's jacket designs employ calligraphy, there are still a great many which employ strictly typographic material. As mentioned previously, ornament is rarely used, but there are exceptions, such

9. *Deutsches Theater* (Büchergilde Gutenberg).

10. Gisèle Prassinos, *Der Mann mit den Fragen Erzählungen* (Hanser).

as the borders using Zapf's own typographic ornament designs on the jacket for Hoffmannsthal's *Ausgewählte Werke* (Büchergilde Gutenberg) (figure 8)]. Purely typographic jackets are not uncommon in Zapf's work, such as his ingenious design for *Deutsches Theater* (Büchergilde Gutenberg) (figure 9), incorporating the contents of the book in the typographic design; and the jackets for Zapf's own major publications: *Manuale Typographicum* I (1954) in Sistina Titling capitals and Palatino italic, and II (1968) in Optima. The jacket for *Typographic Variations* (1963) is also set in Zapf's own Optima typeface, utilising only roman upper and lower-case in three sizes, printed in red, blue, and black on brown paper. The layout is repeated on the title-page design.

Often a seemingly simple arrangement of elegant types carefully placed yields a striking jacket, such as Gisèle Prassinos's *Der Mann mit den Fragen Erzählungen* (Hanser) (figure 10), set in Zapf's Optima type with decoration composed of a repetition of a simple square and triangle printed in color; or *Das Lehrgespräche* (1956) in Palatino and Michelangelo capitals.

Zapf's creativity is far-reaching, and he often applies his thorough technical knowledge of the printing processes to new and innovative effect on his jackets. For example, we have already mentioned his use of letterpress blind debossing on the *Odyssey* and Hoffmannsthal jackets. For *Das Ohr des Malchus* (Büchergilde Gutenberg) Zapf cleverly uses only two colours (red and black) to achieve a varied effect by printing a solid black panel over dates in red writing resulting in a subtle sheen.

Throughout the fifties and sixties Zapf designed dust-jackets for a variety of commercial publishers in Germany. His work in jacket designs continued in the seventies and eighties for some of those same publishers, as well as for more specialised houses such as Ludwig Reichert, for whom Zapf designed a number of jackets, and Hermann Emig, whose series of books and their jackets were designed by Zapf from the late fifties through to the nineties.

Today dust-jacket designs have moved in new directions, as is inevitable. Jackets are perhaps more 'graphic' and commercial in appearance, looking more like a modern advertising brochure than a literary work. Calligraphy on dust-jackets (as seen on the majority of Zapf's jackets; and on a good portion of the jackets designed by Wolpe for Fabers; and almost all the jackets by George Salter for numerous publishers in the United States; among many others) has all but disappeared. What little hand-lettering there is is usually of the slick, glitzy style generally seen on romance novels.

A review of Zapf's jacket designs for assorted publishers may help to give an overview of his remarkable talents in the fields of calligraphy, type design, and graphic design, and shed light on this little-known aspect of his graphic design. The examples reproduced here speak for themselves, and are another facet of the work revolving around letters which Zapf has given the world.

Jerry Kelly is a free lance designer, calligrapher, and printer. Before establishing his own business in 1999 he was a designer/representative for the Stinehour Press (1991–1999) and the Press of A. Colish (1981–1991). Since 1978 he has been a partner in the Kelly/Winterton Press, a private press that prints small editions, mainly by letterpress from hand-set type. He is also a calligrapher, producing hand lettering for assorted publishers and organizations. His work has won awards, from, among others, the Type Directors Club, the Society of Typographic Designers, and AIGA (more than 20 book designs chosen among the annual AIGA '50 books'), and he has been a finalist for the Premio Felice Feliciano. His articles on typography and calligraphy have been widely published in various books and journals, including *Matrix*, *Letter Arts Review*, *Fine Print*, the *AIGA Journal*, *Calligraphy Review*, *Bookways*, and the *Papers of the Bibliographical Society of America*. He is a member of the Grolier Club, an Honorary Member of the Double Crown Club, a Corresponding Member of the Bund Deutscher Buchkunstler, a member of the Typophiles, a trustee of the American Printing History Association, and a Professional Fellow of the Pierpont Morgan Library. He earned his BFA from Queens College, and studied with Hermann Zapf at the Rochester Institute of Technology.

Index

Page references in italics are to illustrations and their captions.

COLOPHON

*

While there was great temptation to set this book in Caslon
(a British type cut by William Caslon in the eighteenth century, and *Matrix*'s
signature type since its beginning), something different was deemed appropriate.

Therefore this volume has been set in the rarely seen Comenius font,
designed by Hermann Zapf for Berthold in 1976. Comenius is a clear, modern type
design, with a large x-height and open counters.

The folios and a small amount of other matter are set in Zapf Renaissance,
designed by Hermann Zapf in 1984 for URW, as an appropriate complement to
the Comenius type employed for the main text.

The captions and author biographies accompanying each article are set in Gill Sans,
designed by Eric Gill for the British Monotype Corporation, released in 1928–1930.
Gill Sans remains a fresh-looking letter more than 70 years after its initial release.

In addition, many other typefaces (too numerous to mention) have been used
in this book for various special purposes, much as has been the practice
in the original issues of *Matrix*.

*

The Special Edition of 80 copies has been hand bound & slipcased, and contains
separate prints of some of the type specimens specially designed for this volume,
in addition to other selected items.

Type & Typography: A Matrix Anthology has been designed by Jerry Kelly.